CONTENTS

Vertical Tab

The vertical tab on the right-hand margin of each double-page spread is a navigational tool designed to help you find your way around the guide. The top section lists the individual chapters, while the lower section highlights the part of the chapter you are currently reading.

D1511130

FOREWORD

After three and a half years of development, *Metal Gear Solid 4: Guns of the Patriots* is finally ready for you to play and I hope you enjoy it. When I created *MGS2*, I expected it to be the end of the series. When people wanted to experience and understand the game universe more, I created *MGS3* – but demand continued and so completion has actually only been achieved now in the fourth of the series. With *MGS4*, I wrap everything up. Although the game is a story in its own right, it is also the continuation and resolution of everything that came before.

MGS4 is designed to give you, the player, a lot of choices – outside of the cinematic sequences, only you decide how the story of the actual game, the "battlefield narrative", evolves. In certain places, you may choose to sneak through a scene or you may wish to get directly involved in each confrontation. Some players may think "How would Snake deal with this?", and then try to remain silent, only disabling opponents when absolutely necessary, as indeed he would. Others might instead look at the number of weapons and gadgets they have found, and decide that fighting the PMC soldiers is the best course of action. The truth is that there is no right or wrong way to play.

The first time you play *MGS4*, you can only react to events. When something happens, you need to make an instantaneous decision. You never know what the consequence will be, and that holds right up until the story ends. Although completing *MGS4* marks the end of the story, it's only the beginning of *MGS4* as a game. Once you know where to go, and generally know what to do, that is when you can start experimenting, pushing yourself on harder levels, or searching for secrets and different tactical approaches.

This guide is the result of a collaboration between Piggyback and Kojima Productions. It has been created to enhance your understanding of everything that occurs during Snake's final mission and it has been designed to complement your *MGS4* experience. Every effort has been made to help you enjoy the game for yourself, at your own pace and without spoiling any surprises. That's not to say that any secrets have been omitted, rather that the guide has been developed to help you beat and savor the game in the first instance, and then master it thereafter. This respect for both game and player's experience is unique.

I hope you enjoy my game very much, and that this book helps you to explore and treasure every last moment of it.

Hideo Kojima

1 HOW TO PLAY

The opening moments of *Metal Gear Solid 4* are so spectacular, and confront you with so many new features, that even experienced players may feel somewhat disorientated. The following pages are designed to help you be fully prepared to get started in the best possible fashion. Generally speaking, we've taken great care to avoid any spoilers at this early stage. For this reason, you will find more in-depth information on certain topics held back until the relevant point in the Walkthrough.

■ BASICS
COMMANDS

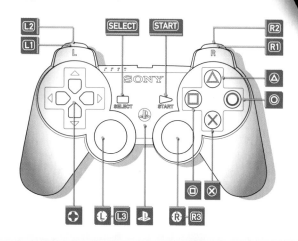

COMMAND	MENUS	GAMEPLAY
L (left stick)	Scroll through menus	Move Snake (press lightly for a slower, quieter pace, firmly for maximum speed)
R (right stick)	Scroll map	Move the camera/crosshairs
✛ (directional buttons)	Scroll through menus	Zoom in and out while using a scope or the Solid Eye's Binos mode; lean slightly left or right in FPS mode (standing/crouching posture only), or while using Binos
⊗	Confirm selection; swap weapon in Weapons menu; swap item in Items menu	Crouch (short press); crawl (long press); roll (while running)
◎	Back	Reload; disable animation/audio track and skip to next dialogue caption (Codec conversations)
△	Change map viewing angle in pause menu (where available); purchase ammo in Weapons menu	Context-sensitive moves (when △ and action icon appear onscreen); FPS mode (when weapon is drawn); fast-forward Codec conversations
▢	Remove weapon in Weapons menu; remove item in Items menu	Toggle Auto Aim on or off (if "Lock-On (Auto Aim) Settings" is fixed to "On" in the Options menu)
R1	Zoom in on map (where available)	Use weapon (with L1 held); CQC (weapon holstered)
R2	Zoom out on map (where available)	Open in-game Weapons menu
L1	View weapons/items in the respective menus View receipt in Drebin's shop	Aim weapon
L2	Customize weapon in Weapons menu	Open in-game Items menu
R3	Toggle between current position and objective location on map	Reset camera to forward-facing position; toggle weapon position (with L1 held; doesn't apply to knife)
L3	-	-
START	Main Menu (at title screen)	Display pause menu; pause cutscenes (select "Skip" to end them); end Codec conversations
SELECT	-	Display controller configuration/activate Codec (if " SELECT Button Function" setting in Options menu is fixed to "Use Codec")
(PS button)	-	-

ONSCREEN DISPLAY

The following annotated screenshot (Fig. 1) shows a typical gameplay screen.

1 **Life Gauge:** Represents Snake's physical wellbeing. An empty Life Gauge means Game Over.

2 **Psyche Gauge, Stress Percentage:** Represents Snake's psychological wellbeing. A diminished Psyche bar and a high Stress percentage will impair Snake's combat ability (particularly in terms of accurately aiming weapons).

3 **Alert Meter:** This appears when the enemy has spotted Snake and raised the alarm. The three stages are Alert, Evasion and Caution, with enemy aggression decreasing through each level.

4 **Solid Eye Radar:** Only available when the Solid Eye is active, this radar indicates the relative position of all living creatures or vehicles within a fixed radius. The brighter "circle within a circle" centered on Snake's position indicates how much noise he is making. A similar (though smaller) circle appears around moving entities – even incidental fauna such as rats and chickens. When the Solid Eye is not active, this display is replaced by a simple compass; the red circle that appears indicates the direction of the next objective.

5 **Camo Percentage:** Snake's current level of camouflage; the higher this is, the better. When potential assailants are distracted by current events in a particular area (for example, if PMC troops are engaged in open combat with local rebel forces), the text is blue. This usually indicates that detection is less likely. If they are actively scouring the environment for signs of movement, the color is orange – which is your cue to move with greater caution.

6 **Threat Ring:** Indicates the proximity and position of mobile entities (soldiers, vehicles, et al). The higher the "waves", the closer they are.

7 **Weapons Window:** Shows the currently selected weapon.

8 **Items Window:** Shows the currently selected item. If this item is battery powered, the Battery Gauge appears under this window.

9 **Auto Aim:** This text is displayed when Auto Aim is active.

10 **Special Action:** An icon appears in this area whenever you can press Ⓐ to perform a context-sensitive action.

■ Main Menu

The Main Menu (Fig. 2) can be accessed from the title screen by pressing (START). This calls up the following options:

New Game: Choose one of four difficulty levels and start a new game

Load Game: Brings up a list of your saves. As well as a useful illustrative screenshot, you can see the date and time that each file was stored. If you pause for a moment as you highlight an entry, additional details will appear, including the total play time and a short text description of the current story status.

Mission Briefing: This enables you to view any Mission Briefing cutscenes that you have unlocked. You will be prompted to choose a save file after selecting this option. If you chose not to load a file, only the Mission 1 Briefing will be available.

Options: Use this to customize and configure MGS4 to suit your preferences. Most of the settings are fairly self-explanatory, with a help message at the bottom of the screen offering useful guidance. As far as gameplay is concerned, you'll find the most pertinent options on the Controls page.

Photo Album: Use this option to view photographs taken with the Camera once you find it. We cover this in greater detail in the Extras chapter, but we strongly recommend that you don't visit that chapter until you have finished your first playthrough – it's packed with extremely serious spoilers.

Virtual Range: A virtual reality training area where you can practice using weapons, items and Snake's many moves against passive target dummies – including CQC techniques. Select "Start with saved data" to enjoy access to all the weapons and items you have acquired in a saved file, or "Start without saved data" to begin with a very basic collection of standard weapon types.

Metal Gear Online: The multiplayer game. Our dedicated MGO chapter begins on page 132.

Extras: Again, this is covered in our spoiler-laden Extras chapter, and isn't something that you should worry about until you have completed MGS4 for the first time.

■ Pause Menu

You can call up the pause menu (Fig. 3) by pressing (START) during play. This screen features an interactive map (with helpful onscreen control tips), with details

on current weather, temperature and wind strength located in the top right-hand corner. Note that some menu options only appear once you reach a particular point in Act 1.

Codec: Access the Codec screen. You can use this to reach Otacon at any time for advice – simply select his frequency with ⬅, then press ⊗ to establish contact. Additional Codec correspondents are added as the story progresses, and you should feel free to experiment with random channels (it's something of a Metal Gear tradition).

Weapons: This is where you can select the weapons accessible from the in-game R2 menu. Simply choose a weapon in the central window (use ⬆ to cycle through the available categories), and then assign it to a slot in the left-hand panel. You can equip up to five weapons simultaneously. The currently highlighted object appears in the right-hand side window, along with useful statistics such as weight and ammo capacity. You will also notice a series of icons that rate firearms and grenades in six categories: "S" is the best, with the subsequent ranks descending from "A" to "E". Press L1 to view background information on a highlighted weapon; once you gain access to Drebin's Shop, you can also use L2 to customize firearms, and △ to purchase additional ammunition.

Items: The Items menu works in the same way as the Weapons menu. Select an item from the central window, and simply equip it in one of the eight available slots. Press L1 to read additional information in the Viewer.

Camouflage: The Camouflage screen enables you to change the settings of the Sneaking Suit, and equip Command Vests, special disguises and outfits. Leaving the OctoCamo on Automatic mode is the best option to begin with; the Manual mode is best left to a second playthrough. Refer to page 20 for more on this subject.

Drebin's Shop: Enter Drebin's Shop to buy weapons, upgrades and ammo. Shopping there is easy – just use ⬆ to highlight an object, then ⊗ to bring up the purchase window. Drebin's Shop is explained in the Walkthrough chapter.

Briefing: A presentation of the many moves available to Snake, with illustrative diagrams designed to help you visualize each action. This also covers gadgets such as Metal Gear Mk. II.

Options: This menu is functionally identical to its equivalent found at the Main Menu.

Save: Use this option to store your progress. Metal Gear Solid 4 uses a checkpoint system – look out for the onscreen prompts that appear when you reach them. When you save your game, only your progress up to the last checkpoint is recorded.

MOVES LIST

The following table recaps all the moves available to Snake.

CATEGORY	MOVE	BUTTON COMMAND	NOTES
Movement	Walk/Run	🕹	Tilt slightly to creep, more firmly to run.
	Crouch/Crawl	⊗	From a standing position, tap ⊗ once to crouch, and hold it to lie down. While crouching, tap ⊗ once to stand or hold it to lie down. While prone, tap ⊗ once to crouch, hold it to stand up.
	Crawl	🕹	Tilt slightly to creep at the slowest possible pace, and more firmly to crawl with greater purpose.
	Crouch-walk	🕹	Tilt slightly to creep, more firmly to run.
	Move camera	🕹	Move the camera around freely with 🕹.
Roll	Roll forward	⊗	Press ⊗ when running to roll. Hold the button while rolling to drop to a crawl.
	Roll and drop	⊗ (hold)	Press and hold ⊗ while running to roll and drop to a crawl.
	Roll to the side	L1 (hold) + 🕹 + ⊗	Hold L1 and tilt 🕹 in the required direction, then instantly press ⊗ to execute a side roll. Do the same from a prone position to roll on the ground.
	Roll over	△	Tap △ once when Snake is prone to make him roll over, and again to make him roll back.
Suspension	Grip edges	△	Press △ when close to gaps to hang over the edge.
	Shimmy	🕹	While hanging, shimmy left or right with 🕹.
	Drop down	⊗	Drop down from a ledge by pressing ⊗.
	Grab ledges	△	When falling, grab ledges or ladders by pressing △.
	Climb up	△	To climb back up, press △ while hanging.
Wall Press	Press against wall	△	Face a surface and use △ to press against it. Press △ again to move away.
	Walk along	🕹	While pressing against a wall, walk along it with 🕹.
	Peek	🕹	When you reach the end of a surface, hold 🕹 in the appropriate direction to peek. You can then open fire normally.
	Jump-out shot	🕹 (hold) + L1 (hold) + R1	While peeking, hold L1 to aim and press R1 to open fire.
Attack	Shoot	L1 (hold) + R1	To attack with a weapon, press L1 to aim (or simply ready it with Auto Aim active), then R1 to fire. With thrown objects such as grenades, hold L1 and use 🕹 to position the targeting circle, then press R1 to throw.
	Manual Aim	🕹	Use 🕹 to aim.
	Switch shoulder view	R3	While aiming manually, press R3 to shift the position of the weapon in Snake's hands and move the camera position to the opposite shoulder.
	Aim mode	⊡	Press ⊡ to toggle Auto Aim on and off (only if the "Lock-On (Auto Aim) Settings" option is set to "On").
	Change scope	L1 (hold) + △, then up or down on ✛	While in FPS mode wielding a weapon with a scope, press up or down on ✛ to change the magnification.
	Reload	◎	Press ◎ to reload.
	FPS mode	L1 (hold) + △	Press △ while aiming to switch to first person view. Snake is free to move in this mode, but his speed is greatly reduced.
	Lean (FPS mode only)	◁, ▷	Lean slightly to the left and right.
CQC	Throw	🕹 + R1 (hold)	Press 🕹 towards the target and press and hold R1 to throw them to the ground for an instant KO.
	Grab	R1 (hold)	Grab the target by pressing and holding R1 when close to them.
	Disarm	R1 (hold) + R1	Press R1 again just as you grab a target to knock their weapon away from them.
	Restrain	R1 (hold longer)	Continuing to hold R1 after you grab someone will restrain the target if you have a one-handed weapon. With a two-handed weapon, Snake will knock the target backwards.
	Choke	R1 (hold longer), then R1	After first grabbing an opponent, press R1 again to choke your victim and KO them.
	Restrain and throw	R1, then 🕹 + R1 (hold)	After restraining your target, press R1 while tilting 🕹 to throw them to the ground.
	Restrain to the ground	R1, then 🕹 + R1 (hold) (crouching)	If you move to a crouching position while restraining a target, use this move to force them to the ground and smother them.
	Finish off	R1 (hold longer), then △	After restraining your target, press △ to slit their throat.
	Shield	R1 (hold longer), then L1	After restraining a target, press L1 to use them as a human shield and aim your weapon. You can then press R1 to fire.
Distraction	Knock on wall	△, then R1	While pressing against a wall, use R1 to knock and attract attention.
	Throw empty Magazine	L1 (hold) + R1	These empty ammo clips are thrown in the same way as grenades. Remember to aim them at the position you would like your target to investigate.
	Play dead	△	Hold △ when Snake is prone, or simply don't move after being stunned by an attack.
	Place a Playboy/ Emotion Mag	L1 (hold) + R1	Hold L1 and R1 to open the publication, then tap ◎ to flip through the pages. Release both shoulder buttons to place it on the ground.
Equipment	Collect items/equipment	🕹	Simply move over items to pick them up, unless you have your full quota for that item.
	Select item	L2 (hold), ✛	Hold L2 and use ✛ to scroll through the available items, then release the button to make your selection.
	Select weapon	R2 (hold), ✛	Hold R2 and use ✛ to scroll through the available weapons, then release the button to make your selection.
	Steal items	△ (hold then release)	By picking up a (dead or unconscious) body then releasing it, you can sometimes obtain an item.
	Hold up	L1	Creep up behind a target's back and press L1.
	Body search	L1, then △	When you hold up a target, move to the front and press △ to execute a body search. Press △ again when the onscreen prompts appear to find items.
Gadgets	Activate OctoCamo	-	Lie motionless for a second while prone or pressed against a wall to blend in with your surroundings.
	Activate Threat Ring	-	Lie motionless while prone or crouched to activate the Threat Ring. The Threat Ring will remain active if you crawl, or crouch-walk slowly.
	Solid Eye	L2 + ✛	Select the Solid Eye in the Items menu (hold L2), and use the ⊡, △ and ◎ buttons to select its three operating modes.

DIFFICULTY LEVELS

There are four difficulty levels in *MGS4*. Your choice is made when you first select the New Game option (Fig. 4).

Liquid Easy is the lowest setting, and should be used by complete beginners who have not previously played an action game, or who lack confidence in their ability. This is a great way to practice before taking the step up to a higher difficulty level.

Naked Normal is a natural progression from Easy. It's challenging, but won't hamper your enjoyment of the game by making things too difficult or frustrating. A good first choice for anyone not too familiar with the *Metal Gear Solid* games.

Solid Normal is the default difficulty level. It's the perfect setting for your first playthrough if you've finished all previous *MGS* games, and relish a stern test of your gaming prowess.

Big Boss Hard makes everything much more difficult. To complete the game at this level you will need both a very good understanding of *MGS4's* gameplay, as well as a solid knowledge of enemy behavior. In this mode, you will almost always need to favor stealth over action. An excellent choice if you want to increase the challenge on a second playthrough.

Select a difficulty level
LIQUID EASY
NAKED NORMAL
SOLID NORMAL
BIG BOSS HARD

For players who are skilled at action games (NORMAL setting for Europe and North America).

04

Generally speaking, as the difficulty level increases:

- There may be fewer items available to collect.
- Soldiers (both friendly and hostile) tend to drop fewer items.
- The stocks of items you can carry at once become smaller.
- The total ammo you can carry is significantly reduced.
- Enemies become more accurate and inflict greater damage, and conversely Snake inflicts less damage on them.
- Enemies become more watchful, and generally tougher.

■ CONTROLS

Forget PMC troops, and other battlefield hazards: your first conflict in *Metal Gear Solid 4* will be between you and your fingers. Mastering basic commands and camera control may take a few hours or so, depending on your gaming ability, but acquiring an all-encompassing appreciation of its numerous (and entirely optional) special moves and techniques will take far longer. Don't be intimidated, though: with a little patience and preparation, you can avoid unnecessary frustration. We know that you're itching to dive feet-first into the action, but reading the following introductory guide before you start will be a purposeful and practical first step.

SNAKE'S CONTROLS

■ Movement

To walk or creep, tilt ● slightly; press it more firmly to run. Don't forget that stealth is key in the *Metal Gear Solid* games, though: running is noisy, and best left for unavoidable combat situations, emergency escapes, or when you're absolutely sure that the coast is clear. From a standing position, tap ⊗ once to crouch, and hold ⊗ to lie down. To stand straight up from a prone position, hold ⊗; tap it to rise to a crouching position. You will probably find that you spend most of the game crawling, which is the stealthiest form of movement, or crouch-walking, which offers a reasonable compromise between sneakiness and speed. As an added bonus, crouching and going prone enable the most efficient use of the Threat Ring and OctoCamo respectively. (Both of these are discussed later in this chapter.)

For optimum stealth, tilt ● lightly while prone to crawl at the slowest pace, which – unlike other movement speeds – does not reduce your Camo rating. Tilt the stick further to move at a more practical speed, but note that your relative visibility will increase as a consequence. Typically, you can expect a 10% reduction in your Camo percentage. Crawling has another (rather less obvious) function: it enables Snake to safely defuse and collect primed explosives, such as Claymores.

CROUCH / CROUCH-WALK

WALK / RUN / CREEP

12

To roll, press ⊗ when running; hold ⊗ while rolling to drop to a crawl. This deft tumble can be used to cross small gaps, and to roll over low obstructions. It's particularly useful if you need to move down a flight of stairs quickly, or to drop down from a ledge. Naturally, it's also an effective evasive maneuver during firefights.

explain any necessary usage instructions. As a rule, objects that restore Health or Psyche must be activated with ⊗ while the menu is active; others, such as gadgets like the Solid Eye, become operational when you release L2 to return to the game. You can only have one "active" item during play.

► HOW TO PLAY

WALKTHROUGH

INVENTORY

METAL GEAR ONLINE

EXTRAS

► BASICS
► CONTROLS

MGS4 PRIMER

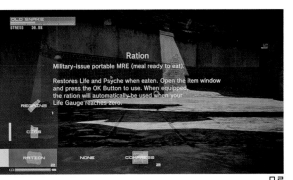

To execute a side roll (Fig. 1), hold L1 and tilt ● left or right, then immediately press ⊗. If you do this from a prone position, Snake will roll on the ground.

To make Snake flip onto his back, press △ when he's lying on his stomach; press the button again to return to the standard crawling position. This is particularly handy when you need to use a weapon at short notice. If you quickly rotate the camera to face an adversary, pressing L1 to aim the weapon will cause Snake to rapidly swing around for a clear shot. You can also throw grenades when in this posture.

Though there are few occasions where you will need to use it, press △ to grab a nearby ledge or ladder as Snake is falling. Usually, if you walk slowly over an edge, the veteran soldier will perform this automatically. Shimmy left and right with ●; press ⊗ to drop down (you should attempt to land on an enemy at least once), or press △ to haul yourself back up if there is sufficient floor space above.

Another key sneaking move is the Wall Press. Face a wall and press △ to push Snake's body against it. With OctoCamo active, using the Wall Press makes you blend in with your surroundings (after a short pause to enable the suit to adjust, of course). While pressed against a wall, you can walk along it and take a peek when you reach an opening with ●. To move out and line up a shot, hold L1.

■ Using Items

To use an item, you must first ensure that the required object has been assigned to one of eight available slots (pause menu → Items). Hold L2 to temporarily pause the action, and use ✛ or ● to cycle through the list (Fig. 2). Pay attention to the onscreen tips – these usually

LIE PRONE / CRAWL / SCOUT-CRAWL

PLAY DEAD

ROLL

SIDE ROLL (PRONE)

SIDE ROLL (STANDING)

KNOCK ON WALL

ROLL ON YOUR BACK

SWIM

CQC: RESTRAIN

CQC: THROW

AIM WEAPON

CQC: DISARM

CQC: RESTRAIN TO THE GROUND

Using Weapons

As with items, you need to first assign a weapon to one of five available slots (pause menu → Weapons) before you can equip it. To change a weapon, hold down R2 and scroll through the available options with ✪ or Ⓛ. Release R2 to make your choice and return to the game. Hold L1 to aim and press R1 to fire. Reload with ◎.

Holding L1 will bring up a target reticule, and move the camera view behind Snake's shoulder; use Ⓡ to aim. Note that you can switch the position of the weapon in Snake's hands and move the camera to the opposite shoulder by pressing R3 (Fig. 3). This is extremely useful when firing from behind cover. Activate FPS Mode with △ for greater accuracy, or to use a scope if a weapon is equipped with one. You can move freely in FPS Mode, but Snake's speed is vastly reduced. You can also press ✪ & ✪ to lean slightly to the left or right in FPS Mode, and ✪ & ✪ to use a scope's zoom function. Some weapons have a variety of firing modes (including single-bullet, burst and full-auto). You can activate these while the weapons window is onscreen – just follow the onscreen instructions.

03

As well as guns, you have plenty of other weapons at your disposal via the Weapons menu. These include grenades, which you aim by pressing L1 and throw with R1. Other "weapons" that you will find include men's publications such as Playboy, which can be used to distract guards, Claymore anti-personnel mines, and empty magazines which can be thrown to create noise.

Many weapons can be customized with a variety of accessories once the Drebin's Shop option becomes available in the pause menu. We explain how this can be achieved in the relevant section of the Act 1 walkthrough.

If "Lock-On (Auto Aim) Settings" is set to "On" at the Options screen, you can press ▣ during play to toggle between Manual Aim and Auto Aim. When Auto Aim is active, a notification appears above Snake's head.

Auto Aim, as its name suggests, causes Snake to automatically target hostile combatants when L1 is held. A red circle will appear to indicate where he is aiming; on human assailants, this will be the subject's torso. You can switch between multiple targets with Ⓡ. Should a target move behind cover, the lock-on will be lost.

Though undoubtedly handy when you face numerous opponents at once, Auto Aim is a feature that we advise you to use sparingly. Its principle weakness is that it does not allow you to target weak spots – for example, the head. This can be a massive problem on the Solid Normal and Big Boss Hard difficulty settings, where your adversaries can withstand much greater damage to the body area before falling. Manual Aim may be tricky to get to grips with at first, but we guarantee that you'll benefit by persevering with it in the long term.

CQC: HOLD UP

CQC: SLIT THROAT

CQC: BODY SEARCH

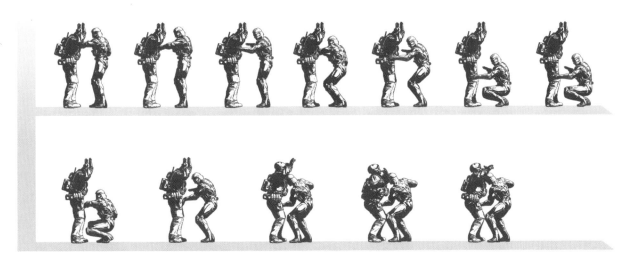

◼ CQC

Close Quarters Combat (CQC) moves can be used to silently take down your opponents, disarm them, or even use them as human shields (Fig. 4). CQC can only be performed in close proximity to a target, and the options available to you depend on your currently equipped weapon. To enjoy the full range, equip a pistol; with a two-handed weapon, your choices are seriously limited. You can refer to our Moves List table on page 11 or consult the in-game Briefing option to learn the necessary button commands.

Mastering CQC takes a little effort, with the delicate positioning and timing being something that most players will need to practice. The Virtual Range is the perfect place to begin, though there's no reason you can't start a new game on a lower difficulty level and hone your prowess in a "live" combat situation. Note that CQC cannot be performed when certain weapons are equipped. Look for the red CQC text above a weapon icon in the bottom right-hand corner before you attempt it.

CQC: SHIELD

SHIMMY

METAL GEAR MK.II

Knock on wall

Disarm mine traps

CAMERA CONTROLS

The wide variety of camera options available to you in *MGS4* is one of the features that mark it as a great leap forward over previous installments. In the standard Third Person View, you have complete control over the camera angle with ⓡ. Additionally, you can also opt to move around in FPS Mode – simply hold ⓛ and tap ④ (Fig. 5).

Other custom viewpoints include Corner View and Intrusion View. Corner View will kick in automatically during a Wall Press when you reach an opening or the end of a surface and continue tilting ⓛ in the same direction, enabling you to peek around corners and fire from behind cover. Intrusion View gives you a dynamic first person viewpoint when Snake is swimming underwater or crawling through air ducts.

◼ MGS4 PRIMER

The disorientation you feel at the start of *Metal Gear Solid 4* can be quite daunting. Though previous *MGS* players will be able to draw on prior experience, players less familiar with the "Stealth Action" gameplay philosophy should resist the urge to go in with all guns blazing. Try to muscle your way through even the early stages of Act 1, and you'll soon be staring blankly at the "Game Over" screen, wondering what exactly you did wrong. The answer to that question, of course, will be a point-blank: "Everything."

If you want to succeed, you must remember the golden rule of *MGS*: a smart Snake is a *stealthy* Snake. As you make progress, you'll realize how much more complex *MGS4's* gameplay is than previous installments, and that the tactical options available to you are incredibly varied. This section is designed to help shape and inform the many decisions you will make during play, and give you a broader understanding and appreciation of how Kojima-san's masterpiece works.

GAUGE MANAGEMENT

There are four gauges that you will need to watch constantly, whether sneaking through patrol lines or engaged in frenzied combat. You'll find that judicious management of these gauges will help you to preserve precious resources, such as Rations, as well as ensure that Snake is at peak condition for each challenge he faces.

◼ Life Gauge

Snake's Life Gauge is the thicker bar in the top left-hand corner of the screen. When it's empty, it's Game Over – as simple as that. Even if you don't regularly check the meter, you'll soon notice when Snake is ailing: the lower his Life Gauge is, the more signs of physical distress he'll exhibit. The gauge will start blinking when reduced to the 25% mark or below (Fig. 1); you'll also hear a distinct warning tone.

Keeping the Life Gauge topped up is therefore vital, but it's just as important not to panic and keep filling the gauge unnecessarily with precious items. Though you can replenish it with healing objects such as Rations and Noodles, you should take care not to waste them – especially on higher difficulty levels. Using a Ration when Snake's Life Gauge is 80% full, for example, is plain foolish. You usually don't need to even think about refilling the gauge until it drops below 25%. During boss fights or difficult skirmishes, you should instead equip Rations, Noodles or Regain and position them as an "active" item. Once Snake's health reaches zero, these will be automatically used until your stocks are exhausted.

One other method of restoring Snake's health is simply to find a safe hiding place and let him stand still. After a few seconds the Life Gauge will slowly start to creep back up. If you crouch or go prone, it will refill more quickly. If you have good cover, you'll find that this even works during boss battles. This can be a great way of refilling your Life Gauge for free – essential when playing on a high difficulty level. Note that recovery speed depends on the condition of Snake's other main gauge, the Psyche Gauge; the higher the Psyche Gauge, the quicker the Life Gauge refills. (Incidentally, if you have an extended break from playing *MGS4* that lasts for more than 24 hours, you may notice that Snake's Life and Psyche gauges are refilled by 20% per day. It's hardly necessary, but a nice touch nonetheless.)

Psyche Gauge

The Psyche Gauge is situated directly below the Life Gauge, appearing as four separate blocks. This represents Snake's psychological wellbeing, which has a direct effect on his performance. Essentially, the more stressed Snake is, the less effective he becomes. Keeping him as calm and focused as possible should be your main goal in terms of managing this meter.

The Psyche Gauge can be refilled with certain healing items, such as Noodles; dedicated Psyche-related objects such as the Compress do not directly refill the gauge, but instead temporarily increase the speed at which it is replenished. Cigs can also be equipped to regain Psyche, but to the detriment of the Life Gauge.

As with the Life Gauge, the Psyche Gauge can also be refilled simply by staying still, and more quickly by crouching or going prone. The better Snake feels generally (not too cold, hot, wet, dirty, or overloaded) the faster his Psyche will replenish. You can tell when he's not feeling great by observing his behavior or murmurs of discontent – if he starts feeling his age, it's usually a direct sign that something is wrong. Finding solutions to assuage these symptoms is usually just a matter of common sense. If Snake is freezing in cold water for instance, get him out of there; if he's overheating in direct sunlight, find some shade where he can cool down.

One of the major effects of a low Psyche Gauge is that it will severely hamper Snake's ability to aim accurately. The more stressed and hyped up he is, the more his aim will be impaired; this can have a particularly detrimental effect when he's using a sniper rifle. Try using a scope when Snake is over-anxious and you'll see how his unsteady hands make it thoroughly difficult to make a clean headshot. The Pentazemin item can be used to temporarily improve his marksmanship when required, but preventative maintenance is always better.

The Psyche Gauge is affected by Snake's Stress level, which is depicted by a number that appears underneath it. If Snake is sweltering in a hot, evil-smelling location, or alternatively shivering in a freezing location, his Stress level will rise. He will also become stressed if his equipment is too heavy (over 70 kg), or during an Alert phase. When Snake's Stress level exceeds 50%, the display will turn red and he will begin to lose Psyche. As his Stress rating continues to increase, his Psyche will diminish at a great

rate. However, as long Snake is not experiencing a Combat High, his Stress level can only reach a maximum of 80%.

A Combat High will kick in if Snake shoots with a gun more than 100 times during the Alert phase. Notification that he is currently experiencing a Combat High will appear next to the Life Gauge (Fig. 2). During this enhanced state, Psyche does not decrease, and any damage caused by enemies is halved. But it's not all good news: during a Combat High, Snake's Stress level can shoot up as far as 100%. It's a short-term boon, but the repercussions can be painful.

When Snake is swimming, or hanging from a railing, the Psyche Gauge is replaced by the O2 Gauge or Grip Gauge respectively (Fig. 3). When the O2 Gauge is depleted, Snake has run out of oxygen and his Life Gauge will start to shrink rapidly. When his Grip Gauge empties, he will fall.

Camo Percentage

The Camo percentage is the figure that appears in the top right-hand corner of the screen. This represents the degree of camouflage protection that Snake has at that particular moment. The higher the percentage, the harder it is for the enemy to see Snake (Fig. 4), so you should always aim for the best possible Camo rating whenever an enemy is likely to spot you. Your Camo percentage can be increased by wearing the right outfits and by crouching, wall-pressing, or (for maximum efficiency) crawling.

Battery Gauge

The Battery Gauge in the bottom left-hand corner represents the amount of juice that Snake still has left in his Battery, which is essential for powering certain items. You can extend the life of the gauge with upgrades – we'll tell you where these are during the walkthrough. Every additional Battery that you find adds an extra bar to the gauge, represented in numerical form (Fig. 5). The maximum number of Batteries depends on your chosen difficulty level – the higher the setting, the fewer upgrades are available. If power is running low and you need to replenish it, simply refrain from using any Battery-powered equipment until it is restored. You'll notice that some gadgets are more energy-hungry than others, so be careful how you use them.

CHOOSING THE RIGHT EQUIPMENT

Weapons

When it comes to selecting weapons, you have two important choices to make – which five weapons you have available by pressing R2 (which you decide in the pause menu), and which one of these five weapons you will actually wield (which you decide in the Weapons window – Fig. 6). Your chosen five should always be balanced. A good configuration would be to have a silenced weapon, a powerful submachine gun for close-range action, a sniper rifle, a grenade type, and one diversionary item such as an empty Magazine. The weapon you actually hold should obviously always reflect your immediate needs.

There are many ways to obtain new weapons or ammo. The most obvious is to search for "hidden" collectibles and pick up weapons from the battlefield, but you can also search corpses or pay a visit to Drebin's Shop.

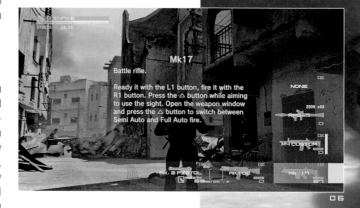

Items

As with weapons, you have two important choices to make here: which eight items you will have available to you by pressing L2 (which you decide in the pause menu), and which one of these eight you actually use (which you decide in the Items window – Fig. 7). The eight that you choose should also be balanced, although this decision is less critical than with weapons. However, the one "active" item you opt for is very important. At first, you will probably tend to equip the Solid Eye most of the time, because it gives you a better understanding of your surroundings. As you eventually acquire the knack of using the Threat Ring instead of the Solid Eye, though, you'll soon be able to free up the item slot for something else – such as a Ration during boss fights.

To obtain new items, you can either pick up any that you find (as shown on the maps in this guide) or search bodies. You can't buy any from Drebin so take great care not to waste anything (especially healing items such as Rations).

Weight

Items and weapons in the game have a weight stat. If the burden of Snake's load (five weapons and eight items) exceeds 70 kg, his Stress will increase, thus reducing his Psyche and overall effectiveness. Just be sensible when it comes to weight distribution, and make sure you compensate for particularly heavy objects with at least one light one if you notice that you are approaching the 70 kg mark. This is generally only a danger when preparing Snake for a boss fight, as there's a natural tendency to bring out rocket launchers and the like for such occasions.

MAKING THE MOST OF YOUR GADGETS

You have many gadgets and interesting objects at your disposal throughout the *MGS4* story. Some of these are made available during Act 1, while others can be found later in the game. Here's a brief guide to the most indispensable of these devices.

▶ HOW TO PLAY

WALKTHROUGH

INVENTORY

METAL GEAR ONLINE

EXTRAS

BASICS

CONTROLS

▶ MGS4 PRIMER

■ Solid Eye

When you first obtain this item, you'll find life in the field infinitely easier if you keep the Solid Eye selected in your items window most of the time. This gadget, which enables the Baseline Map radar function when active, has three modes: Normal, NV and Binos.

When selected, the Solid Eye will display basic data for both enemies and allies, such as which faction they belong to. As it can be all too easy to accidentally open fire on your allies during a hectic firefight, this information can be decisive. You'll find that "friendlies" are much less likely to help you if you start spraying lead indiscriminately, and they may even turn on you if suitably provoked. The information shown is color-coded. Gold, the default color, denotes a neutral character, blue indicates an ally, and red signals an enemy (Fig. 8). The Solid Eye is also invaluable in helping you locate hard-to-spot collectable items, as it increases their visibility by placing a digital frame around them.

The Solid Eye additionally has an intuitive radar system, which translates the vibes that Snake picks up from enemies, including sound and movement. It shows the relative location of all targets around you, but keep in mind that it also detects animals – which can be rather disconcerting if you're in a location filled with rats, for example.

The NV or Night Vision mode is a special goggle that enables you to see more clearly in dark areas, as well as spot hidden items more easily. Scanning a dark room with NV active is sometimes the quickest way to assess its contents. If you wish to zoom in to view a distant point, simply select the Binos option, and then press up or down on ✛.

OctoCamo

Snake's OctoCamo system goes way beyond the camouflage system found in *Metal Gear Solid 3*, and has several different modes. In Automatic mode (generally speaking, the most effective), it enables Snake to blend in with the textures and colors of his surroundings. In order to enjoy the functionality of Automatic mode, Snake must either be prone (Fig. 9) or pressed up against a wall and motionless. After a short pause, you will notice his suit change to match his surroundings; a sound effect accompanies this process. If you check the Baseline Map in the top right-hand corner, you will see Snake's Camo percentage increase as the transformation takes place.

In Manual mode, you choose one specific camo pattern for Snake that doesn't automatically adapt itself to the environment. This is only really effective if you are prepared to alter it as Snake's surroundings change, and is also limited to "memorized" surfaces and terrains that have been previously stored. This is something we examine later in the guide, and isn't anything you should concern yourself with during your first playthrough.

Threat Ring

The Threat Ring is a translucent circle that appears round Snake's body when he crawls or crouches for a few seconds. The best way to explain its function would be to describe it as Snake's "intuition": it indicates the presence of any people, creatures or active objects (such as vehicles) within Snake's immediate vicinity. Any such dangers are represented visually by waves that correspond with the position of each potential threat.

The higher the "wave", the closer (and, sometimes, larger) it is. For example, a soldier that is standing some way away from Snake will only appear as a faint bump in the ring, while multiple enemies standing close by will cause the Threat Ring to undulate like a digitized Rocky Mountains (Fig. 10). It's a brilliantly instinctive way of instantly assessing Snake's current situation. Once you get to grips with it, you'll find that the Threat Ring can be just as reliable as the Solid Eye in terms of enemy detection.

The Threat Ring stays permanently active whenever you crawl, or when you crouch-walk at the slowest speed. If you stand up, move at a faster pace, or ready a weapon, it will immediately disappear. Its efficiency is governed by Snake's current Psyche level: the lower the gauge gets, the smaller and more difficult to "read" the Threat Ring becomes.

Metal Gear Mk. II

Metal Gear Mk. II is a mobile terminal that can be selected from the Items menu and controlled manually. Use ● to move it around, but don't forget to activate its stealth camo function with ⊗ if there are potential aggressors nearby. This ensures that

THE ART OF STEALTH

Mk. II is hidden from the naked eye, though it can still be detected by infrared sensors. Use Mk. II to remotely reconnoiter areas while Snake lies low, or even have it knock out isolated soldiers with its electric shock device by holding ⒧ and then pressing ⒭ (Fig. 11). You can also press ⒜ while controlling the robot to perform a variety of context-sensitive actions, such as disarming traps, knocking on walls to distract enemies, and flicking light switches. When you're done, tap ⒧ or change to a different item to return control to Snake.

Mk. II may not be big enough to wreak havoc in the manner of its much larger namesake, but it's never less than useful – especially if you favor stealth over direct confrontation. It's also invaluable during the Mission Briefing cutscenes at the start of each Act, where you can use it to explore the Nomad and collect hidden items. It's also handy for exploring ventilation shafts, removing the need for Snake to crawl laboriously for minutes at a time.

However, the use of Mk. II is not without drawbacks. The most important thing to remember is that Snake is vulnerable to discovery and sneak attack while piloting it. Secondly, Mk. II consumes battery power at a voracious rate, particularly when its stealth functionality is active. Finally, the device has a limited range, so it's not possible to use it to explore large areas unless you regularly reposition Snake.

It can't be emphasized enough; stealth is the key to success in *Metal Gear Solid 4*, just as it was in all previous installments. Certainly there will be times when direct aggression is best or unavoidable – especially in your first playthrough – but for the most part it's vital that you learn the art of sneaking. How you move and the stance you adopt is of paramount importance. Though there will be occasions when it's safe for you to run upright without a care in the world, you'll usually find that it's best to adopt either the crouch-walk or crawl stance. Bear in mind, though, that you're far from immune to detection when crouch-walking – it can still be rather noisy, with the reduced Camo rating reflecting Snake's increased visibility.

Trust your senses and let your ears be your guide. If you can hear Snake pattering across a wooden floor, then so can the enemy. Slow it down, and above all be patient. Crawling is always more effective than crouching in stealth situations. With your body flattened to the floor, making regular pauses to enable the OctoCamo to adapt to new surfaces, you can easily maintain a Camo rating in excess of 65%, even while moving. On the downside, you're slower to react when crawling on your belly, especially if you're attacked from close range.

Observation of the enemy is another key aspect of effective sneaking. It won't matter in the slightest how quiet you are if you inadvertently stumble directly into the path of a patrolling soldier. Take time to study the enemy's patterns of movement from behind cover. Careful observation should enable

you to figure out when to move and when to stay put. Whether you wish to use this information to bring targets down silently, or merely to sneak past when their back is turned, is entirely up to you. It's also prudent to make use of the gadgets and objects at your disposal. For example, Metal Gear Mk. II is a vital tool for scouting an area without attracting unnecessary attention.

As far as weapons are concerned, nothing arouses the attention and ire of surrounding troops like a deafening hail of machine gun fire. It's no good diligently crawling with care in full camouflage gear, only to bring the enemy swarming to your position with an ill-judged salvo of bullets. Use of silenced weapons or CQC is absolutely essential. One well-aimed headshot or smoothly-executed CQC attack will fell your quarry instantly and silently, but botched attacks or poor marksmanship can give your target the chance to call for help. A headshot is also more potent with anaesthetic weapons – it generally results in a swift takedown, with enemies losing consciousness instantly.

Your Solid Eye's Night Vision function can be extremely effective when it comes to tracking enemy movements, as it reveals the footprints left by patrolling guards (Fig. 12). Don't overuse NV, though, as it actually emits a low noise while active, and may alert a sharp-eared soldier. Finally (for this section at least – we'll offer more advanced tips throughout the guide), should you come across a guard who is blocking the way, you can lure him or her elsewhere by tossing an empty ammo Magazine, or distract a patrolling soldier by placing a copy of Playboy on the ground (Fig. 13).

12

13

MAXIMIZING EFFICIENCY DURING BATTLES

"Efficiency" actually depends on what your goals are. Naturally, if you're trying to achieve a no-kill playthrough, you won't have the same priorities as when your bloodlust dictates that you shoot everyone and everything in sight. But overall, the following tips are true in most instances.

- Aiming for the head works a treat (headshots usually result in instant death/unconsciousness, or increased damage on bosses).

- Using upgraded weapons (scopes, red dots, et al) makes you more accurate and effective.

- When surrounded, activate Auto Aim mode to quickly eliminate all enemies (change targets by pressing left or right on **R**). This is less effective on higher difficulty settings, though.

- Choosing the right location is important. For example, a high vantage point works best if you are sniping, it pays to operate from a defensible position during combat, and picking a secluded spot to silently take down a target is always sensible.

- Press **R3** to turn Snake to face the camera direction. This even works when he's lying down or manning a turret.

- Make sure militia/rebel fighters are friendly to you (Fig. 14) by helping them out as much as possible during battles, especially when they ask you to. Make a point of not aiming at or (however inadvertently) shooting them.

- Never fight if you're in a weak or dangerous position, especially a location that exposes you to fire from several directions. If in doubt, bolt for cover.

- Always try to eliminate your most dangerous opponents first. Snipers and turret operators should obviously be your principle targets.

- Be sure to reload frequently to avoid the dreaded "dead man's click", and have weapons prepared in reserve for more unrelenting assaults.

- Conserve valuable items and ammo, and try to save your most powerful weapons for the strongest targets.

OBSERVING YOUR ENVIRONMENT

MGS4 is a game packed with surprises and secrets. While it's possible to just race through the game, getting the job done and speeding onward to the end, doing so will deny you the chance to fully explore and observe the intricately constructed environments. A good deal of the fun comes from the sheer range of possibilities the game offers, from tactics (optional routes through areas, alternative strategies), to bonuses (hidden locations or objects, entirely optional battles) to secret Easter eggs (such as bizarre enemy behaviors, or even Codec conversations that can be hilarious or instructive).

Take your time: this is a game built for repeat play, and there's simply no way you can enjoy everything it offers in a single sitting.

WALKTHROUGH

2

Whether you are looking for an occasional helping hand during your first attempt to beat *Metal Gear Solid 4*, or seeking detailed step-by-step advice for a "perfect" playthrough at a later date, this chapter has all the guidance you might conceivably need. The "two tier" walkthrough style used throughout is unique, though, so we suggest that you reach the brief User Instructions section overleaf before you continue.

USER INSTRUCTIONS

INTRODUCTION

Metal Gear Solid 4 is a complicated, feature-packed adventure, so we've gone to great lengths to design the sophisticated walkthrough it so richly deserves. We understand that you'd rather dive into the action than read what we have to say here, but trust us: less than five minutes of your time will help you to get the most out of both this chapter and the game itself.

In the (very likely) event that we have a tenuous grip on your attention, we'll begin with the most essential facts.

- *Metal Gear Solid 4* is divided into five "Acts", and so is this chapter. We include a large overview map at the start of each Act, with the box outlines detailing the sections that are covered on the pages that follow.

- In the walkthrough, **left-hand pages** feature magnified, annotated map portions, accompanied by screenshots and extended captions. We know that many players will want to complete their first *MGS4* playthrough without too much assistance, and these left-hand pages offer spoiler-free explanations, tips and general guidance.

- The **map portions** feature, among other things, the locations of all collectibles in each zone. However – and this is very important to know – *MGS4* occasionally adjusts the types of ammunition, items and weapons found in each location in accordance with the equipment you have in your inventory, and your chosen difficulty level. You'll almost certainly encounter slight variations as you play.

- **Right-hand pages** feature detailed walkthroughs written for the Big Boss Hard difficulty level, but the advice offered is also applicable to the Liquid Easy, Naked Normal and (default) Solid Normal settings – you'll just encounter fewer potential enemies, and certain challenges may be less demanding than we suggest. It's actually impossible to unlock all secret features in *MGS4* during your initial run (see "First Playthrough"), but the tactics and strategies we offer are high-level techniques designed to help you achieve "perfect" completion on a subsequent attempt. That's not to say that you can't unlock some cool bonuses on your first sitting, though…

- There are occasional exceptions to the walkthrough format detailed above, but these are very easy to follow.

FIRST PLAYTHROUGH

On your initial run through *Metal Gear Solid 4*, we strongly recommend that you just concentrate on having fun. Enjoy the story, use any weapons or tactics that seem appropriate, and feel free to make as much noise as you like when the urge becomes too great to resist. When you've completed *MGS4* once, you can then try for a "perfect" playthrough. (If you're curious, the requirements for this are no Alert Phases, no continues, no kills, no health items, no "special" items, and a play time of less than five hours – and all on a difficulty level you can't actually access yet. Suffice to say, it's not something you're going to achieve straight away.)

We generally favor a pacifist style of play with an onus on pure stealth in our main walkthrough, because this approach leads to the best post-game rewards. However, without revealing any spoilers, we should let you know that the requirements for certain unlockable features are extremely stringent: think in terms of "zero kills" and "no Alert Phases". Attempting to achieve either goal on a first playthrough is *not* a good idea, because you'll need to repeat both feats (and much more besides) to win the best post-game rewards and accolades at a later date.

Walkthrough: Left-Hand Page
This page offers basic tips to help you through each area of the game on your first sitting, accompanied by illustrative screenshots.

Engaging the Gekko is a fruitless endeavor – you don't have the hardware to destroy them at this early stage, and there's no specific reward for even attempting to. Instead, avoid them by weaving your way through the buildings and back streets. The objective is to reach the exit pictured above. Simply run through it to initiate the next cutscene.

Just in case you miss Otacon's prompt, don't forget that you need to visit the pause menu to assign weapons and items to R2 and L3 respectively. There's more on this in the How to Play chapter (see page 10). For now, ready the AK102 in a spare slot before you press forward.

There are items hidden *everywhere* in *MGS4*, and your hoarding instinct should kick in immediately as you notice a Ration under the truck directly ahead of your starting position. Hold ⊗ to move Snake into a crawling position in order to collect it.

NOTE: MISSION 1 BRIEFING

Metal Gear Solid 4 is divided into five main "acts", each [...] story elements. The Mission Briefing for Act 1, unlike th[...] probably a good idea to save your game and view it [...] East, and gives interesting background information on [...]

ICON	REPRESENTS
▲	Your starting point(s) on each map
◎	Zone exit or mission objective
╳	Blocked path
⊒	Ladder
⊤	Turret
◹	Mortar
⚠ ⚠ ⚠	Enemy presence indicators, from light to heavy
⚠	Mines/traps
⬆ ⬇	Elevation indicators (upper/lower floor)
A ① ②	Walkthrough waypoints
⬍	Elevator

Map Section
The detailed map portions are extremely easy to use; "up" is always north, and the number above each one corresponds with the same portion of the overview map. Just in case you're confused by the presence of certain icons, we've prepared a concise legend (see table on the left).

Lettered Paragraphs

The core of the main walkthrough. As an aid to easy navigation, the letters used as headlines correspond with those that appear on each map.

Tab System

The tab system on the right-hand side of each double-page spread is designed to help you find the required walkthrough section without skipping too far ahead – naturally, evil spoilers await for those who flick through the chapter indiscriminately…

METAL GEAR SOLID 4
GUNS OF THE PATRIOTS TACTICAL ESPIONAGE ACTION

A Crawl underneath the truck directly ahead to collect a Ration, then squeeze beneath the next truck along to resume the extended introductory sequence. If you linger in this opening area the game code will automatically move Snake forward – so don't forget to pause should you need to take a break for any reason. You can take this opportunity to practice a few basic moves if you like, as many things have changed since *MGS3*.

B Collect the AK102. If you move to the left or right, you'll trigger the next cinematic sequence. We suggest that you walk to the right – this puts you in the best position for the next section. Note that your choice of direction alters the cutscene played, which is something to bear in mind for future playthroughs.

Backtrack along the street, away from the Gekko standing next to Snake as play resumes, then run through the broken wall located directly ahead where the road curves to the right. Head for the militia soldier standing in the doorway and wait (briefly) for the Gekko outside to pass. When its back is facing the door, sneak behind it, across the street and into the next house along. Run through this shattered building and into the bombed-out shell of the next house – you can vault through the window by pressing up against the ledge and hitting Ⓐ. Wait in here until the Gekko to your left moves away, then make a dash for the exit – it's a simple U-turn to the right from the doorway that the Gekko was standing outside. The whole process should take no more than 30 seconds.

ALTERNATIVE STRATEGIES

Bar Rations and ammunition dropped by the stricken militia forces, there's nothing of interest in this area – and, therefore, little reason to explore alternative routes. Broadly, though, you can take any path you please, as long as you're prepared to wait for each Gekko to move before darting to the next cover point. Players attempting a playthrough without initiating a single Alert Phase should note that being detected by these Gekko does not count towards the final total.

BRIEFING: GEKKO

Though it's better to run through this area without being detected by the Gekko, let alone engaging them in combat, you'll benefit by knowing a few facts about these monstrous war machines. In addition to ballistic attacks, they can perform a variety of vicious kicks and stamps with their long legs – including a powerful roundhouse sweep that you'll do well to avoid – and will even leap on top of their targets, killing them instantly. They can also throw grenades to flush their prey from cover.

Don't underestimate the sheer mobility and tenacity of the Gekko – they can pop up in surprising positions. For a startling example of this, head upstairs in one of the bombed-out buildings and cause a little noise.

FLASHBACK: SUMMARY

The opening cinematics (and optional Mission Briefing) introduce several characters. To help MGS series newcomers get up to speed – and to refresh the memories of everyone else – here's a quick round-up of the most important faces.

Otacon: A technological genius and inventor of Metal Gear REX, he met Snake at Shadow Moses (MGS1), and now plays a vital supporting role in his friend's missions.

Sunny: Abducted at birth by the Patriots (a shadowy organization that we will return to in a future Flashback), Sunny was later freed by Raiden – the secret agent at the heart of the Big Shell Incident (MGS2), now missing. This delicate child prodigy lives with Snake and Otacon aboard the Nomad.

Roy Campbell: Snake's superior during his time as a United States operative, Campbell has since retired from military life. He now works for the United Nations in an advisory capacity, investigating the activities of Private Military Companies (PMCs).

Liquid: Snake's twin, also a child of Les Enfants Terribles. Unlike Snake, Liquid chose to follow in Big Boss's footsteps, and instigated the events of the Shadow Moses Incident (MGS1). Liquid was killed by a nanovirus (FOXDIE) but his spirit lives on, now occupying and controlling the body of Ocelot – himself a key figure in the events of MGS1, MGS2, MGS3 and MGS: Portable Ops.

Solid Snake: A product of the Les Enfants Terribles project, Snake is a clone of Big Boss. As a government agent, he defeated his "father" in Outer Heaven and Zanzibarland (Metal Gear 1 & 2), before confronting his twin brother in the Shadow Moses Incident (MGS1). He later founded the Philanthropy agency with Otacon in order to prevent the proliferation of Metal Gear technology (MGS2).

FOXDIE: An experimental, highly lethal nanovirus designed to attack specific programmed targets. Snake was injected with FOXDIE during the Shadow Moses Incident (MGS1), but acted merely as its vector – he appears immune to its effects.

■ Remember: if you have the Ration and, later, Noodles or Regain healing objects selected as your current item, Snake will automatically use one whenever his health reaches zero until his stocks are depleted. This can be (literally) a life-saver, with the added benefit of reducing the inevitable wastage that occurs through "manual" use.

■ You can replenish Snake's Psyche and health gauges by finding a safe, ideally concealed position, then leave the veteran soldier to lie in a prone pose. This piece of knowledge can save you a lot of trouble when you play on the Big Boss difficulty level.

OUND ZERO

A

...cutscene that explains Snake's objectives and reveals key ...cessed from the Main Menu. Though entirely optional, it's ...s to establish why Snake is tracking Liquid in the Middle...

Walkthrough: Right-Hand Page

Right-hand pages offer a detailed walkthrough with an emphasis on stealthy infiltration and avoidance. They also regularly feature box-outs marked "Alternative Strategies", "Secret", "Briefing" and "Flashback". The first is pretty self-explanatory, "Secret" indicates a hidden feature, "Briefing" is used to explain new gameplay elements, and the short "Flashback" paragraphs are designed to give a little background information and context when major characters are first introduced.

Margin Notes

You can find notes in the right-hand margin of each right-hand walkthrough page. These reveal tips, tactics, hidden features and interesting observations.

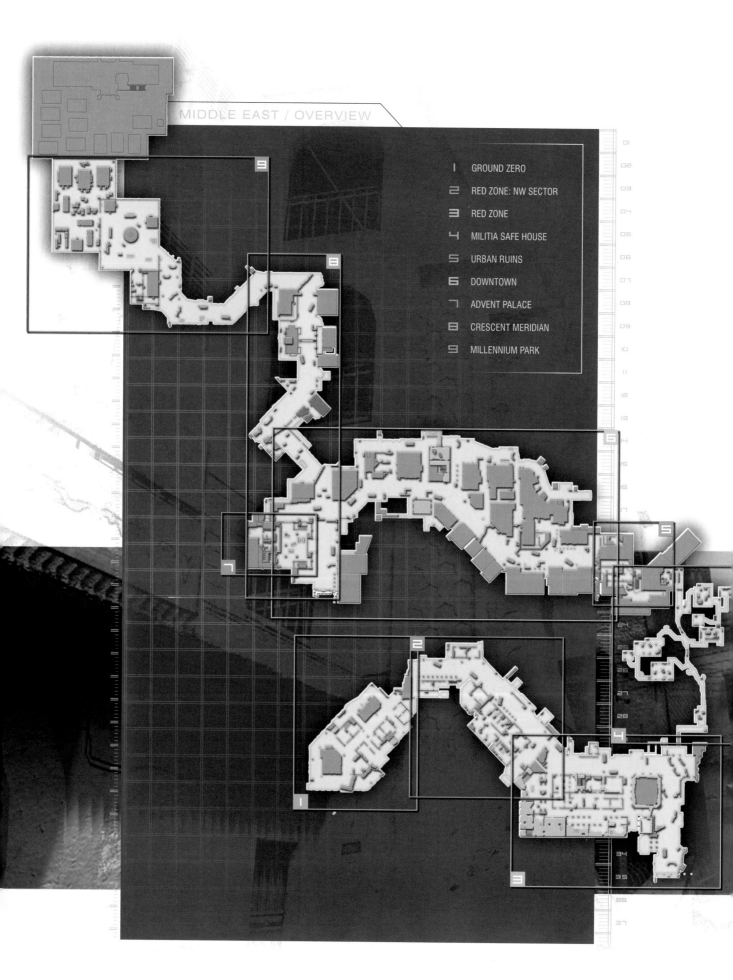

1 GROUND ZERO

2 RED ZONE: NW SECTOR

3 RED ZONE

4 MILITIA SAFE HOUSE

5 URBAN RUINS

6 DOWNTOWN

7 ADVENT PALACE

8 CRESCENT MERIDIAN

9 MILLENNIUM PARK

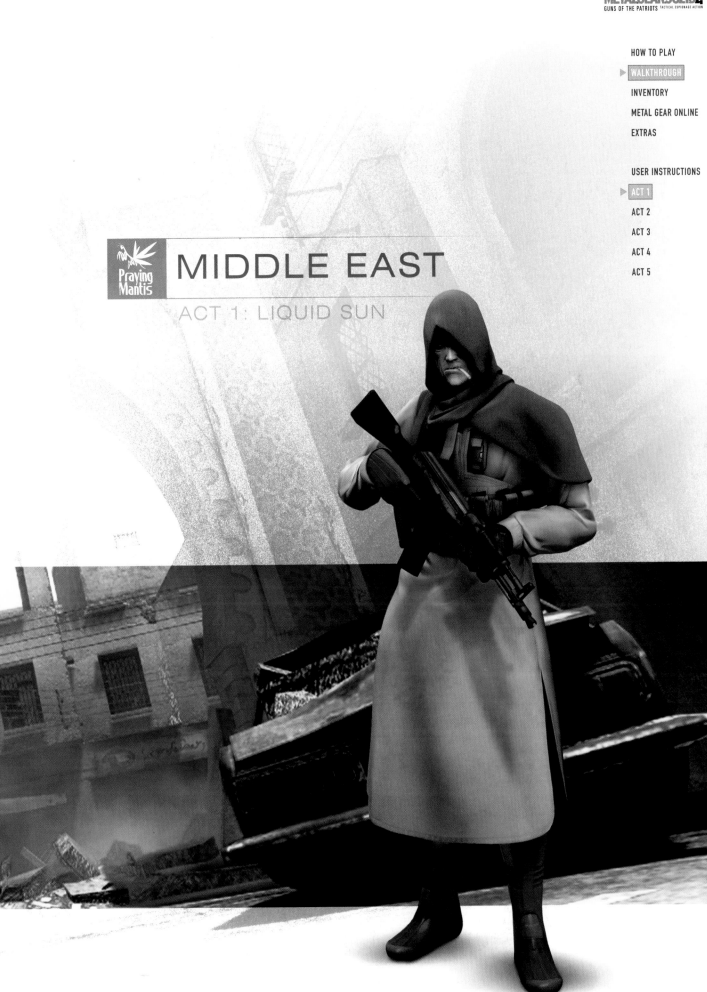

Praying Mantis

MIDDLE EAST
ACT 1: LIQUID SUN

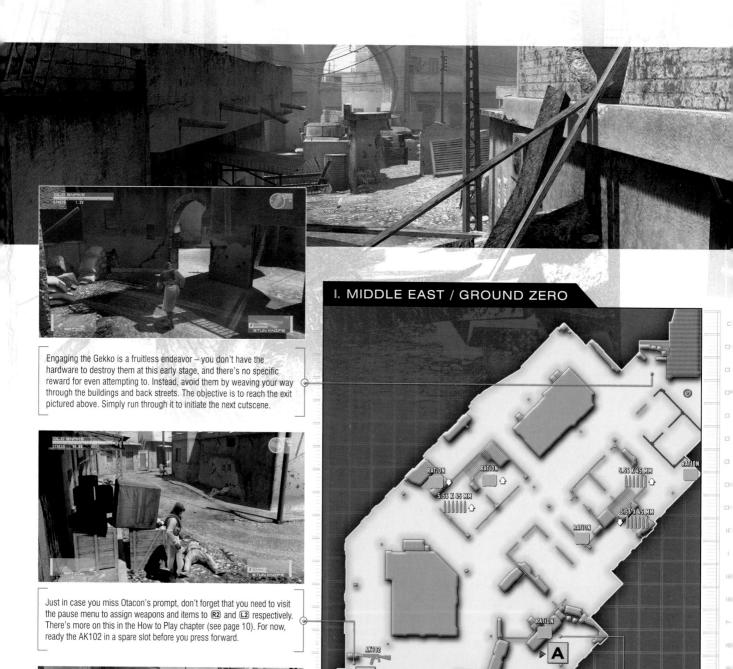

Engaging the Gekko is a fruitless endeavor – you don't have the hardware to destroy them at this early stage, and there's no specific reward for even attempting to. Instead, avoid them by weaving your way through the buildings and back streets. The objective is to reach the exit pictured above. Simply run through it to initiate the next cutscene.

I. MIDDLE EAST / GROUND ZERO

Just in case you miss Otacon's prompt, don't forget that you need to visit the pause menu to assign weapons and items to [R2] and [L2] respectively. There's more on this in the How to Play chapter (see page 10). For now, ready the AK102 in a spare slot before you press forward.

There are items hidden *everywhere* in *MGS4*, and your hoarding instinct should kick in immediately as you notice a Ration under the truck directly ahead of your starting position. Hold ⊗ to move Snake into a crawling position in order to collect it.

NOTE: MISSION 1 BRIEFING

Metal Gear Solid 4 is divided into five main "acts", each prefaced by a Mission Briefing cutscene that explains Snake's objectives and reveals key story elements. The Mission Briefing for Act 1, unlike those that follow, can only be accessed from the Main Menu. Though entirely optional, it's probably a good idea to save your game and view it after escaping the Gekko – it helps to establish why Snake is tracking Liquid in the Middle East, and gives interesting background information on the world of 2014.

A Crawl underneath the truck directly ahead to collect a Ration, then squeeze beneath the next truck along to resume the extended introductory sequence. If you linger in this opening area the game code will automatically move Snake forward – so don't forget to pause should you need to take a break for any reason. You can take this opportunity to practice a few basic moves if you like, as many things have changed since *MGS3*.

B Collect the AK102. If you move to the left or right, you'll trigger the next cinematic sequence. We suggest that you walk to the right – this puts you in the best position for the next section. Note that your choice of direction alters the cutscene played, which is something to bear in mind for future playthroughs.

Backtrack along the street, away from the Gekko standing next to Snake as play resumes, then run through the broken wall located directly ahead where the road curves to the right. Head for the militia soldier standing in the doorway and wait (briefly) for the Gekko outside to pass. When its back is facing the door, sneak behind it, across the street and into the next house along. Run through this shattered building and into the bombed-out shell of the next house – you can vault through the window by pressing up against the ledge and hitting ⊿. Wait in here until the Gekko to your left moves away, then make a dash for the exit – it's a simple U-turn to the right from the doorway that the Gekko was standing outside. The whole process should take no more than 30 seconds.

ALTERNATIVE STRATEGIES

Bar Rations and ammunition dropped by the stricken militia forces, there's nothing of interest in this area – and, therefore, little reason to explore alternative routes. Broadly, though, you can take any path you please, as long as you're prepared to wait for each Gekko to move on before darting to the next cover point. Players attempting a playthrough without initiating a single Alert Phase should note that being detected by these Gekko does not count towards the final total.

■ Remember: if you have the Ration and, later, Noodles or Regain healing objects selected as your current item, Snake will automatically use one whenever his health reaches zero until his stocks are depleted. This can be (literally) a life-saver, with the added benefit of reducing the inevitable wastage that occurs through "manual" use.

■ You can replenish Snake's Psyche and health gauges by finding a safe, ideally concealed position, then leave the veteran soldier to lie in a prone pose. This piece of knowledge can save you a lot of trouble when you play on the Big Boss difficulty level.

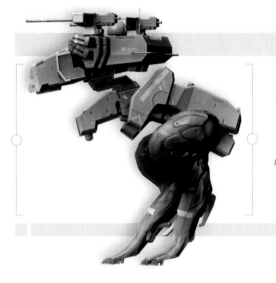

BRIEFING: GEKKO

Though it's better to run through this area without being detected by the Gekko, let alone engaging them in combat, you'll benefit by knowing a few facts about these monstrous war machines. In addition to ballistic attacks, they can perform a variety of vicious kicks and stamps with their long legs – including a powerful roundhouse sweep that you'll do well to avoid – and will even leap on top of their targets, killing them instantly. They can also throw grenades to flush their prey from cover.

Don't underestimate the sheer mobility and tenacity of the Gekko – they can pop up in surprising positions. For a startling example of this, head upstairs in one of the bombed-out buildings and cause a little noise.

FLASHBACK: SUMMARY

The opening cinematics (and optional Mission Briefing) introduce several characters. To help MGS series newcomers get up to speed – and to refresh the memories of everyone else – here's a quick round-up of the most important faces.

Solid Snake: *A product of the Les Enfants Terribles project, Snake is a clone of Big Boss. As a government agent, he defeated his "father" in Outer Heaven and Zanzibarland (**Metal Gear 1** & **2**), before confronting his twin brother in the Shadow Moses Incident (**MGS1**). He later founded the Philanthropy agency with Otacon in order to prevent the proliferation of Metal Gear technology (**MGS2**).*

Otacon: *A technological genius and inventor of Metal Gear REX, he met Snake at Shadow Moses (**MGS1**), and now plays a vital supporting role in his friend's missions.*

Sunny: *Abducted at birth by the Patriots (a shadowy organization that we will return to in a future Flashback), Sunny was later freed by Raiden – the secret agent at the heart of the Big Shell Incident (**MGS2**), now missing. This delicate child prodigy lives with Snake and Otacon aboard the Nomad.*

Roy Campbell: *Snake's superior during his time as a United States operative, Campbell has since retired from military life. He now works for the United Nations in an advisory capacity, investigating the activities of Private Military Companies (PMCs).*

Liquid: *Snake's twin, also a child of Les Enfants Terribles. Unlike Snake, Liquid chose to follow in Big Boss's footsteps, and instigated the events of the Shadow Moses Incident (**MGS1**). Liquid was killed by a nanovirus (FOXDIE) but his spirit lives on, now occupying and controlling the body of Ocelot – himself a key figure in the events of **MGS1**, **MGS2**, **MGS3** and **MGS: Portable Ops**.*

FOXDIE: *An experimental, highly lethal nanovirus designed to attack specific programmed targets. Snake was injected with FOXDIE during the Shadow Moses Incident (**MGS1**), but acted merely as its vector – he appears immune to its effects.*

PETRO BOMB
C. BOX
COMPRESS
NOODLES
PETRO BOMB

5.56 X 45 MM
COMPRESS
5.56 X 45 MM
RATION
RATION
5.56 X 45 MM
5.56 X 45 MM
5.56 X 45 MM
5.56 X 45 MM
COMPRESS
5.56 X 45 MM
RATION
5.56 X 45 MM
NOODLES
RATION
COMPRESS
5.56 X 45 MM

C
D

5.56 X 45 MM
REGAIN
5.56 X 45 MM
5.56 X 45 MM

There's nothing you can do to prevent the slaughter of the militia in this area, and the presence of the Stryker – an armored vehicle with a powerful turret – means that any attempt will end badly. It's best to stick to the cover available inside the buildings on the right-hand side of the main street.

Be careful to stop and wait for PMC soldiers to move forward whenever necessary. The route to the next zone isn't too complicated – it's just a case of sticking to the right-hand side of the map throughout. You only need emerge into the daylight once before the final crawl to the exit, and in that instance the entrance to the next house along is just around the corner.

Be very quiet in the final building, and pause until the coast is clear before sneaking to the right-hand exit. Note that an Alert Phase will carry forward to the next area, so it's probably better to find somewhere to hide and wait for the commotion to subside if you are discovered.

WEAPON LOCKS

Snake can collect any weapon he finds on the battlefield, but many of these – particularly those wielded by PMC troops – are "locked" by the SOP System. There is a way to circumvent this restriction, but you'll need to make do with the AK102 and CQC for the immediate future.

HOW TO PLAY
▶ WALKTHROUGH
INVENTORY
METAL GEAR ONLINE
EXTRAS

USER INSTRUCTIONS
▶ ACT 1
ACT 2
ACT 3
ACT 4
ACT 5

C

Head around the corner onto the main street, then immediately enter the doorway to your right to avoid the two soldiers on the street. A brief cutscene is triggered as you move through the second room, which announces the arrival of the Stryker and additional PMC troops. You can pause to watch the battle through the doorway if you like, but we strongly advise that you don't get involved. Squeeze through the gap in the wall, then wait as you exit for the PMC troops to move on. Crawl towards the pavement, pausing for a moment to enable the OctoCamo to adjust to the new surface, then – carefully! – move around the corner and enter the next building on the right.

Collect items and AK102 ammunition from the two rooms, then crawl through the gap underneath the rubble to continue.

D

Be careful as you creep beneath the debris. Sometimes (but not always), you are confronted by the grizzly sight of a local rebel being executed in cold blood by a PMC soldier. Wait until you are sure that there is no one immediately outside, then crawl out and to the right.

From this point forward, you should stay to the far right of the map. Usually, you will need to creep slowly as you move parallel to a pair of PMC soldiers as they search for survivors, but this isn't always the case; there are occasions when two soldiers will approach from the north instead. You'll be perfectly safe as long as you stay in the shadows to the right of them, and pause to enable the OctoCamo to adapt to new surfaces when you reach them. Crouch or lay down to activate the Threat Ring and reveal the relative location and proximity of patrolling PMC troops.

Take care as you approach the exit. You should see two soldiers moving away from your position on the road outside, towards another Stryker. If so, wait for them to reach it. Check the path to your left (a glance at the Threat Ring might suffice) then crawl out onto the street and immediately head towards the door (to your right on the opposite side of the street) to progress to the next zone.

ALTERNATIVE STRATEGIES

Attempting to sneak to the exit via the left-hand side of the map just isn't practical – there are two Strykers and patrolling PMC soldiers to avoid, with much less cover than our recommended route. You can easily crawl across the very start of the street to pick up a Petro Bomb collectible on the other side (note that this triggers the arrival of the Stryker containing PMC reinforcements), then return and follow the standard path. If you're especially brave or experienced, you can continue past the burning car and enter a doorway just beyond it. This house contains a handful of items (see map), but nothing that warrants the increased danger – you'll acquire these elsewhere soon enough.

Our recommended path through Red Zone: NW Sector uses the exit on the right, and for good reason – the exit on the left puts you in immediate danger of discovery when you arrive in the next zone. It's definitely something worth trying on a subsequent playthrough, though.

■ If you pick up and drop dead bodies or unconscious soldiers (press Ⓐ when the onscreen prompt appears), they will often release a hidden object – usually a common item or box of ammunition.

■ Note that you can also open lockers, which sometimes contain useful items. You can also hide inside them, but doing so is no guarantee that Snake won't be discovered…

BRIEFING: STEALTH TACTICS

Though MGS4 doesn't directly prohibit a more aggressive approach, it can become extremely difficult unless you learn how to evade detection through silent movement and intelligent use of OctoCamo. There's no substitute for first-hand experience, but reading the following guidance is definitely a good starting point.

- *Get into the habit of glancing at the **camouflage rating** in the top right-hand corner of the screen on a regular basis. If you're serious about being as stealthy as possible, you should aim for a minimum 65% whenever there is a danger of detection.*

- *We may be laboring an obvious point, but **crawling** is by far the most effective way to avoid detection. The OctoCamo suit enables Snake to easily blend in with floor surfaces, which can conceal him from vigilant eyes at surprisingly close range. The movement speed may at first feel torturously slow to players accustomed to fast, fluid motion in FPS games, but persevere: once you get a feel for the distinct "rhythm" of creeping in this way, it actually becomes second nature. There's also the fact that crawling leaves no footprints – a definite advantage when sneaking through heavily guarded areas.*

- *The **crouch-walk** is fine if Snake is operating behind cover, if there are no enemies in your immediate vicinity, or when creeping behind a soldier. The **standing posture**, however, should be avoided unless you're absolutely sure that there's no one around, or if you're actively engaged in a combat situation. Sprinting from pillar to post in an upright pose makes Snake as stealthy as a capering clown.*

- ***Movement speed** is important in two respects. Patrolling PMC soldiers are generally looking for any sign of life, usually with a view to extinguishing it, and rapid motions (even while crawling) will attract their attention. Secondly, faster movement creates more noise. Use the full range of analog movement on the left thumbstick to vary your pace as required and, if in doubt, stop dead and wait for potential aggressors to pass by before you continue.*

- *Take **environmental factors** into account. Bright sunshine makes Snake more visible and will reduce his camouflage rating by a small amount. Whenever possible, stick to the shadows. Additionally, just because a PMC soldier can't see you, it doesn't mean they can't hear you. If you clumsily knock over bottles and pots, or blunder through surface water, there's a high probability that a nearby soldier will come to investigate.*

- *To **change the current OctoCamo pattern**, simply pause briefly while crawling, or when pressed up against a solid surface. You don't have to wait for the sound effect and suit transition to complete before moving on – you're safe to get moving as soon as the camouflage percentage is updated.*

- *While crawling, take the different floor surfaces into account. In dangerous situations, you'll need to **pause regularly** to allow the suit to adapt. Pay attention to details such as transitions between rubble and floor tiles, and pavement and street, and be vigilant for potential "detection traps" – for example, brightly colored rugs inside houses.*

*Only available after the introduction of Metal Gear Mk. II

5.56 X 45 MM

RPG-7

RATION

C. BOX

COMPRESS

E

EASTER EGG

5.56 X 45 MM

5.56 X 45 MM

RPG-7° 2ⁿᵈ NOODLES

5.56 X 45 MM

ANEST. (.22)°

5.56 X 45 MM

PLAYBOY

COMPRESS

RATION

RATION

G

RATION

RATION

REGAIN

F

RATION

Though there are three potential routes to the objective, hugging the south side of the map is once again the least complicated path to take. We suggest that you go up the staircase and neutralize the soldier at the top (pictured), then crawl along the end of the upper floor level to avoid detection.

5.56 X 45 MM

5.56 X 45 MM

As there are more soldiers in this area, following patrol routes that cast prying eyes over a wider range of surfaces, there's a much greater chance that Snake might be spotted. Should that happen, attempting to fight your way through the maze of broken walls and alleyways would be unwise – it's better to just make a break for the objective. Any active Alert Phase will be cancelled when the ensuing cutscene ends.

After the interlude, you simply need to reach the entrance to the Militia Safe House area – a short and relatively uncomplicated journey. However, you can gain the friendship of the militia forces by assisting them in the battle against the PMC soldiers, especially by destroying the Stryker that arrives (use the RPG-7 weapon situated near to the exit). This course of action is strongly recommended if this is your first *MGS4* playthrough.

E You'll encounter two soldiers directly ahead as you enter Red Zone, so try not to draw attention to yourself before they move on. Pick up the Cardboard Box and Compress hidden beneath the exposed staircase, then slowly head to the right-hand side of the area. There are numerous PMC troops on patrol throughout this zone, with gaps in broken buildings complicating matters no end – it's hard to anticipate when you might be visible to an unseen enemy.

Head up the staircase in the south-west corner of the map (right of the entrance), then – carefully – crawl up until approximately halfway on the second flight. A PMC soldier with a short patrol route is positioned up here. Wait until he stands outside the doorway at the top of the stairs. You then have two choices: either follow him (use a slow crouch-walk), disable him with CQC and stuff his body into one of the conveniently placed lockers, or sneak past as soon as his back is turned. Either way, you need to (quickly, in the latter instance) creep east and jump over the broken wall section. Go prone as soon as you land – it's better to be safe.

F From this position, you need to crawl approximately east to the end of the shattered building, where you can safely drop back down to the ground. There's an ever-present danger of being spotted by the soldiers patrolling below, and the variable floor surfaces are an additional complication. If you're diligent, moving steadily and positioning your camera to spot potential dangers to your left, it's an easy journey. Should a soldier become suspicious, though, it's not a disaster – he will need to climb a nearby ladder to investigate, which will give you sufficient time to creep to a suitable hiding spot. When you reach the Ration, make sure that the coast is clear, then drop to the ground.

Check to the left to ensure that no one is approaching you from that direction, then move around the corner to the right to reach the street after the two patrolling soldiers move on. You'll need to immediately crawl into the corner of the shady area with the dumpster, as two more soldiers approach from the east. When they pass, move around the corner and through the entrance – take care not to disturb the pots and bottles either side of it – to trigger a cutscene.

G The acquisition of two silenced weapons – the Operator and Mk. 2 Pistol – makes the process of sneaking through enemy lines much, much easier. You now need to make your way through a pitched battle between PMC troops and local militia. If you crawl around the corner from your starting position, you'll see PMC forces massing for a charge on the rebel position. The best plan is to wait for them all to leave their position behind the sandbags before you move forward, but you can also use either pistol (aim for the head, naturally) to neutralize them from cover if you're in a hurry.

Crawl over to the opposite side of the street, steadily make your way forward, towards the battle, and go through an opening on your right. The PMC soldiers won't notice you if you keep a low profile. Once inside, crawl or crouch-walk to the end of the corridor. You can then crawl through the trench behind the besieged rebel forces and, from there, into the entrance to the Militia Safe House area.

> ■ If you're detected near the entrance to this area, there's an extremely novel way to hide until the all-clear is sounded – simply approach the sculpture, climb onto the plinth and follow the onscreen prompt. We won't spoil the surprise, but note that it's worth trying this a few times…
>
> ■ You can hide bodies or incapacitated soldiers in storage lockers – first open the door, then drag them into position. This is especially useful on harder difficulty levels, as soldiers sleeping off the effects of tranquilizers or a vigorous bout of CQC inside a locker will not regain consciousness before you leave the area.

ALTERNATIVE STRATEGIES

There are technically three routes you can take to the meeting with Metal Gear Mk. II and Otacon. The first (and easiest) is to hug the right-hand side of the map, as detailed in the main walkthrough, but you can also move through the center of the zone – a much trickier proposition. In this instance, you can reach a staircase in the maze of broken walls, climb up, and balance precariously in clear view during a short walk over a narrow broken wall. You can then drop down and carefully make a break for the objective. The third option is to follow the buildings on the left, which is the most plausible route if you entered the area from the left-hand entrance in Red Zone: NW Sector. This involves dodging regular patrols, with a high probability of detection and little reward in terms of concealed items.

Though our walkthrough focuses on stealth, you can actually help the militia forces win the battle that takes place after you collect Metal Gear Mk. II. Indeed, to enjoy an easy, uneventful route through the Militia Safe House zone that follows, you actually need to endear yourself to the local rebel forces. The easiest way to achieve this is to use the RPG-7 positioned next to the area exit to destroy the Stryker that arrives during the battle. To help the militiamen triumph, though, you'll need to help eliminate all PMC soldiers, and destroy a second Stryker in the south-west corner of the area. The latter task requires additional RPG-7 ammo, and you can find the necessary single rocket by climbing a staircase in approximately the center of the map, then walking across a narrow wall (as described in the previous paragraph). Note that this weapon only appears *after* Snake's conversation with Otacon.

You'll know when the battle is won when the air resounds with cries of "We did it!" from the jubilant rebels. By way of reward, you're then free to explore the map to collect its many items without fear of reprisals.

If you insist on going through while your relationship with the militia is still neutral, you'll be challenged by almost every individual that you encounter. Freeze every time you are noticed. Should you move, ready a weapon, or do anything likely to cause alarm, the soldiers can and *will* attack. If you wait until they run over and examine Snake, though, you'll be free to move on as soon as they recognize and dismiss him. This process will be repeated several times before you reach the exit.

If you haven't befriended the militia forces at this stage, you can still go back outside right now – and it's a good idea to do so if this is your first playthrough.

BACKTRACKING TO RED ZONE

If you passed through the Red Zone area without getting directly involved in the conflict between the local militia and PMC forces, you'll find that the battle is a little different should you return. If you didn't destroy either of the two Strykers, you'll encounter one speeding along the street towards you as you emerge from the Militia Safe House, coming to a halt just in front of the sandbags. The militia forces now occupy the end of the street where the PMC soldiers were initially stationed during your first visit. The objectives remain the same (destroy both armored vehicles and eliminate PMC troops), but these subtle alterations change the nature of the fight. It's definitely something that you should try on a later playthrough.

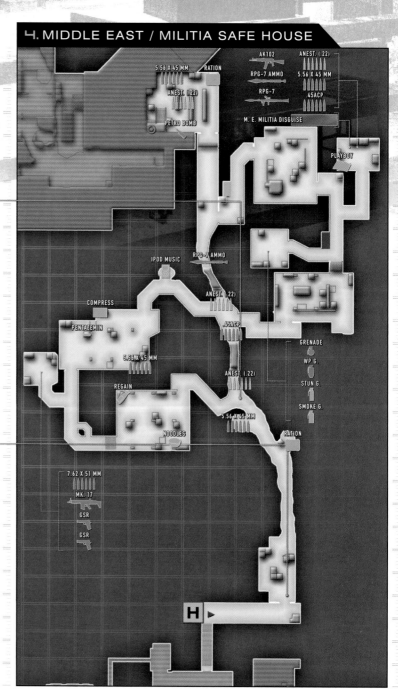

4. MIDDLE EAST / MILITIA SAFE HOUSE

HOW TO PLAY
▶ WALKTHROUGH
INVENTORY
METAL GEAR ONLINE
EXTRAS

USER INSTRUCTIONS
▶ ACT 1
ACT 2
ACT 3
ACT 4
ACT 5

H

If you've befriended the militia forces by causing sufficient havoc in Red Zone (especially by destroying one of the two Strykers), you can stroll happily through the Militia Safe House area and collect its many items until you reach the exit.

ALTERNATIVE STRATEGIES

First-time players (or those who already have PMC blood on their hands) should follow the guidance to the left – this information is for hardcore sneaking experts only. If you are attempting a "pure" stealth/no kill playthrough, though, these tips will guide you safely through the Militia Safe House without disturbing a single one of its denizens. Don't worry about picking up items (you can return to collect them with ease shortly), and try not to rely too heavily on the Threat Ring or Solid Eye in here – the effectiveness of both is reduced by ambient background interference, particularly from chickens and rats. From the top, then:

• Lie down on the left side of the boxes to hide from the first guard, then move forward when he walks past.

• Continue on until you reach two dead ends. Enter the one on the left and wait for the three soldiers to pass.

• As you exit the room with the chickens, look for a narrow gap to your right. Crouch-walk into this and press yourself up against the wall to avoid the next batch of soldiers running to aid their comrades outside.

• Crawl behind the soldier attending to a wounded ally in the makeshift infirmary, taking care not to get too close.

• In the next corridor, you'll again reach another pair of dead ends to the left and right. Move into the one on the right and position Snake in the far corner, then deploy Metal Gear Mk. II. Activate its stealth function, then approach the soldier standing guard outside the next doorway along. He should start a patrol at this point, walking straight past Snake without noticing him. Sneak over to the door as soon as he has strolled by.

• Be extremely cautious in the next room – there are two militia soldiers having a conversation in the middle. Move around the outside of the room, but inch forward at the very slowest crawling pace when Snake is most exposed. One of the two men will leave, but the other that remains can be highly sensitive to noise and movement. Be extra careful as you head for the steps – it's better to wait until he turns his back to you.

• At the top of the steps, immediately crawl along to the left to avoid two further soldiers. Wait until they move on, then return to the corridor and take the next right.

• Inside the small room, collect the Middle East Militia Disguise from the center locker and immediately equip it – select "Camouflage" from the pause menu, then "Cloth", and then "Change Costume".

With a foolproof disguise in place, you can travel anywhere in the basement and collect its many treasures.

BRIEFING: MILITIA FORCES

Though assisting (and therefore allying yourself with) the local militia army is purely optional, it does make the process of sneaking through Act 1 a little easier.

• *If Snake's relationship with the militia forces is neutral (the default state), they may react with suspicion or surprise when they encounter him. In a worst-case scenario, they will raise their weapons and order him to stop while they identify him. If they say "Don't move!" or "Stop right there!", they really mean it.*

• *If you have gained the favor of the militia army, hearts will appear over their heads when they spot you. You may find that individual soldiers will even give you items or ammunition.*

• *Arousing the ire of the militia army by threatening (be careful where you point your gun!), assaulting or killing its members is extremely inadvisable.*

• *Celebratory cries of "We did it!" from militia indicate that the PMC troops within a localized area – or, in some instances, an entire zone – have been defeated. This usually means that you're free to hunt for collectibles and explore your immediate environment. Note that it is not always possible to eliminate the PMC presence in an area.*

BRIEFING: PMC FORCES

You should have a basic appreciation of how PMC soldiers behave by now, but the following tips should help you in future encounters.

• *If PMC soldiers spot you they will immediately raise the alarm, initiating an Alert Phase. This will often lead them to request reinforcements. However, these are not always available – listen to the radio dialogue for clues.*

• *If you disable PMC soldiers before they can shout out or use their radios, you can cancel a newly started Alert Phase instantly should no other soldiers witness the event.*

• *If you neutralize a soldier while he is speaking with his HQ, but before he reports the specifics of a situation, you will generally find that a few troops will be sent to his location to investigate. It's wise to move on (and, if you're sufficiently confident, hide his body) before they arrive.*

• *Listen carefully while sneaking past PMC patrols. If you do anything to arouse a soldier's suspicions, you'll hear them make a remark – most commonly, something along the lines of "Huh?" or "What was that?". They will usually run to your position to investigate, which is your cue to quickly (but carefully) move elsewhere. A comment such as "I swear I saw something" indicates that the soldier has satisfied his curiosity, and will return to his standard patrol route.*

• *Even if you get involved with battles between PMC and militia forces, try to avoid detection at all times. If you trigger an Alert Phase, much more gunfire will be directed at Snake.*

■ When you are hunting for treasure in item-rich locales such as the Militia Safe House, activating the Solid Eye's Night Vision function will increase the visibility of all collectibles.

■ Alternative costumes (such as the Middle East Militia Disguise) are useful in specific situations, but are significantly less effective than OctoCamo for general sneaking. Don't forget to switch back to Snake's standard suit before you enter dangerous areas.

5. MIDDLE EAST / URBAN RUINS

When you reach the area pictured here, either press up against the wall and inch across the narrow ledge, or drop over the edge and traverse until you reach the other side. The exit is then a short stroll away. If you move over to the far right before you drop down to the lower level, you can collect three items before the next checkpoint, which removes the need to backtrack after the cutscene.

When you reach the two militia soldiers, wait until they are shot by enemies down below, then sneak past. There's little point in taking pot-shots at the PMC soldiers outside (expect no reward or, indeed, no form of resolution if you do), so just carry on until you encounter a collapsing wall section.

To reach three of the collectables at the start of this area, you need to climb the two flights of stairs to the very top, then drop down at the position pictured here. You'll find a Dot Sight – worth a cool 20,000 DP at this point – an RPG-7, and a Sleep Gas Mine. The way forward can be found in the rubble to the left of the staircase.

BRIEFING: NON-LETHAL FORCE

As you may have noticed, our main walkthrough relates the stealthiest route through each area. Direct combat is (whenever possible) treated as optional; we also regularly suggest that you "disable" or "neutralize" assailants, but never specify the means by which you do so.

There are two reasons for this. Firstly, stealth is generally the most rewarding and effective style of play. While it's enjoyable to get involved in battles, MGS4 is a "stealth action" game – not an FPS. Secondly, the most significant post-game reward is only available if you (among other things) go through the entire adventure without killing a single person or triggering an Alert Phase. This categorically isn't something that you should attempt to achieve on your first playthrough (where it's practically impossible not to "go loud" on a fairly regular basis, either through inexperience or design), but it's a good idea to acquire certain good habits at an early stage.

FLASHBACK: JOHNNY SASAKI

Johnny (aka Akiba) first appeared in *Metal Gear Solid*, where his uniform was stolen by Meryl Silverburgh, a young soldier who assisted Snake in his mission. He is known for his gastrointestinal "difficulties" – as demonstrated in the noisy, almost palpably fragrant cutscene that introduces him in *MGS4*…

I Urban Ruins is a small and linear area, with no real enemies or challenges to concern you. If you need step-by-step guidance, simply follow the instructions on the left-hand page.

BRIEFING: DREBIN

The meeting with Drebin in the cutscene prior to the Urban Ruins zone opens up a variety of new gameplay features. In this extended Briefing section, we explain key concepts and offer a selection of useful guidelines.

Drebin Points

Commonly abbreviated to "DP", Drebin Points are a currency used to acquire weapons, customizable parts, ammunition and items from the personable yet decidedly amoral arms dealer. These can be obtained in three ways:

1: Collecting weapons from the battlefield. Once Snake has a firearm in his inventory, all subsequent weapons of this type are automatically sold to Drebin. A small onscreen message in the bottom right-hand corner will reveal the funds accrued. (Note that ammunition is added to Snake's supplies.)

2: Destroying non-human assailants. This does not apply to vehicles that contain pilots or drivers.

3: There are also additional DP bonuses awarded for miscellaneous achievements. We'll discuss these later in the walkthrough.

The sum of Drebin Points awarded for each weapon is usually dependant on how common it is. There is actually an audio cue that indicates the level of reimbursement whenever you collect a weapon, which saves you the trouble of looking to see how much DP has been given every time. The longer this sound effect lasts (listen for the distinctive rising tone), the more generous the payment.

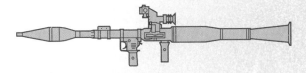

Drebin's Shop

This 24-hour weapons store is very easy to use, so we won't bore you by explaining how to shop there. There are a number of things that aren't immediately apparent, though, so we'll quickly run through those here.

- Different weapons and items are added as you progress through the story, so don't rush to spend all of your Drebin Points straight away. These are thoughtfully marked with "NEW!" to bring them to your attention.

- Note that the color of an object indicates its purpose. Lethal arms and munitions are red, whereas weapons and items designed to merely incapacitate assailants are blue.

- Weapons and items are occasionally unavailable, but you can almost always buy ammunition – though expect to pay a premium in certain situations. As there are certain battles that might consume ammo at a voracious rate, it's always worth saving at least 30,000 DP in reserve. This is especially true for harder difficulty levels.

- When you purchase a weapon, it's prudent to check the type of ammunition it requires beforehand. If it uses a variety that can't be commonly found within your current Act, buying bullets or rockets for it may prove costly.

- Don't feel obliged to spend Drebin Points – you can acquire ample resources for each mission through incremental rewards, by diligently exploring each area for valuable hidden objects (our maps will definitely help with this), and general battlefield scavenging. If you're sufficiently frugal, you'll find it much easier to afford objects of desire that appear much later in the game (or, indeed, during subsequent playthroughs).

HOW TO PLAY

▶ **WALKTHROUGH**

INVENTORY

METAL GEAR ONLINE

EXTRAS

USER INSTRUCTIONS

▶ **ACT 1**

ACT 2

ACT 3

ACT 4

ACT 5

! ■ Drebin Points and any adjustments you make in the pause menu (such as weapon and item configurations, customizations, and so forth) are lost if Snake is killed before you reach a checkpoint. It's therefore a good idea to leave protracted bouts of inventory management until you reach a zone exit, then move forward and save as soon as you arrive at your next destination.

■ Weapons dropped by soldiers during battle are automatically cleared from the map after a short period of grace, so you need to be quick to scoop them up if you're looking to maximize your DP haul.

• If you play MGS4 on Wednesdays or Sundays, you'll enjoy a 20% discount at Drebin's Shop throughout the day.

Customization

Most (but not all) weapons can be enhanced by adding new parts, such as silencers and laser sights. You'll find these occasionally as you progress, but you also have the option of buying add-ons from Drebin. If you decide to upgrade a favorite weapon, it's best to do so via the Weapons menu. Highlight the gun you want to customize, then press L2. Now select the particular area you want to work on (use ⬆ or ⬇) from the available options, and press ⊗. In the list that appears, a "solid" illustration to the left of the text description indicates that you have that item in your inventory; a faded picture means that you'll need to buy it from Drebin first. Conveniently, you can purchase all enhancements directly from this screen.

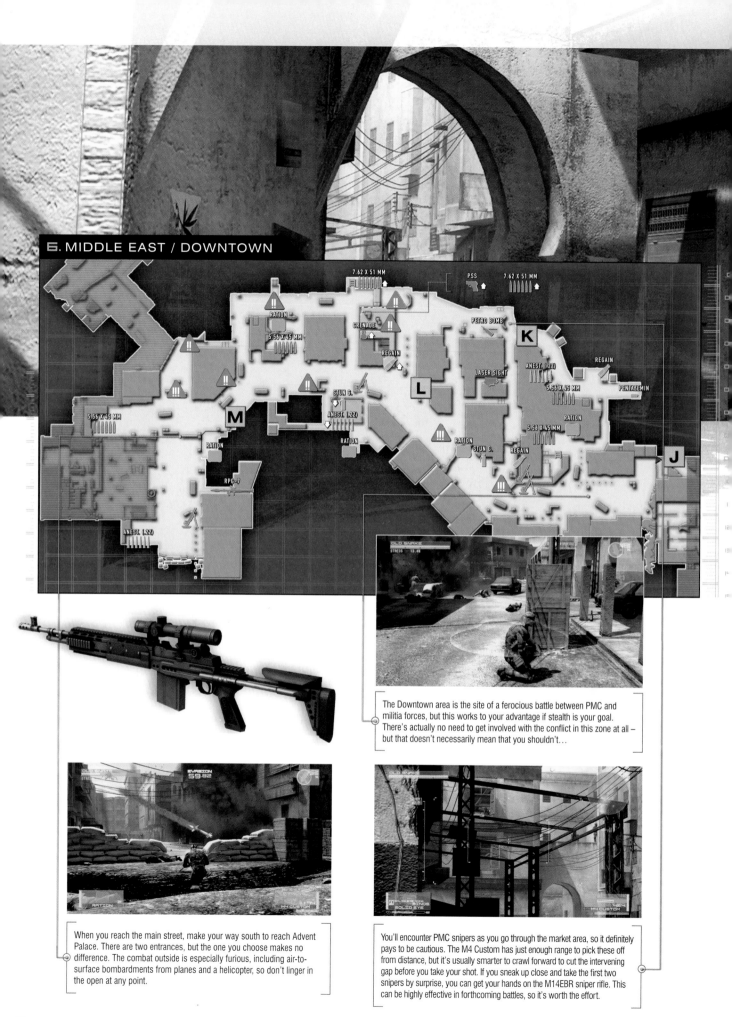

7.62 X 51 MM

PSS   7.62 X 51 MM

RATION

GRENADE

5.56 X 45 MM

PETRO BOMB

REGAIN

K

ANEST. (.22)

REGAIN

LASER SIGHT

5.56 X 45 MM

PENTAZEMIN

L

STUN G.

ANEST. (.22)

RATION

5.56 X 45 MM

M

RATION

RATION

STUN G.

REGAIN

5.56 X 45 MM

RPG-7

RATION

STUN G.

REGAIN

J

ANEST. (.22)

The Downtown area is the site of a ferocious battle between PMC and militia forces, but this works to your advantage if stealth is your goal. There's actually no need to get involved with the conflict in this zone at all – but that doesn't necessarily mean that you shouldn't…

When you reach the main street, make your way south to reach Advent Palace. There are two entrances, but the one you choose makes no difference. The combat outside is especially furious, including air-to-surface bombardments from planes and a helicopter, so don't linger in the open at any point.

You'll encounter PMC snipers as you go through the market area, so it definitely pays to be cautious. The M4 Custom has just enough range to pick these off from distance, but it's usually smarter to crawl forward to cut the intervening gap before you take your shot. If you sneak up close and take the first two snipers by surprise, you can get your hands on the M14EBR sniper rifle. This can be highly effective in forthcoming battles, so it's worth the effort.

METAL GEAR SOLID 4
GUNS OF THE PATRIOTS TACTICAL ESPIONAGE ACTION

HOW TO PLAY
▶ WALKTHROUGH
INVENTORY
METAL GEAR ONLINE
EXTRAS

USER INSTRUCTIONS
▶ ACT 1
ACT 2
ACT 3
ACT 4
ACT 5

J Head south along the nearest stretch of pavement on the main street, keeping low to avoid the PMC soldier in the distance, then take the first right. You're safe to stand up for the time being once you enter this side street, and through the market area beyond it – even if you're not allied with the militia army, the soldiers here won't react negatively to your presence.

K Crawl carefully out of the market area – there are at least two snipers operating directly ahead (one in the top window, the other to the right of him), with other PMC troops supporting them below. Rather than attempt to sneak through this flashpoint, take the alleyway to the left. Stand up as soon as you pass out of view, then squeeze through the gap between the buildings on the right – use ⊕ to press Snake up against the wall. Don't forget to turn around and pick up the Laser Sight on the other side (it's a valuable custom part). Follow the path until you reach the next alley, then turn right. Get into a crouching position, then inch carefully to the right again – there's a Stryker to your left, surrounded by PMC soldiers. Cross the small street and enter the next narrow alleyway – it's just slightly to the north, on your left as you approach it.

L As you emerge onto the main road, note the tall building in the distance; there are snipers operating from two different floors. Militia soldiers occupy the left-hand side of the street; PMC troops return fire from the right. With due caution, crawl to the opposite pavement, then through the small gap underneath the building ahead. When you exit, move back onto the pavement. You're now sufficiently close to disable the nearest marksman in the building ahead with a silenced weapon, but it's not strictly necessary to do so. Move forward until you reach the boxes, then around to the left, but pause for a moment – often, the car ahead will explode as it is hit by stray bullets. Wait for the flames to die down should that happen, then follow the pavement to the end.

M From here, it's a short (but dangerous) crawl through the bomb crater to reach the next area. There are PMC forces to the right, and militia to the left, but there's no reason why either should notice you if you're careful. When you reach the other side, approach the blue door (a zone transition message will pop up when you are close). Check behind you to ensure that the coast is clear, then quickly switch to a crouching position and head through the door.

ALTERNATIVE STRATEGIES

If you're siding with the local militia, there are four separate battles that you can involve yourself with as you pass through the Downtown area. We assume that you intend to employ lethal force in this section, and recommend that you use the M4 Custom equipped with a Suppressor and, if you collected it in the Urban Ruins zone, a Dot Sight for improved long-distance marksmanship.

Main Street (J): As you approach the PMC soldiers at the far end of this road, a Stryker arrives to offer support from behind an impassable barricade. Rather than wasting ammunition and risking detection, take the first right, then climb the ladder to the left. Drop down onto the balcony, then run over to use the mortar emplacement. Destroy the Stryker first, then bombard all PMC troops in range. You can then snipe any remaining soldiers from the gap on the right, or drop down and engage them up close.

Market Courtyard (K): There are actually two ways to approach this battle. You can either pick the two snipers off with your M4 Custom, then eliminate the remaining soldiers, or sneak around the back. The latter strategy involves slipping through the gap mentioned at point **K**, then reaching the main road. When you arrive, sneak through the first entrance on the right. Pick off any PMC troops outside through the window, check that the ground floor is clear, then go upstairs. Silently execute the two snipers (note that there may be a third PMC soldier in the upstairs room), then listen out for sounds of jubilation from the streets below. As a fringe benefit, you get to collect the weapons used by the two marksmen: the excellent M14EBR automatic sniper rifle.

Road (L): Head out onto the main street, and find a safe position with a good view of the large building to the south. Dispatch the two snipers with headshots, then crawl along the left-hand side of the street. The PMC soldiers to your right are continually replaced until you move to position **M** so, bar dispatching a few to secure a clear path forward, there's no reason to linger here.

In the final area (**M**), the PMC soldiers behind the barricades to the right are effectively infinite in number – no matter how many you dispatch, more will arrive to replace their fallen allies. Before you even try it, we can tell you that bludgeoning your way through to the back of their bolt-hole won't work – they simply arrive from the street side if you do that. What you can do, however, is shoot down a helicopter with the RPG-7. There's no bonus for this, bar the satisfaction of seeing what happens, but the resultant explosion is definitely a sight to behold.

> ■ As you encounter gunfire from multiple directions in the Downtown zone, you'll probably notice that Snake is occasionally hit by stray shots. This is far more common on higher difficulty levels. The best way to avoid being caught in the crossfire is to crawl (or use cover) at all times while sneaking through battles.

> ■ The Drum Can and Cardboard Box can be handy places to hide if there's really no other option, but be warned: PMC soldiers are not stupid, and will investigate if the appearance of either seems at all incongruous to them. Incidentally, you can press ⊗ to tip the Drum Can on its side, then use ◑ to roll it – and yes, cannoning into PMC troops is a possibility. However, Snake will become sick if forced to roll for too long, and will lose a large chunk of Psyche.

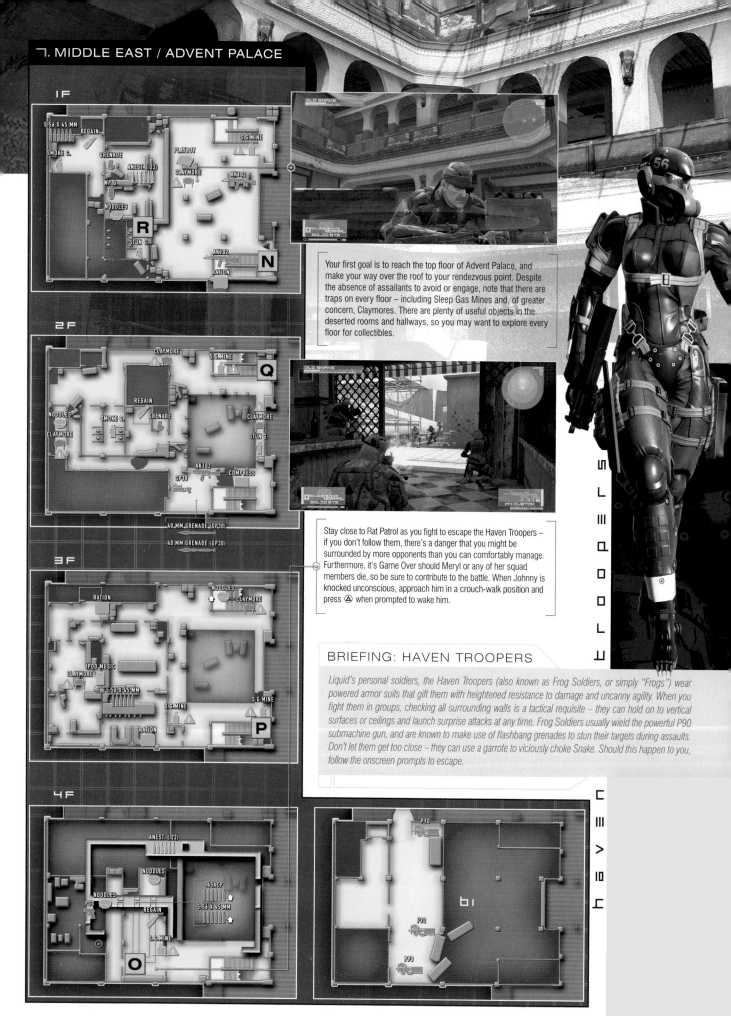

1F

5.56 X 45 MM
REGAIN
SMOKE G.
GRENADE
ANEST. (.22)
PLAYBOY
CLAYMORE
S.G.MINE
WP G.
AK102
NOODLES
R
STUN G.
AK102
RATION
N

2F

CLAYMORE
S.G.MINE
Q
NOODLES
REGAIN
GRENADE
SMOKE G.
CLAYMORE
CLAYMORE
STUN G.
GP30
COMPRESS
AK102
40 MM GRENADE (GP30)
40 MM GRENADE (GP30)

3F

NOODLES
RATION
CLAYMORE
IPOD MUSIC
CLAYMORE
5.56 X 45 MM
S.G.MINE
S.G.MINE
RATION
P

4F

ANEST. (.22)
NOODLES
.45ACP
NOODLES
5.56 X 45 MM
PSS
REGAIN
S.G.MINE
O

P90
P90
b1
P90
P90

OLD SNAKE

Your first goal is to reach the top floor of Advent Palace, and make your way over the roof to your rendezvous point. Despite the absence of assailants to avoid or engage, note that there are traps on every floor – including Sleep Gas Mines and, of greater concern, Claymores. There are plenty of useful objects in the deserted rooms and hallways, so you may want to explore every floor for collectibles.

OLD SNAKE

M4 CUSTOM

Stay close to Rat Patrol as you fight to escape the Haven Troopers – if you don't follow them, there's a danger that you might be surrounded by more opponents than you can comfortably manage. Furthermore, it's Game Over should Meryl or any of her squad members die, so be sure to contribute to the battle. When Johnny is knocked unconscious, approach him in a crouch-walk position and press ⊕ when prompted to wake him.

BRIEFING: HAVEN TROOPERS

Liquid's personal soldiers, the Haven Troopers (also known as Frog Soldiers, or simply "Frogs") wear powered armor suits that gift them with heightened resistance to damage and uncanny agility. When you fight them in groups, checking all surrounding walls is a tactical requisite – they can hold on to vertical surfaces or ceilings and launch surprise attacks at any time. Frog Soldiers usually wield the powerful P90 submachine gun, and are known to make use of flashbang grenades to stun their targets during assaults. Don't let them get too close – they can use a garrote to viciously choke Snake. Should this happen to you, follow the onscreen prompts to escape.

sleepool troopers

haven

METAL GEAR SOLID 4
GUNS OF THE PATRIOTS TACTICAL ESPIONAGE ACTION

HOW TO PLAY

▶ WALKTHROUGH

INVENTORY

METAL GEAR ONLINE

EXTRAS

USER INSTRUCTIONS

▶ ACT 1

ACT 2

ACT 3

ACT 4

ACT 5

N Stealth isn't an issue in Advent Palace, so don't worry about how much noise you create. However, there are several traps positioned throughout the building, and some are pretty cunningly placed. As primed explosives aren't highlighted by the Solid Eye, you should be especially vigilant. You may even prefer to activate Night Vision mode, which makes the devices clearly visible. You can safely collect primed explosives of all varieties by either defusing them with Metal Gear Mk. II, or by crawling over them. Any traps dealt with in this manner are automatically added to Snake's inventory. (Note that the infrared beam trap located in one corridor cannot be disarmed; disregard this completely for now.)

Your objective point is on 4F and, though some routes are blocked, it's really not hard to get there – use the staircase at the north-east end of the building to reach 3F, then head for the stairs in the south-east corner to reach 4F. Once you arrive, head into the bar and collect everything you want; to trigger the next cutscene, enter the corridor beyond. Oh, and ready a few suitable weapons beforehand…

O The Haven Troopers launch their assault immediately after the conclusion of the cutscene. As with all human assailants, headshots work best; players aiming for a no-kill playthrough should be pleased to learn that the Mk. 2's anesthetic darts work perfectly well against them. From behind the bar counter (or, if you prefer, a prone position to the side of it), aim for headshots until you defeat the initial attack wave. Follow Rat Patrol downstairs when the coast is clear.

P Prepare for another batch of assailants to attack from the opposite balcony when you reach 3F. When Rat Patrol move into the diner area, be careful not to get left behind. Your party will now be attacked from both sides – from the area you just left, and the kitchen area ahead. To best protect your companions, it's sensible to first neutralize the Haven Troopers attacking from the rear, then follow your associates through the restaurant area. If you stay low, only popping up to fire when you have a clear shot, you'll find that Meryl and her squad do a pretty good job of clearing the way forward (or, at least, drawing attention away from you). Your assailants will usually stay within the kitchen area, but it's prudent to watch the Solid Eye radar – you may be attacked from a different doorway.

Q Haven Troopers attack from both balconies when you reach 2F, which can prove problematic. Stay low and disable a few on the upper level first, then deal with those on your level when there's less danger of being shot at from above. Again, Rat Patrol moving forward is your cue to follow.

When Johnny is knocked out, approach him in the crouch-walk pose and press ⓐ to wake him. This part of the fight can be particularly nasty on the Big Boss difficulty setting; within such close confines, and with Haven Troopers approaching from the newly formed hole in the wall and the route behind you, it's hard to know which direction to defend. The trick, we found, is to concentrate on one area in particular. However, note that Haven Troopers will jump from the elevator shaft if you defend the rear, which can be an unpleasant shock if you don't expect it.

Check the immediate area for survivors, then follow Rat Patrol through the hole in the toilet wall. Once Johnny disables the infrared beams, roll over the gap in the floor to reach a secret cache of items, including a GP30 grenade launcher add-on for the AK102. When you're ready, drop down to continue the fight.

R The battle on 1F takes place with Snake and Rat Patrol situated behind a counter, and Haven Troopers on the other side. It's actually easier to operate from one of the two rooms, firing through the doorway rather than struggling to pick shots from an awkward crouching position – though be careful not to hit your allies as they move back and forth.

When the last Haven Trooper falls, grant yourself the luxury of a big sigh of relief. Drop down into the basement via the lift shaft, collect the items down there and head up the rubble slope to continue.

SECRET: FROG SOLDIER DOLL

If you defeat the Haven Troopers without recording a single kill, you can find the exclusive Frog Soldier Doll in the small Advent Palace Garage area (the last part of Advent Palace before you exit to Crescent Meridian). Though winning the battle with the Mk. 2 pistol alone is challenging, it's an eminently achievable feat. The Frog Soldier Doll will appear on the upper deck of the Nomad in all subsequent Mission Briefing cutscenes.

FLASHBACK: THE PATRIOTS

An organization thought to have been founded in the early 1970s, The Patriots is a secret committee believed to wield an enormous, practically unchecked degree of influence (though some theorists say "control") over world governments and major corporations.

▣ There is an air duct entrance on 4F (it's just to the right of the bar entrance) that Snake can crawl through, but trust us – it takes an absolute epoch to explore it in this fashion. Instead, use Metal Gear Mk.II to zip through and pick up the collectibles inside, including the useful PSS silenced pistol. You can actually crawl through the air duct to ambush the Haven Troopers on 3F during the battle to escape, though this is something that only experienced players should attempt.

▣ Ed and Jonathan are named after the two principle protagonists in *Policenauts* – a 1994 Hideo Kojima adventure that, lamentably, was never given an official release outside Japan. The names Meryl Silverburgh and FOXHOUND were also first used in that game, and miscellaneous references to it abound throughout the *Metal Gear Solid* series – particularly *MGS4*.

FLASHBACK: MERYL SILVERBURGH

Daughter of Roy Campbell, Meryl met (and, indeed, assisted) Snake during the Shadow Moses Incident. She later enlisted in an organization dedicated to monitoring Private Military Companies, and became the leader of Rat Patrol Team 01: a special unit composed of herself, Jonathan, Ed and Johnny.

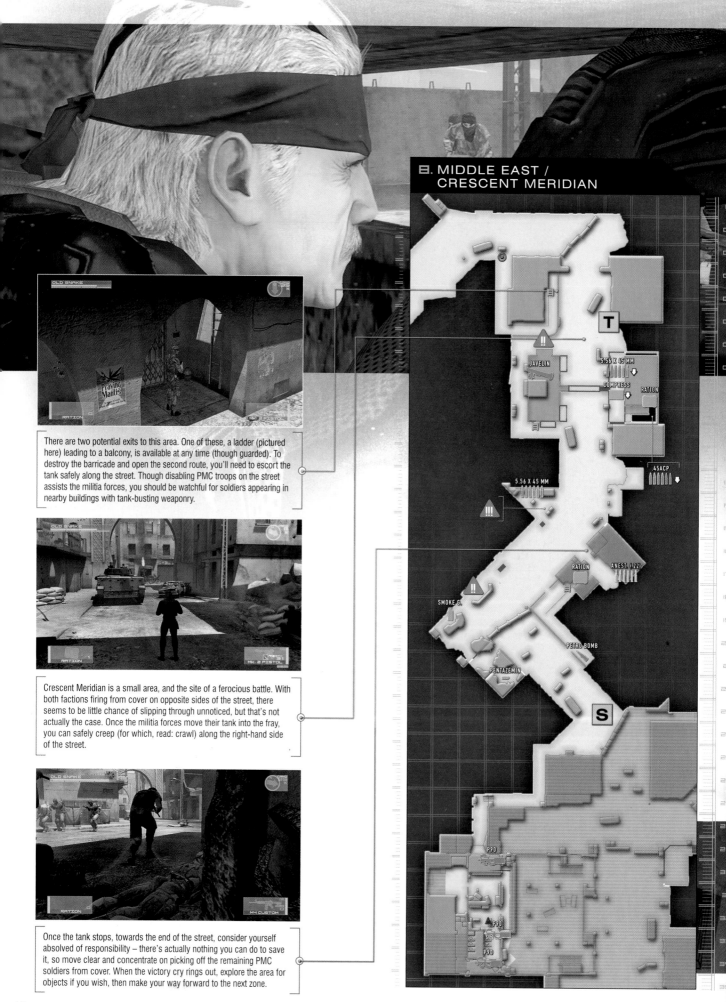

There are two potential exits to this area. One of these, a ladder (pictured here) leading to a balcony, is available at any time (though guarded). To destroy the barricade and open the second route, you'll need to escort the tank safely along the street. Though disabling PMC troops on the street assists the militia forces, you should be watchful for soldiers appearing in nearby buildings with tank-busting weaponry.

Crescent Meridian is a small area, and the site of a ferocious battle. With both factions firing from cover on opposite sides of the street, there seems to be little chance of slipping through unnoticed, but that's not actually the case. Once the militia forces move their tank into the fray, you can safely creep (for which, read: crawl) along the right-hand side of the street.

Once the tank stops, towards the end of the street, consider yourself absolved of responsibility – there's actually nothing you can do to save it, so move clear and concentrate on picking off the remaining PMC soldiers from cover. When the victory cry rings out, explore the area for objects if you wish, then make your way forward to the next zone.

BRIEFING: DUMPSTERS

Snake can hide or take cover inside any dumpsters that he encounters – simply press ⓐ to climb inside. Hold ✪ or tilt the SIXAXIS controller up to peek outside. If you have a one-handed weapon equipped, you can press Ⓛ1 to lift the lid and aim the weapon in first-person mode; as usual, tap Ⓡ1 to fire. To leave the dumpster, press ⓐ again.

A side-effect of hiding in dumpsters is that Snake can be rather fragrant as he exits, with an entourage of flies accompanying him on his journey. The foul smell will cause Snake's Stress level to rise, and also make him easier for PMC soldiers to detect. To remove the odor and lose the flies, you'll need to either change your outfit temporarily (if possible), or find a quiet spot to roll around to dislodge the worst of the grime. Water is immediately effective, but is rarely available. You can actually enjoy a couple of optional Codec conversations with Otacon if you contact him while Snake is covered in grime.

ALTERNATIVE STRATEGIES

If you decide to support the militia attack on the PMC barricade, it's best to have a sniper weapon. If you collected the M14EBR in the Downtown area, you'll find that it's perfect here. If not, the M4 Custom should suffice. With either weapon, it's best to switch to single-shot mode (bring up the Weapons menu with Ⓡ2, then press ⓐ to toggle) for greater accuracy. There's no reason why you can't use the Mk. 2 if you have stubborn pacifist tendencies, but be warned – having PMC troops regain consciousness later in the battle can lead to complications.

After the tank arrives, head over to the opening on your right, then creep over to the exit that leads to the street. From here, you can safely pick off the PMC troops on the opposite side of the road. When the tank draws level, try to follow it on the right-hand pavement, but don't get too close – getting caught underneath its tracks spells instant death.

When the tank reaches the curve in the road, watch the window in the building that faces the street just to your left. A PMC trooper with a Javelin missile launcher will appear; aim for a swift headshot to prevent him from taking aim. Immediately turn your sights to the shattered house on the right-hand side of the street, where another Javelin-carrying soldier will rush into position. Once again, you'll need to react quickly to stop him from firing.

As the vehicle approaches the end of the street, it will blow up the road block. This effectively marks the end of its use to you. Two more PMC troops with missile launchers will appear on the upper floor of the building just beyond the shattered barricade, and it's certainly easy enough to snipe both of these. After that point, however, subsequent PMC guided missile attacks are launched from a concealed position to the south-east. The tank is doomed, so it's prudent to move clear before it's destroyed.

At this point, the flow of PMC reinforcements stops, and you can finish off the last few soldiers to end the battle. Before you move on to the next zone, it's worth gaining access to the rooftops in the middle of Crescent Meridian. The principle reason for your visit is to collect the Javelin guided-missile launcher. This powerful weapon costs a cool 15,000 DP to launder at this point, so don't rush to equip it now – but rest assured that it will come in handy later. Be careful how you return to the ground, as Snake *will* die if he falls from this height.

■ If you accidentally shoot (or even kill) a militia soldier during a battle and unwittingly instigate an Alert Phase, all is not lost. If you manage to escape their immediate onslaught or give them several rations, you can regain their grudging favor by killing a few PMC troops.

■ While Snake is in a prone position (back or front), simply rotate the camera and then press Ⓛ1 to make him spin instantly and aim in the specified direction. This is much quicker than turning normally, which makes a real difference in combat situations.

S From your position after the first cutscene ends, head through the opening on the right. Turn to the right again when you reach the corner and, after creeping past the next opening to your left, crawl through the gap beneath the building. Take a left as you exit, then carefully crawl onto the pavement, allowing the OctoCamo to adjust when you get there.

The situation is very simple: PMC soldiers are stationed on the left side of the street, with militia forces mounting their assault from the right. Your task is to creep alongside the militia, sticking as close to the buildings on that side as possible. This can sometimes be a little awkward, as you'll discover when you reach the dumpster positioned just off the pavement ahead. Militia soldiers will usually take cover behind it, which means that you need to go around the front of the container instead. This might seem like a risk, but rest assured – the PMC soldiers have more pressing concerns to attend to.

For the rest of this journey, you simply need to dodge the trampling feet of militia soldiers until you reach a burned-out car just before the road block at the end of the street. As long as you don't get careless, it's actually a painless journey.

T From your position behind the car, you need to make a daring crawl across the street in broad daylight towards a ladder on the opposite side. Be very careful when you reach the pavement – don't create unnecessary noise, as the two PMC soldiers to your left will react angrily and immediately if disturbed. When you arrive at the foot of the ladder, turn the camera to check that both are facing away from you. Once ready, switch to a crouching position and press ⓐ to mount the ladder. Climb slowly to the top, then go prone. Follow this balcony to its end and then drop down to move to the next zone.

Map labels: .45ACP · 7.62 X 51 MM · SUP. (OP.) · NOODLES · 5.56 X 45 MM · C. BOX · REGAIN · SUP. (OP.) · RATION · PSS · ANEST. (.22) · COMPRESS · .45ACP · ANEST. (.22) · SUP. (M4) · W · NOODLES · SMOKE G. · RATION · IPOD MUSIC · PLAYBOY · V · ANEST. (.22) · U

If you are detected in this final area, you should probably just make a break for the objective. From your entrance point, it's a red door near the far right-hand corner. Be prepared to fight your way out of Act 1 if there is an Alert Phase in progress, though – reinforcements actually enter this zone via your exit…

If you go through the building, watch out for a PMC soldier standing guard inside. Once you arrive at the square with a fountain at its centre, there are two more troops to avoid. The final area of this zone, through the opening in the wall, is heavily guarded. If sneaking isn't your strong suit, you should ready a powerful weapon before you head inside just in case.

Quickly run around to collect the weapons dropped by the unfortunate militia soldiers for an easy boost to your DP, then follow the road. There are two patrolling PMC troops to either engage or avoid straight away and, beyond them, three more soldiers behind the road block – and, you should note, two turrets. It's easier to sneak through the house directly ahead as the road turns to the right, but you could bully your way through with suitable ranged weapons.

U

Stick to the pavement on the left of the street. Crawl to avoid the two PMC troops as they begin their patrol – it's safest to pause until they pass – then continue until you reach a wooden box, with the road block ahead in plain view. Wait until the soldier's patrol route causes him to face away from you, then crawl on until you reach the wire fence. When the soldier pauses, stop dead; with additional forces behind him, including one manning a turret, revealing your position now would be a costly mistake. When he resumes his walk, crawl into the gap between the two buildings directly to the south.

V

Enter the building through the broken wall, but be quiet – there is a soldier standing guard on the floor above. Cautiously crawl up the staircase, and pause as you reach the midway point on the second flight. When the PMC soldier here walks towards the window, you can either ghost over to the left, or disable him silently to be safe. Either way, slip through the first door, then – as quietly as you can – lower Snake through the gap in the floor to return to ground level. Crawl as you approach the broken wall that leads outside, as there are two patrolling soldiers in the area beyond.

W

You need to be calm and patient to successfully sneak through this final section. It should go without saying that crawling, and competent use of OctoCamo, are requisite throughout.

Watch the closest PMC trooper before you move outside, and get a feel for his patrol route – it's a figure eight, of sorts, and fairly easy to read. Wait until he walks to the right of your position, then crawl into the grass directly ahead. Stay there until he completes another circuit, then crawl over behind the large pile of wood while his back is turned. Ignore the hole in the wall, and instead head over to the patch of grass to the left of the large crate. Use the camera to observe the movement of the two soldiers as you move there and, if at all concerned, stop and wait.

When the soldier to your right turns away from you, inch forward out of the grass to the edge of the wall on your left (though not beyond), and use the camera to watch and wait for a soldier to arrive beside the large truck in the next area. He'll approach Snake's position, and eventually stand there for a moment before continuing to the left. He has a fairly lengthy patrol route, which gives you a reasonable amount of time for the precision sneaking that awaits you.

This part can be very difficult, so pay close attention. After checking to the right, crawl through the opening to the gray container almost directly ahead. Don't move too far forward – position Snake to lie behind it, but ensure that his head doesn't poke out at the far side. Stop in this spot and wait for another soldier to approach. He'll pause twice before walking to the south end of the area, which is your cue to crawl quickly around the corner to the right, then left behind the tent. This may take a couple of attempts to perfect, but don't worry: after you get over the initial uncertainty (judging overlapping patrol routes can be tricky), it's really not as hard as it first seems.

Carry on until you reach the corner of the enclosure, then turn left. After a brief pause, a soldier will begin walking towards you. Though you can hide in the nearby dumpster, it's easier to let him draw close, then knock him out with a Mk. 2 headshot. You're now safe to crawl directly south to the red exit door, but watch your radar/Threat Ring and keep the camera trained to the left to be safe.

ALTERNATIVE STRATEGIES

As a footnote to the existing stealth walkthrough, we should point out that you can go through the hole in the wall mentioned briefly at **W**, and follow the outer perimeter of the enclosure to reach the final doorway. Be warned, though: this route, though initially easy, can become alarmingly complicated once you arrive at the tower. To reach the exit from there, you have to take three patrol routes into account (not to mention the soldier standing watch above), and the timing is rather delicate. From the pile of wood by the corner nearest to the door, you need to make a break for the exit (first crawling, then crouch-walking) as soon as the nearest soldier passes you on the return leg of his patrol, and there's really little margin for error. It's a strategy that experts should experiment with, and everyone else should probably avoid.

For those who prefer direct action and don't enjoy too much creeping around, there are a few instances where disabling PMC soldiers with the Mk. 2 or another silenced weapon can make the infiltration process easier, but this is an area clearly designed for stealth. The items in the final area of Millennium Park really don't warrant risky exploration if you're set on sneaking, but it's worth noting that soldiers in this zone sometimes drop the Masterkey under-barrel shotgun attachment for the M4 Custom, a rather fine add-on with a standard price-point of 30,000 DP.

HOW TO PLAY
▶ WALKTHROUGH
INVENTORY
METAL GEAR ONLINE
EXTRAS

USER INSTRUCTIONS
▶ ACT 1
ACT 2
ACT 3
ACT 4
ACT 5

■ You can acquire the useful Magazines by fully emptying a rifle or pistol clip. These empty ammunition cases can then be thrown to distract hostiles and encourage them to leave a patrol route or guard post.

■ **Flashback Update:** Just to clear up any potential confusion (especially if you missed *MGS2*), we'll recap who Liquid Ocelot is. He's the *body* of Ocelot (an important figure in all *MGS* games) possessed by the *spirit* of Liquid Snake (Solid Snake's twin brother, ostensibly killed at the conclusion of *MGS1*). See? It all makes perfect sense.

FLASHBACK: NAOMI HUNTER

An orphan, Naomi Hunter was taken in by the man who (unbeknownst to her) murdered her parents: Frank Hunter, alias Gray Fox. After her adoptive brother was defeated by Snake (*Metal Gear*, *Metal Gear 2*), Naomi attempted to gain revenge by injecting him with the FOXDIE virus at the beginning of his Shadow Moses mission (*MGS1*). She later made her peace with Snake.

I	COVE VALLEY VILLAGE
2	COVE VALLEY VILLAGE (HILL)
3	POWER STATION
4	POWER STATION (PART 2)
5	CONFINEMENT FACILITY
6	VISTA MANSION
7	RESEARCH LAB
8	MOUNTAIN TRAIL
9	MARKETPLACE

SOUTH AMERICA

ACT 2: SOLID SUN

SECRET: MISSION BRIEFING

As soon as the Mission Briefing for Act 2 switches to a multiple-camera format, you can take control of Metal Gear Mk. II and explore the Nomad. The controls for these interactive cutscenes are very simple:

● Press L2 to change to full-screen mode.

● Press △ to transpose the two main video windows (or, in full-screen mode, toggle the current active display)

● Press □ to switch the secondary video feed (by default, the smaller window in the top right-hand corner) between the camera upstairs, and direct control of Metal Gear Mk. II.

You control Metal Gear Mk. II in the same way as you would during a mission, though certain functions are disabled. On the lower deck, you can find a Battery next to the helicopter, and the Camera gadget behind Sunny's computer desk. Upstairs, you'll locate an iPod® tune, a box of ammunition, and a pot of Noodles. The additional Battery doubles the maximum running time of gadgets you use on the battlefield, while the Camera can be used to take snapshots during missions. We'll introduce the more interesting applications of this device later in the walkthrough.

SOUTH AMERICA / OVERVIEW

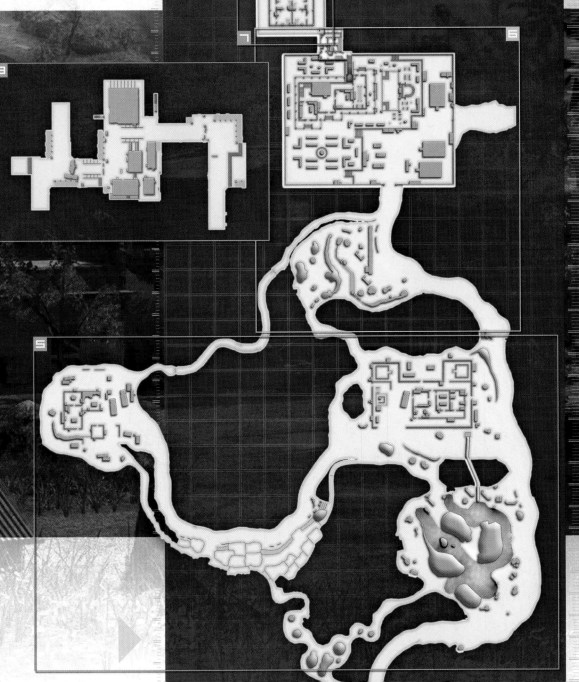

ANEST. (.22)
REGAIN
5.56 X 45 MM
SUP. (M4)
IPOD MUSIC
PETRO BOMB
5.56 X 45 MM
REGAIN
RATION
SVD
SMOKE G.
ANEST. (.22)
7.62 X 54 R
PENTAZEMIN
C4
NOODLES
SOUTH AMERICA DISGUISE
PLAYBOY
5.56 X 45 MM
STUN G.
AN94
MUÑA
5.45 X 39 MM
12 GA. (00 BUCK)
12 GA. (V.RING)
TWIN BARREL
A

There are some interesting items hidden in the buildings here, including the powerful SVD automatic sniper rifle and C4 explosives. You can only collect the former by rolling across the gap to reach the platform it is hidden on. If you experience difficulties with the timing of this acrobatic feat, try tapping ▲ repeatedly to make Snake grab for a firm purchase before he falls.

SECRET: MUNITIONS STORE

Attack the PMC soldiers guarding a group of prisoners held at gunpoint as the mission begins, and you can obtain access to a secret area. If you prevent the PMC troops from murdering their prisoners immediately (smart sniping is a must), the surviving rebels will open the locked door to the small building near your starting position. Among the six collectibles you can find inside are the Twin Barrel shotgun, the South American Rebel Disguise, and some Muña. The latter item is a medicinal plant that helps prevent altitude sickness and replenishes Psyche at a faster rate when equipped.

The scene below your starting position practically begs for a bout of concealed sniping, though time is of the essence – as you'll discover if you wait to see where each rebel prisoner is being taken.

HOW TO PLAY

▶ WALKTHROUGH

INVENTORY

METAL GEAR ONLINE

EXTRAS

USER INSTRUCTIONS

ACT 1

▶ ACT 2

ACT 3

ACT 4

ACT 5

A

The opening scenario at Cove Valley Village presents dedicated stealth experts with something of a moral dilemma: can you simply ghost by as the captive rebels are taken one by one and executed? This walkthrough assumes that you are, indeed, a callous yet pragmatic soul, and intend to avoid any involvement.

From your starting position, crawl down the slope to the back of the buildings. Pause as you reach the area at the end of the first house, and allow the patrolling PMC soldier to pass. Continue straight ahead until you arrive at the end of a corrugated metal wall, then rotate the camera to face around the corner. There is a second patrolling soldier just beyond, so wait until he turns away from you before you crawl into the grassy area. Creep behind the metal huts, then move along to the end. When you're sure the nearby soldier isn't watching, you should be safe to make a break for the shadows just beyond the corner of the building ahead. Stay very low here – there's usually another soldier on the balcony above, and there may be more directly ahead. When all eyes turn away from you, crawl through the shade to the grass, then onto the sloped path.

ALTERNATIVE STRATEGIES

Stealth Walkthrough Beta

For this second stealth/no-kill strategy, you'll need to invest in the Mosin-Nagant sniper rifle from Drebin's Shop. At 60,000 DP (48,000 DP on Wednesdays and Sundays), it's certainly not cheap. However, the investment will definitely pay off if you experience difficulties with the main stealth walkthrough.

Once you have the rifle equipped, crawl to the edge of the grassy outcrop. The Mosin-Nagant is a bolt-action rifle, with only five tranquilizer darts per reload, so you really need to make every shot count. You have seven targets to hit, and should need to reload no more than once. From the top, then:

• Your first target is the soldier closest to you – he should be near (or approaching) the building just ahead.

• Behind him, at the far end of the row of buildings, a PMC soldier will run to investigate. Hit him with a dart straight away.

• Now turn your attention to the two PMC troops guarding the rebel prisoners. If you're really quick, they will not have time to react.

• A soldier will open a door and emerge from the house below you. He's in the best position to do the prisoners the most harm, so deal with him promptly.

• Your penultimate target is to the north-east, and should by now be firing at the rebels from a position near to the fire-damaged building. Use the zoom function (⊙ & ⊙) to get a clear shot.

• Finally, look directly north for the last PMC soldier. He's invariably the last of the troops positioned here to react, and should be either firing at the rebels, approaching one of his downed colleagues, or even obliviously continuing his patrol behind the far row of houses. Don't forget about him – it only takes one soldier to revive all the rest, ruining your plans.

If you complete this shooting spree in an orderly and timely fashion, you won't even encounter a Caution Phase. For some reason, the PMC troops seem more confused than overtly alarmed as their colleagues fall bloodlessly to the turf. Try to snipe with a standard rifle, though, and you'll see a definite change in their behavior.

On the Big Boss Hard difficulty level, you should have just enough time to race around to collect the most desirable items in the buildings (including the contents of the munitions store unlocked by the prisoners) before the PMC soldiers begin to wake up. In the meantime, the rebels that you freed will be attacking the guards on the hill area.

Extreme Force Addendum

If you're really not happy unless you're causing maximum chaos, feel free to use a standard sniper rifle – the M14EBR is very efficient for this kind of medium-distance wetwork. The targets you need to hit are pretty much the same as those detailed in the Stealth Walkthrough Beta text, though there's one big difference: the use of lethal force will initiate a near-immediate Caution status and different reactions from the soldiers, even if you have a Suppressor equipped. The reinforcements will arrive from the hillside path, so be ready for them.

FLASHBACK: VAMP

A henchman of Solidus during the Big Shell Incident, Vamp murdered Otacon's sister, Emma (*MGS2*). Apparently killed by an accidental shot to the head (the bullet was actually aimed at someone else), his continued existence is something of a mystery.

FLASHBACK: **SOLIDUS**

Known as George Sears during his tenure as U.S. President, Solidus – the secret third spawn of the Les Enfants Terribles project – instigated the Shadow Moses Incident in an attempt to escape from his masters, The Patriots (MGS1). Subsequently responsible for the terrorist attack on the Big Shell facility (MGS2), Solidus learned before his death that his every action had been not merely anticipated by The Patriots, but actively encouraged…

FLASHBACK: **ROSEMARY**

*Rosemary (or simply Rose) is the former partner of Raiden, the main protagonist of **Metal Gear Solid 2**. The pair separated after the Big Shell Incident, with Rose now (rather scandalously) cohabiting with Roy Campbell.*

■ Look through the window of the first building you pass after the mission starts – you'll see a PMC soldier inside perusing a copy of Playboy.

■ Tranquilizer darts don't knock PMC soldiers out for very long on the Big Boss Hard difficulty level, so you really need to think a few steps ahead whenever you use them. If you linger in an area where you've sent potential assailants to sleep, listen carefully for the tell-tale yawns that indicate that they've clambered to their feet.

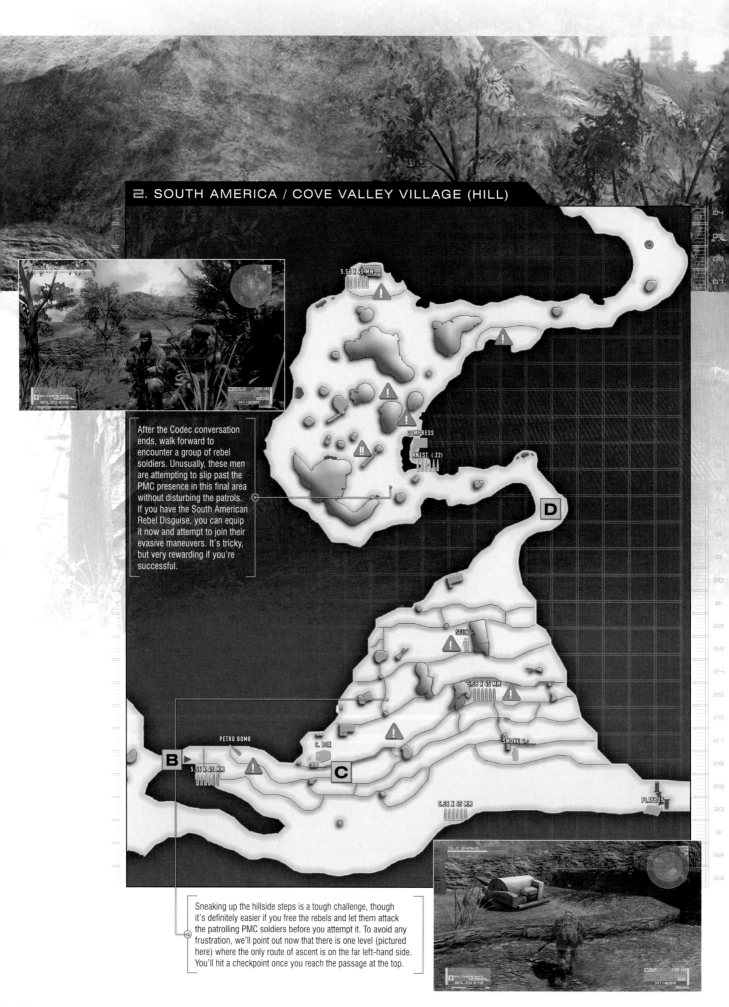

5.56 X 45 MM

COMPRESS

ANEST. (.22)

D

STUN G.

5.56 X 45 MM

PETRO BOMB

SMOKE G.

B

5.56 X 45 MM

C. BOX

C

5.56 X 45 MM

PLAYBOY

After the Codec conversation ends, walk forward to encounter a group of rebel soldiers. Unusually, these men are attempting to slip past the PMC presence in this final area without disturbing the patrols. If you have the South American Rebel Disguise, you can equip it now and attempt to join their evasive maneuvers. It's tricky, but very rewarding if you're successful.

Sneaking up the hillside steps is a tough challenge, though it's definitely easier if you free the rebels and let them attack the patrolling PMC soldiers before you attempt it. To avoid any frustration, we'll point out now that there is one level (pictured here) where the only route of ascent is on the far left-hand side. You'll hit a checkpoint once you reach the passage at the top.

B

Stick to the shade just in front of the rock ledge, and follow the path until you spot a PMC soldier patrolling above; stop just after the grass ends, and you'll notice him pause very close to your position. When he turns to walk the other way, follow him carefully. Quickly switch to a crouching position and climb onto the first step to your left, then approach the next ledge – the spot you should aim for is just in front of a wooden fence section with a tree ahead of it. When the patrolling PMC soldier makes his return walk and passes your position, you should again change to a crouching pose, and press ⓐ to climb to the next level. Crawl forward into the grass.

C

Don't be alarmed at the sudden cries of "We've got contact!" and "We've got company!" – these actually refer to the three rebel soldiers that attack from a location just above you. This is a definite hindrance, so you'll need your wits about you. Immediately crawl through the grass until you reach two low steps; this reduces the likelihood that the soldier you passed moments before will accidentally stumble on Snake while engaging the rebels. While you shouldn't get involved, have the Mk. 2 or another silenced weapon of choice trained at his head until the danger passes. If the PMC soldier gets too close, neutralize him. This isn't ideal (it increases the danger of detection), but it's better than an Alert Phase.

If you're lucky, the surprise rebel attack will have taken out at least one of the PMC troops in this area. Pause and get a "feel" for your surroundings before you climb the two steps to the next level; it's best to hold up until the soldier just behind you (if he's still conscious or alive) approaches, then turns away. Hop up the two ledges, then crawl straight into the grass to your left. Wait for the soldier further ahead to walk away from you (consult the Solid Eye radar for guidance if you can't actually see him), then climb the two ledges to your left, next to the large rock wall. Crawl into the grass behind the boulder, and freeze until the patrolling soldier on this level arrives on the other side, then turns to walk away.

Quickly climb up on the ledge to your left, then hide in the large patch of grass just ahead. When the soldier to your right turns his back to you, move further forward until you're almost parallel to the crates to the left, but still completely concealed by the grass. Making a break for the next ledge without disturbing the guard below is extremely awkward, so – though stealth purists may disagree on this point – it's probably better to send him to sleep with a Mk. 2 headshot, then make a careful dash for the checkpoint at the top.

D

If you opted for the pure stealth route, there's a chance that the sneaking rebels will not take kindly to Snake creeping up behind them. At best they'll act with consternation, which disrupts their progress and increases the likelihood of detection. This is the most common state of affairs. At worst, they may even open fire on Snake, assuming him to be an enemy.

Taking this into consideration, it's advisable to keep low, and follow from a safe distance at first. Hug the rocks to the right until you reach a corner of sorts, and wait in a prone pose. Ready the Mk. 2. When a solitary PMC soldier arrives at the gap between the rocks ahead, hold until he approaches you, then hit him with a dart to the head. (Handily, this is usually noticed by the attentive rebels, who will subsequently refrain from attacking Snake, even if they might have appeared trigger-happy on previous attempts.)

Press forward quickly, staying low through the grass once you reach it, and crawl past the rebel soldier stationed on the ledge to the right. You can sometimes brazenly crouch-walk behind him if his back is turned. The zone exit is then a short walk away.

ALTERNATIVE STRATEGIES

Stealth Walkthrough Beta

Continuing our alternative stealth strategy, follow the route set out in the main walkthrough to reach the top of the hill. The difference, though, is that the rebel attack should have led to the deaths of at least two of the patrolling PMC troops, which makes the climb much less fraught with danger.

After the checkpoint, you get to enjoy a secondary benefit for saving the prisoners: equip the South American Rebel Disguise to enjoy an exhilarating old-school infiltration exercise. Approach the rebels when they stop, then watch the hand signals of the lead soldier. Follow the two men on the right and dart from hiding place to hiding place as they do, always watching for the silent prompts of the man on point. There are a handful of stops to make and, as we've noticed distinct variations between different sessions, the best tips we can offer are to use the camera to check that you're sufficiently concealed, and to stick tight to your companions. Finally, don't take up too much room – if your inconsiderate use of valuable hiding space forces one of the rebels to stand in an exposed position, you'll rue the consequences. Getting through (*sans* OctoCamo) without you or any of the rebels alerting the PMC troops is not a trivial accomplishment, so grant yourself the luxury of a wide satisfied smirk if you achieve it.

Extreme Force Addendum

Fighting your way up the hillside "steps" is much more complicated when there is PMC backup arriving from the top, so it still pays to avoid an outright Alert Phase if you can. In the area after the checkpoint, the same applies – it can get a little intense if you have a large group of additional PMC troops moving in from the zone exit. If you're desperate to try out the Twin Barrel appropriated from the secret munitions store earlier, though, this ambush-friendly locale is a good stalking ground if enemy numbers are of no concern to you.

> ■ Attempting to follow the rebel soldiers closely after the checkpoint really doesn't seem to work unless you have the South American Rebel Disguise – their reactions to Snake interrupt the rhythm of the carefully orchestrated runs between cover, and make detection practically inevitable.
>
> ■ If Snake's Psyche gauge is low, use Pentazemin to immediately steady his hands. It's especially valuable if you need to use a sniper rifle while the old soldier is in less than peak condition.

There's a break in play for a lengthy cinematic interlude when you approach the rusty Stryker in the north-west corner of the map, just outside the power substation's walls. It's followed by a checkpoint.

There are some useful items inside the buildings, so it's worth the risk of sneaking in – the entrance on the east side is usually the safest. If there are soldiers guarding it, you can hide underneath the nearby truck until either they move on, or you silently neutralize them. While you're there, don't forget to destroy the control panel pictured here.

There are two ways to approach the power transmission substation. You can go straight ahead, and attempt to sneak past the PMC machine guns raking the no-man's land in front of the south wall, or head right to access the hill area. The latter path brings you into contact with enemy soldiers, but going up there enables you to pick off the two PMC snipers terrorizing the rebel forces below. It also offers an excellent overview of the battlefield.

PLAYBOY

REGAIN

12 GA. (00 BUCK)

SLEEP GAS SATCHEL

PLAYBOY

COMPRESS

RATION

7.62 X 54R

ANEST. (7.62 MM)

NOODLES

PENTAZEMIN

12 GA. (SLUG)

PSS

FIM-92A

C4

RATION

G

F

SMOKE G

REGAIN

E

HOW TO PLAY

▶ WALKTHROUGH

INVENTORY

METAL GEAR ONLINE

EXTRAS

USER INSTRUCTIONS

ACT 1

▶ ACT 2

ACT 3

ACT 4

ACT 5

■ If you can collect the machine guns dropped by the warring factions – particularly the PKM carried by the rebels, and the M60E4 used by certain PMC troops – they'll come in very handy in a forthcoming battle. There's also a rebel armed with an M72A3 anti-tank rocket launcher attacking from the east side of the base.

■ If you're on a speed run, there's no need to wait until the rebels beat the PMC forces – just blow the control panel, then make a dash for Drebin's location at the north-east of the facility. Rebel control will be established by the time play resumes.

SECRET: DISABLING THE SUBSTATION

The destruction of the control panel inside the substation cuts off all electricity, and adds unrelenting momentum to the rebel attack – once it blows, their victory in this zone is assured. This has a profound effect on what happens after you trigger the next cutscene (and checkpoint) by approaching the north-west corner of the map. If the substation is sabotaged (either by you or the rebels) before you meet Drebin, all PMC forces are removed from the Power Station and Cove Valley Village zones. If, however, the substation is still active when the cinematics begin, all rebel forces are removed from the area, with an increased PMC presence instead guarding both zones. Naturally, the latter scenario makes things more complicated and reduces potential rewards.

A secondary benefit of disabling the power station is that it allows access to a secret area. From the control room, head out to the enclosure just beyond (it's the south-west section of the facility) with a large metal structure at its center. Climb the ladder to reach the upper level, then approach one of the two heavy wires that link it to the adjacent pylon. Use △ to jump over the edge of the barrier, then traverse along one of the wires until you are suspended over the walkway on the pylon; press ✕ to drop down. Check your Psyche gauge before you attempt this – if it's low, Snake's grip gauge will be reduced during the climb, which may not give him sufficient time to reach safety.

The treasures in this secret area include a valuable Rifle Scope, an FIM-92A surface-to-air launcher, and a PSS silenced pistol in addition to a few boxes of useful ammunition. To reach the Pentazemin collectable on the high boxes at the back, simply perform a forward roll off the nearby rusty crates; from there, you can hop over the wall to return to your starting position.

E

Crawl on the path near the rock wall to the left when the rebels begin their attack. From there, continue forward in the shadow beneath the rock overhang, being careful not to attract the attention of the PMC snipers. Follow the narrow path ahead until you reach a grassy mound. Pause here and observe the battle. As you can see, PMC soldiers are raking the field in front of the power transmission substation with a wall of bullets fired from two fixed gun emplacements. To avoid incidental injury, crawl over to the path on the right, and follow it until you see a fallen log; this should provide sufficient cover. Crawl into the grass on the right as soon as it seems safe to do so.

F

If you observe the terrain ahead, you'll notice strips of grass that lie between two trees. You need to creep through this area cautiously until you reach the second tree. Pause and watch the PMC soldiers. There should be one (perhaps two) stationed on the east side of the substation, not far ahead from your position. When these are killed, reinforcements arrive from inside the facility to replace them. The challenge here is to watch carefully, and use the Solid Eye radar to correctly judge the best moment to break from cover; use the Mk. 2 to accelerate this process if you wish. When the path is temporarily clear, crawl forward on the right-hand side of the sandbag wall until you reach the truck. Hide underneath it for a moment, then crawl through the opening in the wall, and turn left to clamber up the small set of steps leading into the station. Check the door to your right (there may be PMC soldiers in that room), and slip by to the left once you're sure that no one is looking your way.

G

You're now in the main transmission substation control room. Generally, on a stealth playthrough, you can lie in wait here for rebel forces to blow the control panel (shown on the left-hand page), which disables all power in the facility and usually spells the end of PMC resistance. If you're keen to expedite the process, which can take a while, you can perform this act of sabotage yourself. Head over to the Stryker behind the power station to initiate a cutscene with Drebin when the coast is clear. You'll reach a checkpoint when it ends.

ALTERNATIVE STRATEGIES

As sneaking through the lower east side of this zone on the approach to the substation is pretty simple, visiting the raised area to the west is only necessary or appropriate if you're looking to get directly involved in the battle.

If you're keen to try the alternative scenario that ensues when the rebels fail to gain control of the area (see "Disabling the Substation"), there is a short-cut to the meeting with Drebin. When you reach the grassy mound mentioned at point **E**, you can actually move to a path that runs alongside the left-hand side of the area. You can follow this all the way to the side of the substation with little chance of discovery, though you'll need to be cautious as you pass the nearest turret. Drop into the trench as you round the corner, then make your way to the end to trigger the cutscene.

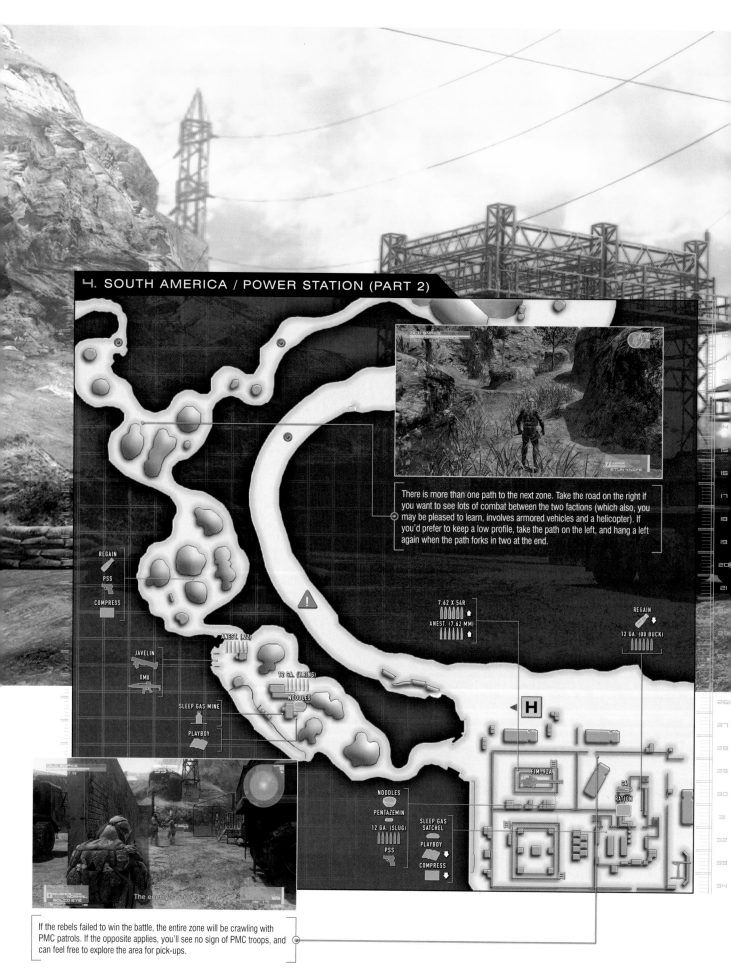

4. SOUTH AMERICA / POWER STATION (PART 2)

There is more than one path to the next zone. Take the road on the right if you want to see lots of combat between the two factions (which also, you may be pleased to learn, involves armored vehicles and a helicopter). If you'd prefer to keep a low profile, take the path on the left, and hang a left again when the path forks in two at the end.

REGAIN

PSS

COMPRESS

ANEST. (.22)

JAVELIN

XM8

12 GA. (V.RING)

NOODLES

SLEEP GAS MINE

PLAYBOY

7.62 X 54R

ANEST. (7.62 MM)

REGAIN

12 GA. (00 BUCK)

H

FIM-92A

C4

RATION

NOODLES

PENTAZEMIN

12 GA. (SLUG)

PSS

SLEEP GAS SATCHEL

PLAYBOY

COMPRESS

The enemy's here!

If the rebels failed to win the battle, the entire zone will be crawling with PMC patrols. If the opposite applies, you'll see no sign of PMC troops, and can feel free to explore the area for pick-ups.

HOW TO PLAY
▶ WALKTHROUGH
INVENTORY
METAL GEAR ONLINE
EXTRAS

USER INSTRUCTIONS
ACT 1
▶ ACT 2
ACT 3
ACT 4
ACT 5

ALTERNATIVE STRATEGIES

If you opted against sabotaging the power station, and met with Drebin before the rebels could gain access to the facility, you'll need to sneak past PMC patrols to reach the next zone. There are broadly two ways to reach the Confinement Facility in this alternative scenario, and the following stealth-focused walkthroughs explain how to reach them without raising the alarm. If you have an itchy trigger finger, there's no reason why you can't adapt our strategies to encompass some form of creative violence, but we suggest that you use silencers. If you end up in a firefight during a full Alert Phase, you'll find that the lack of defensible positions can make it easy for reinforcements to flank and surround you.

Right Exit (Road)

Two PMC soldiers approach your position from the road as soon as the cutscene ends, so go prone and crawl back a little to avoid detection. They'll pause for a moment when they reach the crates ahead, then continue walking along the west substation wall. Crawl at first, then get up and crouch-walk rapidly along the road. Pay attention to the path ahead. Hug the wooden barrier when you reach it, get as close to the two barrels as you can, then equip the Drum Can just before the next pair of patrolling soldiers move into view. The Solid Eye radar will help you with the timing here. Wait until both saunter by, oblivious to your presence, and then make the short walk forward to the next zone.

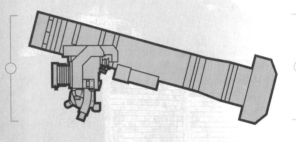

Left Exits (Valley Path)

If you're quick, you can crouch-walk straight to the narrow passage, avoiding the need to wait for the two patrolling PMC troopers on the road to pass by. Slow down as you approach the entrance, as you'll find a PMC soldier walking directly ahead. Follow him through from a safe distance. When you arrive at the first patch of open space, he'll walk to the left, around the large rock, before pausing. He'll then continue forward and pass by the second patrolling PMC soldier in this area.

Crawl forward, staying close to the left-hand wall, until you reach a patch of grass behind a pile of wood; you'll see a sloping path leading up to your left. Pause until the first soldier returns to the start of the area, and then watch his colleague closely. When he resumes his walk and disappears behind the second pile of wood, crawl onward until you reach another patch of grass just in front of a boarded-up mine shaft. Wait here: the soldier you passed moments before will be returning shortly.

Pick up the two collectibles in front of the mine (the powerful XM8 rifle and a Javelin missile launcher), then crawl into the next patch of grass at the entrance to the narrow passageway (from the collectibles, it's the first left). Be very quiet and careful – there's a danger of being spotted from behind, and another soldier may be just ahead.

In the next open area, one soldier walks a long circular patrol between its entrance, by the large rock you should see in front of you, and the level exit further along. His route is slow and clockwise, so it's fairly easy to predict where he'll be after watching for a moment. There's plenty of cover here, so no massive risk of detection, but the most pragmatic solution is simply to tranquilize him.

The final PMC soldier beats a path between the two exits, and barely warrants a mention if you took the sensible step of disabling the previous guard; there are plenty of places to hide without fear of someone stumbling upon you from behind. You can now hold your position until the path of your choice is clear.

> ■ Playboy isn't merely a way to distract enemies – you can also use it to restore Psyche at a fairly rapid rate. Equip it in the weapons menu, then hold [L1] and [R1] as normal. However, rather than releasing these to place it on the ground, press ⊙ to enter first-person mode. You can then press ◎ to flip pages.
>
> ■ You can dive through low windows by pressing ✕. It's one of the least stealthy things you can do, and perhaps all the more enjoyable for that reason.

H

[**Note:** If the first sight you see after the cutscene is two PMC soldiers approaching you along the road, skip to "Alternative Strategies".]

Having destroyed the power station, you're now free to explore the entire zone for collectibles; indeed, you can even backtrack to Cove Valley Village if you wish, as it's now also under rebel control.

Once you're ready to move on to the next zone, we strongly suggest that you take the "valley path" (the opening to the left of the road), and follow it until you reach a fork at the end. Take the exit to the left – this is by far the best choice for anyone making a pure stealth/no kill/speed playthrough.

If you're looking for action, or a new challenge on a subsequent run through the game, take either of the other two exits. These lead directly into the heart of a battle in the south-east region of the Confinement Facility zone, and are only recommended if you're searching for a little chaos, or a sterner test of your sneaking prowess. The main road is perhaps the toughest route to take, as you start in a very exposed position.

J

I

Broadly speaking, the Confinement Facility zone can be separated into three distinct sections: the pitched battle in the south-east sector, the contested main building at the north-east of the map, and the lightly patrolled roadway leading to and including the small (but well-guarded) area to the north-west. Two of the zone entrances put you straight into the conflict in the south-east corner, while the third (as covered in our main walkthrough) is the best sneaking route, and begins just off the road at the center of the map.

The Confinement Facility is possibly the largest zone in *Metal Gear Solid 4*, and there are plenty of sights to see – you can visit it a few times and still not truly know all of its secrets. For that reason, you can find an enlarged annotated map on the double-page spread that follows, marked with all collectable items and accompanied by tips and useful observations.

How you approach this zone is purely a matter of personal preference. There really isn't a "right" or "wrong" way to make your way to its two exits if you're playing with no specific end goals in mind. However, try not to loiter in exposed positions on the east side of the map – with rockets and mortars pummeling the area, and bullets flying freely, "accidental" hits are a distinct hazard.

HOW TO PLAY
▶ WALKTHROUGH
INVENTORY
METAL GEAR ONLINE
EXTRAS

USER INSTRUCTIONS

ACT 1
▶ ACT 2
ACT 3
ACT 4
ACT 5

I ‎ Despite its large size, the Confinement Facility zone is surprisingly simple to sneak through once you know the best route to take. From the start, crouch-walk along the path and drop down the first three ledges as it bends to the left. Stop after the third, and wait for a PMC soldier to arrive in front of you. When he turns away, carefully crawl further forward and wait for him to walk out onto the road. You can then sneak past and continue along the left-hand path. (There's no point in disabling him, and nor for that matter should you try – annoyingly, another soldier always runs from the road to investigate.)

J ‎ You can crouch-walk behind the cover of the rock face until you reach a wooden fence at the top of the slope, where you should switch to a safer crawl. Continue until you arrive at a patch of grass in front of a large tree, then stop and observe the area ahead. You should notice a soldier patrolling alongside a truck, a sniper in a watchtower, and (with the help of the Solid Eye radar) espy another on the road behind your position. There are more moving around to the left behind the buildings, but these are not immediately apparent.

Wait until the soldier walking the short route between the two trucks turns away from you, then crawl down the slope. Turn right at the bottom, and move along to the far end of the stack of wooden posts. Pause here until the soldier's patrol brings him close to you. When he turns, take a quick glance at the watchful sniper in the guard tower (if he's facing away, you're perfectly safe), then crawl straight over to the truck on the right and hide beneath it. Crawl to the front when you see legs pass to your left, and take a long, hard look at the guard in the tower above. When he turns to the right, that's your cue to crawl out and to the right, and then hide behind another pile of wood. Look back to check that there's no danger of discovery from behind, then crawl through the grass and, beyond that, the zone exit.

FLASHBACK: RAIDEN

A former child soldier, Raiden was the central protagonist (for which, read: "puppet") at the heart of the Big Shell Incident (*MGS2*), where he received assistance from Snake and Otacon. Estranged from his long-term partner Rosemary as he struggled to come to terms with his chequered past, he was responsible for the rescue of Sunny from The Patriots. His more recent whereabouts are something of a mystery.

▦ You can find a box of Chaff Grenades in the main building. These will be valuable in a future battle if you're attempting a no-kill playthrough.

▦ Due to the neverending supply of combatants, the Confinement Facility is a good place to "farm" for ammunition and Drebin Points. However, you should note that the DP profits are worth approximately 10% of a weapon's full value when you kill the owner (and even less on Big Boss Hard).

ALTERNATIVE STRATEGIES

There are several ways to reach either of the Confinement Facility's two exits, with our suggested paths simply being the most expeditious and low-risk. There's no reason why you can't enter the zone via the road entrance from the Power Station in the south-east area, and then attempt a daring "marathon" route that ends at the exit in the north-west corner. You can find additional tips (and an enlarged map overview) over the page.

No-Alert Speed Run
Starting from the zone entrance south of the map (just off the road that connects the east and west sectors), take the first right. With one eye on the passing Stryker, tranquilize the PMC soldier just ahead. You can then drop down to the road and sprint until you reach the main compound. As soon as you spot a PMC soldier near a row of sandbags, switch to a careful crawl (though it's sometimes possible to boldly crouch-walk past). Take the first left, and make your way through the gap between the rocks; you can crouch-walk for a short stretch here to shave seconds from your time.

Once the cover to your right ends, you'll encounter the final (and most testing) part of this high-speed strategy. There's a very high probability that you will see a PMC soldier close to your right, or just ahead; worse, there's a good chance that additional soldiers will run from the side exit of the compound. The risk of detection is extremely high so, having readied a fully loaded Mk. 2 in advance, neutralize any nearby troops with headshots. Wait for a moment to ensure that no others come to investigate, then make the brief crawl (or even shorter crouch-run) to the exit just ahead. A good par time for this stealth sprint through the zone is around 90 seconds, though more daring players will be able to slash this to something closer to a minute.

The ∞-Year War
If subtlety isn't your strong suit, opting to shoot your way through the Confinement Facility zone is a perfectly reasonable tactic. However, don't attempt to "win" the battle – it's simply not possible. No matter how many PMC soldiers you clinically dispatch, yet more will arrive to take their place. In actual fact, using lethal force puts you at a distinct disadvantage if you're set on exploring and collecting items: any soldier killed is almost immediately replaced like-for-like with another. However, tranquilized or unconscious soldiers will remain inactive until they awaken or are revived, and won't be relieved by reinforcements. It's something to bear in mind, especially if you're set on saving the four rebel prisoners (see overleaf for details).

ANEST. (7.62 MM)

ANEST. (7.62 MM)

45ACP

9 X 39 MM

VSS

9 X 39 MM

7.62 X 51 MM

STUN G.

REGAIN

COMPRESS

PLAYBOY

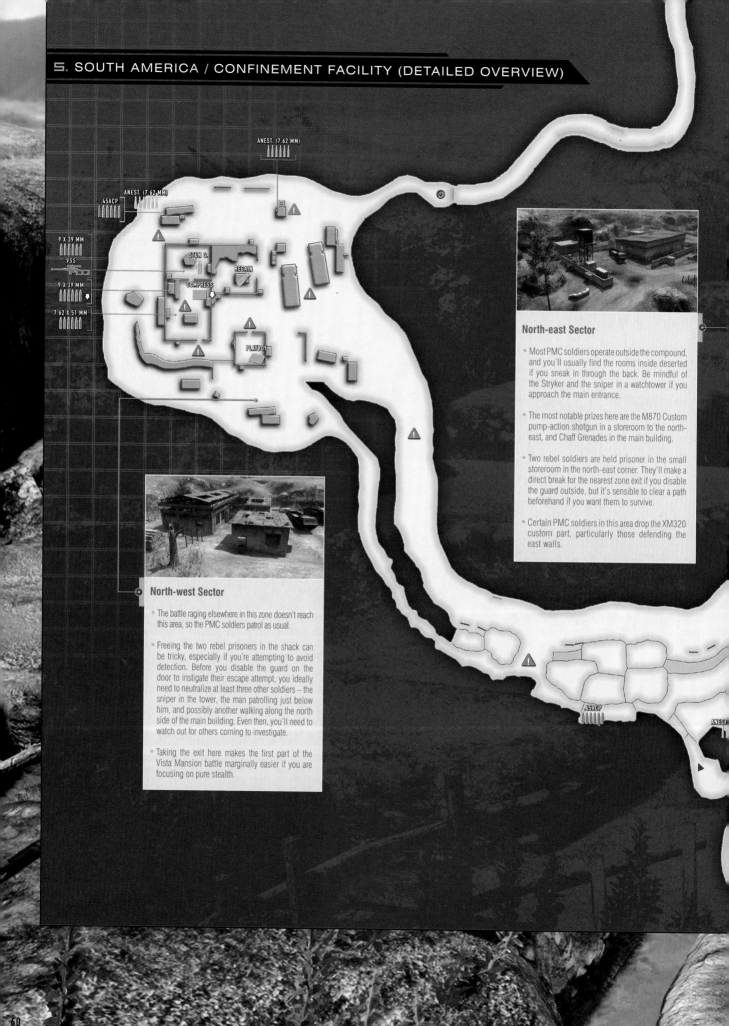

North-east Sector

• Most PMC soldiers operate outside the compound, and you'll usually find the rooms inside deserted if you sneak in through the back. Be mindful of the Stryker and the sniper in a watchtower if you approach the main entrance.

• The most notable prizes here are the M870 Custom pump-action shotgun in a storeroom to the north-east, and Chaff Grenades in the main building.

• Two rebel soldiers are held prisoner in the small storeroom in the north-east corner. They'll make a direct break for the nearest zone exit if you disable the guard outside, but it's sensible to clear a path beforehand if you want them to survive.

• Certain PMC soldiers in this area drop the XM320 custom part, particularly those defending the east walls.

North-west Sector

• The battle raging elsewhere in this zone doesn't reach this area, so the PMC soldiers patrol as usual.

• Freeing the two rebel prisoners in the shack can be tricky, especially if you're attempting to avoid detection. Before you disable the guard on the door to instigate their escape attempt, you ideally need to neutralize at least three other soldiers – the sniper in the tower, the man patrolling just below him, and possibly another walking along the north side of the main building. Even then, you'll need to watch out for others coming to investigate.

• Taking the exit here makes the first part of the Vista Mansion battle marginally easier if you are focusing on pure stealth.

45ACP

ANEST

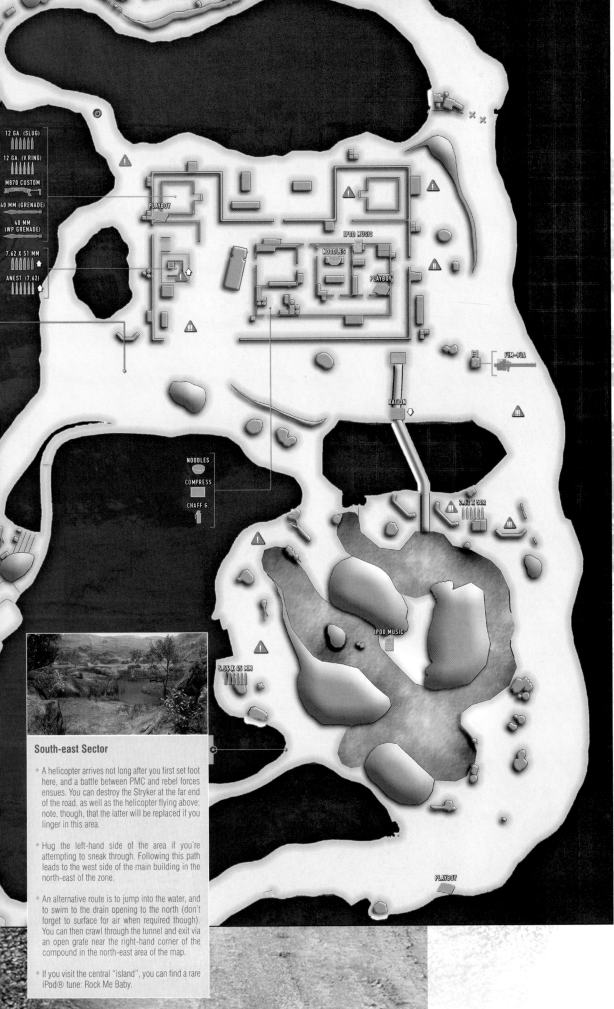

■ The Wednesday and Sunday discounts at Drebin's Shop end at midnight prompt. However, they also start when the clock strikes twelve, which can be of benefit during late-night Tuesday or Saturday sessions.

■ If you free the four soldiers held captive in the Confinement Facility zone, you'll improve your relationship with the rebel faction. Additionally, you'll have a further two rebels fighting alongside you in the Vista Mansion area that follows.

Map labels

12 GA. (SLUG)
12 GA. (V.RING)
M870 CUSTOM
40 MM (GRENADE)
40 MM (WP GRENADE)
7.62 X 51 MM
ANEST. (7.62)

PLAYBOY
IPOD MUSIC
NOODLES
PLAYBOY
FIM-92A
RATION
NOODLES
COMPRESS
CHAFF G.
7.62 X 54R
IPOD MUSIC
5.56 X 45 MM
PLAYBOY

South-east Sector

- A helicopter arrives not long after you first set foot here, and a battle between PMC and rebel forces ensues. You can destroy the Stryker at the far end of the road, as well as the helicopter flying above; note, though, that the latter will be replaced if you linger in this area.

- Hug the left-hand side of the area if you're attempting to sneak through. Following this path leads to the west side of the main building in the north-east of the zone.

- An alternative route is to jump into the water, and to swim to the drain opening to the north (don't forget to surface for air when required though). You can then crawl through the tunnel and exit via an open grate near the right-hand corner of the compound in the north-east area of the map.

- If you visit the central "island", you can find a rare iPod® tune: Rock Me Baby.

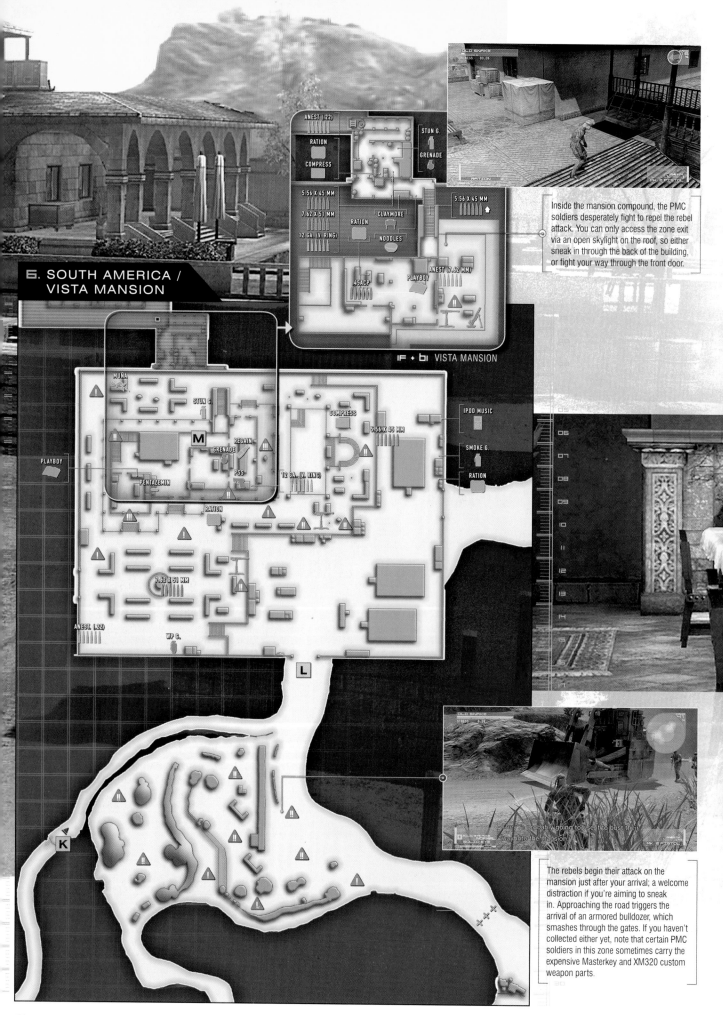

6. SOUTH AMERICA / VISTA MANSION

VISTA MANSION (inset map labels)

ANEST (.22)

RATION

COMPRESS

STUN G.

GRENADE

5.56 X 45 MM

7.62 X 51 MM

12 GA. (V. RING)

RATION

CLAYMORE

NOODLES

5.56 X 45 MM

45ACP

PLAYBOY

ANEST (7.62 MM)

IF + bi VISTA MANSION

Inside the mansion compound, the PMC soldiers desperately fight to repel the rebel attack. You can only access the zone exit via an open skylight on the roof, so either sneak in through the back of the building, or fight your way through the front door.

Main map labels

MUNA

STUN G.

COMPRESS

IPOD MUSIC

5.56 X 45 MM

SMOKE G.

M

REGAIN

GRENADE

PSS

RATION

PENTAZEMIN

PLAYBOY

12 GA. (V. RING)

RATION

7.62 X 51 MM

ANEST (.22)

WP G.

L

K

The rebels begin their attack on the mansion just after your arrival; a welcome distraction if you're aiming to sneak in. Approaching the road triggers the arrival of an armored bulldozer, which smashes through the gates. If you haven't collected either yet, note that certain PMC soldiers in this zone sometimes carry the expensive Masterkey and XM320 custom weapon parts.

K If you entered the Vista Mansion zone from the Confinement Facility exit specified on page 59, you'll find yourself on a raised pathway above patrolling PMC soldiers below. A rebel attack will begin shortly after your arrival. This will draw attention elsewhere, which facilitates an easy crawl all the way around to the road. As you approach this, a brief cutscene will show the arrival of an armored bulldozer. Stay where you are when play resumes, and wait for the rebel driver to smash through the main gates. All PMC soldiers will subsequently be removed from this part of the zone.

If you start in the lower area, you simply need to sneak to the road to initiate the cutscene. It's slightly harder to avoid detection, granted, but it's not something that should present too many problems at this point in the game.

L Crawl through the broken gates and head to the right, behind the first large tent. When you arrive at the corner of the mansion compound, you can usually crouch-run to the north wall without fear of detection. Check that the path ahead is clear, then sprint over to the steps. Drop to a crawl when you reach them, and stay as far away as you can from the PMC soldiers to your left as you sneak past.

The mansion's back door is just over to the left, but you'll often find that one PMC soldier will annoyingly linger in this area, and sometimes even go inside. While you can make a break for the door if you're sure there's no one around, the safest way to get inside is to continue along the wall until you reach a window. Approach it, take a glance at the Solid Eye radar to ensure that nobody is in the immediate vicinity, then run and press ⊗ to smash through the glass.

M Move along the hallway and turn left when you reach the reception area. Switch to a crouch-walk as you near the staircase, and quickly jog over and press yourself against the wall between the two pot plants. Two PMC soldiers will run downstairs en route to join the fray outside, pausing for a moment before they separate. Stay perfectly still, and neither will notice you. When they pass, run upstairs to the bedroom. Look through the small window to ensure that there are no soldiers on the roof (it's almost invariably clear, but such caution is always wise), then head through the door. Drop through the skylight to reach the basement, but be warned – backtracking is impossible once you hit the ground. You can run freely through the tunnels, collecting the items stashed in this area, before climbing the ladder leading to the next zone.

HOW TO PLAY

▶ **WALKTHROUGH**

INVENTORY

METAL GEAR ONLINE

EXTRAS

USER INSTRUCTIONS

ACT 1

▶ ACT 2

ACT 3

ACT 4

ACT 5

■ If you didn't collect it earlier, you can find the Muña item in the north-west corner of the compound. This unique item increases the rate of Psyche renewal when equipped, which makes it a vital tool if you're attempting to complete *MGS4* without using any healing items.

■ The "Sailor" iPod® tune is located between a crate and the outer east wall of the mansion area. This restores Snake's health when you listen to it, so it's worth picking up on your way past.

ALTERNATIVE STRATEGIES

There's no reason why you can't opt to sneak around to the left once you enter the mansion compound, though there's a greater chance of being hit by stray bullets if you do. You'll also need to crawl for most of the way, but you're free to run once you move behind the west wall of the building.

One side effect of a "pure" stealth playthrough is that it leaves you a little under-equipped for certain set-piece battles. This isn't a problem during the largely infiltration-focused situations up until this point, as – naturally – you can concentrate on simply slipping by unnoticed, or using CQC and the Mk. 2 to temporarily disable troublesome guards. It's no great spoiler to reveal that boss battles await you, though, and only having a modest range of basic pistols and rifles at your disposal can make these potentially much harder.

While you can buy weapons from Drebin if absolutely necessary, it's possible to save DP by locating a machine gun before you head into the mansion. If you don't already have one, your best bet is the PKM carried by certain rebel soldiers (or even the M60E4 wielded by PMC troops). 200 rounds would be a good figure to aim for. Again, you could buy additional ammunition from Drebin later. However, the luxury of immediate delivery has a handsome price: 1,200 DP per 30 bullets.

BACKTRACKING TO THE CONFINEMENT FACILITY

When the armored bulldozer smashes through the mansion gates, it signifies the end of the conflict in the Confinement Facility zone. As the rebels actually win the battle, this means that you can make a return visit to collect valuable items that you almost certainly missed earlier. Of particular note are the Chaff Grenades and M870 Custom inside the main building, which will prove extremely useful in the not-too-distant future. You can get by without either, but our walkthrough presumes that you will take the time to collect both.

SECRET: AKINA MINAMI

Climb onto the bed when you reach the upstairs room of the mansion, and then look up to discover a picture of Akina Minami. If you examine this in FPS view, Snake will briefly speak to acknowledge the Japanese fashion model. If his Psyche bar is less than full, it will be replenished at a vastly increased rate until you turn his gaze elsewhere.

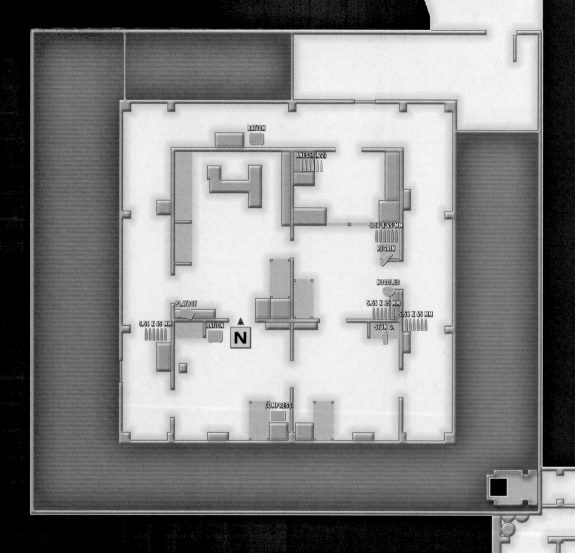

When the Caution Phase ends, stay in the central area and ready your weapons for the forthcoming battle before you proceed to the outer corridor. We find that a machine gun and a shotgun is the best all-purpose combination, though there's nothing to stop you from breaking out heavy artillery if you've been itching for an excuse to do so

Before you reach the main course of this fight (a tip from the maître d': expect seafood), try not to fill yourself up on the appetizer of several Haven Troopers. These will enter via the exterior windows, often dropping from the ceiling to begin their assault, and will use Stun Grenades in addition to their P90 submachine guns if the initial Caution Phase is escalated. If you're swift and cunning, you can beat them without being spotted once.

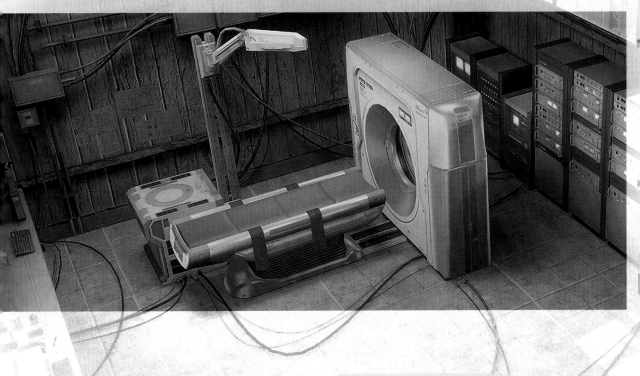

METAL GEAR SOLID 4 GUNS OF THE PATRIOTS TACTICAL ESPIONAGE ACTION

HOW TO PLAY
WALKTHROUGH
INVENTORY
METAL GEAR ONLINE
EXTRAS

USER INSTRUCTIONS
ACT 1
ACT 2
ACT 3
ACT 4
ACT 5

■ Always check your weapon after cutscenes! *MGS4* occasionally changes your equipment when they end, which can lead to confusion (and accidental kills) for Mk. 2 devotees.

■ If you're on a no-kill playthrough and would like to appease your inner humanitarian – or just be certain that you won't ruin that perfect 100% fatality-free Act 2 session – you can move unconscious Haven Troopers to a safe spot behind the CT scanner before you head to the outer corridor to trigger the arrival of Laughing Octopus. They usually drop a good range of ammunition, so it's not *all* selfless toil…

N There's a Caution Phase in effect when the final cinematic sequence ends. Unless you want this to escalate to an Alert Phase, you'll need to hide Snake before the Haven Troopers arrive. The best way to fight this battle without being detected, we've found, is to lie down by the front end of the bed in the bottom-right room. If you move Snake's legs under the bed, you'll find that it's an ideal location – it provides a clear view of the two areas where the Haven Troopers tend to pause while searching for you, with a perfectly serviceable Camo percentage of around 70%.

Ready the Mk. 2 pistol, and wait for the first pair of Haven Troopers to arrive. They will eventually make their way to the top-right* room directly ahead of you, so knock them out with clean headshots once they move into view. From this point forward, more Haven Troopers will usually arrive in the top-left room. By using R3 to adjust Snake's firing stance, you can hit these the moment they land. If your marksmanship is less than stellar, or if you're a little unlucky, you may find that a Haven Trooper approaches your position. You usually have a split-second to hit her with a headshot before Snake is detected, but this really isn't hard at short range.

When the Caution Phase ends, it's safe to stand up. Quickly collect any items you need in the central rooms, then prepare your inventory. Refer to the nearby "Briefing: Preparation" section for tips on what you should do before you continue. Once ready, run to the outer corridor to move to the next phase of this fight.

* Just so you know, directions such as "top-right room" and "bottom-left" room refer to the locales as they appear on the mini-map.

SECRET: CUTSCENE INTERACTIONS

There are hidden cutscene interactions involving Naomi during the cinematic sequences that fall before the Haven Trooper attack. Though the L1 prompt doesn't appear as usual, you can still press the button on these occasions to view the scientist from a first-person perspective. If Snake's Psyche gauge is at all depleted, each sly glance will lead to a sudden bar increase.

Hold L1 when:
- *Naomi sits on the bed and attempts to pick up the cigarette dropped by Snake.*
- *Naomi sits down in front of Snake (just before she says "There's something I have to tell you.")*

BRIEFING: SYRINGE

When used, the Syringe provided by Naomi gives Snake a temporary boost to his Psyche rating, replenishing it instantly, with the flashing gauge frozen while its effects are active. However, use this very sparingly – as Naomi warns, its efficiency wanes with repeated abuse, and Snake will begin to experience increasingly unpleasant side effects after relatively few applications. When equipped as your current item, you can administer a dose to soldiers held in a CQC hold by pressing △. This has a really quite profound effect on PMC troops…

BRIEFING: PREPARATION

This short section is designed to help players prepare for the battle that follows once all Haven Troopers have been neutralized.

- *Equipping the right weapons and having a good "feel" for the lab environment is absolutely essential. The best way to defeat the powerful adversary awaiting you is to take control of the battle, never giving her a moment to dictate proceedings.*

- *If you're on a no-kill playthrough, note that you can use lethal force on Laughing Octopus until she sheds her suit without spoiling your zero kills statistic. A shotgun/machine gun combination works best: the former often knocks her over immediately, and the latter inflicts large amounts of damage. Explosive weapons (grenades, rocket launchers) are less than ideal, as there's a danger that unconscious Haven Troopers might be caught in the blast.*

- *Defeating Laughing Octopus with purely non-lethal weapons leads to a special reward – see "Secret: Laughing Octopus Doll" overleaf for more details. If you decide to take this approach, equip Stun Grenades and a shotgun loaded with V-Ring ammunition. She's rather good at dodging and deflecting tranquilizer darts, so use the Mk. 2 only as a last resort.*

- *Familiarize yourself with the layout of the lab. Note the location of all items that Snake can stand on (particularly boxes and beds), and the position of any low windows he can roll through. These will be extremely useful later.*

The rolling attack performed by Laughing Octopus is extremely powerful, so we've marked this area map with the locations of places where Snake can stand to avoid it, or windows/low walls that he can vault or roll over as she approaches.

 Indicates a bed, crate or box that Snake can stand on.

 Places where Snake can dive through windows or vault over low walls as the rolling Octopus approaches.

Laughing Octopus will use her camouflage ability to conceal herself from Snake on several occasions. While hiding, her taunts and other utterances will briefly reveal her location on the Solid Eye radar. Use Night Vision to pinpoint her exact position, and open fire when you find her. The key to this battle is intelligent use of cover. Snake will fare badly if you attack too aggressively, so try to operate from defensible positions that don't leave him too exposed.

Once she sheds her suit, there are two potential stages to the Laughing Beauty fight. In the first, she will pursue Snake around the lab, dodging swiftly to the left and right when he aims at her, and catching him in a tender yet deadly embrace if she moves within range; waggle ⓛ to escape. If three minutes pass with no resolution, her health and Psyche gauges will be replenished, and the action will resume in an ethereal "white world". If not killed or disabled in a further three minutes, Laughing Beauty will automatically die.

﹁. SOUTH AMERICA / RESEARCH LAB

BRIEFING: FACECAMO

You are provided with the FaceCamo device after the battle ends. This new gadget can be equipped at the Camouflage menu, and typically improves Snake's Camo percentage by 10% to 15% when worn.

SECRET: LAUGHING OCTOPUS DOLL

If you defeat Laughing Octopus with non-lethal weapons, you'll find an exclusive collectible figurine on the bed in the bottom-left corner of the top-right room after she sheds her powered suit. It can only be collected during phase one of the Laughing Beauty confrontation (that is, before she is disabled or the "white world" sequence begins), so don't forget to pick it up straight away. This item, along with the Frog Soldier Doll found in the Advent Palace Garage in Act 1, and three other dolls located in Acts 3, 4 and 5, is required to unlock a secret weapon that can be used on subsequent playthroughs.

◯ LAUGHING OCTOPUS

The tips that follow are designed to assist players who would like to complete a "perfect" defeat of Laughing Octopus – that is, using no healing items, without harming sleeping Haven Troopers, and with a non-lethal conclusion.

Attacks

If you're really good – or at least moderately practiced – you can dodge every type of assault that Laughing Octopus attempts. We strongly recommend that you avoid the outer corridor and stay in the inner rooms during attack phases.

- Her standard attack is to use a P90. This can be withering if Snake is caught in an accurate volley on higher difficulty levels, so always stay close to some form of cover (ideally a doorway). Laughing Octopus generally stops firing once your bullets start to hit home (and especially if hit squarely and knocked from her feet with a shotgun blast), so don't relent until she falls.

- Laughing Octopus is extremely agile, and will use her tentacles to move rapidly to new locations. She can arrive from any position, at any time.

- When knocked down, she fills the air around her with an impenetrable smoke. If you're close, back away immediately. More often than not, this cloud masks the launch of slow-moving but tenacious homing missiles. Though you can shoot these down (temporarily activate Auto Aim if you want to make this really easy), it's generally safer to dodge them. Stay out of their range, and they'll eventually explode automatically.

- At short range, Laughing Octopus will make dizzying melee attacks, so don't get too close – or if you do, knock her down with a shotgun blast immediately. Later in the battle, she usually attempts an alternative ranged melee attack. Launching one of her tentacles forward, she'll attach it to Snake and electrocute him. If you're prudent with your use of cover, this need never be a danger.

- We've saved the worst till last, of course. When Laughing Octopus rolls into a ball and begins spinning on the spot, you have literally a second to find something to stand on; after a brief pause, she'll fire herself at Snake's position with unerring accuracy. You generally encounter this later in the battle, and it's not something to be casual about: a direct hit can drain approximately 75% of a full health bar on higher difficulty levels. The only reliable way to dodge it is to climb straight onto a crate, box or bed. From safety, blast her with a shotgun as she rolls to a halt. This is why you should, whenever possible, operate from the two rooms at the bottom of the map – you can simply run onto either bed without pausing to climb.

Hiding Places

Watch the radar to judge Octopus's general location, then use NV to find her. If Snake is injured, this is the perfect time to go prone and wait for his health and Psyche levels to replenish. Generally speaking, winning the battle is much easier if you can exact maximum damage each time you discover one of her hiding places.

Laughing Beauty

For the final section of the fight, aim your tranquilizer darts at Laughing Beauty's torso. There's usually a brief delay between her dodge attempts, which is the best time to strike, but expect to waste a fair amount of Mk. 2 ammo nonetheless. Stun Grenades are extremely effective if you can aim them ahead of her, though. Your reward for this merciful resolution will be the exclusive Laughing Beauty FaceCamo.

■ If you place Snake in a prone position, face up, on a bed during the first phase of the Laughing Beauty fight, she will climb on top and cuddle him. Unfortunately, this really hurts. Waggle ◐ to throw her aside.

■ The cutscene that follows this battle changes depending on whether you knocked Laughing Beauty out, or attacked her with a lethal weapon type. This is something to look out for on a second playthrough.

OCTOPUS'S HIDING PLACE/POSE	NOTES
Against wall/on ceiling	Use a machine gun/shotgun.
Against painting	Use a machine gun/shotgun.
CT Scanner/inside box	Her tentacles appear convincingly as cables, but the illusion is shattered with NV. Use a shotgun.
Medical mannequin	This shouldn't show up in white on NV; take a quick glance in the direction she is facing to learn how Laughing Octopus is attempting to make a dummy out of *you*. Use a machine gun/shotgun.
Posing as Metal Gear Mk. II	The scale makes this a comparatively clumsy subterfuge. Use a machine gun (or a Stun Grenade if you're aiming to obtain the secret Laughing Octopus Doll), and don't follow the illusion!
Posing as an unconscious Haven Trooper	This is an evil deception if you're on a no-kill playthrough. You can discern which body is her by looking at the health and Psyche bars on the Solid Eye readout; the figures will correspond with those in the top left-hand corner. If she's lying on top of (or even very near to) a sleeping Haven Trooper, though, it's safer to just leave her. Otherwise, use a machine gun; a Stun Grenade is fine if you're working to reduce her Psyche gauge instead.
Posing as Naomi	A cheap trick, but a clever one. Use a machine gun, and don't stop firing when the smoke appears. Unlike other instances, you can sometimes drain additional health before she actually moves.

This tracking section is enormous fun. If this is your first playthrough, we advise you not to consult the more detailed instructions to the right unless you become irreparably stuck. Listen to the advice that Otacon and Raiden have to offer on using Night Vision and reading footprints, and you'll be all set to find your own unique way through this zone. There are at least a handful of occasions where going the "wrong" way is the most enjoyable part…

It pays to be a little more vigilant after you pass the river (and, you should notice, a checkpoint), as there are Haven Troopers to worry about in the second part of the zone. Use the Solid Eye's NV function very sparingly from this point forward: activate it briefly, examine the ground, then switch it off before potential adversaries notice its telltale sound.

P To avoid potential confusion in this maze-like zone, we've divided the standard stealth walkthrough into bite-sized chunks. These include tips on all the other things you can look out for while tracking Naomi – though as pathways that deviate from the ideal route usually lead to ambushes, they are purely optional.

Q **Stealth:** Follow the path to the north-west, and crouch-walk over the bridge. There's a soldier patrolling in the area beyond, so go prone when you reach the boxes on the other side.

Optional: Take the path to the north to encounter a PMC soldier enjoying a bathroom break. You can sneakily collect a Fore Grip B custom weapon part from beside him while he concentrates on the matter in hand, so to speak.

R **Stealth:** Watch the patrolling soldier carefully, and make your way to the north-east path once it's safe to do so.

Optional: The north-west path leads to a dead-end where you'll find a pot of Noodles booby-trapped with a Claymore hidden in the grass just behind it. The path directly north leads to a small building where a PMC soldier is waiting to spring a surprise attack. If you crawl carefully to the right, you can hit him with a Mk. 2 dart through the back window, though the rewards are fairly modest – a box of Stun Grenades, a Playboy and a PSS collectible. You can puzzle over the meaning of the rather cryptic white sign if you like, though we can tell you now that it has no specific purpose.

S **Stealth:** Crawl over to the path to the east, and listen out for the comment made by the PMC sniper on the rock above as you pass him for a little comic relief. Stop before you reach the first tree in the next open area.

Optional: The path to the north leads to a raised area above the small building discussed at **R**. You can slide down the slope if you wish. The path to the south is much more interesting. If you were wondering what the sniper mentioned above was focusing on, look to the bra discarded on the rock; a little *too* casually, it transpires. Follow the path around, and you'll be forced to deal with three PMC soldiers: one patrolling, another admiring a Playboy in the ruined building, and a final one hiding behind boxes just before the river.

T **Stealth:** Look to your right – there's a PMC soldier lying in wait. Pause until he looks along the path he is defending before you move. The alternative, as ever, is simply to send him to sleep with a tranquilizer dart, or to use Metal Gear Mk.II to entice him elsewhere. Either way, cross the river once you pass him.

Optional: The path to the east also leads to the river, but takes you far too close to the soldier mentioned above.

U **Stealth:** There's a checkpoint here, so save your progress. Follow the (left-hand) path to the east.

Optional: The path to the south leads to an ambush – a Haven Trooper is hiding on the other side of a large log, with another behind a tree around the corner.

V **Stealth:** Crawl over to the north-east path, but be quiet – there's a Haven Trooper not far to your right. Stay low throughout, and take special care when you sneak past a second Haven Trooper (look left) at the end. She has her back turned to you, so just crawl straight by to the right. Stop when you reach the tree stump.

Optional: As you approach the path to the south, you'll hear brief sounds of a woman in distress. Follow it around, and the spoken entreaties become a little … well, listen for yourself. Espying the Haven Trooper sniper on the ledge above the small building should make things crystal clear; a tranquilizer shot will enable you to pick up the collectibles here without too much fuss. The path directly north leads to another pair of Haven Troopers poised to shoot on sight. You'll find a Ration there, but if you're composed and experienced enough to retrieve it without causing a scene, you undoubtedly won't need it.

W **Stealth:** There is a PMC soldier planting a Claymore just off to your right, but you can usually crawl past safely if you stick to the rocks on the left. As the best route forward is to take the south pathway, which makes him a distinct liability, it's sensible to simply tranquilize him. However, doing so before he moves away from the explosive device will cause him to fall directly on top of it – with obvious consequences. This isn't counted as a "kill" (we've checked), but it's hardly the most subtle way to deal with the situation…

Optional: The dead-end to the north-east features an Easter egg: a metal plate covered with handprints and signatures from the *MGS4* development team (including Hideo Kojima, Yoji Shinkawa and Mineshi Kimura, among others). Lie Snake down on this, and you can then register the exclusive Hand Camo pattern in the Camouflage menu. Follow the path to the south-east, and you'll encounter a pair of women's shoes. Unfortunately, but perhaps predictably, they're closely watched by a Haven Trooper sniper.

X **Stealth:** Your ideal route leads to the west, but a PMC soldier usually walks along this path as soon as you arrive in the area. Crawl after him (don't get too close!), then take the first left before he reaches the end of his patrol. Turn right and enter the underground tunnel to exit the zone.

Optional: There's nothing of real note in this final region – a PSS, a couple of additional PMC patrols, and that's it. You'll almost wish that your curiosity hadn't been sated…

■ If you backtrack to the Research Lab, you can pick up Noodles and a box of ammo for the Mk. 2. You can't enter the lab, but the collectibles are worth the short journey if you're running low on healing items and tranquilizer darts.

■ If you follow the path mentioned at point U in the walkthrough, you'll encounter a flattened circle of grass that is rather redolent of a crop circle. Stand in the center of it to hear a mystery monologue. If you wait until it ends, you'll get a DP bonus.

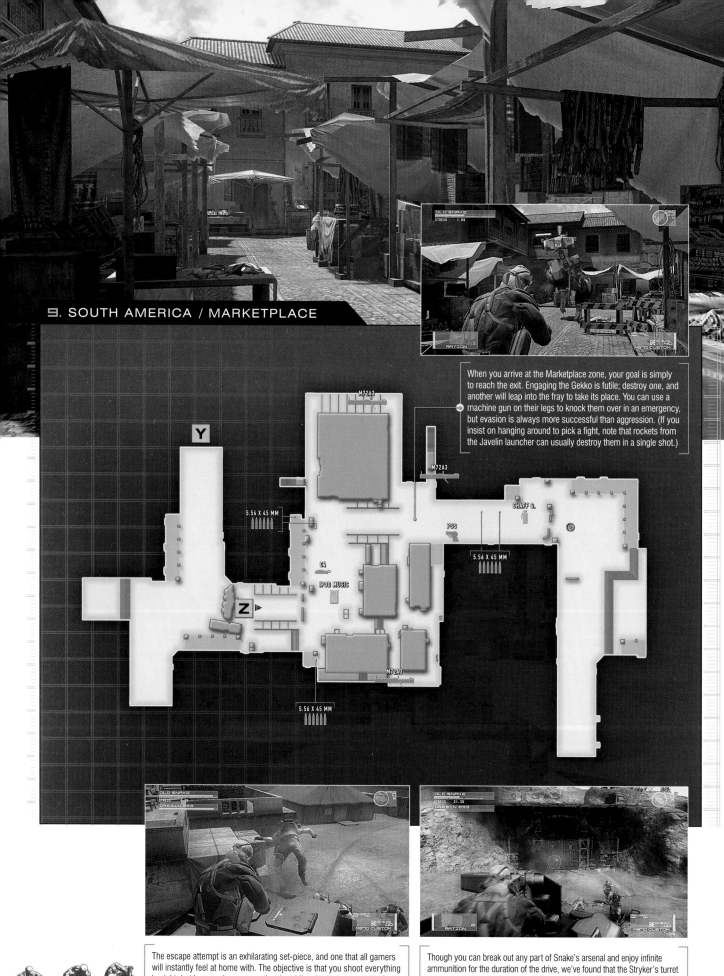

9. SOUTH AMERICA / MARKETPLACE

When you arrive at the Marketplace zone, your goal is simply to reach the exit. Engaging the Gekko is futile; destroy one, and another will leap into the fray to take its place. You can use a machine gun on their legs to knock them over in an emergency, but evasion is always more successful than aggression. (If you insist on hanging around to pick a fight, note that rockets from the Javelin launcher can usually destroy them in a single shot.)

M72A3

Y

M72A3

CHAFF G.

5.56 X 45 MM

PSS

5.56 X 45 MM

C4

IPOD MUSIC

Z

M72A3

5.56 X 45 MM

The escape attempt is an exhilarating set-piece, and one that all gamers will instantly feel at home with. The objective is that you shoot everything in sight, but keep a close eye on the shambling, brain-damaged PMC soldiers. When they climb onto Drebin's Stryker, you'll need to use CQC (or, for maximum efficiency, a shotgun) to knock them off.

Though you can break out any part of Snake's arsenal and enjoy infinite ammunition for the duration of the drive, we've found that the Stryker's turret is actually the most potent weapon you can use. This is especially applicable when you reach the locked gates in the Power Station zone – though it might seem that explosives will be quicker, that's not actually the case.

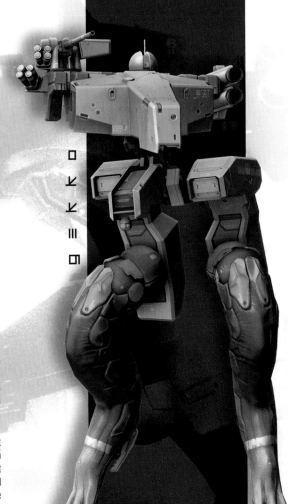

Y

The escape aboard Drebin's Stryker presents a novel challenge for players attempting a no kill/no health items playthrough. The swarming PMC soldiers may have been reduced to staggering, insensible husks, but they're still living creatures – and therefore count as kills at the final Act 2 performance summary.

Phase 1: Vista Mansion

As soon as you gain control of Snake, equip Chaff Grenades and the M870 Custom (though any shotgun will suffice, even the Masterkey add-on) set to fire the non-lethal Vortex Ring Shot ammo type. Just in case you haven't done this before, hold R2, and then press ◎ to cycle through the available ammo types. Tranquilizer darts have no effect on the assailants you face in this area, so holster your trusty Mk. 2 for the time being. Ensure that your shotgun is loaded as you pass through the mansion gates.

When the soldiers wearing powered suits attack, throw a Chaff Grenade to prevent them from firing at Snake or the Stryker. You can then use targeted blasts with Vortex Ring Shot to deter the surrounding PMC soldiers. It's also very efficient at knocking off anyone who is clinging to the side of the vehicle; effective crowd and passenger control here will make the next phase a little easier. Whenever the distinctive chaff disappears (or just before that point if you're well organized), quickly throw another grenade to restore the jamming effect.

If you neglected to collect the Chaff Grenades in the Confinement Facility earlier, all is not lost. You can expect to sustain greater damage, granted, but you can attempt to minimize this by crouching just behind the Stryker's turret. Concentrate on knocking PMC soldiers down as they climb up, and Drebin will eventually drive the Stryker through the gates.

Phase 2: Confinement Facility

Man the turret and use it to blast the Gekko, prioritizing them in terms of proximity – the nearer they are, the more dangerous they are. If a Gekko gets too close it will jump over the Stryker and attack from behind, so try to take them down as quickly as possible. You can also deploy occasional Chaff Grenades to prevent them from firing their weapons, and use CQC or Vortex Ring shotgun blasts to get rid of PMC soldiers when they clamber aboard the Stryker.

The thick, acrid cloud of smoke that develops as you destroy Gekko can mask the approach of others. Activate the Solid Eye's NV function to enjoy a clearer view of proceedings. Finally, always aim at the top "head" section of the Gekko. Not only does this destroy them quickly, it also minimizes the possibility that you will accidentally hit and kill a PMC soldier.

Phase 3: Power Station

This is a blessedly simple section once you know what is expected of you. Ignore the tank – you can't do anything about it – and simply pummel the locked green gates with the turret from the moment they appear in view. The only danger here is that you might accidentally shoot a PMC soldier while he climbs onto the Stryker, but this happens very rarely.

Phase 4: High Woodlands Highway

Again, this is a relatively easy sequence if you're moderately accomplished in your use of the turret. There are no PMC soldiers to worry about, so you can concentrate exclusively on shooting Gekko. Focus on destroying individual units in turn, as this reduces the number of potential weapons firing at you; as a bonus, you'll accrue a greater sum of bonus DP (see margin note) by the time you reach the final Marketplace area.

Z

When play resumes, go prone in the shade to the left to regain Life and Psyche if you would like to avoid using healing items. Ready the two Chaff Grenades collected earlier if you have them. You need to pick a way through the market stalls and rampaging Gekko, avoiding their deadly feet and insistent weapons systems. A single kick can result in instant death on Big Boss Hard, and the presence of innocent civilians precludes any attempt to use explosive weaponry to clear a path.

The solution, as with the opening of Act 1, is to just make a run for it. As the Gekko can turn up in a variety of positions, it's impossible to recommend a foolproof path to the zone exit. However, the following route seems to be the most consistently reliable.

- Run directly ahead from your starting position, then take a left behind the first set of market stalls.

- Throw a Chaff Grenade if you have one, then dart from cover to reach the small section of metal fence. You can vault over this to avoid the Gekko that usually blocks the path to your left.

- Sprint straight over to the stall just ahead and to your left, and hide behind it. You can find an M72A3 missile launcher here.

- Wait for the Gekko just beyond the stall to smash through the marketplace area leading to the zone exit, thoughtfully destroying all obstructions that block your safe passage through. Let it return and pass by your position, then throw your final Chaff Grenade and sprint for the zone exit.

- Don't look back: just run. A final Gekko will land at the opening between the two low barriers, but there's absolutely nothing you can do about this. Run directly towards it and, just before it can sweep its leg around to lash out, roll through the gap with Snake angled slightly to the right to make an extremely narrow escape.

> ■ Destroying "unmanned" vehicles – that is, artificial creatures that have no human pilot, such as the Gekko – results in a small DP bonus. This does not count towards the "Kills" total displayed at the end of each Act.

> ■ Collectable items can randomly appear when Gekko destroy stalls in the small Marketplace zone. Granted, you're usually too busy attempting to avoid being kicked to death by giant killing machines to worry about stockpiling assorted comestibles, but we thought it worth a mention nonetheless.

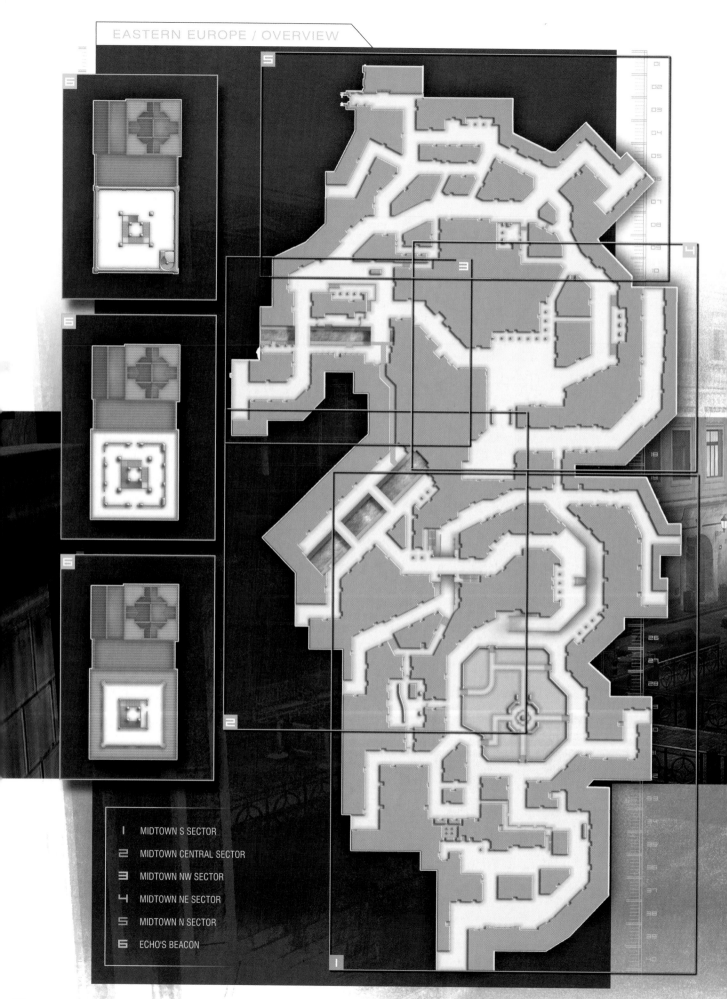

I   MIDTOWN S SECTOR

2   MIDTOWN CENTRAL SECTOR

3   MIDTOWN NW SECTOR

4   MIDTOWN NE SECTOR

5   MIDTOWN N SECTOR

6   ECHO'S BEACON

EASTERN EUROPE

ACT 3: THIRD SUN

SECRET: MISSION BRIEFING

As with the Act 2 Mission Briefing, wait until the screen changes to a multiple-camera format, then take control of Metal Gear Mk.II by pressing ⊙. You can find two boxes of ammunition just beyond the helicopter. Upstairs, you'll encounter another Battery, an iPod® tune ("Shin Bokura no Taiyou Theme"), plus a Compress in the toilet.

You can bump Metal Gear Mk. II into each of the following characters to gain unique FaceCamo types. If the collision is successful, you'll hear the distinct "click" sound effect used to indicate item collection.

CHARACTER	WHEN?	FACECAMO TYPE
OTACON	When interactive cutscene starts	Octacon
NAOMI	After she stands up approximately five minutes into the cutscene	Cyborg Raiden – Visor Closed
SUNNY	When she leaves her chair, around three minutes after Naomi gets to her feet	Cyborg Raiden – Visor Open

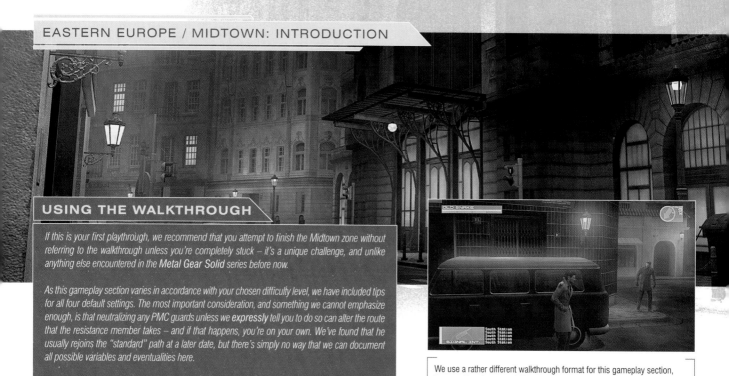

USING THE WALKTHROUGH

If this is your first playthrough, we recommend that you attempt to finish the Midtown zone without referring to the walkthrough unless you're completely stuck – it's a unique challenge, and unlike anything else encountered in the Metal Gear Solid series before now.

As this gameplay section varies in accordance with your chosen difficulty level, we have included tips for all four default settings. The most important consideration, and something we cannot emphasize enough, is that neutralizing any PMC guards unless we expressly tell you to do so can alter the route that the resistance member takes – and if that happens, you're on your own. We've found that he usually rejoins the "standard" path at a later date, but there's simply no way that we can document all possible variables and eventualities here.

You meet your first resistance target in Midtown S Sector shortly after play resumes, and take a similar route through this zone irrespective of your chosen difficulty level. To use our stealth-focused walkthrough, simply follow the guidance designed for your setting, and then jump to the specified page when you reach the zone exit. We've placed two color-coded route lines on each relevant area map – one for the path taken on Liquid Easy, Naked Normal and Solid Normal, the other for the tougher Big Boss Hard path – which will make the process of following your target much simpler.

We use a rather different walkthrough format for this gameplay section, because there's a very definite emphasis on stealth – try to shoot your way through the city streets, and you won't get very far. Your first task is to find a resistance member, which is the easy part. The second is to successfully stalk him through the heavily patrolled streets to the secret resistance HQ without raising the alarm. There are five map "zones" in total between you and the objective. How many of these you visit, and the route you take, depends on both your actions and the chosen difficulty setting.

GENERAL TIPS

- *As long as you don't lose track of the resistance member, there's no need to use the Signal Interceptor. The Solid Eye is a much more valuable tool. Besides, your target won't usually continue with his walk until you approach his position.*

- *Unless you actively want to complicate matters, discard Snake's default disguise and switch to full OctoCamo (including FaceCamo). You should crawl in most instances, switching to a crouch-walk if you're absolutely certain there's no risk of detection. Only adopt a standing posture if discovered and in need of a rapid escape.*

- *There are regular checkpoints after each load break, so save your progress at each one. In a worst-case scenario, you can then reset and reload if things go badly.*

- *The resistance member will pause and wait whenever he encounters a PMC patrol that he cannot pass; this is signposted by a change in music, from the standard area theme to a moody, bass-heavy piece. If you wait, he'll eventually choose a different path.*

- *If the resistance member is spooked – by your clumsiness, or if you disable PMC soldiers while he is watching – he'll run for a hiding place. Wait for a while, and he'll return to resume his journey. He's sometimes very careless when he sprints for cover, though, and may encounter PMC troops, who will arrest him on sight.*

- *Though you can save the resistance member by neutralizing his captors if he is arrested, it's sometimes too risky to attempt it. If you leave him, he will be marched to one of several road blocks, and then escorted from the zone – this is shown in a brief cutscene.*

- *If a resistance member dies or is captured, just wait patiently. After a while, another will arrive via the entrance passed through earlier, and will make his way to your position. However, this supply of resistance members is not boundless – if too many are caught or killed, it's Game Over.*

- *Watch your environment carefully for potential hazards. Searchlights are to be avoided at all costs, and even litter (particularly cans) can reveal your location if disturbed.*

Make too much noise, or stand incautiously in plain view, and the man you are tailing will become suspicious. If you're seriously indiscreet and he actually sees or hears you, he will usually run for a hiding place – but he may even draw a weapon and open fire. In these instances, find somewhere to hide, and wait for him to resume his walk. You really don't need to get too close – the Solid Eye radar will enable you to keep track of his movements.

In most areas (particularly on lower difficulty settings), you can simply follow the resistance member's lead as you slip by PMC patrols, which can include helicopters sweeping the area below them with searchlights and even road vehicles fitted with turrets. In certain instances, though, you may find that you need to act as a "guardian angel" for your target, either taking improvised steps to prevent PMC soldiers from detecting him, or disabling his captors should he be arrested.

I. EASTERN EUROPE / MIDTOWN S SECTOR

HOW TO PLAY

WALKTHROUGH

INVENTORY

METAL GEAR ONLINE

EXTRAS

USER INSTRUCTIONS

ACT 1

ACT 2

ACT 3

ACT 4

ACT 5

■ Easter egg 1: As you follow the resistance member, you may notice a mysterious man in a trench coat and hat occasionally leaning out from a place of concealment to watch you. When you attempt to look directly at him, though, he'll move behind cover, and will vanish if you run over to investigate.

■ Easter egg 2: When you reach the park, there is a plinth with an empty "space" for a missing statue, much like the one encountered in Act 1. If you climb up and hold △, you can use it as a place to hide from PMC soldiers or the resistance member — though, naturally, Snake will need to be wearing OctoCamo for this to work. There are amusing consequences if you choose to hide here straight away after reaching the park …

Big Boss Hard ——— Solid Normal, Naked Normal & Liquid Easy ———

BIG BOSS HARD

1 From your starting position, walk onto the road and take the first left to trigger a brief cutscene. Hide behind the van until the resistance member walks by, then trail him from a safe distance.

2 When his progress is halted by the presence of two guards, hide behind the metal enclosure until he turns around. This should take approximately 30 seconds. Follow him onto the balcony above the guards, then carefully crawl after him.

3 Stay at the top of the ladder as the resistance member stands below, watching the PMC soldier at the end of the street. When he opts to take another route, climb down and follow him into the park.

4 Hide behind the hedge and wait until he relieves himself, then crawl along the path after him. He'll pause behind two PMC guards. Conceal yourself in the long grass behind the tree in the north-east corner of the park.

5 When the resistance member throws a grenade, wait in your hiding place until the Caution Phase ends, then go down the nearby steps. Head north, and take the road on the right. Your target will be admiring a poster of Minami Akina, but will move on when you approach.

6 Go prone on the right-hand pavement as the patrol vehicle passes by, then follow the resistance member to Midtown Central Sector (turn to page 76).

SOLID NORMAL, NAKED NORMAL & LIQUID EASY

As Big Boss Hard up to point **6**, but with fewer PMC guards; note that the patrol vehicle doesn't appear at all on Liquid Easy. Trailing him from a safe distance, follow the resistance member to Midtown NE Sector (turn to page 78).

ALTERNATIVE STRATEGIES

This is purely a tip for players attempting a speed run on Big Boss Hard, as it helps to shave a few minutes from the Midtown section. Go straight to the balcony mentioned at **2**, and climb down the ladder at the other side. Tranquilize the soldier at the end of the road (mentioned at point **3**), and hide his body behind the nearby car. Now hide and wait for the resistance member to arrive. He'll take a completely different route to Midtown Central Sector, skipping the park area entirely, and will eventually return to the "standard" path at point **2** of the walkthrough on page 76.

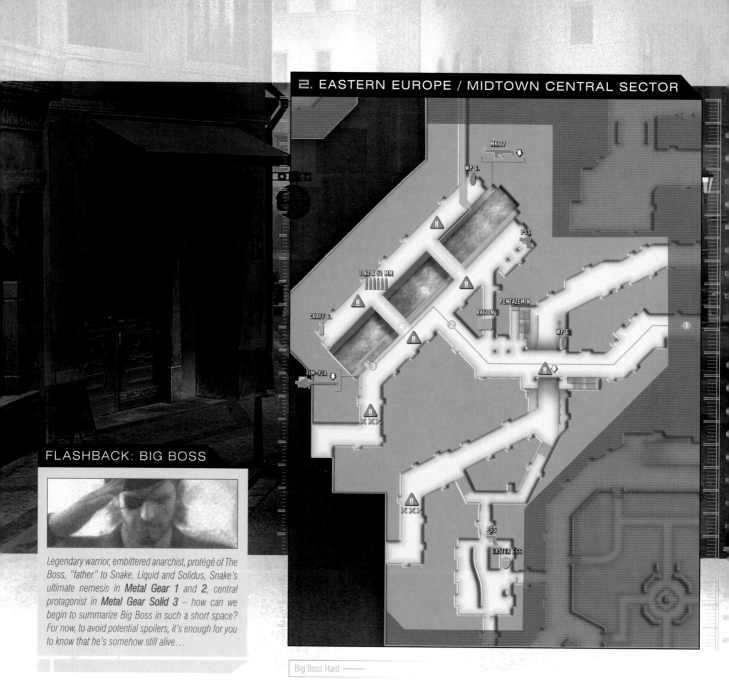

MK.17

WP 6.

PSS

7.62 X 51 MM

PENTAZEMIN

CHAFF 6.

RATION

4

2

WP 6.

1

3

FIM-92A

×××

×××

PSS

EASTER EGG

Big Boss Hard ————

FLASHBACK: BIG BOSS

Legendary warrior, embittered anarchist, protégé of The Boss, "father" to Snake, Liquid and Solidus, Snake's ultimate nemesis in **Metal Gear 1** *and* **2**, *central protagonist in* **Metal Gear Solid 3** – *how can we begin to summarize Big Boss in such a short space? For now, to avoid potential spoilers, it's enough for you to know that he's somehow still alive…*

BIG BOSS HARD

1 The resistance member can be found just around the corner, gazing at another poster of Minami Akina. Go prone and wait from a safe distance, even as he begins to walk away. As you'll soon discover, his longing for the Japanese (and, evidently, worldwide) icon becomes too much to bear, and he sprints back along the bridge for another private moment with the photograph. When he leaves for a second time, follow him until he reaches the square.

2 Don't panic about the whereabouts of your target should he disappear from view in this section – the most important thing is to avoid detection yourself. He's heading down to the waterway, so you'll catch up with him soon. There's a helicopter with a searchlight flying overhead, and being caught in full view by its beam will lead to an instant Alert Phase. Crawl beside the first two parked vans, staying in the road and rotating the camera to keep the helicopter in sight, until you reach a larger van. Move around behind it, and onto the pavement. There are two guards not far behind this last vehicle, so making any noise will be a potentially fatal mistake.

3 Crawl to the top of the steps, and study the opposite side of the waterway to observe the PMC soldier over there. As long as you are not directly in his field of view, it's safe to move down. When his peripheral vision might potentially encompass Snake's position, either stop dead, or inch forward at the very slowest crawling speed. Don't rush this – you usually have a period of grace before the searchlight moves towards your position, and you'll be reasonably safe once you reach the shadow underneath the bridge ahead. When you get there, stop and watch the progress of the searchlight.

4 As soon as the searchlight passes overhead, move carefully along your current side of the waterway until you reach the shadows beneath the second bridge. Once you're sure that the resistance member is sufficiently far away, drop into the water and cross to the path on the other side. Glance back at the chopper to ensure that you have enough time, then approach the opening that the resistance member walked through. Be very careful here – he will turn to face your direction, cautiously backing along the passage, fearing that someone is following him. If you wait behind the wall, out of sight, he'll eventually turn and exit the zone. Follow him to Midtown NW Sector.

META GEAR SOLID 4
GUNS OF THE PATRIOTS TACTICAL ESPIONAGE ACTION

HOW TO PLAY

▶ **WALKTHROUGH**

INVENTORY

METAL GEAR ONLINE

EXTRAS

USER INSTRUCTIONS

ACT 1

ACT 2

▶ **ACT 3**

ACT 4

ACT 5

∃. EASTERN EUROPE / MIDTOWN NW SECTOR

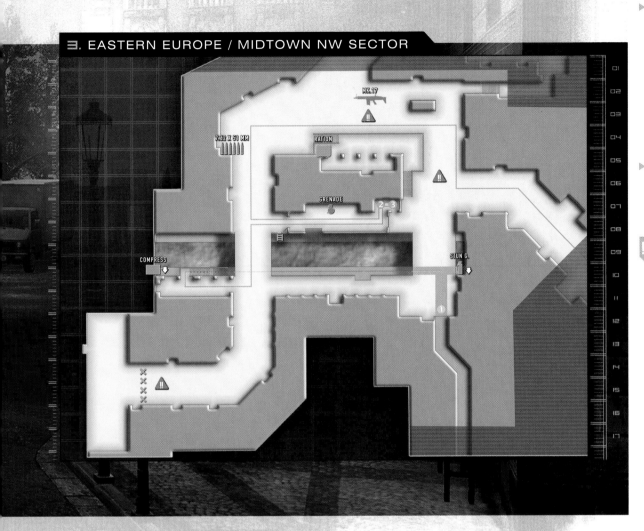

■ An alternative way to follow the resistance member through the two waterways is to dive into the water and stay submerged to dodge the spotlights. However, if you are spotted, note that you cannot perform CQC while wading.

■ Though there's nothing of vital importance, you can collect some useful items and ammunition in the city streets. Getting Snake to each collectible is a tough task, though, so it's better to utilize the services of a cloaked Metal Gear Mk.II if you espy anything that catches your eye.

BIG BOSS HARD

1 Switch to a crawling position immediately, and wait for a moment – if you're too hasty you'll spook your quarry straight away, which can lead to difficulties. Carefully crawl out and observe as he wades through the water. There's actually no need to follow him, as he'll be returning to your current side when he reaches the next bridge. Wait for the searchlight to pass overhead (note that you need to wait towards the back of the shadowy area – too far forward, and the helicopter crew will spot you), and then creep over to the alcove on the left if you need an immediate hiding place, or otherwise make straight for the shadow under the second bridge. Crawl up to the top of the steps, then turn left. Cross the bridge and take the first right.

2 Slowly approach the hole in the wall to the left of the second set of (closed) gates, then deploy Metal Gear Mk. II and engage its stealth function. Move it (or, if you prefer to anthropomorphize, *him*) through the opening, and turn left. You need to bump into the can just behind the two PMC soldiers at speed to knock it clearly away from its current position; towards the right side of the road (from your starting position) would be best. Once you've accomplished this feat, continue north and around the corner to the left. Do exactly the same with the second can behind the next PMC duo, then deactivate Metal Gear Mk. II.

3 Pause for a few seconds to allow the soldiers to get back to their original positions, then return to the road. Turn right, and sneak along the pavement until you spot the resistance member. Crawl carefully behind both sets of PMC soldiers, then follow your target to Midtown NE Sector.

ALTERNATIVE STRATEGIES

With video games, the most effective way to solve a problem isn't always the most enjoyable. In our walkthrough for the Midtown NW Sector, we reveal how to sneakily move the two tin cans that the resistance member might accidentally stumble on, leading to his arrest in both instances. If you follow our guidance to the letter in that area, you'll miss an amusing experience. The first can is a trial, but when you encounter the second without prior warning, you can't help but snigger – even if it is through slightly gritted teeth. You can almost hear the Kojima Productions design team chuckling as you attempt to save the resistance member from a second bout of calamitous clumsiness…

BRIEFING: SIGNAL INTERCEPTOR

*The Signal Interceptor only works in this one part of **MGS4**, and has no further use thereafter. Its sole function is to highlight the general "area" that a resistance member is located in on the pause menu map. It's worth a try if you get hopelessly lost on a first playthrough and don't want to resort to using our maps unless absolutely necessary, but the Solid Eye is actually a much more useful tool in general.*

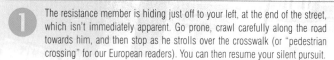

ANEST. (.22)

7.62 X 51 MM

SMOKE G.

NOODLES

.45ACP

4

RATION

5.56 X 45 MM

Big Boss Hard ——— Solid Normal, Naked Normal & Liquid Easy ———

BIG BOSS HARD

1 This is a very short and easy area to get through, as long as you don't do anything too hasty. Creep along the street in pursuit of your lead, and wait around the corner as he stands in the doorway. Crawl along and follow him to the left.

2 Trail him from a safe distance as he moves from pillar to pillar, keeping quiet to avoid arousing the suspicions of the nearby guards. Once you round the corner, you simply need to follow him to Midtown N Sector.

SOLID NORMAL, NAKED NORMAL & LIQUID EASY

1 The resistance member is hiding just off to your left, at the end of the street, which isn't immediately apparent. Go prone, crawl carefully along the road towards him, and then stop as he strolls over the crosswalk (or "pedestrian crossing" for our European readers). You can then resume your silent pursuit.

2 Crawl through the arch, and around to the right. There is a helicopter hovering over the square, scouring the shadows with a searchlight; there are also a few PMC soldiers (the exact number depends on your chosen difficulty setting). As long as you stay low on the pavement behind the parked vehicles, there's little danger of detection.

3 Follow the resistance member along the next street until it bends to the left, then wait and watch from a concealed position as he creeps behind two PMC soldiers (note: only one on Liquid Easy). Unfortunately, concentrating on his would-be captors, he fails to notice an empty metal container at his feet and accidentally knocks it over. This leads to his immediate arrest.

From your hiding position, ready your Mk. 2 pistol and track the movements of the PMC soldiers. You need to hit both with two precise headshots; for a "perfect" takedown, you should neutralize the soldier walking slightly behind first. More often than not, the resistance member will run up the nearby steps and hide for a moment, before resuming his journey. There is a chance, though, that he will make the ill-judged decision to run back into the previous square, only to be arrested for a second time. Should that happen, you'll just have to wait until he is taken into custody, then hold your position until a second resistance member arrives.

(If marksmanship isn't your strong suit, note that you can sit idly by as the resistance member is escorted away. Once the coast is clear, run over and kick the metal container clear of the pavement. When a second resistance member arrives, you can be assured that he won't make the same mistake.)

4 Finally, once safely beyond the previous flashpoint, simply tail the resistance member until he reaches the exit to Midtown N Sector – your next (and final) destination in the Midtown area.

5. EASTERN EUROPE / MIDTOWN N SECTOR

HOW TO PLAY
▶ WALKTHROUGH
INVENTORY
METAL GEAR ONLINE
EXTRAS

USER INSTRUCTIONS
ACT 1
ACT 2
▶ ACT 3
ACT 4
ACT 5

All difficulty levels

■ If you're attempting a "perfect" playthrough (no kills, no alerts, no healing items used, and so forth), the next section of the game is *extremely* difficult on higher difficulty levels. Unless you already have one, you can tip the odds slightly in your favor by acquiring a Twin Barrel shotgun from Drebin's shop before you exit this zone. It's by no means mandatory that you do so, but it can definitely help.

■ If you hold up the resistance member by sneaking up behind him with a weapon drawn, he may drop an iPod® tune when you search him.

BIG BOSS HARD

1 Wait until the resistance member emerges from the courtyard just ahead in his crude yet effective PMC disguise, then crawl after him. You can't follow him onto the main road, so take the path to the right instead. Cross the next street and move onto the pavement, then head left. Crawl down to the side of the white van.

2 There is a PMC patrol vehicle driving in a loop around this area, so wait until it passes before you inch out to the right. Be careful while moving around the corner – Snake has a tendency to stand up if he bumps into corners while crawling, and that could spell disaster here. Sneak behind the two guards, and onto the pavement of the road leading north-west. It's usually wise to pause behind the parked car until the patrol vehicle has made a second pass.

3 Crawl up the slope to the end of the pavement and, when the coast is clear, across to the pavement on the opposite side. Stop as the patrol vehicle drives by for a third time, then take the next left. When you round the corner, you'll see the resistance member standing with three PMC soldiers. One of these will immediately peel off to the right; the other two will accompany your target to the end of the alleyway, where another will depart to the left. The final soldier will move along a path to the right shortly afterwards.

4 Check to ensure that the patrol vehicle is a safe distance away, then follow the resistance member across the road. There are no PMC soldiers to worry about here.

5 At the end of the alleyway, listen out for an approaching patrol vehicle, then crawl over the road in pursuit of the resistance member. Be very careful as you approach the top of the slight slope. When you reach a barrel beside a road sign, stop and wait. There is a PMC soldier on a very short patrol route on the side-street to your right. Tranquilizing him isn't an option, because his body will fall in plain sight, so you'll need to time your crossing to perfection. Pause until the vehicle passes, then wait for the soldier to turn away from you. Crawl past the entrance immediately: there's just enough time to get behind the cover of the next building before he turns to face you.

SOLID NORMAL, NAKED NORMAL & LIQUID EASY

As with Midtown S Sector, the route you take is functionally identical to Big Boss Hard, though there are fewer PMC guards on lower difficulty levels. The biggest change is that you won't encounter a patrol vehicle at **2**, and that there isn't a soldier at **5**. On Liquid Easy, you can even crawl straight over the junction rather than taking a detour at **1**, as there are actually no guards there at all.

6 Move to the end of the pavement, then hold until the patrol vehicle makes a final pass. You're then safe to crawl straight over the road to the sloped driveway. When the resistance member removes his disguise, follow him to the left to exit the zone.

This sequence is similar to the one in South America, but with one principle difference – Snake, riding pillion, occupies a fixed position throughout. This means that being accurate with your chosen weapons is vital. Hold L1 to aim, and R1 to fire as usual; if you release the former, the camera returns to a default position, usually to the side of the bike. When you next press L1, the camera will generally adjust to the direction of the most imminent danger, which is a useful trick to know. You have no access to Drebin's Shop while on the bike, but the gift of infinite ammunition for the duration of the journey is more than adequate compensation for this inconvenience.

There are three sections to the bike chase, with each one packed with numerous assailants. Vehicles with turrets are the principle danger, though you shouldn't underestimate the threat posed by large groups of PMC troopers or Haven Troopers. In the third section, Raging Raven will attack with her army of Sliders. Any damage that you inflict upon her here will be carried over to the boss battle that follows, so it's worth targeting her specifically whenever the opportunity arises.

FLASHBACK: EVA

A pivotal figure in the events of Operation Snake Eater (MGS3), EVA failed in her secret mission to seize control of The Philosophers' Legacy for the Chinese government. The cutscenes that you have just viewed pretty much cover everything else.

III
<
OI

BRIEFING: SLIDERS

Though glimpsed briefly back in Act 1, Sliders make their first appearance as an enemy that you can actually fight during this bike chase; they're also an integral part of the combat that takes place in the next zone. There's little need for extended tactical guidance, though, as they're actually very simple to destroy – a few well-placed bullets is always sufficient. As with other non-human assailants, you'll receive a nominal DP bonus for each one you dispatch.

A PREPARATION

Note: This walkthrough section is intended for players attempting a no-kill playthrough. If that doesn't include you, just break out the big guns (or at least those that can be wielded with one hand), and enjoy the opportunity for a little indiscriminate shooting. The tips to your left should be sufficient to get you to the end of this spectacular sequence.

As soon as you gain control of Snake, ready the Mk. 2, Stun Grenades and (optionally, though optimally) a Twin Barrel shotgun loaded with V-Ring ammunition. You can also ready a submachine gun if you would like to earn a little extra DP by shooting down the Sliders when they enter the fray, but this isn't mandatory. Before you begin, there are two things you should know. Firstly, a single tranquilizer dart to a PMC soldier or Haven Trooper is sufficient to knock them out during this sequence. Secondly, be careful where you throw Stun Grenades – when you're moving at high speed, you're more likely to harm Snake and his companions than enemy soldiers.

B CHURCH COURTYARD

- This is the shortest part of the journey, and the least complicated. Due to the high speed of the chase here, use of Stun Grenades is inadvisable. Concentrate on knocking down as many PMC soldiers with tranquilizer darts as you can manage, and you should squeeze through with no more than a couple of hits.

- One part that warrants further mention is the second Gekko encounter. Ignore the giant war machines, and instead focus on disabling the PMC soldiers directly ahead. Once most of these are out cold (or all of them, if you're really good), turn your attention to the group that arrives to your left.

C RIVERSIDE WEST

- There are several soldiers at the first corner. Throw a Stun Grenade immediately to disable some of them, switching to the Mk. 2 or Twin Barrel. With good aim (or a lucky bounce) and a few shots as you pass, you can get by without any damage.

- When the PMC vehicle arrives, don't worry about it – it's not actually a danger to you. Dislodge the Haven Trooper that lands on the roof of the van for a little target practice.

- When you pull out onto the riverside road, throw a Stun Grenade towards the vehicles to your right. As EVA turns to the left, throw another Stun Grenade to the left of the roadblock ahead; most of the PMC soldiers arrive from the alley and congregate in this position. We had a lot of success with looking down at the ground and throwing more Stun Grenades at their feet, though accomplished marksmen will probably fare just as well with the Mk. 2. There's not a great deal that you can do about the turret operators from this range, but we've noticed that their firing accuracy is usually less than impressive. When EVA turns the bike around, quickly reload your weapons.

- This is the unpleasant part. Ready either the Mk. 2 or Twin Barrel. When EVA makes the jump beside the two PMC vehicles, you need to disable one (or, ideally, both) of the turret operators before the slow-motion sequence ends. If you don't, you're going to take a lot of damage. When the bike lands, concentrate on the turret operators (if still conscious), then turn your attention to the PMC troops.

- There are no further stops until you reach the next zone, though the streets are crawling with Haven Troopers. If you managed to get past the second roadblock with Snake's Life gauge approximately half full (a difficult yet achievable goal), you should be able to reach the next load break without using a single restorative item.

D RIVERSIDE EAST

- Snake's Life and Psyche gauges are replenished after the cutscene. Equip a submachine gun. Shoot as many of the Sliders as you can, and try to hit Raging Raven to bring down her health. If you intend to collect the secret Raging Raven Doll, you'll need to hit her with tranquilizer darts or V-Ring shotgun blasts.

- After a while you'll pass a PMC vehicle, which will give chase. Use the Twin Barrel to disable the turret operator.

- From this point forward, you'll need to alternate between a submachine gun to shoot Sliders, and the Mk. 2 or Twin Barrel to pacify Haven Troopers and PMC gunners. As you're moving at such speed during this section, Stun Grenades are generally a poor choice.

- When you reach the section where the streets are packed with Haven Troopers, use the Mk. 2 exclusively. Try to disable as many as you can from range; accuracy is absolutely vital here.

- The last dangerous stage is when EVA turns right and heads down two sets of steps. Use the Mk. 2 to render the Haven Troopers unconscious as you approach them. Once you pass this area, you're free to holster your weapons and enjoy the fireworks if you wish.

If you're attempting a perfect playthrough after completing *MGS4* at least once, the "no healing items" requirement makes this otherwise enthralling on-rails sequence something of a trial. Getting through it without using a single Ration is perfectly possible – just very, very hard on the highest difficulty setting. The tips we offer here are broadly designed with this challenge in mind, but there are a few additional tricks that we don't reveal here to avoid unnecessary spoilers. You can find these on page 170 of the Extras chapter.

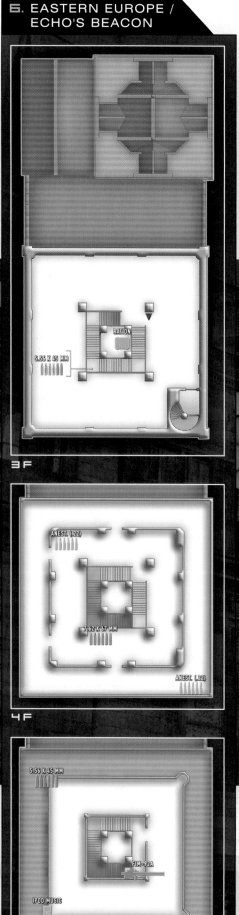

Outright aggression is the best strategy against Raging Raven. If you attempt to play a cat-and-mouse game, staying inside to sneak occasional pot-shots at passing targets, the Beast and her swarms of Sliders will wear you down by unexpectedly flying by from various directions, often firing as they pass by. Worse still, Raging Raven has some powerful melee attacks. To make the battle as painless as possible, you should head straight up to the top floor and go on the offensive.

Your priority throughout this set-piece battle is to reduce the number of Sliders flying around the tower to a bare minimum. Not only does this limit the number of aggressors you face, it also plays a vital role in exacerbating Raging Raven's foul temper. The angrier she becomes, the less likely it is that she will use her more devastating attacks. Keep moving at all times on the upper walkway, and pummel her with powerful weapons as you dodge her grenades. As with the confrontation with Laughing Octopus, the initial Beast stage is followed by a brief fight against Raging Beauty.

3 F

4 F

5 F

82

 RAGING RAVEN

Preparation

- If Snake is ailing after the motorbike sequence, move underneath the stairs and lie down to recover health. This position is usually completely safe at the start of the fight. You can actually return here whenever your Life gauge is running low to catch your breath, though there's no guarantee that you won't be attacked on subsequent visits.

- In the upcoming boss battle, your choice of weapons depends on what you intend to achieve. Ideally you should favor a sniper rifle (the Mosin-Nagant if you're looking to obtain the secret Raging Raven Doll), and a suitably powerful automatic rifle to use against the Sliders. Raging Raven tends to dodge regularly, so should you choose explosive ordnance, be sure that it's sufficiently fast to reach her before she moves. Finally, if you plan to spend any time inside the building on the lower floors, which we don't explicitly recommend, a shotgun (optionally loaded with V-Ring ammunition) will help you to deter the advances of the Beast if she comes looking for you.

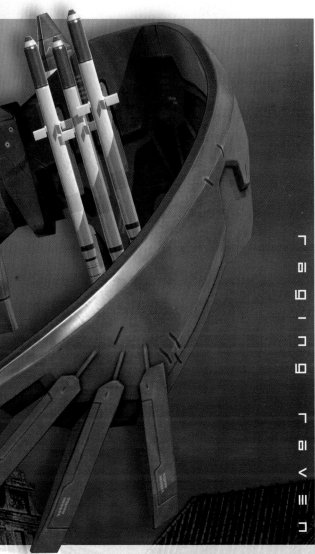

Attacks

If you approach this battle in the correct way, you need never experience the more deadly parts of Raging Raven's offensive repertoire. Just for your information, though, these are the potential assaults you can expect to endure if things really aren't going your way...

- If you're operating on the outer walkway of the middle floor or the top floor, Raging Raven will fire grenades towards Snake. They destroy sections of the brickwork on contact, and Snake can be knocked over the edge in areas where the barrier has been smashed. Press ④ to make him haul himself back up. A less common attack type is when she unleashes a barrage of grenades; this can be avoided by simply turning tail and running until she empties her clip.

- Raging Raven uses different grenade types, including flashbang and incendiary varieties. The latter can set Snake ablaze. If this happens, use forward rolls to extinguish the flames.

- Raging Raven and her Sliders will regularly fly through the building if you stay inside. If they are aware of Snake's position, they may fire a projectile in his direction. If you don't do enough to manage Slider numbers and foolishly loiter inside the building for extended periods, they may even fly through in a "swarm" of sorts.

- When she enters the tower interior, Raging Raven's standard attack is to fire a rapid barrage of grenades at Snake.

- Once her Life bar is below 75%, Raging Raven will begin to perform "grab" attacks whenever Snake is on the two lower floors of the building. Waggle ⑤ to free him. If you don't escape in time, Snake will be slammed to the ground.

- After Raging Raven has grabbed Snake three times and has performed at least one floor slam, there is another possible outcome. If Snake fails to escape, she will carry him above the building, then drop him from a great height. If you press ④ at the correct time, Snake can catch a ledge as he falls past. If you fail, he plummets to his death.

- When you hear beeping, approach a staircase and hold up for a second. As soon as the beeping becomes more insistent, run up or down as applicable. You're usually safe from the large explosion that ensues, as it's generally confined to a single region.

General Guidelines

In the Raging Raven fight, attack really *is* the best form of defense.

- Make your way up to the top floor, then set about destroying as many Sliders as you can find. This infuriates Raging Raven, which is a good thing – she loses focus when she's angry, which usually means that she won't use her most lethal attacks. The Sliders you eliminate are replaced by periodic waves of reinforcements, so thin their numbers regularly.

- Unless you need to go inside to heal or dodge one of her more explosive attacks, you should fight the entire battle on the top floor. Once you've engaged Raging Raven's attention by shooting her as she passes, she'll float and fire grenades at Snake. If you pay attention, these are simple to dodge; a dive to the side will usually move you clear of the blast radius. We found that the best technique is to stay in motion at all times, strafing along the side of the building she is facing.

- Keep track of Raging Raven and hit her with whichever weapon type you prefer. Sniper rifles work brilliantly (especially if you're cool enough to pick a clean headshot while on the move), but using the standard third-person viewpoint is generally fine as well for hitting Raging Raven with body shots.

- If you hear Raging Raven say, "I'm overheating!", she will fly to the roof of a nearby building and temporarily disengage her personal Slider unit. Though she has a tendency to use a Stun Grenade to mask her departure, try to follow her flight path and identify where she lands. Hit her with a sniper rifle shot as soon as you can. As this brief break enables her to cool down, you'll need to set about destroying Sliders to send her into a renewed fury.

Raging Beauty

As with the Laughing Octopus fight, you need to knock Raging Beauty out, kill her, or hold on until the end of the "white world" phase to complete the battle. If you opt for a non-lethal conclusion, you'll receive the Raging Beauty FaceCamo.

SECRET: RAGING RAVEN DOLL

If you found the Frog Soldier Doll in Act 1 and are collecting secret figurines by defeating each Beast with non-lethal techniques (see page 66), you can find the Raging Raven Doll on the top floor during the first stage of the Raging Beauty confrontation.

HOW TO PLAY

▶ WALKTHROUGH

INVENTORY

METAL GEAR ONLINE

EXTRAS

USER INSTRUCTIONS

ACT 1

ACT 2

▶ ACT 3

ACT 4

ACT 5

■ If you feel daring, a quick way to descend to a lower floor is to drop off the edge, press ⊗ to release Snake's grip, then press ④ again to grab a ledge below as Snake falls past.

■ No matter how you choose to end it, you will receive the powerful and versatile MGL-140 grenade launcher once the battle is over.

1 SNOWFIELD, HELIPORT & TANK HANGAR

2 CANYON & NUCLEAR WARHEAD STORAGE BLDG

3 SNOWFIELD & COMMUNICATIONS TOWER

4 BLAST FURNACE & CASTING FACILITY

5 UNDERGROUND BASE & UNDERGROUND SUPPLY TUNNEL

6 PORT AREA

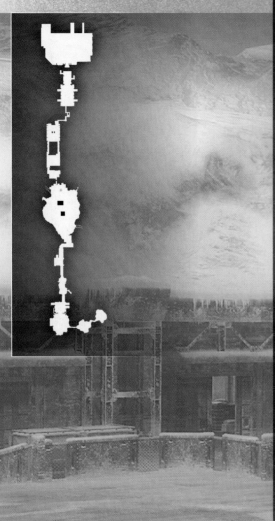

SECRET: MISSION BRIEFING

You know the drill by now: when the Mission Briefing screen switches to a multiple-camera format, take control of your mechanical scout by pressing Ⓞ. Metal Gear Mk. III replaces its unfortunate forebear, but it's functionally identical in terms of control and abilities. You can find a Regain and some ammo on the lower deck, with a Battery and an iPod® tune being your reward for venturing upstairs.

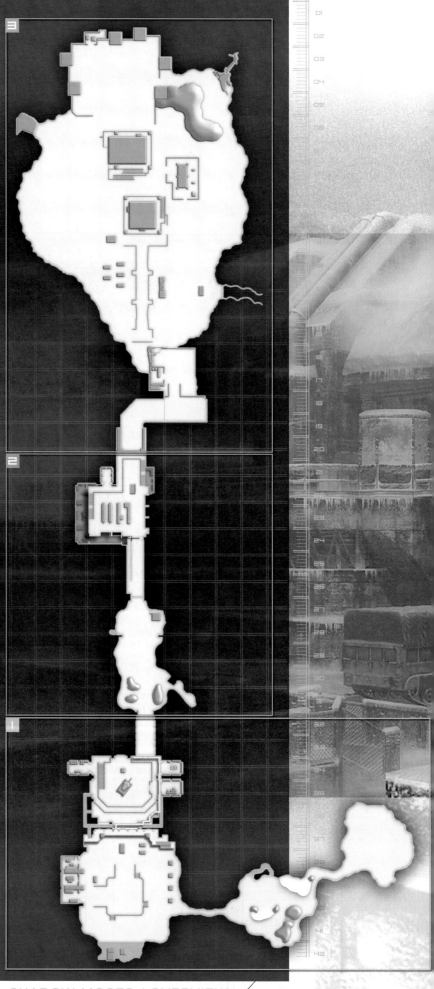

SHADOW MOSES / OVERVIEW

84

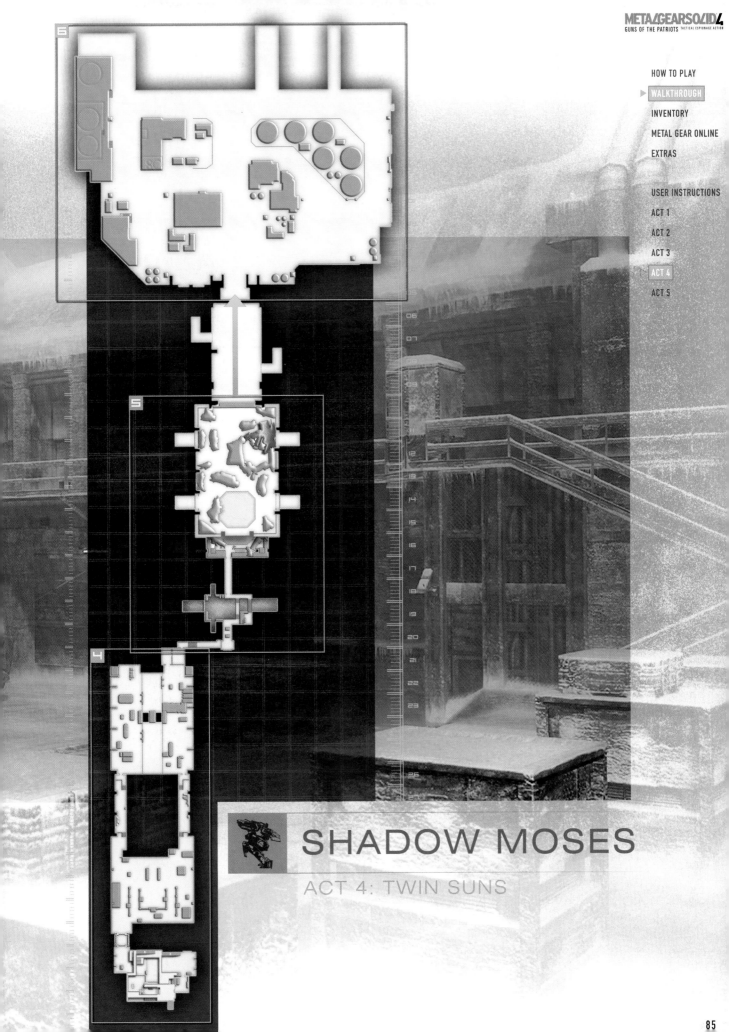

SHADOW MOSES

ACT 4: TWIN SUNS

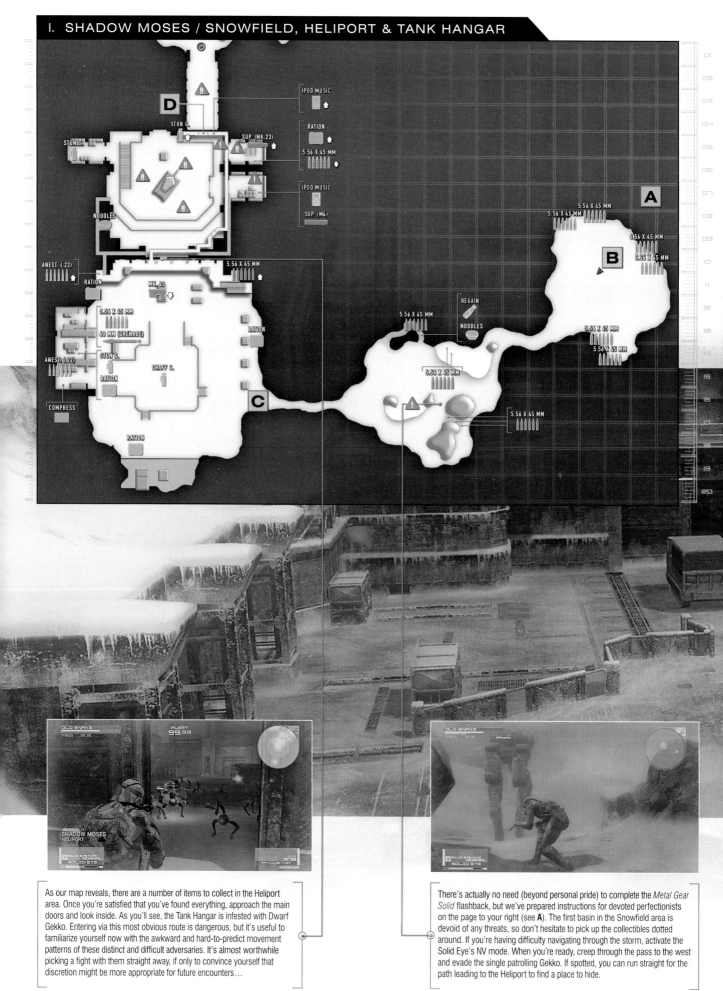

IPOD MUSIC

RATION

5.56 X 45 MM

IPOD MUSIC

SUP. (M4)

STUN G.

STUN G.

SUP. (MK.23)

NOODLES

D

A

5.56 X 45 MM

5.56 X 45 MM

5.56 X 45 MM

B

5.56 X 45 MM

ANEST. (.22)

RATION

5.56 X 45 MM

MK. 23

5.56 X 45 MM

40 MM (GRENADE)

RATION

REGAIN

NOODLES

5.56 X 45 MM

5.56 X 45 MM

5.56 X 45 MM

ANEST. (.22)

STUN G.

CHAFF G.

RATION

5.56 X 45 MM

C

5.56 X 45 MM

COMPRESS

5.56 X 45 MM

RATION

As our map reveals, there are a number of items to collect in the Heliport area. Once you're satisfied that you've found everything, approach the main doors and look inside. As you'll see, the Tank Hangar is infested with Dwarf Gekko. Entering via this most obvious route is dangerous, but it's useful to familiarize yourself now with the awkward and hard-to-predict movement patterns of these distinct and difficult adversaries. It's almost worthwhile picking a fight with them straight away, if only to convince yourself that discretion might be more appropriate for future encounters…

There's actually no need (beyond personal pride) to complete the *Metal Gear Solid* flashback, but we've prepared instructions for devoted perfectionists on the page to your right (see **A**). The first basin in the Snowfield area is devoid of any threats, so don't hesitate to pick up the collectibles dotted around. If you're having difficulty navigating through the storm, activate the Solid Eye's NV mode. When you're ready, creep through the pass to the west and evade the single patrolling Gekko. If spotted, you can run straight for the path leading to the Heliport to find a place to hide.

A

From your starting position in the (amazingly vivid) flashback/dream sequence, head north to the searchlights. Wait for one to move away from you, then quickly sprint after it and escape down the steps to the west. Head north to the (closed) main doors, avoiding the gaze of the security camera to the north-west. On lower difficulty levels, you can take the vent just beneath the camera; if there's a sleeping guard there, you'll need to take a longer route. Sneak east, underneath the security camera, and carefully climb the steps. There is a patrolling guard at the top. When it's safe to do so, hide in the small alcove to the right of the searchlight, and wait for the soldier to reach your position. All you then have to do is follow him – from an appropriate distance, of course – and crawl through the ventilation shaft at the center of the walkway to exit. Note that anything that occurs during the *MGS1* dream sequence does not count towards your post-Act ratings, including Alert Phases and deaths.

B

Leave the first basin, then crawl up the slope to your right. From a safe distance away from the ledge, stop and observe the Gekko in NV mode. The patrol route the mechanical guard follows is very complicated, involving regular turns to sweep large portions of the area with its thin scanning beam. The best time to make your move is when it strides towards the most distant point of its patrol. Slide down the snowy bank, and crawl through the small gap in the rocks. When you get to the other side, it's a short dash to reach the westward slope leading to the Heliport.

SECRET: SECURITY CAMERAS

When you first approach the Heliport area, a song called "The Best is Yet to Come" will play if there is no Alert Phase active. If you reach either of the two rusty security cameras – one to the west of the helipad just inside the southern door, the other to the north-east just by the steps – before this piece of music ends, you'll see one of two "secret" cutscenes with Flashback opportunities. If you approach the latter camera, pause and wait for Otacon to finish his brief radio transmission before you proceed, or the sequence might not start. Note that you can only view one camera cutscene per visit.

BRIEFING: DWARF GEKKO

Don't underestimate these small sentries. Individually rather weak, Dwarf Gekko can overwhelm Snake when they attack as a swarm. They pour into areas in large numbers when an Alert Phase or, to a lesser extent, Caution Phase is active, and will depart when the all-clear is sounded.

- *Their main method of detection is to sweep an area with a blue scanning beam. No matter how well-camouflaged Snake is, being caught in this all-seeing ray will lead to an instant Alert Phase.*

d w a r f   g e k k o

HOW TO PLAY

▶ WALKTHROUGH

INVENTORY

METAL GEAR ONLINE

EXTRAS

USER INSTRUCTIONS

ACT 1

ACT 2

ACT 3

▶ ACT 4

ACT 5

■ Throughout Act 4, you'll encounter regular "flashback" audio sequences taken from *Metal Gear Solid*. If you listen to the end of each one (don't press (START) or trigger an Alert Phase), there's a welcome bonus of 1,000 DP. Some of these happen automatically, but others require a little exploration to find. In the Heliport region, "optional" flashbacks can be found at the center of the helipad, the gates to the south, and just inside the upper ventilation shaft. In the Tank Hangar, there's one on the staircase.

C

The Heliport area is free of potential assailants, which enables you to explore and reminisce in equal measure without fear of alerts. If you're wondering how to obtain the Ration in the north-west corner, you'll need to take the steps in the north-east leading to the upper walkway, make your way back to the north-west corner, then roll over the barrier to land on the metal platform below. As in *Metal Gear Solid*, there are rooms to the west, with the doors to the central area locked; you can reach this location by crawling through small gaps in the wall on either side.

We suggest that you take the stairs to the upper walkway and crawl through the upper ventilation shaft to infiltrate the Tank Hangar. This is the least complicated route to the area exit, and you'll also find the Warhead Storage iPod® tune if you choose this path.

D

Press ⓐ to climb out of the ventilation shaft, then tap ⓧ to drop down once the Dwarf Gekko in the corner moves its scanning beam away. Crouch-walk behind the metal enclosure that extends from the wall at the end of the walkway, and wait there until a trio of Dwarf Gekko scan the area. Watch the floor below, paying attention to the groups of Dwarf Gekko patrolling around the tank at the center of the hangar. As soon as the coast is clear below, vault over the barrier and drop down. Crawl through the gap underneath the doors, but stick to the left to avoid detection.

In the tunnel beyond, wait until the scanning beams move towards a horizontal position, then crouch-walk to the other side before they make their return pass.

- *Dwarf Gekko also have sensitive hearing, and will respond if they hear incongruous noises such as loud footsteps or gunfire. However, their "basic" sight functionality is very poor – Snake can crawl or even crouch-walk in surprisingly close proximity without alerting them to his presence.*

- *They perform melee attacks at close range. If you see a Dwarf Gekko rolling purposefully towards Snake, it's probably planning to kick his legs from underneath him. They will also leap onto Snake's body and administer electric shocks. You can dislodge these immediately with a quick forward roll, or by waggling ⓛ once the electricity begins to flow. Dwarf Gekko self-destruct when they sustain critical damage, and the explosion will injure Snake if he is caught in the blast radius.*

- *Dwarf Gekko carry pistols. The GSR is the most common, though you'll also encounter some that hold the Five Seven or (albeit very rarely) the more expensive D.E.*

- *Finally, Dwarf Gekko can be briefly disabled by hitting one of their "arms" with a tranquilizer dart, or catching them in a Stun Grenade explosion. They are extremely sensitive to Chaff Grenades, being frozen in place while the jamming effect is active.*

45ACP 5.56 X 45 MM

5.56 X 45 MM

1F

5.56 X 45 MM

H

FIM-92A

5.56 X 45 MM

40 MM (GRENADE)

5.56 X 45 MM

RATION

5.56 X 45 MM

COMPRESS

40 MM (GRENADE)

CLAYMORE

RATION

PENTAZEMIN

PLAYBOY

B2

C. BOX

M72A3

G

5.56 X 45 MM

RATION

RATION

C. BOX

IPOD MUSIC

F

5.56 X 45 MM

RATION 5.56 X 45 MM

5.56 X 45 MM

IPOD MUSIC 5.56 X 45 MM

40 MM (GRENADE)

.45ACP

RATION

5.56 X 45 MM

5.56 X 45 MM

E

Congratulations are due if you remembered the security code when prompted to enter it in Otacon's old office, but the real challenge begins when you leave. The first Gekko can be avoided with relative ease, but the second is a much bigger threat. You can protect Metal Gear Mk. III by launching a direct attack if you wish, but there are a couple of enjoyable stealth-oriented strategies that you can try instead – see **H** on the page to your right.

The Canyon area... well, we're actually going to leave you to learn about it for yourself. What we will say, though, is that it's fine to just sprint for the area exit directly ahead if you feel threatened.

E

If you've already completed one playthrough, you'll have a good idea of what to expect here. If not – well, try not to read any further for now. Trust us when we say that you'll *know* when to resume reading.

You can actually get through this area without awakening either Gekko by crawling directly between them. This means that you won't be able to collect all items in the vicinity, but it's a small sacrifice on a no-detection playthrough. If a Gekko rises up, it's generally best to just run straight for the zone exit – there's a brief delay before it begins its patrol.

F

Simply approach the back door here, then use the elevator when prompted. Feel free to collect any items scattered around before you do.

G

Make your way to Otacon's former office to trigger a cutscene. The numbers you type at the console don't actually matter – see "Secret: Security Code" for more details. When the Gekko arrives in the corridor, hide until it moves away from Snake, then sneak behind it to reach the blocked office entrance. Crawl beneath the desk, and into the next room. You can then creep over to the elevator while the Gekko isn't looking, briefly stand up to press the call button, and then make your departure once it arrives.

H

Head over to the back door to trigger a brief cutscene. When the Gekko arrives, you either need to destroy it, or somehow distract its attention until Metal Gear Mk. III opens the exit. If it spots Snake or Metal Gear Mk. III, an immediate Alert Phase will begin – which is obviously something you'll want to avoid on a no-detection playthrough. While there's plenty of scope for experimentation here, we can suggest two strategies that work perfectly well.

Option 1: *"I fear nothing, except needless DP expenditure."*
Crouch-walk over to the truck and wait patiently. When the Gekko moves to the left side of the van (relative to your current position), sneak over to the right and head for the smaller row of canvas-covered crates. Press ⓐ to "press" Snake against them, then tap ℝ1 to make him rap his fist against the surface. It won't create much noise, but it's enough – the Gekko will move over to investigate. Position the camera to enable you to judge which direction it is approaching from, then crouch-walk to the opposite side of the boxes.

You'll need to repeat this process until Metal Gear Mk. III finishes its work, only "knocking" when the Gekko begins walking away. It's a very tense few minutes, but isn't too demanding if you concentrate throughout. We've used the specified row of boxes exclusively on several occasions, and have found that it's the best position to operate from. However, be very careful when the timer counts down to single figures – find a hiding place that the Gekko can't possibly stumble across before the clock reaches zero. There is a brief cutscene when the door is unlocked, and whereas Snake is completely frozen in place while this plays, the Gekko is not. If you knock just beforehand, you'll almost certainly be discovered.

Metal Gear Mk. III engages its cloaking function once the door opens, so you simply need to distract the Gekko one last time, then cautiously make a break for the opening.

Option 2: *"Look, I'm in a hurry – DP is no object."*
This strategy is potentially easier and much faster, but requires a stock of C4 and the super-powerful Javelin missile launcher (which, incidentally, costs 15,000 DP to unlock). Crouch-walk to the left side of the truck immediately, and plant three sticks of C4 on the ground. Move back to the front of the truck and wait. When the Gekko passes, crouch-walk over to the blast door where you first entered earlier, and take cover. Wait until the Gekko stands on the C4, then detonate it with ◎ – note that the C4 must still be your "active" weapon for this to work. Switch to the Javelin, and immediately hit the Gekko with a rocket while it is stunned. There's no time to waste – hesitate for a second, and there's a chance it will turn to see you. One direct hit is sufficient to destroy it completely; a few seconds later, Otacon and Metal Gear Mk. III will (rather inexplicably) manage to unlock the door without further delay.

SECRET: SECURITY CODE

There are two different cutscenes that follow the sequence where you enter the security code. If you enter the password given to you by Otacon earlier (usually 48273 on Big Boss Hard), you'll get the "good" conclusion; if it's wrong, you'll view an amusing alternative sequence in which an embarrassed Snake loses a nominal amount of Psyche. However, if you enter the password 14893 (sound familiar?), you'll hear a laugh from Little Gray. Once this ends, though, you'll receive a massive 100,000 DP bonus.

SECRET: ELECTRIFIED FLOOR

*On your way back from Otacon's former office, you can use an unorthodox trick to get rid of the Gekko mentioned at **G**. Activate Metal Gear Mk. III, engage its cloaking feature, and pilot it to the flashing control panel to the left of the elevator. When you arrive in front of it, stop and press ⓐ once the onscreen prompt appears. Not only is the Gekko destroyed instantly, you'll also receive a 5,000 DP bonus.*

SECRET: LOCKED ROOM IN TANK HANGAR

Once Otacon restores power to the facility and you destroy or evade the Gekko in Nuclear Warhead Storage Bldg 1F, you can backtrack to the Tank Hangar area to visit a previously locked room. Make your way onto the upper walkway, then move over to the east to reach it. Inside you'll find a box of Suppressors for the M4 Custom and an iPod® tune.

HOW TO PLAY
▶ WALKTHROUGH
INVENTORY
METAL GEAR ONLINE
EXTRAS

USER INSTRUCTIONS
ACT 1
ACT 2
ACT 3
▶ ACT 4
ACT 5

■ Here's something that you might not have noticed before now: animals can trigger active traps such as Claymores. We mention this because the temptation to have a little fun with the Gekko while Metal Gear Mk. III opens the doors is something you'll find hard to resist on future playthroughs. If you want to play with fixed explosives, be warned – curious rodents can lead to unexpected developments.

■ You'll trigger an optional audio flashback if you approach the locker in Otacon's old office. As usual, there's a 1,000 DP bonus for listening to the end.

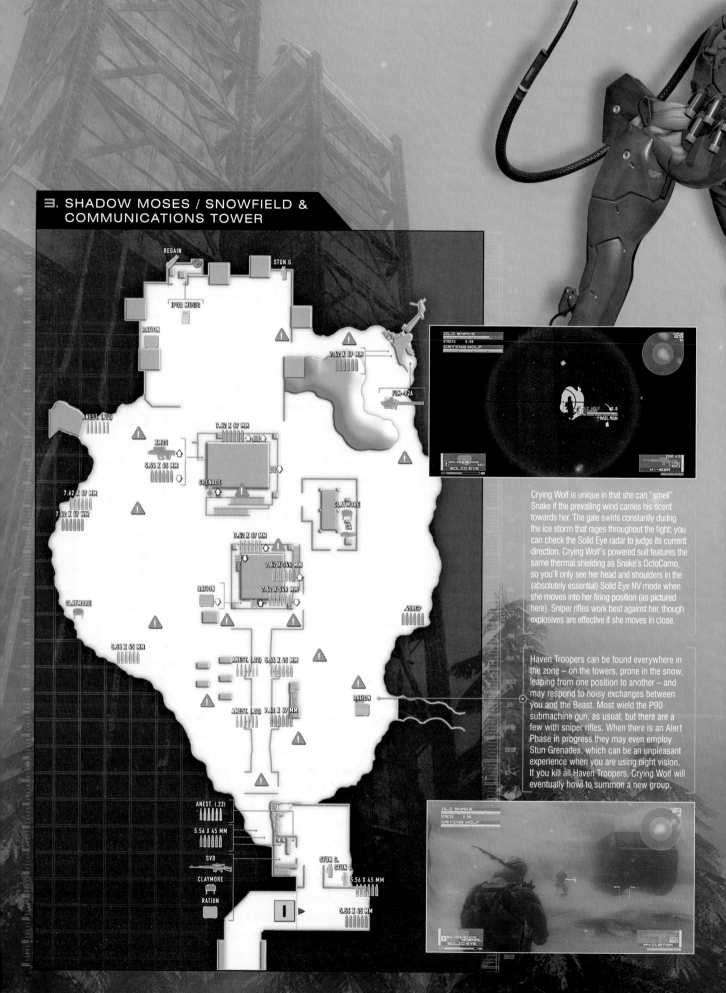

REGAIN

STUN G.

IPOD MUSIC

RATION

7.62 X 67 MM

FIM-92A

ANEST. (.22)

XM25

7.62 X 67 MM

5.56 X 45 MM

GRENADE

CLAYMORE

7.62 X 67 MM

C4

7.62 X 67 MM

7.62 X 67 MM

7.62 X 67 MM

7.62 X 54R MM

RATION

7.62 X 54R MM

CLAYMORE

.45ACP

5.56 X 45 MM

ANEST. (.22) 5.56 X 45 MM

RATION

ANEST. (.22) 7.62 X 67 MM

ANEST. (.22)

5.56 X 45 MM

SVD

STUN G.

CLAYMORE

STUN G.

RATION

5.56 X 45 MM

5.56 X 45 MM

OLD SNAKE
STRESS   0.0%
CRYING WOLF

C. WOLF   RAIL GUN

SOLID EYE MODE
NV
SOLID EYE

Crying Wolf is unique in that she can "smell" Snake if the prevailing wind carries his scent towards her. The gale swirls constantly during the ice storm that rages throughout the fight; you can check the Solid Eye radar to judge its current direction. Crying Wolf's powered suit features the same thermal shielding as Snake's OctoCamo, so you'll only see her head and shoulders in the (absolutely essential) Solid Eye NV mode when she moves into her firing position (as pictured here). Sniper rifles work best against her, though explosives are effective if she moves in close.

Haven Troopers can be found everywhere in the zone – on the towers, prone in the snow, leaping from one position to another – and may respond to noisy exchanges between you and the Beast. Most wield the P90 submachine gun, as usual, but there are a few with sniper rifles. When there is an Alert Phase in progress they may even employ Stun Grenades, which can be an unpleasant experience when you are using night vision. If you kill all Haven Troopers, Crying Wolf will eventually howl to summon a new group.

OLD SNAKE
STRESS   0.0%
CRYING WOLF

SOLID EYE MODE
NORMAL
SOLID EYE

M4 CUSTOM

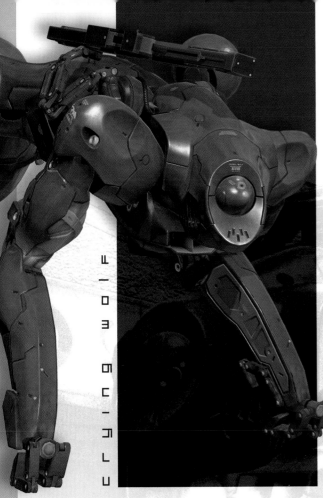

HOW TO PLAY
▶ WALKTHROUGH
INVENTORY
METAL GEAR ONLINE
EXTRAS

USER INSTRUCTIONS
ACT 1
ACT 2
ACT 3
▶ ACT 4
ACT 5

Haven Troopers

- Crying Wolf is not particularly hard to beat on her own – it's the presence of several Haven Troopers that makes this fight complicated, especially during no-alert/no-kill playthroughs. When stationary, the Haven Troopers appear as small (yet nonetheless tangible) dots on the Solid Eye radar. The storm restricts their clear view of the snowfield, so you can enjoy a little more freedom to move (or, indeed, even be blasted from your feet by Crying Wolf) without directly arousing suspicion.

- Haven Troopers will eventually clamber back to their feet if knocked out with a tranquilizer dart. This means that it's vital not to hang around in any one area for too long.

- Finally, Haven Troopers can hear non-silenced weapons over the howling winds if they're sufficiently close. If you're keen to avoid detection, you should disable any nearby hostiles before you fire weapons such as the Mosin-Nagant or SVD.

General Guidelines

- The trick to winning this battle on a "perfect" playthrough is patience. Snake's growing Stress level as he struggles with the biting cold may inspire a direct and rapid approach, but you have more time than you might suspect.

- Whenever possible, stick to the very outside of the map area, and crawl at all times unless you need to dodge an attack. This makes it much easier to avoid detection, even if it does slow your progress down. The central towers may seem inviting, but think about it: they're just *too* obvious. Crying Wolf and the Haven Troopers are not stupid.

- Disable any Haven Troopers that might interfere with your progress, but ignore those that pose no obvious threat – especially when you're actually moving away from them.

- You should ideally aim to be downwind of your opponent at all times, but this isn't always possible. The storm can be annoyingly capricious: you'll encounter moments where the wind will reveal your location to Crying Wolf just as you sneak up to a perfect sniping location. However, you can prevent her from firing by shooting her first.

- Once you have Crying Wolf in your sights, you can usually hit her with three shots before she moves, or up to two with a bolt-action sniper rifle. Watching and listening to her progress as she repositions herself is absolutely vital and – we would argue – the key to beating her without injury or even a Caution Phase. Once you gain the ability to confidently judge her next location, it becomes exponentially easier to win.

- If Crying Wolf spots, smells or hears you before or after she slides back into her suit, she may move only a short distance before emerging to fire once again. If you react quickly, this is an opportunity to inflict additional damage before she moves much further afield.

- While her movements depend on many factors, we've noticed that she tends to head to the north-east when the battle begins. If the wind is in your favor, this can provide you with a great start.

Crying Beauty & Battle Aftermath

You know what to do against Crying Beauty. If you beat her with non-lethal weapons, you'll receive the Crying Beauty FaceCamo; no matter what happens, you'll get your hands on the mighty Rail Gun. There are numerous collectibles in this zone (including the XM25 grenade launcher), so it's worth taking a brisk stroll to pick them up before you depart.

CRYING WOLF

Preparation

- There's no backtracking once you drop down onto the snowfield, so collect the items in the southern area before you proceed. If your Battery level is low, it's prudent to disable the Solid Eye and wait inside for it to recharge – you need to have NV active throughout this confrontation.

- Much like previous Beast battles, your choice of weapons depends on your objectives. If you would like to collect the Crying Wolf Doll, you should choose the Mosin-Nagant and the Mk. 2 pistol. If you're on a standard lethal playthrough any sniper rifle will suffice. The SVD, M82A2, VSS and M14EBR will enable you to get the most hits per sniping opportunity, though you trade power for subtlety with the latter two. The M82A2 is best, but it's not cheap.

- Don't forget to equip FaceCamo – maximum concealment is a must.

Attacks

- Your opponent spends much of the battle waiting in a fixed position, with her suit opened to enable her to snipe with the Rail Gun. Once she detects Snake through sight, sound or smell, she will begin firing as soon as she has a reasonably clear shot. Note that hiding behind trees will not work – the powerful Rail Gun can scythe through them with ease.

- Keep Crying Wolf waiting for too long, and she may come in search of Snake. If you suddenly find the camera intermittently switching to the beast's POV, you're in trouble. She'll charge directly at Snake and, unless her path is blocked, will pounce and knock him to the ground. This drains half of his Life gauge on Big Boss Hard. When control returns, you have a brief moment to dive aside before she slams him with a second attack.

- Crying Wolf will also attempt to bowl Snake over while running past. This isn't especially hard to dodge, though standing up to gain the necessary pace to escape from her may alert nearby Haven Troopers to your whereabouts.

- Finally, Crying Wolf has a tendency to toss grenades at Snake as she passes. These have a reasonably long fuse, though, and can usually be evaded in a crouch-walk posture if you're keen to avoid both detection and damage.

> ■ The four wolves that congregate after the Crying Beauty battle will often follow Snake around the zone once they catch his scent. Don't do anything to annoy them – vaguely supernatural canines are *not* to be trifled with.
>
> ■ You can find four optional audio "flashbacks" in this area after Crying Beauty falls. These can be located in the following positions: just to the south of your starting point once the cutscene ends (near the corner of the north tower), by the crashed helicopter in the north-east, on the lower walkway of the south communications tower, and in the snow-covered "path" at the very south of the map.

SECRET: CRYING WOLF DOLL

After a non-lethal takedown of Crying Wolf in her Beast form, you might fear that the Crying Wolf Doll could be just about anywhere in a large zone like this, but worry not – it's actually just behind your starting position once the Crying Beauty fight begins.

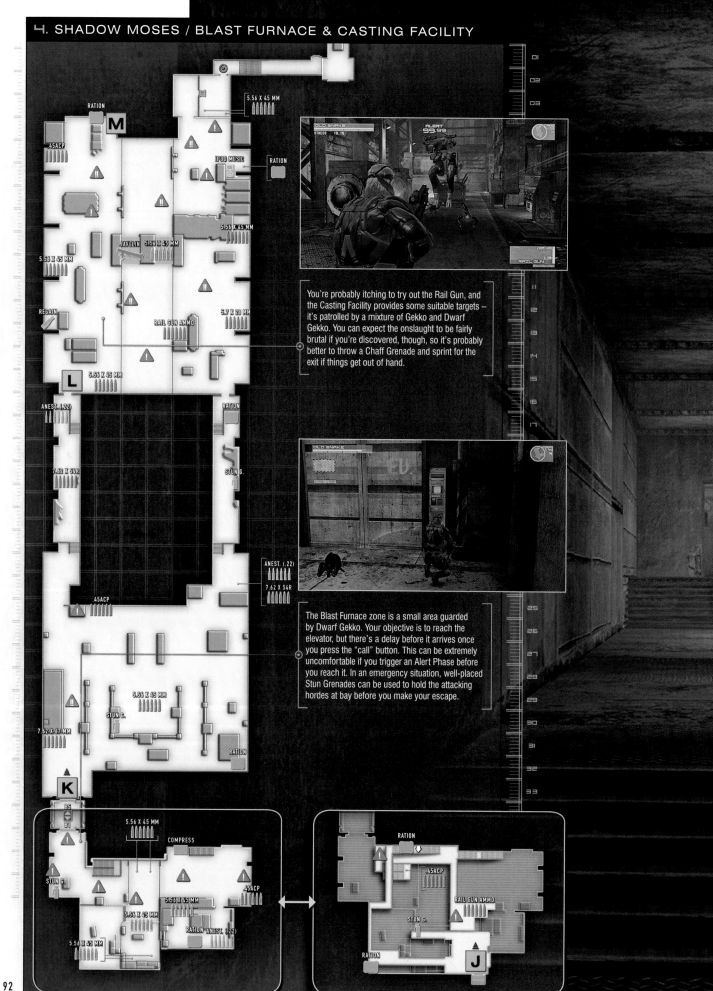

RATION

M

.45ACP

IPOD MUSIC

RATION

5.56 X 45 MM

JAVELIN   5.56 X 45 MM

5.56 X 45 MM

5.56 X 45 MM

REGAIN

RAIL GUN AMMO

5.7 X 28 MM

L

5.56 X 45 MM

ANEST. (.22)

RATION

STUN G.

7.62 X 54R

ANEST. (.22)

7.62 X 54R

.45ACP

STUN G.

5.56 X 45 MM

7.62 X 67 MM

RATION

K

B5

B1

COMPRESS

5.56 X 45 MM

STUN G.

RATION

.45ACP

5.56 X 45 MM

.45ACP

5.56 X 45 MM

5.156 X 45 MM

RAIL GUN AMMO

5.56 X 45 MM

RATION   ANEST (.22)

STUN G.

5.56 X 45 MM

RATION

J

You're probably itching to try out the Rail Gun, and the Casting Facility provides some suitable targets – it's patrolled by a mixture of Gekko and Dwarf Gekko. You can expect the onslaught to be fairly brutal if you're discovered, though, so it's probably better to throw a Chaff Grenade and sprint for the exit if things get out of hand.

The Blast Furnace zone is a small area guarded by Dwarf Gekko. Your objective is to reach the elevator, but there's a delay before it arrives once you press the "call" button. This can be extremely uncomfortable if you trigger an Alert Phase before you reach it. In an emergency situation, well-placed Stun Grenades can be used to hold the attacking hordes at bay before you make your escape.

J There are some useful items and ammunition (particularly the Rail Gun rounds) in the small Blast Furnace zone, but you should have no desperate need to collect them at this point. We've experimented with a variety of routes through the area, but we're going to suggest the most direct path. From your starting position, head to the west wall. Press Snake against it, and inch along the narrow ledge to the next walkway.

Watch the patrol route followed by the two mobile Dwarf Gekko below. When they move to the top of the nearby steps, vault over the side of the barrier by the metal pillar that supports the walkway, and press ⊗ to drop down. It's a big drop, but Snake won't be injured by it; if your timing is good, your landing won't be noticed. Now cautiously crouch-walk over to the elevator (don't disturb the sleeping Dwarf Gekko just outside), and press the call button. When your ride arrives, head for level B5.

K There is a Gekko directly ahead when you exit the elevator, but fortunately it is facing in the opposite direction. Though it may seem a tad counter-intuitive, drop to a crawl and head directly for it. If you move without pausing, you can slip by into the corridor on the left-hand side of the map when the Gekko turns to the right, though you'll need to carefully dodge the scanning beam of the Dwarf Gekko affixed to a nearby wall. It's usually safe to quickly switch to a crouch-walk for this last part.

L When you reach the north section of the Casting Facility, crouch-walk directly ahead, staying reasonably close to the west wall. Quietly sneak past the group of sleeping Dwarf Gekko, then slip by to the left when you reach the scanning beam of their more alert nearby companion.

Hold up for a second when you reach the end of the machinery to your right, and observe the patrol path of the three Dwarf Gekko just beyond. They perform scans in three directions: to the west, to the east (towards the conveyor belt), and finally to the north. When they roll to the right, quickly crouch-walk past to reach the north wall, then hide behind the wheeled machines.

M Crawl towards the conveyor belt to observe the patrolling Gekko; the rusty (and, note, explosive) drums to your right conceal you from the Dwarf Gekko. Look over to where the far conveyor belt meets the north wall, and you'll notice a small gap in the barrier on the other side. This is where you need to go. Wait for the Gekko to turn away, then climb onto the conveyor belt and crouch-walk to the other side. You have approximately 15 seconds before it will turn back to face you. There are three Dwarf Gekko on the other side, so drop down and go prone. This can be tricky; sometimes, through sheer bad luck, they'll detect Snake as he lands. More often than not, though, they'll be rolling away from your position when you arrive, which leaves you free to crouch-walk straight for the exit (just to your left) once they roll to the south. There's a concealed Dwarf Gekko scanning the area just outside, though, so be sure to avoid this on your way through.

■ Here's a neat trick: as Gekko are "cyborgs", having both biological and mechanical components, you can actually tranquilize them. Shoot their legs with approximately five Mk. 2 darts (or as little as two or three if you hit the back of their "knee" joints), and they will fall onto their backs, thrashing and writhing until they regain control of their limbs approximately 20 to 30 seconds later.

■ As long as an Alert Phase isn't in progress, you'll hear another audio flashback during the elevator ride between the Blast Furnace and Casting Facility zones.

ALTERNATIVE STRATEGIES

Taking the path on the east side of the Casting Facility zone is a more challenging route, and we're not convinced that the principle reason for going there – a box of Rail Gun ammunition, plus a few other sundry collectibles – warrants the heightened risk on a no-detection playthrough. Because this path is blocked towards the north-east end of the area, you'll need to either climb onto the conveyor belt and squeeze through one of the two gaps in the large machine, or make your way over to the west side (and, from there, follow our walkthrough). As you hit a checkpoint just beforehand, though, there's no reason why you can't save and reload if things ago awry.

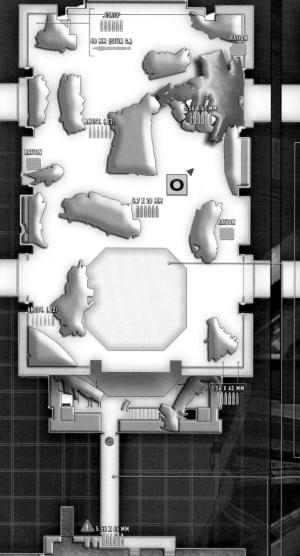

.45ACP

40 MM (STUN G.)

RATION

5.56 X 45 MM

ANEST. (.22)

RATION

O

5.7 X 28 MM

RATION

ANEST. (.22)

5.56 X 45 MM

RPG-7

RAIL GUN AMMO

RATION

P

FIM-92A

5.56 X 45 MM

FIM-92A

RAIL GUN AMMO

5.56 X 45 MM

NOODLES

5.56 X 45 MM

N

The Rail Gun is (without question) the best weapon to use when the Suicide Gekko attack, but you'll need to use fully-charged shots to conserve ammunition. When they jump into the "ring-fenced" area that Snake operates in, you have a short period of time to destroy them before they activate their self-destruct function. These are your absolute priority, no matter what might be happening elsewhere.

Don't fall through the holes in the ground, or into the depths that the bridge spans – this spells instant death. The lack of cover and space in this tiny zone means that an altercation with numerous Dwarf Gekko can be an absolute disaster. If you have a spare Chaff Grenade, your best option is to throw one and make a break for the exit.

The fight with Vamp is not merely a test of your dexterity and marksmanship – it's also a puzzle that you have to solve in order to continue. How do you kill a man who appears to be immortal? We're not going to spoil your enjoyment of this conundrum by casually revealing the solution here, but consider the information revealed in the storyline: Vamp is not a supernatural creature, but a product of technological augmentation. However, if you're really stuck, you'll find the answer you need at point **O** in the main walkthrough.

94

N This tiny zone initially seems like a stern test of your infiltration skills on Big Boss Hard. Fortunately, this is the type of challenge that can be filed in the "easy when you know how" category. Wait until the patrolling Dwarf Gekko scans the short walkway on the south side of the map (just ahead of your starting position), then move over to the barriers. Pause as it scans the bridge, then creep onto the steps when it moves on. Its next destination is just in front of the exit. When it then rolls over to the right, wait for the nearest scanning beam to move off the bridge, then crouch-walk at full speed for the door, hugging the far wall when you reach it. There's little margin for error here, so it's a good idea to save your progress before you start.

If you're brave enough to attempt it, you can actually go back out to pick up the collectibles at the top of the stairs once the patrolling Dwarf Gekko returns to the bridge. You'll need to watch the three Dwarf Gekko closely before you make a dash for the exit, but the return journey is much easier.

O VAMP

Once you know Vamp's secret, this is a short and fairly painless battle. If this is your first fight against him, it's more enjoyable to solve the puzzle for yourself. We reveal how to end the confrontation after the tips that follow, so look away now if you'd rather we didn't ruin the surprise.

General Tips

Automatic rifles, machine guns and submachine guns are a must for this battle. Vamp is extremely fast and mobile, and will regularly leap onto the piles of debris dotted around the zone. Fire in short bursts when he's far away to increase accuracy, and use more sustained barrages when he moves closer.

We advise against using shotguns and launchers with explosive ordnance, as Vamp has an attack which he generally only performs when knocked over by a concussive blast. He'll begin spinning on the spot, and will then throw two or three knives at Snake. These are very hard to avoid. The damage you can inflict with explosive weapon types really won't compensate for the injuries you're likely to sustain.

Vamp's melee assaults are extremely damaging if they hit, but they aren't too difficult to evade with practice. When he performs his leaping attack, release **L1** and angle your run to the left or right to dodge. With his more deadly slashing or kicking attacks, where he charges directly for Snake at high speed, you'll also (as a general rule) need to roll at the very last moment to avoid the blow.

When he throws knives, run and dive aside to dodge them. You can actually shoot them out of the air if you're preposterously swift and accurate (or just plain lucky), but expect to sustain at least a few hits from these during the course of the fight. Temporarily engaging Auto Aim might be a useful trick in this battle.

The coup de grâce

Once Vamp's Life gauge is reduced to a quarter of the last bar, only fire at him when he runs towards you. This is absolutely vital: if he falls while standing on top of a debris pile, or on Metal Gear REX, you'll need to fight him all over again once he regenerates. Run over to him as he lies on the ground, prepare the Syringe as your current active item, and unequip your current weapon (tap **R2** or hold it and scroll to the empty slot). As he stands up, press **R1** to grab him in a CQC lock from behind, then press **△** to inject him. Yes – it's really that simple...

P SUICIDE GEKKO

This flashpoint is more a test of your marksmanship than anything else. However, the following general tips should help you to defeat the Suicide Gekko without too many problems.

Use the Rail Gun exclusively for this fight, and fire it only when fully charged. The current charge level is visible in the bottom right-hand corner, beneath the weapon icon, or appears in the targeting lines you'll see while aiming in FPS Mode. A single maximum-power shot will destroy a Gekko instantly; if you're lucky enough to be able to get two in perfect alignment, you can even destroy more than one at once.

Firing the Rail Gun before it reaches full charge is a waste of ammunition. Even if you haven't collected any additional ammo on your way here, the 30 rounds that the rifle had when dropped by Crying Wolf is more than sufficient for this fight. If your supplies run short, you can find a box of 15 rounds by running underneath Metal Gear REX. If you need any more, you'll have to visit Drebin's Shop.

You should be charging the Rail Gun at all times, even if there doesn't appear to be a target in view. Only fire at Gekko when you're sure you have a clear shot – too many misses, and you'll soon be overwhelmed.

Move constantly to dodge bullets fired by the Gekko. You can also crouch and use the surrounding debris as cover – there's no actual need for you to be in plain sight as the Rail Gun charges.

If you're very efficient at destroying the Gekko, you'll get to watch more of the battle between Raiden and Vamp on the right half of the screen. If you have a moment to spare, look up to see them fighting in "real time". Oh, and try to shoot Vamp if you get a clear shot – it's worth the attempt just too hear Snake's reaction...

■ If you're attempting a "perfect" playthrough, the "no health items" specification makes it a little irritating that your Life gauge is not replenished between the fight against Vamp and the arrival of the Suicide Gekko. However, it's by no means a disaster. You can replenish Snake's health by crouching between waves of Gekko. If you've completed the game at least once before and have the special reward for collecting the Frog Soldier Doll and all Beauty figurines, the Vamp battle actually becomes something of a non-event...

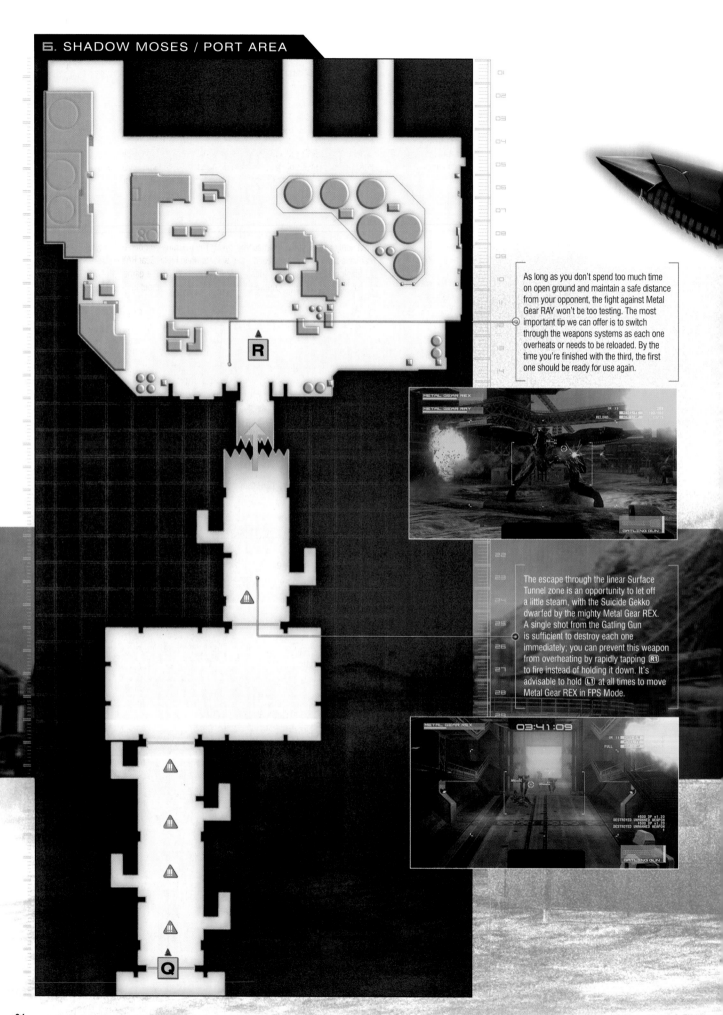

As long as you don't spend too much time on open ground and maintain a safe distance from your opponent, the fight against Metal Gear RAY won't be too testing. The most important tip we can offer is to switch through the weapons systems as each one overheats or needs to be reloaded. By the time you're finished with the third, the first one should be ready for use again.

The escape through the linear Surface Tunnel zone is an opportunity to let off a little steam, with the Suicide Gekko dwarfed by the mighty Metal Gear REX. A single shot from the Gatling Gun is sufficient to destroy each one immediately; you can prevent this weapon from overheating by rapidly tapping R1 to fire instead of holding it down. It's advisable to hold L1 at all times to move Metal Gear REX in FPS Mode.

Q

The ticking counter suggests a high degree of urgency as you escape, but it's actually quite generous: you have plenty of time to reach the exit safely. This makes the Surface Tunnel an outstanding location to farm for Drebin Points. There are certain areas where Gekko will continually enter through side doors if you stand and wait, and you encounter the first of these at the top of the slope just ahead from your starting point. Get into position just outside, and blast as many of the Gekko as you can until there are two minutes left on the clock. You should then charge directly for the exit, blasting every additional hostile you encounter on your way. Using this strategy, you can expect to reach the exit corridor with around ten seconds to spare, and gain more than 100,000 DP for your efforts.

R   METAL GEAR RAY

Even on higher difficulty levels, the (amazingly enjoyable) fight against Metal Gear RAY shouldn't pose you any problems once you absorb the following basic guidelines.

- First things first: engaging Metal Gear RAY in the open is suicide on Big Boss Hard. However, if you try to operate in the south-west corner behind the (indestructible) building, you'll always have a place to hide. As an added benefit, this leaves your opponent with just two potential routes to attack from. Try to emerge only partially from concealment when you move out to fire, as it makes it easier to dodge back behind solid cover when required.

- Your opponent's missile attacks are extremely damaging, but are easily dodged by hiding behind a building, or by shooting individual rockets down with the Gatling Gun. The Water Cutter laser is also powerful, but less commonly seen if you remain behind cover. The machine gun bursts hardly warrant a mention. The greatest danger by far is when Metal Gear RAY makes its lunging attack. Using our trick of playing a cat-and-mouse game around the south-west structure, you won't actually need to worry about it.

- On the off-chance that you do encounter a rapidly-accelerating RAY at close range, hold ● in a horizontal direction and press ✕ to dodge to one side. After evading the lunging attack, you can optionally perform a special melee assault by approaching Metal Gear RAY before it stands. Get up close, and press ▲ when the onscreen prompt appears. Be warned – if you arrive too late, you'll leave yourself wide open to a veritable world of hurt.

- Metal Gear RAY can leap great distances, and will usually do so to escape when faring badly. Take note of the direction it moves in – any momentary confusion that might lead to it sneaking up behind you is definitely to be avoided.

- Last, but not least, we've noticed that Liquid tends to become a little more cagey with his attack strategy once RAY is seriously damaged. Don't get drawn into chasing him, as this is exactly the mistake that he's hoping for. Instead, grind him into submission with long-range Gatling Gun and FE Laser barrages.

■ **Flashback Update:** If you didn't play *MGS1* and are curious about the meaning of the exchange where Snake says "Fox…", and then Liquid completes the phrase a moment later by exclaiming "…die!" during the cutscene that follows, it's actually a reference to Liquid's original death. He was killed by the FOXDIE nanovirus injected into Snake by Naomi Hunter prior to the events of the Shadow Moses Incident.

BRIEFING: METAL GEAR REX

REX has three weapons systems. The Gatling Gun is the default armament. It's prone to overheating if fired continuously in full automatic mode. The AT Missile launcher locks on to targets when you bring the crosshair into contact with them. Its projectiles are slow, but have a homing function; it's best to launch them in a devastating barrage at reasonably close range. You'll need to switch to another weapon while the launcher reloads. Finally, the FE Laser works in a similar way to the Rail Gun. It has five levels of charge based on how long you hold ⓛ1, and is fired as a focused beam once you press ⓡ1. When its energy supply is exhausted, it takes approximately one minute to return to full power.

Metal Gear REX: Basic Controls

BUTTON / STICK	ACTION
●	Move
●	Camera controls/aiming
L1	Aim weapon
R1	Melee kick; fire weapon (with L1 held)
R2	Change weapons
✕	Dash/dodge (with ●)
▲	Context-sensitive functions

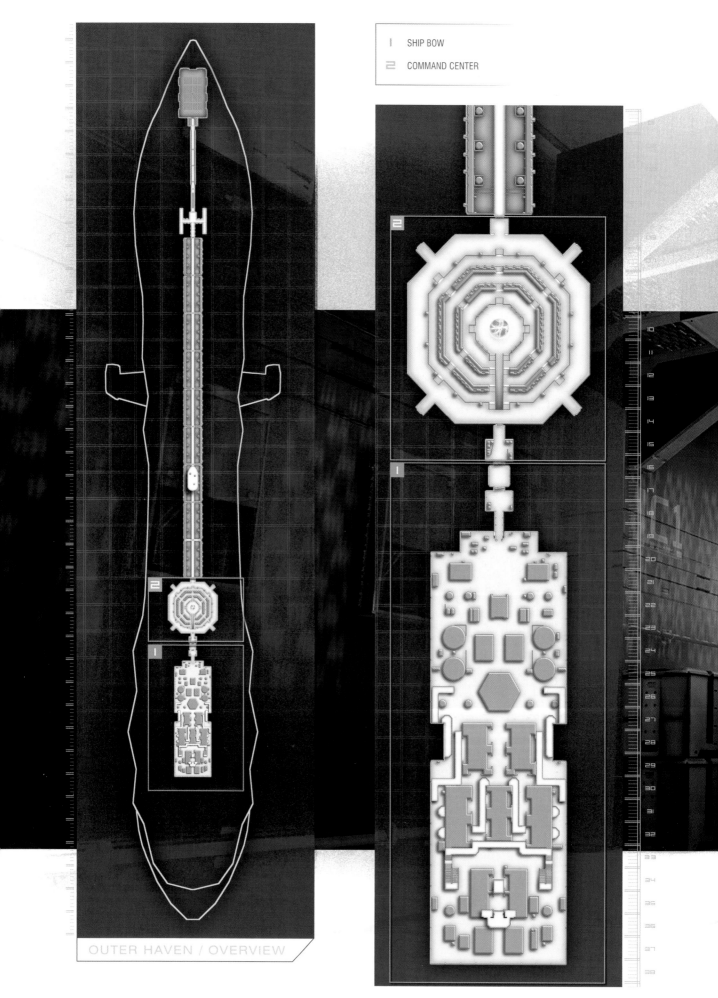

SHIP BOW

COMMAND CENTER

OUTER HAVEN / OVERVIEW

HOW TO PLAY
WALKTHROUGH
INVENTORY
METAL GEAR ONLINE
EXTRAS

USER INSTRUCTIONS
ACT 1
ACT 2
ACT 3
ACT 4
ACT 5

OUTER HAVEN

ACT 5: OLD SUN

SECRET: MISSION BRIEFING

Unlike other Mission Briefings, the Act 5 introduction doesn't take place on the Nomad, and you don't have full control of Metal Gear Mk. III. You can, however, look around the room with **R**, and amuse yourself by moving the image projected onto the screen with **L**.

I. OUTER HAVEN / SHIP BOW

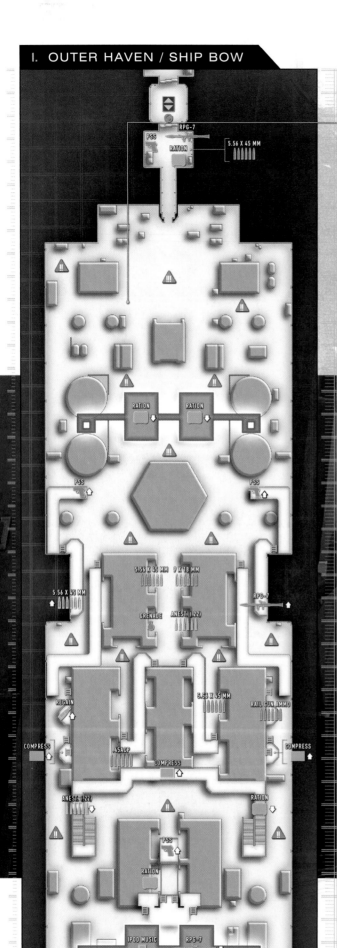

RPG-7

PSS

RATION

5.56 X 45 MM

RATION   RATION

PSS   PSS

5.56 X 45 MM   9 X 18 MM

5.56 X 45 MM

RPG-7

GRENADE   ANEST (.22)

REGAIN

5.56 X 45 MM

RAIL GUN AMMO

COMPRESS   COMPRESS

.45ACP

COMPRESS

ANEST (.22)   RATION

PSS

RATION

IPOD MUSIC   RPG-7

A

Trust us: an Alert Phase is something you'll want to avoid at all costs, because it makes it incredibly hard to escape this zone. The Haven Troopers will just keep on coming and, to the south* of the map, you'll also have Gekko to worry about. The door leading into the ship must be unlocked by rapidly tapping △, and this process is virtually impossible to complete if Snake is being shot at, kicked or stamped on. The best (indeed, only) solution is to hide and wait for the fuss to die down before you sneak to the exit.

* Note that, despite the orientation of our map,
you actually travel to the south in the Ship Bow zone.

There's a Caution Phase in effect the moment the action starts, with Haven Troopers searching for Snake in large numbers. They generally move in pairs, and will respond with their customary blend of extreme violence and nimble athleticism should Snake attract their attention. Keep a low profile, and favor the Mk. 2 when you need to take targets out – lethal force is more likely to spark an Alert Phase.

A Go prone straight away, and equip the Mk. 2. This zone is absolutely crawling with Haven Troopers, with the permanent Caution Phase making them especially twitchy. Attempting a "pure" stealth strategy would be ridiculously complicated, so it's much more sensible to neutralize any Haven Troopers you encounter. They generally move in pairs, so the usual common-sense approach applies: always take out the soldier just "behind" her comrade whenever possible to minimize the risk of detection. It should go without saying that headshots are an absolute requisite.

Our strategy involves sticking to the left-hand side of the ship, and you should crawl at all times unless we suggest otherwise. There's a very definite procedure that you'll need to follow, so try not to deviate from the path we specify.

- The first two Haven Troopers arrive directly ahead. Drop to a crawl and move around to the left, leaving cover. As soon as you have a clear shot, take both of them down and crawl past.

- You'll spot a second pair not long after you pass the first two. Wait until they drop down to your level before you strike.

- This part is potentially complicated. A single Haven Trooper will drop down just to the right as you round the corner; two more arrive further to the south. Take out the closest one first, then the nearest of the pair further ahead. The third Haven Trooper will usually walk away. It's a precision shot, but expert marksmen should be able to hit the back of her helmet at this range. If not, you can gain a larger target to aim for by hitting her torso with a dart to make her turn around, then follow up with a decisive headshot.

Your route on the left-hand side of the ship appears to be blocked by crates, but you can squeeze through the gap by standing up and pressing Snake against the wall. Drop back down and crawl when you reach the other side.

The final two Haven Troopers that you need worry about drop down shortly afterwards.

When you reach the far end of the bow section, crawl over to the right. Wait and watch as the Gekko just outside the door is destroyed by artillery strikes. Once the second Gekko turns away, crouch-walk over to the door and press ⃝ to interact with the opening mechanism; you'll need to tap the button rapidly to turn the wheel. As soon as the door is open, sprint through to reach the safety of the room inside. There are a few useful provisions that you can collect here before you enter the elevator.

HOW TO PLAY

▶ **WALKTHROUGH**

INVENTORY

METAL GEAR ONLINE

EXTRAS

USER INSTRUCTIONS

ACT 1

ACT 2

ACT 3

ACT 4

▶ **ACT 5**

■ Due to the collapse of the War Economy, everything in Drebin's Shop is half-price until the end of Act 5. There's a certain irony to this, though, as you'll doubtlessly have little need for new weapons by this point in the game. However, as DP and weapons can be carried over to your next playthrough, this is the perfect time to invest in the incredibly expensive Tanegashima rifle.

ALTERNATIVE STRATEGIES

The Ship Bow zone is an absolute warren of different paths, ladders and raised walkways. There are even two tunnels below the deck. The first hatch is just by your starting position; the second tunnel is closer to the zone exit, with access points on both sides of the ship. You might imagine that there are many treasures to be had for those bold enough to explore, but no – with the exception of an iPod® tune, there are items in quantity, but nothing of irresistible quality or value.

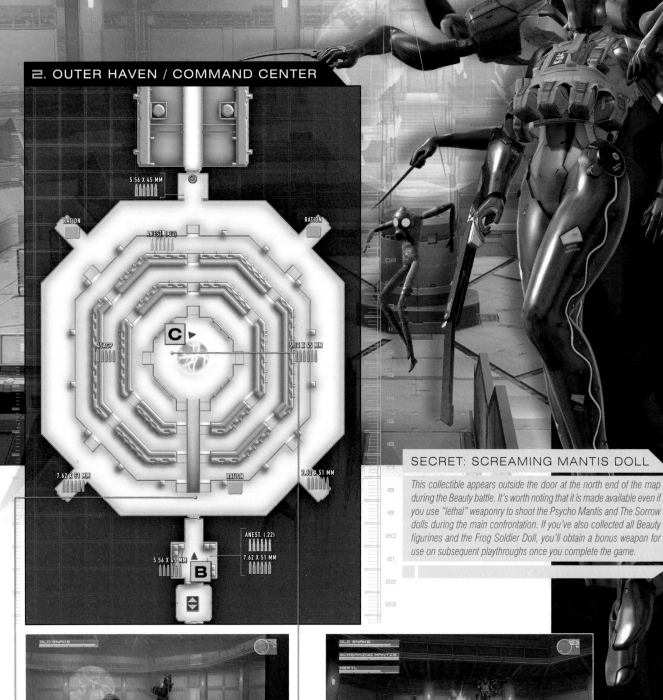

2. OUTER HAVEN / COMMAND CENTER

5.56 X 45 MM

RATION   RATION

ANEST. (.22)

45ACP   5.56 X 45 MM

C ▶

7.62 X 51 MM   RATION   7.62 X 51 MM

ANEST. (.22)
7.62 X 51 MM

5.56 X 45 MM B

08
14
16
18
19
20
21
22
23

SECRET: SCREAMING MANTIS DOLL

This collectible appears outside the door at the north end of the map during the Beauty battle. It's worth noting that it is made available even if you use "lethal" weaponry to shoot the Psycho Mantis and The Sorrow dolls during the main confrontation. If you've also collected all Beauty figurines and the Frog Soldier Doll, you'll obtain a bonus weapon for use on subsequent playthroughs once you complete the game.

Once the cutscene ends, run straight for the raised area to the north*. The small wall here is a good position to fire from, and there are plenty of avenues of escape if you can't neutralize the first group of Haven Troopers before they reach your position. Try to remain crouched until you have a target lined up. If you're in danger of being surrounded, make a break for one of the support pillars on your current level. The second wave of Haven Troopers fire from the balcony above, followed by a final group which will jump down to fight up close.

* Again, note that "up" is south on this map.

This is another boss battle enhanced by the presence of puzzles to solve, so we won't spoil your enjoyment of it by giving away its secrets too casually. If you get really stuck, you can refer to the main walkthrough to the right. What we will tell you is that you'll encounter the Mission Failed screen if Meryl dies, so don't hit her with lethal weapons – use the Mk. 2, Stun Grenades, or a shotgun loaded with V-Ring ammunition if you need to disable her.

Screaming mantis

B Before you head through the door, equip the Mk. 2 and a shotgun loaded with V-Ring ammunition; you can optionally prepare the Mosin-Nagant (if you have it) and Stun Grenades. The battle against the Haven Troopers is a straight fight, so the general advice offered on the page to your left is more than sufficient. Snake's Life and Psyche levels are carried over to the next fight, so you should take the opportunity to crouch and recuperate when there's only one soldier left.

Try to avoid tranquilizing Haven Troopers when they are attached to walls or ceilings – the fall will kill them, which can make the next battle marginally more complicated.

HOW TO PLAY
▶ WALKTHROUGH
INVENTORY
METAL GEAR ONLINE
EXTRAS

USER INSTRUCTIONS
ACT 1
ACT 2
ACT 3
ACT 4
▶ ACT 5

FLASHBACK: PSYCHO MANTIS

Psycho Mantis, the self-styled "world's greatest mind reader and psychokineticist," first appeared in MGS1's most imaginative boss battle. In a humorous breaking of the fourth wall (which can be said to be something of a Hideo Kojima trademark), Mantis demonstrated his supernatural prowess by "reading" certain save files stored on the player's memory card, and by using the rumble function in a player's DualShock controller to move it with the power of his mind. The trick to beating him was to switch your controller to the second port, thereby preventing him from anticipating your every action. His cameo appearance in MGS4, then, is a welcome reminder of one of the most iconic set-piece battles of the first PlayStation era.

C SCREAMING MANTIS

Preparation

There are three distinct stages to this fight, so we'll cover each one in turn. Stick to the Mk. 2 (it's surprisingly accurate as you fire at the dolls, even from long range) and a shotgun loaded with V-Ring ammunition for emergency crowd control; using other weapons will just complicate matters.

Phase 1

If you haven't already guessed the solution to the immediate problem of not being able to hit anything, it's very simple: use the Syringe to suppress Snake's nanomachines and prevent Screaming Mantis from exerting control over him. Run up to the top level row of computer consoles. This is the safest area to operate in at first, as it offers good protection from gunfire and from the blades thrown by Screaming Mantis.

- The second puzzle is how to actually attack Mantis. While her body is impervious to conventional forms of attack, the two dolls she carries are not. Aim exclusively for the doll she holds in her right hand – from your point of view, the one to the left of her body (which attentive *MGS1* veterans will recognize as Psycho Mantis). Hitting this doll will cause Screaming Mantis to temporarily lose control of all "living" puppets (including Meryl). The doll is temporarily invulnerable after you score a direct hit, or while Mantis is performing certain actions. The best time to take a shot is when she is floating in a fixed position.

- In this first phase, the Haven Troopers (alive or dead) and Meryl barely move, so keep moving at all times and just concentrate on shooting the doll.

- Screaming Mantis has two forms of attack. The first is to hurl viciously sharp blades at Snake in a curved trajectory that makes them very hard to dodge in the open. The arrival of each knife is foreshadowed by a cry of "Take that!", so crouch or lie down behind a computer console to avoid them. Her second attack type is to "warp" towards Snake to perform a close-range melee attack. Just run (and, if necessary, dive at the last moment) to avoid this. As the battle progresses, she may occasionally perform a second "follow-up" attack, so don't stop running until she moves further away.

- Mantis also fires glowing, slow-moving darts that enable her to gain control of bodies. If you notice ghostly "strings" appearing as Snake moves and all your shots appear to be inexplicably wayward, it indicates that Snake has been hit by one of these projectiles – you'll need to use the Syringe again.

Phase 2

- After the short cutscene, Screaming Mantis uses more aggressive tactics.

Meryl will actively pursue Snake, firing as she approaches him, while the Haven Troopers will be regularly repositioned. Keep moving at all times, only stopping briefly to shoot the Psycho Mantis doll or to take cover when she begins to throw blades.

- For this phase and the one that follows, some players might find it easier to run around the top level. Should you need to dodge the blade attacks, you can dive over the glass barriers to take cover behind the computer consoles on the next level down.

Phase 3

- This is where things get really tricky. Screaming Mantis will now move all bodies inexorably towards Snake, and those that carry weapons will fire more regularly. Again, you'll need to stay in motion at all times to avoid them.

- Mantis will regularly hold Meryl or Haven Troopers in front of her dolls, which makes it hard to get a clear shot. It's easier to just tranquilize them, then go for the doll.

- When Screaming Mantis finally drops her Psycho Mantis doll, quickly run over to collect it. Equip it in the Weapons menu, then use it to fire at your opponent. Follow the onscreen prompts that appear when you score a direct hit: just hold **L1** and waggle your controller like crazy to shake her into insensibility, ending the battle.

- Alternatively, if you would like to collect the second doll held by Screaming Mantis (it's actually a representation of The Sorrow from *MGS3*), you'll again need to shoot it several times to cause her to drop it. If you have been careful not to kill any Haven Troopers, even accidentally, Screaming Mantis has no available puppets to attack you with, and you'll face her alone for this (purely optional) section of the battle. If you're wondering why this is, the Psycho Mantis doll enables her to control the living, while the second doll (The Sorrow) is used to manipulate the dead (and, incidentally, has no effect on Screaming Mantis). Both dolls can be used during subsequent playthroughs once you complete the game, and are explained in the Extras chapter.

- On the Big Boss Hard difficulty level, Snake will often drop the doll he is carrying if he is hit. Watch out for this – if you don't pick it up straight away, Screaming Mantis will collect it and resume her assault with renewed vigor.

As always, a short Beauty fight follows. Take pity on your adversary, and you'll obtain the Screaming Beauty FaceCamo.

There are a number of amusing references to the Psycho Mantis boss battle in *MGS1* during the fight against Screaming Mantis, and the cutscene that follows once the Beauty falls. If you attempt the *MGS1* solution and reassign your controller to another number before using the Syringe, you'll view a secret Codec exchange between Snake and Otacon. You can also call Rosemary twice via Codec for optional conversations w'th her and Roy Campbell (though these also occur automatically if you don't use the Syringe for an extended period of time). Finally, the outcome of the cutscene featuring Psycho Mantis changes if you play with a DualShock 3 controller – though we definitely think that the Sixaxis conclusion is funnier...

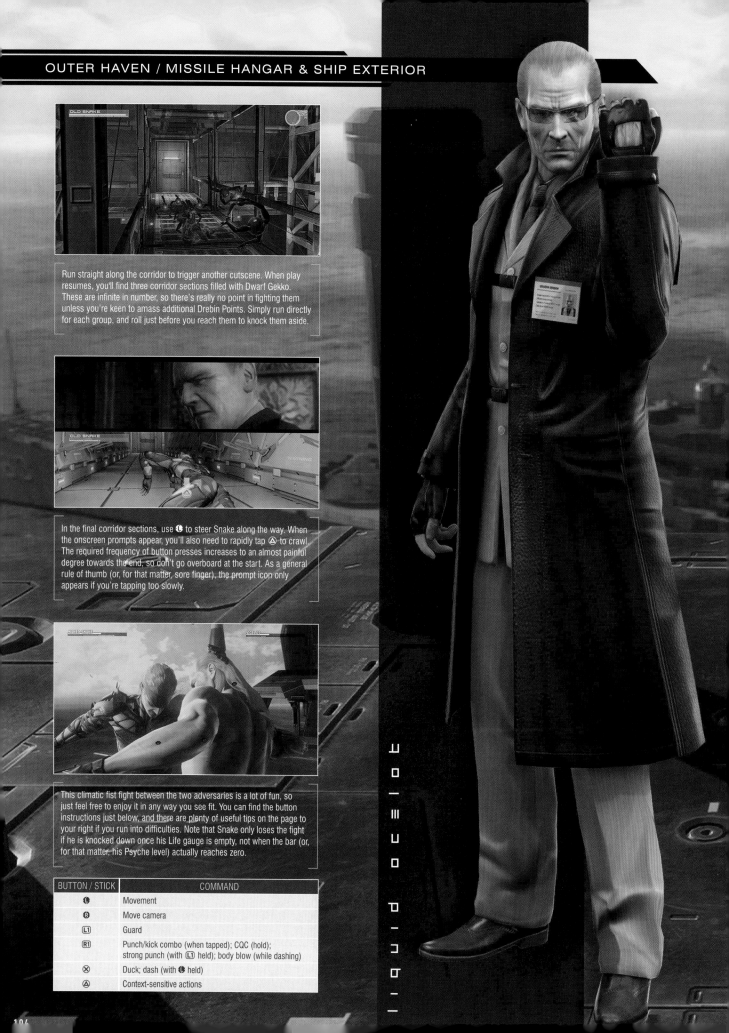

Run straight along the corridor to trigger another cutscene. When play resumes, you'll find three corridor sections filled with Dwarf Gekko. These are infinite in number, so there's really no point in fighting them unless you're keen to amass additional Drebin Points. Simply run directly for each group, and roll just before you reach them to knock them aside.

In the final corridor sections, use ⓛ to steer Snake along the way. When the onscreen prompts appear, you'll also need to rapidly tap △ to crawl. The required frequency of button presses increases to an almost painful degree towards the end, so don't go overboard at the start. As a general rule of thumb (or, for that matter, sore finger), the prompt icon only appears if you're tapping too slowly.

This climatic fist fight between the two adversaries is a lot of fun, so just feel free to enjoy it in any way you see fit. You can find the button instructions just below, and there are plenty of useful tips on the page to your right if you run into difficulties. Note that Snake only loses the fight if he is knocked down once his Life gauge is empty, not when the bar (or, for that matter, his Psyche level) actually reaches zero.

BUTTON / STICK	COMMAND
ⓛ	Movement
ⓡ	Move camera
L1	Guard
R1	Punch/kick combo (when tapped); CQC (hold); strong punch (with L1 held); body blow (while dashing)
✕	Duck; dash (with ⓛ held)
△	Context-sensitive actions

102

D There's no specific coaching required for the final tunnel sequence. The Dwarf Gekko are simple to get past, so probably don't even warrant this quick mention. Once Snake enters the section filled with microwave radiation, you just need to approach the final door before the cutscene in the upper window ends. If you don't manage this, you *will* pay a visit to the Mission Failed screen, but this is actually a highly unlikely outcome. Don't neglect to save your progress when the opportunity arises.

E LIQUID OCELOT

If you're attempting to get through the entire game without using a single continue, the confrontation against Liquid can be really tough at first. This is especially true on the highest difficulty settings. The following tips and guidelines should help you to get through. If you fail, just load your last saved game and try again – it's really much easier with a little practice.

General Guidelines

- Hold L1 to guard whenever you are not actively attacking. Liquid Ocelot is very swift, and will regularly use lunging strikes that enable him to hit Snake when you least expect it.

- Keep moving at all times (we've found it helps to retreat while angling Snake's direction slightly to the left or right), and only attack in response to Liquid's assaults – if you try to take the initiative, he'll pick you off with ease. The best time to strike is just after he completes a sequence of blows that you successfully block, or when he misses entirely. He's especially vulnerable when he fails to hit home with one of his lunging attacks.

- CQC moves are enjoyable, but not practical – they're just too risky. We suggest that you stick with the basic punch/kick combo attack. Even if the initial punches miss, the kicks often don't. Resume your hold on L1 as soon as each sequence ends.

- Last, but not least, whenever Liquid Ocelot poses and taunts Snake, quickly release the guard button and hold △ to restore Snake's Life gauge; Liquid's gauge will also be partially replenished. The swifter you are, the better the results will be. This "secret" feature is almost essential on higher difficulty settings. You can sometimes encourage your opponent to make his gesture of defiance by pressing △ from a safe distance. Liquid most commonly does this after he or Snake clamber back to their feet following a knockdown.

There are four stages to the fight, with short cutscenes and a change in musical accompaniment prior to each one.

With the **first phase**, the general guidelines will see you through. The **second phase** is much tougher. Liquid Ocelot will regularly use a powerful lunging punch, which is tremendously damaging if you fail to block it. It drains a fair amount of Life even if you guard against it. While the obvious solution is to use the "dash" function (⊗) to evade this particular attack, the timing is very delicate – and the consequences should you fail can be pretty dire.

The **third phase** is the most unique. You no longer encounter the lunging assaults found in the first two phases, but your opponent will regularly perform an unblockable headbutt on Snake at close range. It's not all one-way traffic, though, as you can now perform an identical attack by pressing △ when the button prompt appears following consecutive punches. Whenever Liquid Ocelot changes his fighting stance, attack him before he can get too close – if you don't, he'll grab Snake. Follow the onscreen button prompts to escape (or dodge, where applicable) whenever they appear.

In the **fourth stage**, approach your opponent and press R1 repeatedly to punch. The fight is effectively over as a contest here, so there's no cause for further anxiety. Don't leave the room when the credits begin to roll – there's actually more drama to come. The same applies for the second credits sequence.

F AND FINALLY...

After the concluding (audio-only) dialogue sequence ends, you'll view a post-game "Final Results" screen where additional Drebin Points are awarded in accordance with your overall performance. When you've studied this page, press ⊗ to proceed to a screen where you are awarded one or more of forty "Emblems" in recognition of feats achieved during your playthrough. Press R1 to view explanations for each one that you have unlocked. The following screens reveal your completion rewards. No matter how you fared, you'll be given the Race Gun, the Suit "disguise", and five types of colored Command Vests. When prompted to save, select "Yes" and create a new file. This is absolutely essential – if you don't save this data, you won't be able to enjoy your rewards on subsequent playthroughs.

If this is the first time you have completed *MSG4*, don't view this as the end: the *real* challenge begins right now. Finishing the game for the first time also unlocks a new difficulty level: The Boss Extreme. To complete the ultimate "perfect" playthrough – and win the most exclusive potential rewards – you'll need to beat *MGS4* on this elite setting with zero kills, no continues, not a single Alert Phase, and without using a solitary recovery item. This might appear to be a daunting prospect, but we'll be there to help you every (silent) step of the way. Turn to page 154 to reach our secret-packed Extras chapter, where all of *Metal Gear Solid 4*'s remaining secrets are laid bare.

HOW TO PLAY
▶ WALKTHROUGH
INVENTORY
METAL GEAR ONLINE
EXTRAS

USER INSTRUCTIONS
ACT 1
ACT 2
ACT 3
ACT 4
▶ ACT 5

■ Even though weapon ammunition is carried forward to subsequent playthroughs, you can earn a reasonable sum of Drebin Points for future purchases by engaging the Dwarf Gekko in the final tunnel until your ammo runs out. The best place to fight is by the exit to the third corridor section where they attack. If you lie down, Snake will automatically regain Life as you fight.

■ During the third stage of the fight against Liquid Ocelot, there's a hidden sequence that you will not encounter unless you actively look for it. When Snake is held in a chokehold, don't press anything. Eventually, Liquid will plant a kiss on Snake's cheek.

INVENTORY

▶ **SPOILER WARNING!** *Though largely free of content that could potentially ruin revelations in the MGS4 story, be warned that the text that follows reveals certain gameplay-based surprises and rewards.*

This chapter offers a comprehensive, easy-to-use guide to the equipment that Snake has at his disposal during the course of the game. If you're looking to buy a weapon from Drebin's Shop, apply custom parts to an existing favorite, or simply learn the function of a particular item, you've turned to the right section.

WEAPONS

The following tables present a detailed breakdown of the most important characteristics for each weapon type available in the game. The basic structure of each table is easy to follow, but these explanations will help to make everything clear.

Weapon ID:
Weight: The precise weight of each weapon in kilograms.

Range: A weapon's maximum operational distance, expressed in meters (1 meter equals approximately 3.3 feet).

Power: Expresses the raw potency of each weapon type. This only applies to "primary fire" functionality (in other words, not to custom attachments), and often decreases with range. You can find a graph that illustrates this for each armament type in the in-game Weapons menu.

CQC Compatibility: Indicates if Close Quarters Combat moves are possible when the weapon is equipped. As a general rule, you'll enjoy access to the full range of CQC moves while holding a pistol; with compatible rifles, your options are understandably limited.

Firing Modes: When a weapon has more than one firing mode, these are indicated by one star for single shot, three for burst fire, and five stars for full automatic.

Ammo:
Ammo Type: The category of ammo used by the weapon.

Magazine Capacity: The quantity of ammo included in each magazine.

Maximum Ammo:
This reveals the maximum amount of ammo that Snake can carry on each of the five difficulty settings. Practically unlimited in Liquid Easy, these totals are significantly reduced on Big Boss Hard and The Boss Extreme.

Attributes:
This section breaks down the ratings for each of up to seven possible attributes that a weapon may have: Damage, Penetration, Stability, Reload, Lock, Sleep and Stun. "S" is the highest possible rating, and "E" is the lowest. To make this system more intuitive, we're representing each letter in a more visual gauge format. The more color and cell coverage you can see, the better the rating (as illustrated in the following diagram).

E	D	C	B	A	S

Sleep and Stun are attributes that only apply to certain non-lethal weapons. To learn more about the importance of the other ratings, please turn to the "Best Attributes Ratings" table on page 122 of this chapter.

Regular Price (DP):
Some of the weapons are made available in Drebin's Shop at different stages of the game. This line will give you the regular price. Look up in the dedicated section of this chapter for more details on availability. Please note that the weapons with no price indication must be collected from the battlefield.

Customization / Notes:
The final section of the tables outlines any available customizations for the weapon in question, and mentions any extra detail worth noting (for example if a weapon has a special feature). You can learn more about custom weapon parts on page 130 of this chapter.

HOW TO PLAY
WALKTHROUGH
INVENTORY
METAL GEAR ONLINE
EXTRAS

WEAPONS
ITEMS
CAMOUFLAGE
DREBIN'S SHOP
WEAPON MODIFICATION
ENEMIES & ALLIES

MK. 2 PISTOL

PISTOL	
Weight (kg)	1.1
Range (m)	76.0
Power	350
CQC Compatibility	✔
Firing Modes	-
Ammo Type	Anest. (.22)
Magazine Capacity	10
Liquid Easy	9,999
Naked Normal	893
Solid Normal	300
Big Boss Hard	100
The Boss Extreme	50

E D C B A S

DMG, SHK, PNT, STB, RLD, LKD, SLP, STN

Regular Price (DP): -

Customization: -

OPERATOR

PISTOL	
Weight (kg)	1.0
Range (m)	71.0
Power	420
CQC Compatibility	✔
Firing Modes	-
Ammo Type	.45ACP
Magazine Capacity	7
Liquid Easy	9,999
Naked Normal	893
Solid Normal	893
Big Boss Hard	500
The Boss Extreme	300

E D C B A S

DMG, SHK, PNT, STB, RLD, LKD, SLP, STN

Regular Price (DP): -

Customization:
Top Mount: Suppressor (OP)
Bottom Mount: Flash Light (H.G.)

HANDGUNS

Handguns enable Snake to use his full repertoire of CQC moves, and are extremely quick to reload. However, their poor range makes them appropriate for close encounters only. The three types that can be fitted with a Suppressor (the Operator, Mk. 23 and 1911 Custom) are excellent choices if you're aiming for maximum stealth. The staple Mk. 2 pistol fires tranquilizer darts, and is a weapon you'll need to learn to love if you're going to unlock all of *MGS4*'s secrets. A fringe benefit of having a pistol equipped as your current weapon is that Snake runs at a slightly faster pace.

GSR

PISTOL	
Weight (kg)	1.2
Range (m)	63.5
Power	430
CQC Compatibility	✔
Firing Modes	-
Ammo Type	.45ACP
Magazine Capacity	8
Liquid Easy	9,999
Naked Normal	893
Solid Normal	893
Big Boss Hard	500
The Boss Extreme	300

E D C B A S

DMG, SHK, PNT, STB, RLD, LKD, SLP, STN

Regular Price (DP): 3,000

Customization:
Bottom Mount: Flash Light (H.G.)

FIVE SEVEN

PISTOL	
Weight (kg)	0.8
Range (m)	80.0
Power	300
CQC Compatibility	✔
Firing Modes	-
Ammo Type	5.7 x 28 mm
Magazine Capacity	20
Liquid Easy	9,999
Naked Normal	893
Solid Normal	893
Big Boss Hard	500
The Boss Extreme	300

E D C B A S

DMG, SHK, PNT, STB, RLD, LKD, SLP, STN

Regular Price (DP): 6,000

Customization:
Bottom Mount: Flash Light (H.G.)

PMM

PISTOL	
Weight (kg)	0.8
Range (m)	70.0
Power	325
CQC Compatibility	✔
Firing Modes	-
Ammo Type	9 x 18 mm
Magazine Capacity	12
Liquid Easy	9,999
Naked Normal	893
Solid Normal	893
Big Boss Hard	500
The Boss Extreme	300

E D C B A S

DMG, SHK, PNT, STB, RLD, LKD, SLP, STN

Regular Price (DP): 3,500

Customization: -

PSS

PISTOL	
Weight (kg)	0.9
Range (m)	50.0
Power	350
CQC Compatibility	✔
Firing Modes	-
Ammo Type	7.62 x 42 mm
Magazine Capacity	6
Liquid Easy	9,999
Naked Normal	893
Solid Normal	893
Big Boss Hard	500
The Boss Extreme	300

E D C B A S

DMG, SHK, PNT, STB, RLD, LKD, SLP, STN

Regular Price (DP): 5,000

Customization: -

* DMG (Damage), SHK (Shock), PNT (Penetration), STB (Stability), RLD (Reload), LKD (Lock), SLP (Sleep), STN (Stun)

G18C

MACHINE PISTOL	
Weight (kg)	0.9
Range (m)	60.0
Power	300
CQC Compatibility	✔
Firing Modes	* *****
Ammo Type	9 x 19 mm
Magazine Capacity	33
Liquid Easy	9,999
Naked Normal	893
Solid Normal	893
Big Boss Hard	500
The Boss Extreme	300

EDCBAS

Attributes	
DMG	
SHK	
PNT	
STB	
RLD	
LKD	
SLP	
STN	

Regular Price (DP): 8,000

Customization:
Bottom Mount: Flash Light (H.G.)

MK. 23

PISTOL	
Weight (kg)	1.2
Range (m)	90.0
Power	440
CQC Compatibility	✔
Firing Modes	-
Ammo Type	.45ACP
Magazine Capacity	12
Liquid Easy	9,999
Naked Normal	893
Solid Normal	893
Big Boss Hard	500
The Boss Extreme	300

EDCBAS

Attributes	
DMG	
SHK	
PNT	
STB	
RLD	
LKD	
SLP	
STN	

Regular Price (DP): -

Customization:
Top Mount: Suppressor (Mk. 23)

RACE GUN

PISTOL	
Weight (kg)	0.9
Range (m)	60.0
Power	200
CQC Compatibility	✔
Firing Modes	-
Ammo Type	9 x 23 mm
Magazine Capacity	19
Liquid Easy	9,999
Naked Normal	893
Solid Normal	893
Big Boss Hard	500
The Boss Extreme	300

EDCBAS

Attributes	
DMG	
SHK	
PNT	
STB	
RLD	
LKD	
SLP	
STN	

Regular Price (DP): -

Notes:
Features a ricochet function

TYPE 17

MACHINE PISTOL	
Weight (kg)	1.4
Range (m)	80.0
Power	430
CQC Compatibility	✔
Firing Modes	* *****
Ammo Type	.45ACP
Magazine Capacity	10
Liquid Easy	9,999
Naked Normal	893
Solid Normal	893
Big Boss Hard	500
The Boss Extreme	300

EDCBAS

Attributes	
DMG	
SHK	
PNT	
STB	
RLD	
LKD	
SLP	
STN	

Regular Price (DP): -

Customization: -

DESERT EAGLE

PISTOL	
Weight (kg)	2.1
Range (m)	90.0
Power	700
CQC Compatibility	✔
Firing Modes	-
Ammo Type	.50AE
Magazine Capacity	7
Liquid Easy	9,999
Naked Normal	893
Solid Normal	893
Big Boss Hard	500
The Boss Extreme	300

EDCBAS

Attributes	
DMG	
SHK	
PNT	
STB	
RLD	
LKD	
SLP	
STN	

Regular Price (DP): 20,000

Customization: -

* Attributes: DMG (Damage), SHK (Shock), PNT (Penetration), STB (Stability), RLD (Reload), LKD (Lock), SLP (Sleep), STN (Stun)

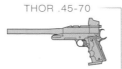

	DESERT EAGLE (LONG BARREL)	1911 CUSTOM	THOR .45-70	SOLAR GUN
	PISTOL	PISTOL	HAND RIFLE	STUN GUN
WEAPON ID				
Weight (kg)	2.1	1.0	2.3	0.5
Range (m)	125.0	100.0	150.0	150.0
Power	710	450	1,500	5,000
CQC Compatibility	✔	✔	✔	✔
Firing Modes	-	-	-	-
AMMO				
Ammo Type	50AE	.45ACP	.45-70	-
Magazine Capacity	7	7	1	-
MAX. AMMO				
Liquid Easy	9,999	9,999	9,999	-
Naked Normal	893	893	893	-
Solid Normal	893	893	300	-
Big Boss Hard	500	500	100	-
The Boss Extreme	300	500	50	-

Attributes (EDCBAS): DMG, SHK, PNT, STB, RLD, LKD, SLP, STN

Desert Eagle (Long Barrel)
Regular Price (DP): -
Customization: -

1911 Custom
Regular Price (DP): -
Customization:
Top Mount: Suppressor (1911)

Thor .45-70
Regular Price (DP): -
Customization: -

Solar Gun
Regular Price (DP): -
Notes: Chargeable; stuns enemies and makes them drop their item(s); secret weapon, see page 166

HOW TO PLAY
WALKTHROUGH
INVENTORY
METAL GEAR ONLINE
EXTRAS

WEAPONS
ITEMS
CAMOUFLAGE
DREBIN'S SHOP
WEAPON MODIFICATION
ENEMIES & ALLIES

P90

SUBMACHINE GUN	
Weight (kg)	3.2
Range (m)	135.0
Power	300
CQC Compatibility	✔
Firing Modes	★★★★★
Ammo Type	5.7 x 28 mm
Magazine Capacity	50
Liquid Easy	9,999
Naked Normal	893
Solid Normal	893
Big Boss Hard	500
The Boss Extreme	300

E D C B A S

Attribute	
DMG	
SHK	
PNT	
STB	
RLD	
LKD	
SLP	
STN	

Regular Price (DP): 5,000

Customization:
Muzzle Mount: Suppressor (P90)
Left Mount: Laser Sight
Right Mount: Flash Light (L.G.)

M10

SUBMACHINE GUN	
Weight (kg)	3.3
Range (m)	73.0
Power	420
CQC Compatibility	✔
Firing Modes	★★★★★
Ammo Type	.45ACP
Magazine Capacity	30
Liquid Easy	9,999
Naked Normal	893
Solid Normal	893
Big Boss Hard	500
The Boss Extreme	300

E D C B A S

Attribute	
DMG	
SHK	
PNT	
STB	
RLD	
LKD	
SLP	
STN	

Regular Price (DP): 3,000

Customization:
Muzzle Mount: Suppressor (M10)

MP7

SUBMACHINE GUN	
Weight (kg)	1.5
Range (m)	140.0
Power	250
CQC Compatibility	✔
Firing Modes	★★★★★
Ammo Type	4.6 x 30 mm
Magazine Capacity	20
Liquid Easy	9,999
Naked Normal	893
Solid Normal	893
Big Boss Hard	500
The Boss Extreme	300

E D C B A S

Attribute	
DMG	
SHK	
PNT	
STB	
RLD	
LKD	
SLP	
STN	

Regular Price (DP): 3,500

Customization:
Top Mount: Dot Sight (MP7);
Scope

SUBMACHINE GUNS

Superior magazine capacity and fully automatic firing modes make the SMG an invaluable tool when you need to deal with multiple enemies at close range. Don't pay too much attention to their ostensibly poor overall ratings: it's the withering rate of fire that makes this weapon type so efficient. For stealth purposes, the P90 and M10 can be fitted with optional Suppressors; the MP5SD2 comes with an everlasting silencer as standard. The P90, first encountered in Act 1, is a gun that you can rely on throughout: it packs a powerful punch, and its magazine capacity is outstanding.

VZ. 83

SUBMACHINE GUN	
Weight (kg)	1.4
Range (m)	75.0
Power	325
CQC Compatibility	✔
Firing Modes	★★★★★
Ammo Type	9 x 18 mm
Magazine Capacity	20
Liquid Easy	9,999
Naked Normal	893
Solid Normal	893
Big Boss Hard	500
The Boss Extreme	300

E D C B A S

Attribute	
DMG	
SHK	
PNT	
STB	
RLD	
LKD	
SLP	
STN	

Regular Price (DP): -

Customization: -

BIZON

SUBMACHINE GUN	
Weight (kg)	2.5
Range (m)	100.0
Power	325
CQC Compatibility	✔
Firing Modes	★★★★★
Ammo Type	9 x 18 mm
Magazine Capacity	64
Liquid Easy	9,999
Naked Normal	893
Solid Normal	893
Big Boss Hard	500
The Boss Extreme	300

E D C B A S

Attribute	
DMG	
SHK	
PNT	
STB	
RLD	
LKD	
SLP	
STN	

Regular Price (DP): 7,000

Customization: -

MP5SD2

SUBMACHINE GUN	
Weight (kg)	3.1
Range (m)	160.0
Power	290
CQC Compatibility	✔
Firing Modes	★★★★★
Ammo Type	9 x 19 mm
Magazine Capacity	30
Liquid Easy	9,999
Naked Normal	893
Solid Normal	893
Big Boss Hard	500
The Boss Extreme	300

E D C B A S

Attribute	
DMG	
SHK	
PNT	
STB	
RLD	
LKD	
SLP	
STN	

Regular Price (DP): 15,000

Notes: Built-in silencer

PATRIOT

HAND RIFLE	
Weight (kg)	1.5
Range (m)	160.0
Power	425
CQC Compatibility	✔
Firing Modes	★★★★★
Ammo Type	5.56 x 45 mm
Magazine Capacity	∞
Liquid Easy	∞
Naked Normal	∞
Solid Normal	∞
Big Boss Hard	∞
The Boss Extreme	∞

E D C B A S

Attribute	
DMG	
SHK	
PNT	
STB	
RLD	
LKD	
SLP	
STN	

Regular Price (DP): -

Notes: Secret weapon, see page 165

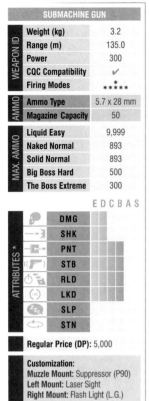
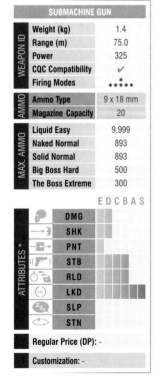

* Attributes: DMG (Damage), SHK (Shock), PNT (Penetration), STB (Stability), RLD (Reload), LKD (Lock), SLP (Sleep), STN (Stun)

METAL GEAR SOLID 4
GUNS OF THE PATRIOTS TACTICAL ESPIONAGE ACTION

HOW TO PLAY

WALKTHROUGH

INVENTORY

METAL GEAR ONLINE

EXTRAS

WEAPONS

ITEMS

CAMOUFLAGE

DREBIN'S SHOP

WEAPON MODIFICATION

ENEMIES & ALLIES

RIFLES

The rifle category includes various types of weapons, which you can use for totally different purposes. Many of them represent good alternatives to submachine guns, as they offer a full auto-firing mode with improved Range and Power ratings. Some of them are additionally highly customizable (especially the M4 Custom), making them extremely versatile.

Sniper Rifles, of course, are in a class of their own. With massive Power and Range ratings, they should always be your first choice whenever you need to take out a target instantly at long range. Of particular note is the M14EBR. It's technically the weakest in its class, but its auto-fire capability, cheap (and readily available) ammunition and support for custom add-ons make it perfect for battles with PMC soldiers and Haven Troopers. If you're looking for raw power in certain set-piece confrontations, though, the M82A2 is almost peerless (though perhaps superseded by the Rail Gun from the end of Act 4), but be prepared to pay generously for the privilege of using it. Finally, anyone attempting a no-kill playthrough should seriously consider investing in the Mosin-Nagant. It's not cheap, but the ability to tranquilize troublesome soldiers from afar is something you'll appreciate on more than one occasion.

AK 102

ASSAULT RIFLE	
Weight (kg)	3.0
Range (m)	200.0
Power	415
CQC Compatibility	✔
Firing Modes	★★★★★
Ammo Type	5.56 x 45 mm
Magazine Capacity	30
Liquid Easy	9,999
Naked Normal	893
Solid Normal	893
Big Boss Hard	500
The Boss Extreme	300

EDCBAS

- DMG
- SHK
- PNT
- STB
- RLD
- LKD
- SLP
- STN

Regular Price (DP): -

Customization:
Bottom Mount: GP30

M4 CUSTOM

CARBINE	
Weight (kg)	5.0
Range (m)	220.0
Power	400
CQC Compatibility	✔
Firing Modes	★★★★★
Ammo Type	5.56 x 45 mm
Magazine Capacity	30
Liquid Easy	9,999
Naked Normal	893
Solid Normal	893
Big Boss Hard	500
The Boss Extreme	300

EDCBAS

- DMG
- SHK
- PNT
- STB
- RLD
- LKD
- SLP
- STN

Regular Price (DP): -

Customization:
Top Mount: Dot Sight; Scope
Muzzle Mount: Suppressor (M4)
Bottom Mount: XM320; Masterkey;
Fore Grip A; Fore Grip B
Left Mount: Laser Sight
Right Mount: Flash Light (L.G.)

MK. 17

ASSAULT RIFLE	
Weight (kg)	4.1
Range (m)	200.0
Power	530
CQC Compatibility	✔
Firing Modes	★★★★★
Ammo Type	7.62 x 51 mm
Magazine Capacity	20
Liquid Easy	9,999
Naked Normal	893
Solid Normal	893
Big Boss Hard	500
The Boss Extreme	300

EDCBAS

- DMG
- SHK
- PNT
- STB
- RLD
- LKD
- SLP
- STN

Regular Price (DP): 3,500

Customization:
Top Mount: Dot Sight; Scope
Bottom Mount: Fore Grip A; Fore Grip B
Left Mount: Laser Sight
Right Mount: Flash Light (L.G.)

G3A3

ASSAULT RIFLE	
Weight (kg)	4.4
Range (m)	250.0
Power	540
CQC Compatibility	✔
Firing Modes	★★★★★
Ammo Type	7.62 x 51 mm
Magazine Capacity	20
Liquid Easy	9,999
Naked Normal	893
Solid Normal	893
Big Boss Hard	500
The Boss Extreme	300

EDCBAS

- DMG
- SHK
- PNT
- STB
- RLD
- LKD
- SLP
- STN

Regular Price (DP): 4,000

Customization: -

FAL CARBINE

CARBINE	
Weight (kg)	4.5
Range (m)	230.0
Power	550
CQC Compatibility	✔
Firing Modes	* *****
Ammo Type	7.62 x 51 mm
Magazine Capacity	20
Liquid Easy	9,999
Naked Normal	893
Solid Normal	893
Big Boss Hard	500
The Boss Extreme	300

E D C B A S

ATTRIBUTES *	
DMG	
SHK	
PNT	
STB	
RLD	
LKD	
SLP	
STN	

Regular Price (DP): 4,500

Customization: -

AN94

ASSAULT RIFLE	
Weight (kg)	4.0
Range (m)	220.0
Power	375
CQC Compatibility	✔
Firing Modes	* *** *****
Ammo Type	5.45 x 39 mm
Magazine Capacity	30
Liquid Easy	9,999
Naked Normal	893
Solid Normal	893
Big Boss Hard	500
The Boss Extreme	300

E D C B A S

DMG	
SHK	
PNT	
STB	
RLD	
LKD	
SLP	
STN	

Regular Price (DP): 5,000

Customization:
Bottom Mount: GP30

XM8

CARBINE	
Weight (kg)	2.8
Range (m)	220.0
Power	400
CQC Compatibility	✔
Firing Modes	* *****
Ammo Type	5.56 x 45 mm
Magazine Capacity	30
Liquid Easy	9,999
Naked Normal	893
Solid Normal	893
Big Boss Hard	500
The Boss Extreme	300

E D C B A S

DMG	
SHK	
PNT	
STB	
RLD	
LKD	
SLP	
STN	

Regular Price (DP): -

Customization:
Bottom Mount: XM320
Notes: Built-in dot sight

TANEGASHIMA

MATCHLOCK GUN	
Weight (kg)	4.0
Range (m)	100.0
Power	725
CQC Compatibility	✔
Firing Modes	-
Ammo Type	Lead Ball
Magazine Capacity	1
Liquid Easy	9,999
Naked Normal	893
Solid Normal	300
Big Boss Hard	100
The Boss Extreme	50

E D C B A S

DMG	
SHK	
PNT	
STB	
RLD	
LKD	
SLP	
STN	

Regular Price (DP): 1,000,000

Notes: Might generate strong winds (likelihood: 30%) in wide open areas that make enemies drop their items; secret weapon, see page 167

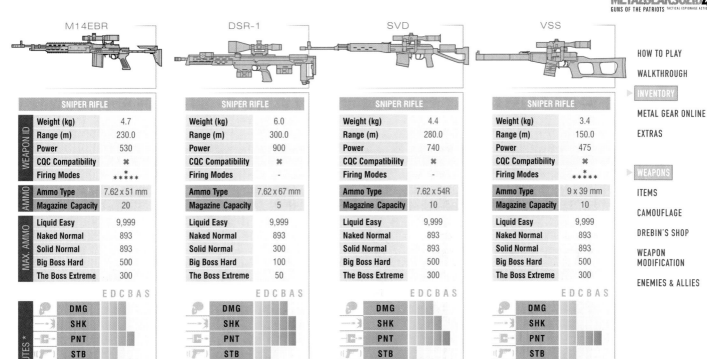

M14EBR

SNIPER RIFLE	
Weight (kg)	4.7
Range (m)	230.0
Power	530
CQC Compatibility	✖
Firing Modes	★★★★★
Ammo Type	7.62 x 51 mm
Magazine Capacity	20
Liquid Easy	9,999
Naked Normal	893
Solid Normal	893
Big Boss Hard	500
The Boss Extreme	300

EDCBAS

DMG	
SHK	
PNT	
STB	
RLD	
LKD	
SLP	
STN	

Regular Price (DP): 9,000

Customization:
Muzzle Mount: Suppressor (M14)
Left Mount: Laser Sight
Right Mount: Flash Light (L.G.)

DSR-1

SNIPER RIFLE	
Weight (kg)	6.0
Range (m)	300.0
Power	900
CQC Compatibility	✖
Firing Modes	-
Ammo Type	7.62 x 67 mm
Magazine Capacity	5
Liquid Easy	9,999
Naked Normal	893
Solid Normal	300
Big Boss Hard	100
The Boss Extreme	50

EDCBAS

DMG	
SHK	
PNT	
STB	
RLD	
LKD	
SLP	
STN	

Regular Price (DP): 20,000

Customization: -

SVD

SNIPER RIFLE	
Weight (kg)	4.4
Range (m)	280.0
Power	740
CQC Compatibility	✖
Firing Modes	-
Ammo Type	7.62 x 54R
Magazine Capacity	10
Liquid Easy	9,999
Naked Normal	893
Solid Normal	893
Big Boss Hard	500
The Boss Extreme	300

EDCBAS

DMG	
SHK	
PNT	
STB	
RLD	
LKD	
SLP	
STN	

Regular Price (DP): 18,000

Customization: -

VSS

SNIPER RIFLE	
Weight (kg)	3.4
Range (m)	150.0
Power	475
CQC Compatibility	✖
Firing Modes	★★★★★
Ammo Type	9 x 39 mm
Magazine Capacity	10
Liquid Easy	9,999
Naked Normal	893
Solid Normal	893
Big Boss Hard	500
The Boss Extreme	300

EDCBAS

DMG	
SHK	
PNT	
STB	
RLD	
LKD	
SLP	
STN	

Regular Price (DP): -

Notes: Built-in silencer

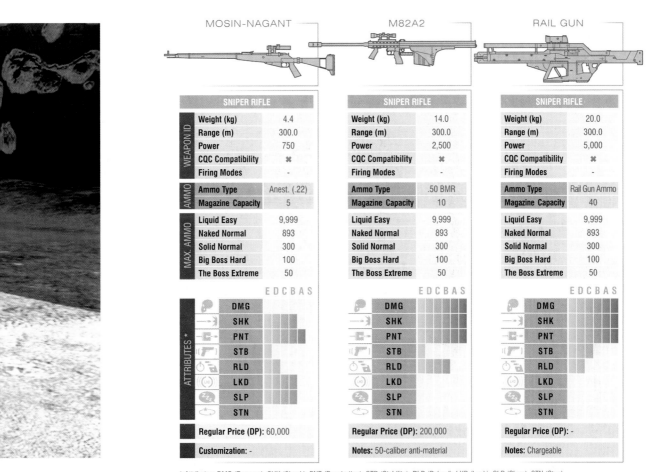

MOSIN-NAGANT

SNIPER RIFLE	
Weight (kg)	4.4
Range (m)	300.0
Power	750
CQC Compatibility	✖
Firing Modes	-
Ammo Type	Anest. (.22)
Magazine Capacity	5
Liquid Easy	9,999
Naked Normal	893
Solid Normal	300
Big Boss Hard	100
The Boss Extreme	50

EDCBAS

DMG	
SHK	
PNT	
STB	
RLD	
LKD	
SLP	
STN	

Regular Price (DP): 60,000

Customization: -

M82A2

SNIPER RIFLE	
Weight (kg)	14.0
Range (m)	300.0
Power	2,500
CQC Compatibility	✖
Firing Modes	-
Ammo Type	.50 BMR
Magazine Capacity	10
Liquid Easy	9,999
Naked Normal	893
Solid Normal	300
Big Boss Hard	100
The Boss Extreme	50

EDCBAS

DMG	
SHK	
PNT	
STB	
RLD	
LKD	
SLP	
STN	

Regular Price (DP): 200,000

Notes: 50-caliber anti-material

RAIL GUN

SNIPER RIFLE	
Weight (kg)	20.0
Range (m)	300.0
Power	5,000
CQC Compatibility	✖
Firing Modes	-
Ammo Type	Rail Gun Ammo
Magazine Capacity	40
Liquid Easy	9,999
Naked Normal	893
Solid Normal	300
Big Boss Hard	100
The Boss Extreme	50

EDCBAS

DMG	
SHK	
PNT	
STB	
RLD	
LKD	
SLP	
STN	

Regular Price (DP): -

Notes: Chargeable

* Attributes: DMG (Damage), SHK (Shock), PNT (Penetration), STB (Stability), RLD (Reload), LKD (Lock), SLP (Sleep), STN (Stun)

HK21E

MACHINE GUN	
Weight (kg)	9.3
Range (m)	250.0
Power	530
CQC Compatibility	✔
Firing Modes	* *** *****
Ammo Type	7.62 x 51 mm
Magazine Capacity	100
Liquid Easy	9,999
Naked Normal	893
Solid Normal	893
Big Boss Hard	500
The Boss Extreme	300

EDCBAS

ATTRIBUTES *	
DMG	
SHK	
PNT	
STB	
RLD	
LKD	
SLP	
STN	

Regular Price (DP): 6,000

Customization: -

M60E4

MACHINE GUN	
Weight (kg)	5.8
Range (m)	260.0
Power	550
CQC Compatibility	✔
Firing Modes	-
Ammo Type	7.62 x 51 mm
Magazine Capacity	200
Liquid Easy	9,999
Naked Normal	893
Solid Normal	893
Big Boss Hard	500
The Boss Extreme	300

EDCBAS

DMG	
SHK	
PNT	
STB	
RLD	
LKD	
SLP	
STN	

Regular Price (DP): 10,000

Customization:
Top Mount: Dot Sight; Scope
Bottom Mount: Fore Grip A; Fore Grip B
Left Mount: Laser Sight
Right Mount: Flash Light (L.G.)

PKM

MACHINE GUN	
Weight (kg)	9.0
Range (m)	265.0
Power	730
CQC Compatibility	✔
Firing Modes	-
Ammo Type	7.62 x 54R
Magazine Capacity	100
Liquid Easy	9,999
Naked Normal	893
Solid Normal	893
Big Boss Hard	500
The Boss Extreme	300

EDCBAS

DMG	
SHK	
PNT	
STB	
RLD	
LKD	
SLP	
STN	

Regular Price (DP): 9,000

Customization: -

MK. 46 MOD 1

MACHINE GUN	
Weight (kg)	10.2
Range (m)	250.0
Power	400
CQC Compatibility	✔
Firing Modes	-
Ammo Type	5.56 x 45 mm
Magazine Capacity	100
Liquid Easy	9,999
Naked Normal	893
Solid Normal	893
Big Boss Hard	500
The Boss Extreme	300

EDCBAS

DMG	
SHK	
PNT	
STB	
RLD	
LKD	
SLP	
STN	

Regular Price (DP): 9,000

Customization:
Top Mount: Dot Sight; Scope
Bottom Mount: Fore Grip A; Fore Grip B
Left Mount: Laser Sight
Right Mount: Flash Light (L.G.)

TWIN BARREL

SHOTGUN	
Weight (kg)	2.3
Range (m)	40.0
Power	1,250
CQC Compatibility	✘
Firing Modes	-
Ammo Type	12 Ga. (00 Buck)
Magazine Capacity	2
Liquid Easy	9,999
Naked Normal	893
Solid Normal	100
Big Boss Hard	50
The Boss Extreme	30

EDCBAS

ATTRIBUTES *	
DMG	
SHK	
PNT	
STB	
RLD	
LKD	
SLP	
STN	

Regular Price (DP): 25,000

Customization: -

OTHER FIREARMS

Weapons in this "everything else" category include machine guns, shotguns, grenade launchers and rocket/missile launchers – in other words, the heavy artillery. Shotguns can be equipped with three different ammo types, each leading to a slight adjustments to their overall performance. Of particular note is Vortex Ring Shot, a special type of non-lethal ammunition that knocks soldiers from their feet and usually renders them unconscious. As for the grenade/rocket/missile launchers, we hardly need to work on a hard sell: they're supremely powerful, though limited ammunition (and high overheads if you purchase more stocks from Drebin) means that you'll often save them for special occasions. The Javelin, king of all things that make other things go boom, even has an impressive guidance system that enables you to adjust the trajectory of its missiles in mid-flight.

Naturally, these firearms aren't exactly what you would call "stealth" weapons, but even if you're trying to achieve a no-kill, no-alert playthrough, you'll be glad to hear that there are no penalties for using them against non-human targets and bosses. Look to the Walkthrough chapter for guidance on when this is possible.

M870 CUSTOM

SHOTGUN

WEAPON ID		
Weight (kg)		3.8
Range (m)		50.0
Power		1,300
CQC Compatibility		✔
Firing Modes		-

AMMO		
Ammo Type		12 Ga. (00 Buck)
Magazine Capacity		4 (+1)

MAX. AMMO		
Liquid Easy		9,999
Naked Normal		893
Solid Normal		100
Big Boss Hard		50
The Boss Extreme		30

ATTRIBUTES * — E D C B A S

DMG, SHK, PNT, STB, RLD, LKD, SLP, STN

Regular Price (DP): 30,000

Customization:
Top Mount: Dot Sight; Scope
Notes:
Built-in tactical light

SAIGA-12

AUTOMATIC SHOTGUN

WEAPON ID		
Weight (kg)		3.8
Range (m)		50.0
Power		1,250
CQC Compatibility		✔
Firing Modes		-

AMMO		
Ammo Type		12 Ga. (00 Buck)
Magazine Capacity		8

MAX. AMMO		
Liquid Easy		9,999
Naked Normal		893
Solid Normal		100
Big Boss Hard		50
The Boss Extreme		30

E D C B A S

DMG, SHK, PNT, STB, RLD, LKD, SLP, STN

Regular Price (DP): 40,000

Customization: -

XM25

GRENADE LAUNCHER

WEAPON ID		
Weight (kg)		5.5
Range (m)		300.0
Power		2,000
CQC Compatibility		✔
Firing Modes		-

AMMO		
Ammo Type		25 mm A.B.G.
Magazine Capacity		6

MAX. AMMO		
Liquid Easy		9,999
Naked Normal		893
Solid Normal		50
Big Boss Hard		30
The Boss Extreme		10

E D C B A S

DMG, SHK, PNT, STB, RLD, LKD, SLP, STN

Regular Price (DP): 80,000

Customization: -

MGL-140

GRENADE LAUNCHER

WEAPON ID		
Weight (kg)		6.0
Range (m)		300.0
Power		2,000
CQC Compatibility		✔
Firing Modes		-

AMMO		
Ammo Type		40 mm (Grenade)
Magazine Capacity		6

MAX. AMMO		
Liquid Easy		9,999
Naked Normal		893
Solid Normal		50
Big Boss Hard		30
The Boss Extreme		10

E D C B A S

DMG, SHK, PNT, STB, RLD, LKD, SLP, STN

Regular Price (DP): -

Customization:
Bottom Mount: Fore Grip A; Fore Grip B
Right Mount: Flash Light (L.G.)

RPG-7

ROCKET-PROPELLED GRENADE LAUNCHER

WEAPON ID		
Weight (kg)		8.5
Range (m)		250.0
Power		3,500
CQC Compatibility		✖
Firing Modes		-

AMMO		
Ammo Type		RPG-7 Ammo
Magazine Capacity		1

MAX. AMMO		
Liquid Easy		9,999
Naked Normal		893
Solid Normal		50
Big Boss Hard		30
The Boss Extreme		10

ATTRIBUTES * — E D C B A S

DMG, SHK, PNT, STB, RLD, LKD, SLP, STN

Regular Price (DP): 60,000

Customization: -

M72A3

ANTI-TANK ROCKET LAUNCHER

WEAPON ID		
Weight (kg)		2.5
Range (m)		200.0
Power		2,450
CQC Compatibility		✖
Firing Modes		-

AMMO		
Ammo Type		M72A3
Magazine Capacity		1

MAX. AMMO		
Liquid Easy		9,999
Naked Normal		893
Solid Normal		50
Big Boss Hard		30
The Boss Extreme		10

E D C B A S

DMG, SHK, PNT, STB, RLD, LKD, SLP, STN

Regular Price (DP): 40,000

Customization: -

JAVELIN

ANTI-TANK MISSILE LAUNCHER

WEAPON ID		
Weight (kg)		22.3
Range (m)		400.0
Power		5,000
CQC Compatibility		✖
Firing Modes		-

AMMO		
Ammo Type		Javelin
Magazine Capacity		1

MAX. AMMO		
Liquid Easy		9,999
Naked Normal		893
Solid Normal		50
Big Boss Hard		30
The Boss Extreme		10

E D C B A S

DMG, SHK, PNT, STB, RLD, LKD, SLP, STN

Regular Price (DP): 150,000

Customization: -

FIM-92A

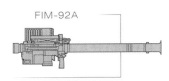

SURFACE-TO-AIR MISSILE LAUNCHER

WEAPON ID		
Weight (kg)		15.7
Range (m)		500.0
Power		3,000
CQC Compatibility		✖
Firing Modes		-

AMMO		
Ammo Type		FIM-92A
Magazine Capacity		1

MAX. AMMO		
Liquid Easy		9,999
Naked Normal		893
Solid Normal		50
Big Boss Hard		30
The Boss Extreme		10

E D C B A S

DMG, SHK, PNT, STB, RLD, LKD, SLP, STN

Regular Price (DP): 100,000

Customization: -

* Attributes: DMG (Damage), SHK (Shock), PNT (Penetration), STB (Stability), RLD (Reload), LKD (Lock), SLP (Sleep), STN (Stun)

EXPLOSIVES

Even the most fresh-faced of novices will have a general idea of when explosives should be deployed. On your first playthrough, you're bound to find yourself in situations that practically beg for a well-placed grenade – for example, to silence a sniper, or to ambush a group of soldiers in close formation. Grenades are cheap, plentiful and easy to use, so don't neglect this useful part of your arsenal. Claymores can be very useful if you have studied an enemy's movements and know where their route will take them, but don't make the rookie mistake of treading on your own device. Like all other mines and traps, they can be collected while primed and ready to blow by carefully crawling over them, or by sending Metal Gear Mk. II to defuse them.

However, it's not all about blowing things up – this category also includes grenades and mines that are compatible with a more stealthy approach, such as Sleep Gas Mines and Stun Grenades. Chaff Grenades have the distinct feature of jamming electronic equipment, preventing most machines (such as Gekko) from firing for a short period. Drebin doesn't stock these in his shop, so use them very sparingly. You will notice that the table reveals special Smoke Grenades which have a unique effect on anyone caught in their effective radius, increasing emotional attributes such as Laugh (Yellow), or Cry (Blue). If you've already completed *MGS4* at least once, you can learn more about soldier emotions on page 165.

GRENADE

FRAG GRENADE		
Weight (kg)		0.3
Range (m)		30.0
Power		2000
CQC Compatibility		✔
Liquid Easy		9,999
Naked Normal		893
Solid Normal		50
Big Boss Hard		30
The Boss Extreme		10

EDCBAS

ATT	DMG	
	SHK	
	STN	

Regular Price (DP): 120
Notes: -

PETRO BOMB

Weight (kg)		0.8
Range (m)		30.0
Power		1000
CQC Compatibility		✔
Liquid Easy		9,999
Naked Normal		893
Solid Normal		50
Big Boss Hard		30
The Boss Extreme		10

EDCBAS

DMG	
SHK	
STN	

Regular Price (DP): 100
Notes: -

WHITE PHOSPHORUS GRENADE

Weight (kg)		0.8
Range (m)		30.0
Power		1500
CQC Compatibility		✔
Liquid Easy		9,999
Naked Normal		893
Solid Normal		50
Big Boss Hard		30
The Boss Extreme		10

EDCBAS

ATT	DMG	
	SHK	
	STN	

Regular Price (DP): 110
Notes: -

STUN GRENADE

FLASHBANG GRENADE		
Weight (kg)		0.5
Range (m)		30.0
Power		2000
CQC Compatibility		✔
Liquid Easy		9,999
Naked Normal		893
Solid Normal		50
Big Boss Hard		30
The Boss Extreme		10

EDCBAS

DMG	
SHK	
STN	

Regular Price (DP): 120
Notes: -

CHAFF GRENADE

ELECTRONIC JAMMING GRENADE		
Weight (kg)		0.8
Range (m)		30.0
Power		-
CQC Compatibility		✔
Liquid Easy		9,999
Naked Normal		893
Solid Normal		50
Big Boss Hard		30
The Boss Extreme		10

EDCBAS

DMG	
SHK	
STN	

Regular Price (DP): -
Notes: -

SMOKE GRENADE

SMOKE GRENADE		
Weight (kg)		0.5
Range (m)		30.0
Power		-
CQC Compatibility		✔
Liquid Easy		9,999
Naked Normal		893
Solid Normal		50
Big Boss Hard		30
The Boss Extreme		10

EDCBAS

DMG	
SHK	
STN	

Regular Price (DP): 100
Notes: -

* Attributes: DMG (Damage), SHK (Shock), SLP (Sleep), STN (Stun)

META/GEAR SO/ID 4
GUNS OF THE PATRIOTS TACTICAL ESPIONAGE ACTION

HOW TO PLAY

WALKTHROUGH

INVENTORY

METAL GEAR ONLINE

EXTRAS

WEAPONS

ITEMS

CAMOUFLAGE

DREBIN'S SHOP

WEAPON MODIFICATION

ENEMIES & ALLIES

SMOKE GRENADE (YELLOW)

SMOKE GRENADE	
Weight (kg)	0.5
Range (m)	30.0
Power	-
CQC Compatibility	✔
Liquid Easy	9,999
Naked Normal	893
Solid Normal	50
Big Boss Hard	30
The Boss Extreme	10

E D C B A S

ATT*	DMG	
	SHK	
	STN	

Regular Price (DP): -

Notes: Increases emotional attribute "Laugh"

SMOKE GRENADE (RED)

SMOKE GRENADE	
Weight (kg)	0.5
Range (m)	30.0
Power	-
CQC Compatibility	✔
Liquid Easy	9,999
Naked Normal	893
Solid Normal	50
Big Boss Hard	30
The Boss Extreme	10

E D C B A S

	DMG	
	SHK	
	STN	

Regular Price (DP): -

Notes: Increases emotional attribute "Rage"

SMOKE GRENADE (BLUE)

SMOKE GRENADE	
Weight (kg)	0.5
Range (m)	30.0
Power	-
CQC Compatibility	✔
Liquid Easy	9,999
Naked Normal	893
Solid Normal	50
Big Boss Hard	30
The Boss Extreme	10

E D C B A S

	DMG	
	SHK	
	STN	

Regular Price (DP): -

Notes: Increases emotional attribute "Cry"

SMOKE GRENADE (GREEN)

SMOKE GRENADE	
Weight (kg)	0.5
Range (m)	30.0
Power	-
CQC Compatibility	✔
Liquid Easy	9,999
Naked Normal	893
Solid Normal	50
Big Boss Hard	30
The Boss Extreme	10

E D C B A S

	DMG	
	SHK	
	STN	

Regular Price (DP): -

Notes: Increases emotional attribute "Scream"

CLAYMORE

MINE	
Weight (kg)	1.6
Range (m)	20.0
Power	2,000
CQC Compatibility	✔
Liquid Easy	9,999
Naked Normal	893
Solid Normal	50
Big Boss Hard	30
The Boss Extreme	10

E D C B A S

ATT*	DMG	
	SHK	
	SLP	

Regular Price (DP): 300

Notes: -

SLEEP GAS MINE

SLEEP GAS MINE	
Weight (kg)	1.5
Range (m)	3.0
Power	5,000
CQC Compatibility	✔
Liquid Easy	9,999
Naked Normal	893
Solid Normal	50
Big Boss Hard	30
The Boss Extreme	10

E D C B A S

	DMG	
	SHK	
	SLP	

Regular Price (DP): 300

Notes: -

C4

-	
Weight (kg)	1.6
Range (m)	3.0
Power	3,000
CQC Compatibility	✔
Liquid Easy	9,999
Naked Normal	893
Solid Normal	50
Big Boss Hard	30
The Boss Extreme	10

E D C B A S

	DMG	
	SHK	
	SLP	

Regular Price (DP): 400

Notes: -

SLEEP GAS SATCHEL

REMOTE SLEEP GAS MINE	
Weight (kg)	1.5
Range (m)	3.0
Power	5,000
CQC Compatibility	✔
Liquid Easy	9,999
Naked Normal	893
Solid Normal	50
Big Boss Hard	30
The Boss Extreme	10

E D C B A S

	DMG	
	SHK	
	SLP	

Regular Price (DP): 400

Notes: -

* Attributes: DMG (Damage), SHK (Shock), SLP (Sleep), STN (Stun)

ETC

In this table you will find various items that are classed as "Weapons" in the game, but may not on first glance actually appear to be so. The empty Magazine, Playboy and the Emotion Mag are all used to distract the enemy, with the latter having the added bonus of increasing an emotional attribute (again, see page 165 for more details if you've already completed *MGS4*). The function of the Stun Knife is obvious; other items that appear here are secret, and are explained in the Extras chapter.

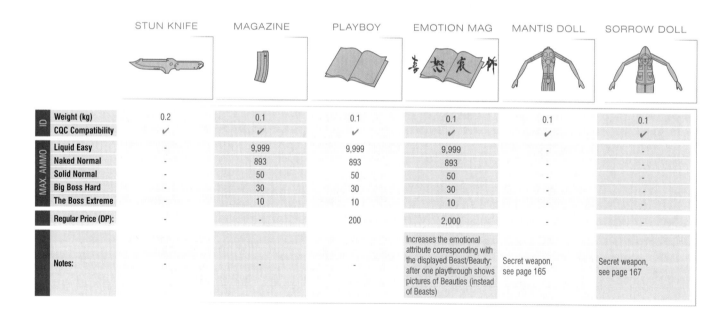

		STUN KNIFE	MAGAZINE	PLAYBOY	EMOTION MAG	MANTIS DOLL	SORROW DOLL
ID	Weight (kg)	0.2	0.1	0.1	0.1	0.1	0.1
	CQC Compatibility	✔	✔	✔	✔	✔	✔
MAX. AMMO	Liquid Easy	-	9,999	9,999	9,999	-	-
	Naked Normal	-	893	893	893	-	-
	Solid Normal	-	50	50	50	-	-
	Big Boss Hard	-	30	30	30	-	-
	The Boss Extreme	-	10	10	10	-	-
	Regular Price (DP):	-	-	200	2,000	-	-
	Notes:	-	-	-	Increases the emotional attribute corresponding with the displayed Beast/Beauty; after one playthrough shows pictures of Beauties (instead of Beasts)	Secret weapon, see page 165	Secret weapon, see page 167

WEAPON RANKINGS

Top 5 Heaviest Weapons

The primary benefit of this list is to show you which weapons you should avoid equipping at the same time to avoid exceeding the 70kg weight limit, which causes Snake's Stress rating to soar at an alarming rate. If you don't wish to see Snake looking even more haggard and decrepit than he already does, it might be advisable to avoid placing these in his backpack at the same time.

MISSILE LAUNCHER, **JAVELIN**, 22.3 KG

SNIPER RIFLE, **RAIL GUN**, 20.0 KG

MISSILE LAUNCHER, **FIM-92A**, 15.7 KG

SNIPER RIFLE, **M82A2**, 14.0 KG

MACHINE GUN, **MK. 46 MOD 1**, 10.2 KG

METAL GEAR SOLID 4
GUNS OF THE PATRIOTS TACTICAL ESPIONAGE ACTION

HOW TO PLAY
WALKTHROUGH
INVENTORY
METAL GEAR ONLINE
EXTRAS

WEAPONS
ITEMS
CAMOUFLAGE
DREBIN'S SHOP
WEAPON MODIFICATION
ENEMIES & ALLIES

Weapons: Longest Range & Highest Power

Power is only a relative attribute; with most weapon types, it decreases with range. Its main function is that it enables you to immediately judge how much inherent "bite" each firearm has in relation to its peers.

Though this doesn't apply to all weapons (a Javelin missile is just as explosive at 100 meters as it is at 200 meters), potential Power diminishes as the distance between Snake and the target increases. For example, an M4 Custom headshot to a PMC soldier wearing a helmet 250m in the distance is much less likely to result in an instant kill than a shot from several meters away.

As a general rule, damage inflicted with Handguns (with the exception of the Mk. 2) and, to a slightly lesser degree, submachine guns, is most affected by range. Both are therefore poor choices against targets that you even remotely have to squint at. Conversely, sniper rifles and Missile/Grenade Launchers maintain their maximum level of damage over much longer distances.

TOP 20 MOST POWERFUL

MISSILE LAUNCHER, **JAVELIN**, PW* 5,000

GRENADE LAUNCHER, **XM25**, PW* 2,000

SNIPER RIFLE, **RAIL GUN**, PW* 5,000

GRENADE LAUNCHER, **MGL-140**, PW* 2,000

STUN GUN, **SOLAR GUN**, PW* 5,000

EXPLOSIVE, **GRENADE**, PW* 2,000

EXPLOSIVE, **SLEEP GAS MINE**, PW* 5,000

EXPLOSIVE, **STUN GRENADE**, PW* 2,000

EXPLOSIVE, **SLEEP GAS SATCHEL**, PW* 5,000

EXPLOSIVE, **CLAYMORE**, PW* 2,000

ROCKET LAUNCHER, **RPG-7**, PW* 3,500

HAND RIFLE, **THOR .45-70**, PW* 1,500

MISSILE LAUNCHER, **FIM-92A**, PW* 3,000

EXPLOSIVE, **WHITE PHOSPHORUS GRENADE**, PW* 1,500

EXPLOSIVE, **C4**, PW* 3,000

SHOTGUN, **M870 CUSTOM**, PW* 1,300

SNIPER RIFLE, **M82A2**, PW* 2,500

SHOTGUN, **SAIGA-12**, PW* 1,250

ROCKET LAUNCHER, **M72A3**, PW* 2,450

SHOTGUN, **TWIN BARREL**, PW* 1,250

TOP 15 LONGEST RANGE

MISSILE LAUNCHER, **FIM-92A**, 500 m

SNIPER RIFLE, **SVD**, 280 m

MISSILE LAUNCHER, **JAVELIN**, 400 m

MACHINE GUN, **PKM**, 265 m

SNIPER RIFLE, **DSR-1**, 300 m

MACHINE GUN, **M60E4**, 260 m

SNIPER RIFLE, **MOSIN-NAGANT**, 300 m

MACHINE GUN, **HK21E**, 250 m

SNIPER RIFLE, **M82A2**, 300 m

ROCKET LAUNCHER, **RPG-7**, 250 m

SNIPER RIFLE, **RAIL GUN**, 300 m

ASSAULT RIFLE, **G3A3**, 250 m

GRENADE LAUNCHER, **XM25**, 300 m

MACHINE GUN, **MK. 46 MOD 1**, 250 m

GRENADE LAUNCHER, **MGL-140**, 300 m

Top 6 weapons with the best Capacity

Weapons with high magazine capacity give you much more bang for your reloading buck, enabling you to do more damage before there's a need to duck behind cover to replace the magazine. These weapons are often good choices when you face multiple opponents, or during boss fights.

MACHINE GUN, **M60E4**, CAP* 200

MACHINE GUN, **MK. 46 MOD 1**, CAP* 100

MACHINE GUN, **PKM**, CAP* 100

SUBMACHINE GUN, **BIZON**, CAP* 64

MACHINE GUN, **HK21E**, CAP* 100

SUBMACHINE GUN, **P90**, CAP* 50

* CAP = Capacity

Best Attributes Ratings

These tables provide an at-a-glance guide to which weapons perform best in each of the six main attribute categories.

Damage (DMG): The higher the rating, the more damage the weapon will deal to a target. This does not apply to non-lethal weapons.

Shock (SHK): Refers to a weapon's force of impact. The higher the value, the less likely the target is to be able to return fire immediately.

Penetration (PNT): Reflects the weapon's ability to pierce body armor on humans and armor on mechanical targets.

Stability (STB): With high STB ratings, the accuracy of Snake's aim is less affected by a low Psyche gauge.

Reload (RLD): The higher the rating, the quicker a weapon can be reloaded. If you cross reference the "Best STB" and "Best RLD" tables, you will see that Pistols offer the most impressive ratings in both attributes, making them good choices if you're looking for accuracy and efficiency at close range.

Lock (LKD): This parameter only applies when Auto Aim is enabled and active. High ratings indicate that a weapon can lock onto a target over greater distances.

BEST SHK RATING

DESCRIPTION	NAME	SHK
		E D C B A S
EXPLOSIVE	C4	
EXPLOSIVE	GRENADE	
EXPLOSIVE	STUN GRENADE	
EXPLOSIVE	CLAYMORE	
EXPLOSIVE	WHITE PHOSPHORUS GRENADE	
SNIPER RIFLE	RAIL GUN	
SNIPER RIFLE	M82A2	
SHOTGUN	SAIGA-12	
SHOTGUN	M870 CUSTOM	
SHOTGUN	TWIN BARREL	
HAND RIFLE	THOR .45-70	
GRENADE LAUNCHER	XM25	
GRENADE LAUNCHER	MGL-140	

BEST DMG RATING

DESCRIPTION	NAME	DMG
		E D C B A S
EXPLOSIVE	C4	
ROCKET LAUNCHER	RPG-7	
SNIPER RIFLE	RAIL GUN	
SNIPER RIFLE	M82A2	
MISSILE LAUNCHER	JAVELIN	
MISSILE LAUNCHER	FIM-92A	

122

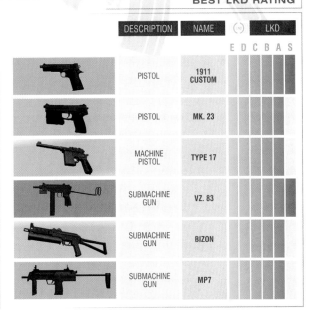

BEST SHK RATING

DESCRIPTION	NAME	SHK					
		E	D	C	B	A	S
MISSILE LAUNCHER	JAVELIN						
MISSILE LAUNCHER	FIM-92A						
ROCKET LAUNCHER	RPG-7						
ROCKET LAUNCHER	M72A3						

BEST PNT RATING

DESCRIPTION	NAME	PNT					
		E	D	C	B	A	S
SNIPER RIFLE	RAIL GUN						
SNIPER RIFLE	M82A2						
SNIPER RIFLE	SVD						
SNIPER RIFLE	VSS						
SNIPER RIFLE	DSR-1						
SNIPER RIFLE	MOSIN-NAGANT						
HAND RIFLE	THOR .45-70						

BEST STB RATING

DESCRIPTION	NAME	STB					
		E	D	C	B	A	S
PISTOL	MK. 2 PISTOL						
PISTOL	RACE GUN						
PISTOL	PMM						
PISTOL	1911 CUSTOM						
PISTOL	PSS						
SUBMACHINE GUN	MP7						

BEST RLD RATING

DESCRIPTION	NAME	RLD					
		E	D	C	B	A	S
MACHINE PISTOL	G18C						
PISTOL	FIVE SEVEN						
PISTOL	RACE GUN						
PISTOL	MK. 23						
PISTOL	PMM						
PISTOL	GSR						
PISTOL	DESERT EAGLE (LONG BARREL)						
PISTOL	DESERT EAGLE						
PISTOL	1911 CUSTOM						
PISTOL	OPERATOR						
PISTOL	PSS						

BEST LKD RATING

DESCRIPTION	NAME	LKD					
		E	D	C	B	A	S
PISTOL	1911 CUSTOM						
PISTOL	MK. 23						
MACHINE PISTOL	TYPE 17						
SUBMACHINE GUN	VZ. 83						
SUBMACHINE GUN	BIZON						
SUBMACHINE GUN	MP7						

All-Round Weapons

The best weapon for a given situation is often one that excels in several different categories. Which "all-rounder" is best for you will very much depend on the situation at hand, not to mention your personal preferences and chosen goals. The purpose of this table is simply to offer you a selection of some of the most reliable weapons in each category.

DESERT EAGLE (LONG BARREL)

PISTOL		
Weight (kg)		2.1
Range (m)		125
Power		710
CQC Compatibility		✔
Ammo Type		.50 AE
Magazine Capacity		7

E D C B A S
DMG
SHK
PNT
STB
RLD
LKD

M60E4

MACHINE GUN		
Weight (kg)		5.8
Range (m)		260
Power		550
CQC Compatibility		✔
Ammo Type		7.62 x 51 mm
Magazine Capacity		200

E D C B A S
DMG
SHK
PNT
STB
RLD
LKD

P90

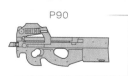

SUBMACHINE GUN		
Weight (kg)		3.2
Range (m)		135
Power		300
CQC Compatibility		✔
Ammo Type		5.7 x 28 mm
Magazine Capacity		50

E D C B A S
DMG
SHK
PNT
STB
RLD
LKD

THOR .45-70

HAND RIFLE		
Weight (kg)		2.3
Range (m)		150
Power		1,500
CQC Compatibility		✔
Ammo Type		.45-70
Magazine Capacity		1

E D C B A S
DMG
SHK
PNT
STB
RLD
LKD

SAIGA-12

SHOTGUN		
Weight (kg)		3.8
Range (m)		50
Power		1,250
CQC Compatibility		✔
Ammo Type		12 Ga. (00 Buck)
Magazine Capacity		8

E D C B A S
DMG
SHK
PNT
STB
RLD
LKD

M82A2

SNIPER RIFLE		
Weight (kg)		14.0
Range (m)		300
Power		2,500
CQC Compatibility		✘
Ammo Type		.50 BMR
Magazine Capacity		10

E D C B A S
DMG
SHK
PNT
STB
RLD
LKD

RAIL GUN

SNIPER RIFLE		
Weight (kg)		20.0
Range (m)		300
Power		5,000
CQC Compatibility		✘
Ammo Type		Rail Gun Ammo
Magazine Capacity		40

E D C B A S
DMG
SHK
PNT
STB
RLD
LKD

M72A3

ROCKET LAUNCHER		
Weight (kg)		2.5
Range (m)		200
Power		2,450
CQC Compatibility		✘
Ammo Type		M72A3
Magazine Capacity		1

E D C B A S
DMG
SHK
PNT
STB
RLD
LKD

ITEMS

RECOVERY ITEMS

The following table presents all the various recovery items available in the game – that is, anything that Snake can carry and use to recover Life or Psyche.

The "Use" column shows you whether an item is "Consumable" (one unit disappears when it is used), or "Permanent" (it remains active while equipped in the items window). Some objects, such as Rations and Noodles, will be used automatically when Snake's Life gauge reaches zero if they are equipped. This is very handy during boss battles where the risk of sudden death is much higher.

The "KG" column is self-explanatory, and really shouldn't be much of an issue – most items are very light, and you need to make an active effort to overload Snake. As a general rule, recovery items do not require an external power source.

The "Effect on Life" and "Effect on Psyche/Stress" columns detail the impact that items have on, amazingly enough, Snake's Life, Psyche and Stress.

The difficulty setting columns at the end of the table show the maximum number of each item that can be found in the game depending on the chosen game mode. As you can see, on Liquid Easy the potential number is practically boundless. With The Boss Extreme, though, you need to make every last oh-so-finite resource count.

Muña is an unusual herb that you can only find in South America, and which slightly increases Psyche restoration speed when equipped. It's permanent, so there's no need to worry about using it all up. The Syringe is another interesting item; it can be used to restore Psyche, but has unpleasant side-effects which you really should take into consideration. Turn to page 169 to learn more.

	USE	KG*	EFFECT ON LIFE	EFFECT ON PSYCHE/STRESS	LE*	NN*	SN*	BBH*	TBE*
CIGS	Permanent	0.1	Slightly reduces Life when equipped	Slightly restores Psyche when equipped.	-	-	-	-	-
MUÑA	Permanent	0.1	-	Slightly increases Psyche restoration speed when equipped.	-	-	-	-	-
RATION	Consumable	0.3	Restores 75% Life	Restores ~5% Psyche.	9,999	15	10	5	3
NOODLES	Consumable	0.1	Restores 100% Life	Restores 25/50% Psyche (in cold/hot environments respectively).	9,999	15	10	5	3
REGAIN	Consumable	0.1	Restores 100% Life	Restores 25/50% Psyche (in hot/cold environments respectively).	9,999	15	10	5	3
PENTAZEMIN	Consumable	0.1	-	Prevents hands from trembling during sniping/aiming.	9,999	15	10	5	3
COMPRESS	Consumable	0.1	-	Temporarily increases Psyche restoration speed.	9,999	15	10	5	3
SYRINGE	Consumable	0.2	-	Restores depleted Psyche in one burst; abuse will dilute effectiveness and lead to unpleasant side-effects, so use sparingly; see page 169 to learn more.	-	-	-	-	-

KG = Weight (kg), LE = Liquid Easy, NN* = Naked Normal, SN* = Solid Normal, BBH* = Big Boss Hard, TBE* = The Boss Extreme

	USE	KG*	IMPACT ON BATTERY	EFFECT ON PSYCHE/STRESS
IPOD®	Permanent	0.1	✗	Use to listen to music files that can be found throughout the game. Some songs can have beneficial effects. Secret item, see page 174.
SOLID EYE	Permanent	0.1	✗	Goggle that enables the Baseline Map radar function; provides basic details about enemies and "friendlies". Has Night Vision and Binoculars modes.
CAMERA	Permanent	0.7	✓	Use to take photographs that are displayed in the Photo Album. Secret item, see page 168.
METAL GEAR MK. II/III	Permanent	0.1	✓	Remote mobile terminal that can be manually controlled to collect items, stun opponents, and explore environments.
CARDBOARD BOX	Permanent	0.6	✓	A blast from the past: equip it and select it to hide from the enemy.
DRUM CAN	Permanent	9.0	✗	The deluxe version of the cardboard box: an oil can big enough for Snake to hide in. You can move when inside the drum, in fact you can even execute a roll attack after which Snake will possibly vomit!
SIGNAL INTERCEPTOR	Permanent	0.5	✗	Use to eavesdrop on PMC radio conversations during one particular mission. See page 74.
SCAN PLUG	Consumable	0.3	✗	Portable scanner that shows the location of all enemies on a map when injected into an individual. Secret item, see page 168.
BANDANA	Permanent	0.1	✗	Gives Snake infinite ammunition when equipped; secret item, see page 168.
STEALTH	Permanent	2.5	✗	Makes Snake invisible; secret item, see page 168.

MISSION SUPPORT ITEMS

"Mission Support" items are gadgets and gizmos that you will find yourself using time and again throughout the game.

As you can tell from the "Use" column, the only "Consumable" item in this category is the Scan Plug. There are no stocks to worry about, but you do need to activate it manually while restraining a target in a CQC lock. All other Mission Support items remain permanently active when selected.

The "KG" column is only of direct relevance with the cumbersome Drum Can.

The items that are Battery-powered are marked in the "Impact on Battery" column. You can find Battery upgrades at the end of each Act, which increase the potential operational life of your gadgets; we reveal the location of these in the Walkthrough chapter. You can only have one of the featured objects in your inventory at any time, so there is no difficulty level information included in the table.

The "Effect" column gives a brief description of the main application of each item, as well as page references to the Extras chapter (warning: spoilers!) where applicable.

▪ CAMOUFLAGE

Is it really necessary at this point to stress that camouflage plays a vital part in *Metal Gear Solid 4*? Generally speaking, good use of camo and sound stealth strategies will offer greater rewards than direct aggression. In this section, we look beyond the standard automatic OctoCamo functionality, and examine the customizable options that you can play with.

COMMAND VESTS

Command Vests can be equipped via the Camouflage option of the pause menu. They have little impact on your Camo percentage, but the various colors allow you to match them with Snake's current outfit. Five vests are available from the start, and a further five are unlocked when you have played through the game at least once.

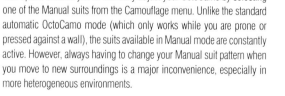

NAME: KHAKI
LOCATION / UNLOCKING CONDITION:
Available from the beginning

NAME: GREEN
LOCATION / UNLOCKING CONDITION:
Clear the game once

NAME: OLIVE DRAB
LOCATION / UNLOCKING CONDITION:
Available from the beginning

NAME: BLUE
LOCATION / UNLOCKING CONDITION:
Clear the game once

NAME: BLACK
LOCATION / UNLOCKING CONDITION:
Available from the beginning

NAME: RED
LOCATION / UNLOCKING CONDITION:
Clear the game once

NAME: GREY
LOCATION / UNLOCKING CONDITION:
Available from the beginning

NAME: ORANGE
LOCATION / UNLOCKING CONDITION:
Clear the game once

NAME: NAVY BLUE
LOCATION / UNLOCKING CONDITION:
Available from the beginning

NAME: TAN
LOCATION / UNLOCKING CONDITION:
Clear the game once

NAME: SNEAKING SUIT
LOCATION / UNLOCKING CONDITION:
Available from the beginning

OCTOCAMO MANUAL

This option enables you to manually adjust your OctoCamo by selecting one of the Manual suits from the Camouflage menu. Unlike the standard automatic OctoCamo mode (which only works while you are prone or pressed against a wall), the suits available in Manual mode are constantly active. However, always having to change your Manual suit pattern when you move to new surroundings is a major inconvenience, especially in more heterogeneous environments.

Though you have a very limited number of Manual patterns available at the start of the game, as you can see here, you can store new Manual patterns while the Automatic mode is active, then use them at a later date. As long as you're patient and don't mind spending plenty of time in the pause menu, registering unique patterns (especially the rare ones, like the "hand print" texture found in a secret South American location) can be a fun challenge.

NAME: OLIVE DRAB
LOCATION / UNLOCKING CONDITION:
Available from the beginning

NAME: TIGERSTRIPE
LOCATION / UNLOCKING CONDITION:
Available from the beginning

NAME: WOODLAND
LOCATION / UNLOCKING CONDITION:
Available from the beginning

NAME: 3-COLOR DESERT
LOCATION / UNLOCKING CONDITION:
Available from the beginning

NAME: MARPAT URBAN
LOCATION / UNLOCKING CONDITION:
Available from the beginning

NAME: CORPSE CAMO
LOCATION / UNLOCKING CONDITION:
Secret camo,
see page 162

FACECAMO

NAME: FACECAMO
LOCATION / UNLOCKING CONDITION:
South America (defeat Laughing Octopus)

NAME: LAUGHING BEAUTY
LOCATION / UNLOCKING CONDITION:
Defeat Laughing Octopus without killing her

NAME: OTACON
LOCATION / UNLOCKING CONDITION:
Hit Otacon with Metal Gear Mk.II during interactive Mission Briefing

NAME: YOUNG
LOCATION / UNLOCKING CONDITION:
Eastern Europe (level start)

NAME: RAGING BEAUTY
LOCATION / UNLOCKING CONDITION:
Defeat Raging Raven without killing her

NAME: RAIDEN A
LOCATION / UNLOCKING CONDITION:
Hit Sunny with Metal Gear Mk.II during interactive Mission Briefing

NAME: YOUNG WITH BANDANA
LOCATION / UNLOCKING CONDITION:
Eastern Europe (level start)

NAME: CRYING BEAUTY
LOCATION / UNLOCKING CONDITION:
Defeat Crying Wolf without killing her

NAME: RAIDEN B
LOCATION / UNLOCKING CONDITION:
Hit Naomi with Metal Gear Mk.II during interactive Mission Briefing

NAME: MGS1
LOCATION / UNLOCKING CONDITION:
Shadow Moses (level start)

NAME: SCREAMING BEAUTY
LOCATION / UNLOCKING CONDITION:
Defeat Screaming Mantis without killing her

NAME: DREBIN
LOCATION / UNLOCKING CONDITION:
Acquire 60+ weapons

FACECAMO

You obtain the FaceCamo after you fight Laughing Octopus during Act 2. This gadget can be equipped at the Camouflage menu, and typically improves Snake's Camo percentage by 10% to 15% when worn. However you can also have fun with collectible preset FaceCamo variants, using them to dramatically change Snake's facial appearance. If you've always felt that Otacon is the true hero, or that *MGS1* Snake has superior bone structure, use this option to enjoy your preferred visage – they even remain active for the majority of cutscenes.

NAME: CAMPBELL
LOCATION / UNLOCKING CONDITION:
Hit Campbell with Metal Gear Mk.II during interactive Mission Briefing

NAME: BIG BOSS
LOCATION / UNLOCKING CONDITION:
Obtain the Big Boss emblem, see page 157

COSTUMES

NAME: CIVILIAN DISGUISE
LOCATION / UNLOCKING CONDITION:
Eastern Europe (level start)

NAME: SUIT
LOCATION / UNLOCKING CONDITION:
Clear the game once

NAME:
MIDDLE EAST MILITIA DISGUISE
LOCATION / UNLOCKING CONDITION:
Middle East (Militia Safe House)

COSTUMES

The Costumes listed here enable Snake to disguise himself, and are purely optional – indeed, two of them are actually reasonably hard to find. Some can only be used in specific locales, while two are game completion rewards. The Walkthrough chapter has tips on the use of the militia and rebel outfits during Act 1 and Act 2 respectively.

NAME: ALTAIR
LOCATION / UNLOCKING CONDITION:
Obtain the Assassin emblem

NAME:
SOUTH AMERICAN REBEL DISGUISE
LOCATION / UNLOCKING CONDITION:
South America (Cove Valley Village)

DREBIN´S SHOP

You'll meet Drebin early in the game. He's a somewhat mysterious figure, who, along with his nappy-wearing, soda-drinking assistant, Little Gray, runs a black-market shop where you can pick up weapons, ammo, and other assorted items. The good news is that you don't actually have to wait for one of his showy-but-timely set-piece entrances to call upon his services – you can simply select his shop from the pause menu, and spend your Drebin Points straight away.

DREBIN'S SHOP

The basics of using the shop couldn't be simpler, and the following table is designed to follow the same layout as the shop, with the same classifications in use. We've included the "regular" price and discount price, with the latter only available on Wednesdays and Saturdays.

The following points are worth noting while browsing for goods:

- As soon as you have collected/bought/unlocked a new weapon, it will no longer be displayed or on sale in Drebin's Shop.

- In most instances, new ammunition types will become available as soon as you have collected/bought/unlocked the corresponding weapons.

- You usually won't find any items on sale at Drebin's Shop. The corresponding section exists, though, and this is because a few special or secret items can appear there if you meet the required conditions. Refer to the Extras chapter to learn more about these, but bear in mind that they are unavailable during your first playthrough.

DREBIN POINTS PRIMER

Drebin Points are your currency both for purchasing equipment from Drebin's Shop, and for "laundering" ID-coded weapons that you acquire. You can earn DP in three ways:

1: Collecting weapons from the battlefield. Once you have a firearm in your inventory, all subsequent weapons of this type are automatically sold to Drebin (though ammunition is added to Snake's supplies).

2: Destroying non-human assailants (this excludes vehicles that contain pilots or drivers).

3: Obtaining bonuses awarded for miscellaneous achievements. These are discussed in the Walkthrough chapter.

In practice, your main source of income will be to diligently explore each area in the game for valuable hidden objects, and meticulously scour busy battlefields for lucrative collectibles. You can also send out Metal Gear Mk. II to investigate areas where you don't want to venture yourself, using its stealth feature to avoid detection while picking up assorted items. In certain instances, it might even be worth using it to stun isolated enemies in order to steal their weapon, especially if it's a valuable one.

There are a few instances in the game where soldiers of different factions will continually respawn, no matter how many are killed. One example of this can be found in the Downtown area in Act 1, just before the entrance to Advent Palace. You can use such opportunities to disable as many opponents as possible, and then pick up equipment that they drop. However, before you rush off to perpetrate mass slaughter to fund your purchase of the Tanegashima, a warning: DP rewards drop *significantly* when you repeatedly collect weapons of similar types.

	NAME	REGULAR PRICE	REDUCED PRICE	FIRST AVAILABILITY
HANDGUNS	GSR	3,000	2,400	Middle East (end)
	Five Seven	6,000	4,800	South America (beginning)
	PMM	3,500	2,800	Middle East (end)
	PSS	5,000	4,000	Middle East (end)
	G18C	8,000	6,400	Eastern Europe (beginning)
	Desert Eagle	20,000	16,000	South America (beginning)
SUBMACHINE GUNS	P90	5,000	4,000	South America (beginning)
	M10	3,000	2,400	Middle East (end)
	MP7	3,500	2,800	Middle East (end)
	Bizon	7,000	5,600	South America (beginning)
	MP5SD2	15,000	12,000	-
RIFLES	Mk. 17	3,500	2,800	Middle East (end)
	G3A3	4,000	3,200	South America (beginning)
	FAL Carbine	4,500	3,600	Shadow Moses (beginning)
	AN94	5,000	4,000	Eastern Europe (beginning)
	Tanegashima	1,000,000	800,000	Middle East (end)
	M14 EBR	9,000	7,200	Middle East (end)
	DSR-1	20,000	16,000	Middle East (end)
	SVD	18,000	14,400	South America (beginning)
	Mosin-Nagant	60,000	48,000	Middle East (end)
	M82A2	200,000	160,000	South America (beginning)
OTHER FIREARMS	HK21E	6,000	4,800	South America (beginning)
	M60E4	10,000	8,000	South America (beginning)
	PKM	9,000	7,200	Eastern Europe (beginning)
	Mk. 46 Mod 1	9,000	7,200	Shadow Moses (beginning)
	Twin Barrel	25,000	20,000	Eastern Europe (beginning)
	M870 Custom	30,000	24,000	Middle East (end)
	Saiga-12	40,000	32,000	South America (beginning)
	XM25	80,000	64,000	South America (beginning)
	RPG-7	60,000	48,000	Middle East (end)
	M72A3	40,000	32,000	South America (beginning)
	Javelin	150,000	120,000	South America (beginning)
	FIM-92A	100,000	80,000	Eastern Europe (beginning)
EXPLOSIVES	Grenade	120	96	Middle East (end)
	Petro Bomb	100	80	Middle East (end)
	White Phosphorus Grenade	110	88	Middle East (end)
	Stun Grenade	120	96	Middle East (end)
	Smoke Grenade	100	80	Middle East (end)
	Smoke Grenade (Yellow)	-	-	Second playthrough onwards
	Smoke Grenade (Red)	-	-	Second playthrough onwards
	Smoke Grenade (Blue)	-	-	Second playthrough onwards
	Smoke Grenade (Green)	-	-	Second playthrough onwards
	Claymore	300	240	Middle East (end)
	Sleep Gas Mine	300	240	Middle East (end)
	C4	400	320	Middle East (end)
	Sleep Gas Satchel	400	320	Middle East (end)
ETC	Playboy	200	160	Middle East (end)
	Emotion Mag	2,000	1,600	South America (beginning)
BULLETS	Anest. (.22)	30	24	Middle East (end)
	Anest. (7.62 mm)	40	32	-
	9 x 23 mm	50	40	-
	.45-70	100	80	-
	.45 ACP	20	16	Middle East (end)
	.50 AE	30	24	-
	.50 BMR	150	120	-
	4.6 x 30 mm	10	8	-

METALGEARSOLID 4
GUNS OF THE PATRIOTS TACTICAL ESPIONAGE ACTION

HOW TO PLAY

WALKTHROUGH

▶ INVENTORY

METAL GEAR ONLINE

EXTRAS

WEAPONS

ITEMS

CAMOUFLAGE

▶ DREBIN'S SHOP

WEAPON MODIFICATION

ENEMIES & ALLIES

	NAME	REGULAR PRICE	REDUCED PRICE	FIRST AVAILABILITY
BULLETS	5.45 x 39 mm	20	16	-
	5.56 x 45 mm	15	12	Middle East (end)
	5.7 x 28 mm	30	24	-
	7.62 x 42 mm	30	24	-
	7.62 x 51 mm	30	24	-
	7.62 x 54R	40	32	-
	7.62 x 67 mm	50	40	Eastern Europe (beginning)
	9 x 18 mm	10	8	Eastern Europe (end)
	9 x 19 mm	25	20	-
	9 x 39 mm	40	32	-
	Rail Gun Ammo	200	160	Shadow Moses (end)
	Lead Ball	40	32	-
	12 Ga. (00 Buck)	50	40	-
	12 Ga. (Slug)	60	48	-
	12 Ga. (V.Ring)	50	40	-
	40 mm G. (GP30)	120	96	-
	40 mm (Grenade)	130	104	Shadow Moses (beginning)
	40 mm (WP Grenade)	120	96	Shadow Moses (beginning)
	40 mm (Stun Grenade)	130	104	Shadow Moses (beginning)
	40 mm (Smoke Grenade)	100	80	Shadow Moses (beginning)
	25 mm A.B.G.	150	120	-
	RPG-7 Ammo	250	200	-
	M72A3	200	160	-
	Javelin	350	280	-
	FIM-92A	300	240	-
CUSTOM PARTS	Masterkey	30,000	24,000	Middle East (end)
	GP30	30,000	24,000	Middle East (end)
	XM320	60,000	48,000	Middle East (end)
	Suppressor (OP)	200	160	Middle East (end)
	Suppressor (Mk. 23)	200	160	-
	Suppressor (1911)	200	160	-
	Suppressor (P90)	200	160	-
	Suppressor (M10)	200	160	-
	Suppressor (M4)	200	160	Middle East (end)
	Suppressor (M14)	200	160	-
	Dot Sight	20,000	16,000	Middle East (end)
	Scope	35,000	28,000	Middle East (end)
	Laser Sight	30,000	24,000	Middle East (end)
	Flash Light (H.G.)	3,000	2,400	Middle East (end)
	Flash Light (L.G.)	7,000	5,600	Middle East (end)
	Fore Grip A	2,500	2,000	Middle East (end)
	Fore Grip B	2,500	2,000	Middle East (end)
ITEMS	Scan Plug	-	-	After playing MGO more than 10 hours
	Bandana	-	-	Second playthrough onwards
	Stealth	-	-	Second playthrough onwards

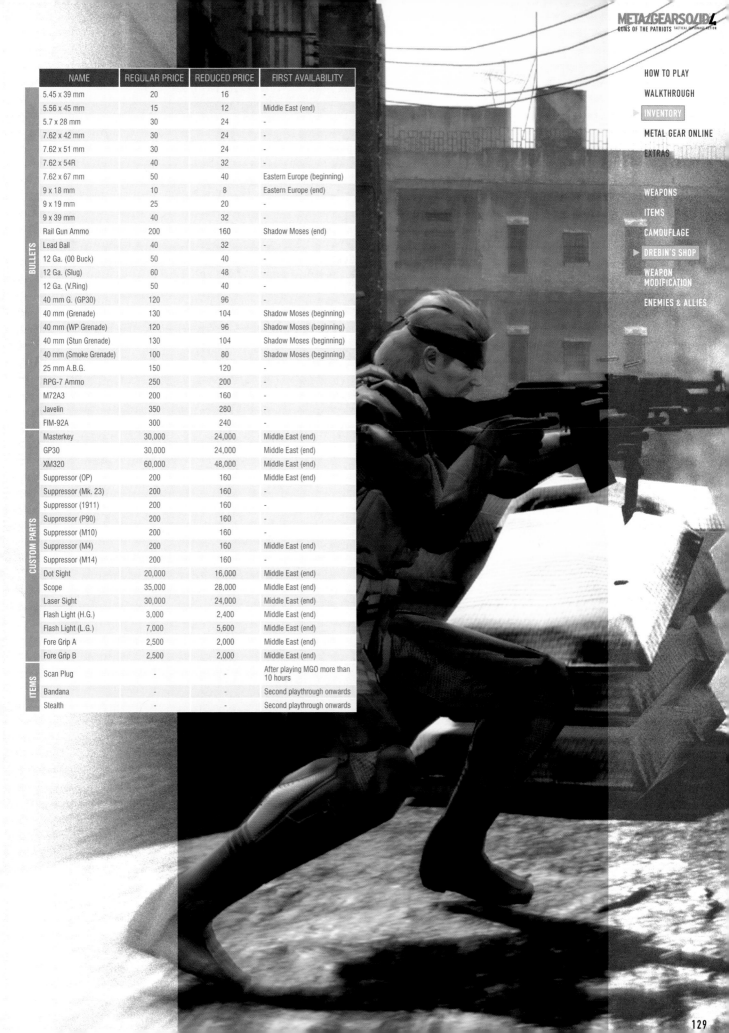

WEAPON MODIFICATION GUIDE

In addition to its stunningly wide range of armaments, *MGS4* also has a large number of upgrades and enhancements that you can apply to specific weapons.

WEAPON MODIFICATIONS

Weapon modifications are a way to upgrade and enhance your basic weapons. They can be purchased using Drebin Points, found in hidden locations, or dropped by soldiers.

	NAME	DESCRIPTION	PRICE (DP)
	SUPPRESSOR	Silences the firing noise of a weapon. Though cheap, these are specific to the weapons that support them – you can't use an M4 Custom Suppressor on a P90, for example. Note that Suppressors wear out after a certain number of shots.	200
	SCOPE	Used to zoom in on targets, thereby increasing your accuracy over long distances.	35,000
	DOT SIGHT	A targeting sight that improves on the standard iron sights. Only visible in FPS Mode.	20,000
	LASER SIGHT	A thin laser beam that projects a red dot onto your target, boosting Auto Aim accuracy for relevant weapons. Makes aiming from the third-person viewpoint much easier.	30,000
	FLASHLIGHT	Use this to temporarily blind enemy soldiers at close range before you shoot them. Sends your Camo rating plummeting to -100%.	3,000 (H.G.) 7,000 (L.G.)
	FORE GRIP A & B	Enhance stability, which is good for improving aiming precision and for reducing recoil. These increase accuracy when firing in the third-person viewpoint. There are two different types of Fore Grip, but both are functionally identical.	3,000
	MASTERKEY	An under-barrel shotgun that can be attached to the M4 Custom. A very potent combination if you want to tote both a shotgun and a rifle at the same time. Press R2 to fire it while aiming.	30,000
	GRENADE LAUNCHERS	Similar to the Masterkey, these two attachments fit under the barrel of compatible rifles. Press R2 to fire them while aiming.	30,000 (GP30) 60,000 (XM320)

CUSTOMIZATION COMPATIBILITY

The following table reveals the custom parts that you can add to each weapon type. However, note that you can only have one modification active in each category. With the Top Mount slot, for example, you can have either a Dot Sight or a Scope, but not both at the same time.

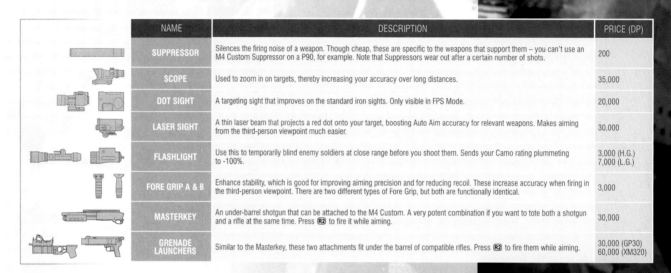

	HANDGUNS						SUBMACHINE GUNS			RIFLES						OTHER FIREARMS			
	OPERATOR	GSR	FIVE SEVEN	G18C	MK. 23	1911 CUSTOM	P90	M10	MP7	AK 102	M4 CUSTOM	MK.17	AN94	XM8	M14EBR	M60E4	K.46 MOD 1	M870 CUSTOM	MGL-140
SUPPRESSOR	▲				▲	▲	●	●			●				●				
SCOPE										▲	▲	▲				▲	▲	▲	
DOT SIGHT										▲	▲	▲				▲	▲	▲	
LASER SIGHT									◀		◀	◀				◀	◀	◀	
FLASH LIGHT (H.G.)	▼	▼	▼	▼															
FLASH LIGHT (L.G.)									▶		▶	▶				▶	▶	▶	▶
FORE GRIP A & B											▼	▼				▼	▼		▼
MASTERKEY											▼								
GRENADE LAUNCHER (GP30)										▼			▼						
GRENADE LAUNCHER (XM320)											▼			▼					

▲ = Top Mount   ● = Muzzle Mount   ▼ = Bottom Mount   ◀ = Left Mount   ▶ = Right Mount

ENEMIES & ALLIES

The following table presents a detailed list of all NPCs you can expect to encounter. It is divided horizontally according to the different types of NPCs. Because of how the game is set up, certain alliances and allegiances can be fluid. It's possible to fight on the side of the Rebel forces, or against them; it's up to you.

The final column reveals the weak points for each enemy type. Obviously, you can find more information and strategies to defeat your opponents – especially bosses – on the corresponding pages of the Walkthrough chapter.

	NAME	WEAK POINT(S)
REBELS	Middle East Rebels	Head
	South America Rebels	Head
	Paradise Lost Army	Head
PMCS	Haven Troopers	Head
	Praying Mantis (Middle East)	Head
	Pieuvre Armement (South America)	Head
	Powered Suit (South America)	Head
	Raven Sword (Eastern Europe)	Head
UNMANNED	Gekko	Legs, Head
	Dwarf Gekko	Head
METAL GEARS	Metal Gear REX	-
	Metal Gear RAY	-
BOSSES	Crying Wolf	Head
	Screaming Mantis	Dolls
	Laughing Octopus	Head
	Raging Raven	Head
	Vamp	CQC (Syringe)
	Liquid	-

METAL GEAR ONLINE

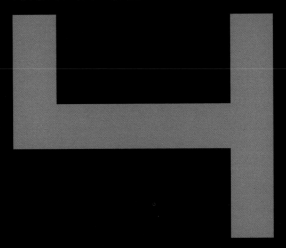

Metal Gear Online is not *Metal Gear Solid 4*'s multiplayer component: it's actually a completely separate game in its own right, with enormous potential for future expansion. This chapter is designed as a primer for readers who are using the *MGO* client packaged with *MGS4* for the first time, offering explanations and tips to help players find their feet – and then stay on them for as long as possible…

GETTING STARTED

This short section is intended to help you understand the structure and contents of the most important menus in *MGO*. It will lead you smoothly from the title screen to the beginning of your first match. If you're a veteran of other online games or simply confident in your ability to find your way on your own, you can skip directly to the next section on page 136.

01

02

START MENU

Once you log in using your Game ID and password, you are taken to the Start Menu (Fig. 1).

The Start Menu has several useful entries, all of which are quite self-explanatory and accompanied by handy help messages. Select the first one, Start Game, when you're ready to create your online identity.

If this is your first time at the Character Select screen, you have to create the soldier that you will use in the game. You'll need to choose a name, appearance, voice and accessories (Fig. 2). Note that clothing is purely cosmetic, and has no effect on gameplay. Most of these parameters (bar character name, face, and voice, which are final once you register them) can later be changed via the Personal Data screen.

You can also assign Skills to your character, with each level costing 1 point. The level of each Skill is shown using a simple bar display (one block per level, up to a maximum of three). Essentially the higher the level, the more effective the Skill. For example, the Runner Skill will make you move faster at level 3 than it will at level 1. You have 4 skill points to spend in total.

Until you gain experience on the battlefield, the maximum Skill level you can access in each discipline is level 1. As a successful sniper, you will eventually gain the option of increasing your Sniper Rifle+ Skill by an additional level, and later to 3; however, your maximum Skill budget is still 4, so you'll need to sacrifice other aptitudes to make the upgrade. Some players will eventually opt for specialization, while others will prefer to remain as all-rounders; the choice, naturally, is yours to make. There's no "right" or "wrong" way to spend Skill points, but it goes without saying that you should favor those that you're likely to regularly use in combat.

SKILL	DESCRIPTION
Handgun+	Skill wielding handguns. Reduces recoil and reload time.
SMG+	Skill wielding submachine guns. Reduces recoil and reload time.
Assault Rifle+	Skill wielding assault rifles. Reduces recoil and reload time.
Shotgun+	Skill wielding shotguns. Reduces recoil and reload time, and makes pump action faster.
Sniper Rifle+	Skill wielding sniper rifles. Reduces recoil and reload time, and makes bolt action faster.
Hawkeye	Increases the zoom rate when aiming in FPS mode (but not when using a scope).
Surveyor	Extends the maximum lock-on distance (which is the same as increasing the LKD rating in the single-player game).
Quarterback	Enables you to throw weapons farther.
Trickster	Enables you to set up traps more quickly.
CQC+	Allows you to restrain targets and use advanced CQC, and increases knockout damage.
Blades+	Allows you to move while attacking with a knife, and makes knife attacks faster.
Runner	Increases your movement speed.
Monomania	Displays enemies you've attacked (data can be shared through SOP). Display time is improved with levels.
Sixth Sense	Displays nearby traps (data can be shared through SOP). Range increases with levels.
Narc	Displays attacking enemies when they target you and damage is sustained (data can be shared through SOP). Display time is improved with levels.
Scanner	Press ⓐ while restraining an enemy to display link info (data can be shared through SOP). Scanning time is improved with levels. Requires CQC+ Skill, and the Scanning Plug item.

As a general rule, you should try to choose your Skills to complement those of your teammates, so that your force becomes a cohesive unit with a balanced pool of abilities at its disposal. Note that you can change the Skills assigned to your character from the Briefing Menu before each game.

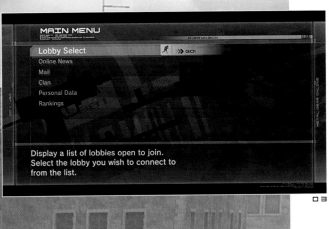

Display a list of lobbies open to join.
Select the lobby you wish to connect to
from the list.

03

THE MAIN MENU

After you have selected the character you want to use, you will arrive at the Main Menu, your central hub (Fig. 3). This menu features the following options:

Lobby Select	Gives you access to three types of Lobby. More on this below.
Online News	Check the latest news available.
Mail	Use this to send and receive mail. You can store up to 16 messages in your Inbox, and up to 5 emails in your Sent folder.
Clan	A Clan is a group of players who join together and play as a team. You can use the Clan screen to join a Clan or form your own, and then to keep in touch with all members. If you check the Clan Roster, you can see which Lobbies your fellow Clan members are playing in. The Clan leader can additionally edit the Clan emblem, which is an easy way of identifying Clan-mates during play.
Personal Data	Allows you to change a series of personal settings.
Rankings	Character and Clan rankings are listed here. Rankings are divided up according to rules, and host ratings.

■ Lobby Select

You have access to three different types of Lobby (Fig. 4): Automatching, Free Battle, and Training.

Automatching – Select this Lobby if you want to simply plunge straight into the action. This will automatically create a game with other characters that are (as a general rule) at a similar level to you. Once a suitable group of players has been located, you will either join a new match or arrive in the middle of a battle that is already underway. Automatching is the best option if you're a complete newcomer to *MGO*, or still feel as if you're trundling on training wheels from indignity to disaster. Games in this Lobby influence your level, score, record and Skills, but not your grade.

Free Battle – In this Lobby, you can either join a game that is already up and running, or create a new one that you will host, specifying your own rules, maps and settings (including the number of rounds). You can register up to 15 stages in a game.

Training – In Solo Training, you use dummies and targets to hone your skills. To learn all about the basics of gameplay in the *Metal Gear Online* world, it's best to select Novice Training. Join Combat Training allows you to receive combat training from veteran players called Instructors. In Combat Training, you train other players as an Instructor. What you do in the Training Lobby has no effect on your level, score, record or Skills.

Automatically create a game with characters
close to your level.

More Details

04

■ Personal Data

This entry lets you change many personal parameters (Fig. 5).

Skill Settings	Enables you to change the Skills you chose when creating your character.
Appearance Setting	Your choices here only affect your character's appearance, and have no impact on performance.
Personal Stats	Details of your past battles, sorted by game modes. This includes how many times (and how) you brought down enemies, and how they got the better of you. You'll also find various stats regarding your play time, as well as noteworthy feats you may have accomplished.
Friend List	Edit your Friend List, send mail or move to a game where a friend is playing. You can have up to 32 friends in your list.
Block List	You can block up to 32 players you don't want to interact with.
Match History	View a list of characters you have faced online.
Player Search	Search for logged-in players matching the name you enter.
Gameplay Options	Adjust a series of self-explanatory options (similar to those in the solo game), and prepare keyboard macros or preset messages.
Photo Album	View the pictures you've taken with the Camera item.

THE BRIEFING MENU

This is the menu that appears prior to every game (Fig. 6). You can use it for several purposes – among other things, to consult the map (though you will probably find the maps used in this guide more handy), to change teams if you need to balance the distribution of players, or to modify your Skills to best suit the game mode. Other entries in this menu are straightforward and speak for themselves.

Press ⊚ to display the Chat Log Screen, and (START) to confirm you're ready.

■ MULTIPLAYER BASICS

For some players, *Metal Gear Online* will be their first ever experience of multiplayer gaming. However, even battle-scarred veterans of online warfare will find that the world of *MGO* is unique. The following section is designed to get you up and running with a minimum of fuss.

CONTROLS

Generally speaking, controls in *Metal Gear Online* are the same as in those in *MGS4*. If you've already played *MGS4* for a while prior to making your debut in *MGO* (and really, you should), the process of moving your character around will feel instinctively comfortable.

Note that you can practice the basics of controlling a character via the Novice Training option in the Training Lobby. You can also refer to the How to Play chapter of this guide (see page 8).

There are very few commands that are specific to *MGO*. Essentially, pressing (SELECT) once opens the Preset Messages window (Fig. 1), and pressing it a second time brings up the Chat menu. With both of these, make your selections with ⊙. You can also adjust the map with (R3).

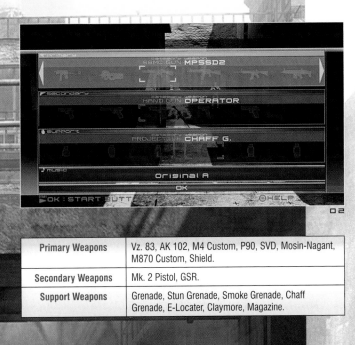

Primary Weapons	Vz. 83, AK 102, M4 Custom, P90, SVD, Mosin-Nagant, M870 Custom, Shield.
Secondary Weapons	Mk. 2 Pistol, GSR.
Support Weapons	Grenade, Stun Grenade, Smoke Grenade, Chaff Grenade, E-Locater, Claymore, Magazine.

DEFAULT EQUIPMENT

At the beginning of each game, you are offered the chance to choose your equipment. Most of the weapons available also exist in *MGS4*, and can therefore be found in this guide's Inventory chapter. Each firearm has special attributes and applications, so you really need to make your selection in accordance with the game mode you're about to play (different objectives require different equipment), your personal preferences, and whether or not you have teammates. In any case, try to adopt a balanced configuration that will enable you to adapt your strategies as new situations arise.

You must choose one weapon per category (the table shows a representative selection of the weapons you will usually have access to). This preset list corresponds to the default weapons available (Fig. 2). Extra weapons can be acquired only if the "Drebin Points Enabled" option has been activated.

The items you have by default include the Cardboard Box, Binos (which you use like the Solid Eye's Binos mode), and the Camera. These work exactly as they do in *MGS4*. More can be acquired either by finding them on the battlefield (they are then only available for the duration of the corresponding stage), or by fulfilling certain special conditions.

THE SOP SYSTEM

Just like in *MGS4*, the SOP System is a network of nanomachines inside the bodies of participating soldiers. This links teammates together and enables them to share information.

To benefit from this system, you must first activate it. To do so, face a teammate at close range and press △. If you are standing, you will salute (Fig. 3); in other stances, you will point with your finger. When your teammate's body flashes your team color, it means the link is complete. If the linked teammate is also in direct communication with other squad members, you will automatically join this network. However, the SOP System remains active for only as long as you live: if you die and respawn, you start in an unlinked state.

You can see linked teammates as outlines even when there are obstacles in the way, which enables you to coordinate and participate in sophisticated tactical strikes on enemy positions — but, naturally, this also applies to your opponents. The range of data provided depends on your stance and the current conditions, but you may be able to see not only their position, but also their status and which direction their radio messages arrive from. This information is accompanied by the following identifying icons:

⊙	Preset Message sent	♥	Reading a magazine
★	Knocked out	☠	Dead
z	Sleeping	!	In combat

With certain Skill settings, when a teammate deals damage to an opponent or is injured by an enemy or trap, the corresponding enemy or trap will appear temporarily on linked teammates' screens.

The SOP System's main function is to provide information on teammates. However it can also be used to reveal data about your enemies. This is only possible if you have the required Skills, and possibly a specific item, as shown in the following table.

CONDITION REQUIRED	EFFECT
Monomania Skill	Displays enemies you've attacked to all linked teammates.
Sixth Sense Skill	Displays nearby traps to all linked teammates.
Narc Skill	Displays the location of enemies targeting or damaging your soldier to all linked teammates.
CQC+ Skill Scanner Skill Scanning Plug item	Restrain an enemy through CQC (Fig. 4), then press ⓐ to inject the Scanning Plug. This will transmit the outlines of all enemies linked to the one you captured to teammates in your current network.

Needless to say, knowing the position of enemy forces will give you and your team a significant advantage in any game.

MULTIPLAYER DIFFERENCES

Overall, you play *MGO* exactly as you play *MGS4*. The controls are identical, the equipment is used in the same way, and even the onscreen display is broadly similar in both games. This means that all of the time you spend having fun in the single-player adventure is experience you build for the multiplayer game.

There are, however, a few features that make *MGO* very distinct, as you generally don't have access to certain gadgets and tools that are staples of *MGS4*. The most notable difference is that, as a rule, you do not have the OctoCamo suit to help you blend in with environments. The lack of OctoCamo means that it's generally more difficult to hide; naturally, intelligent use of cover is a must. (The game modes where you play as Snake are an obvious exception – he does, of course, get to use OctoCamo.)

OctoCamo isn't the only thing you're deprived of in *MGO*: the same applies for the Threat Ring and Solid Eye (unless you're playing as Snake in a Sneaking Mission). On the other hand, a radar is constantly displayed in the top-right corner of the screen, giving you a reliable overview of objectives and allies around you (but not enemies). More generally, the equipment at your disposal is considerably limited compared to the incredible resources offered by *MGS4*. The fact that you have no recovery items whatsoever, and that you cannot recuperate by crouching or lying down, means that you cannot refill your Life and Psyche gauges – straying into the line of fire really matters. Basically, you have three weapons per stage, and bar a few support items such as the Binos, this is pretty much all you have to work with.

Another difference from single-player *MGS4* is that the names and Life gauges of allies are displayed above their heads at all times, but enemy names and Life gauges are only shown when you point a weapon at them. If there's no writing over the head of someone approaching you, shoot first and ask questions later!

You don't have Drebin's Shop in *MGO*, but certain game types offer the facility to buy more weapons and upgrades with the Drebin Points that you earn during the match. You also get a default sum of DP to start with. The more people you defeat and bases or targets you capture, the greater the sum of points you earn to spend the next time you are killed, or when a new round starts if you manage to survive until the end.

You cannot collect ammo or weapons anywhere in the online game. Once your clip is empty, that's it: you must switch to your secondary weapon, the default Stun Knife, or resort to CQC if you have the corresponding (and requisite) CQC+ Skill.

Skills are unique to *MGO*, and your chosen aptitudes – as well as those of your teammates – have a massive bearing on the tactics available to you individually and as a group. Other special features include the E-Locater (a grenade that, once it explodes, renders all enemies visible within a set range – Fig. 5), and the Shield (a primary "weapon" that you can use to protect yourself against gunshots and explosions – ready it with L1, and press R1 to strike with it).

MGO has a friendly-fire lock that kicks in if you start firing on a teammate. It doesn't work with CQC, but it's a handy feature that helps to avoid accidental betrayals.

Finally, the catapult is a fantastic device that enables you to fly through the air and reach rooftops (Fig. 6). It's extremely fun to use, is a great way to reach a new location quickly, and has obvious strategic value, but be warned: enemy snipers will often target it specifically, as soldiers are completely vulnerable in the moments before they are launched through the air.

MULTIPLAYER TIPS

GENERAL TIPS

Let's start with a fundamental basic. On the subject of reloading, the following wisdom always applies: *reload or die*. We really can't overstate how important it is to enter battles with a full clip. When choosing weapons, reload times and ammo capacity are important considerations.

Don't neglect to use your secondary weapon. If you hear the dreaded "dead man's click" during a firefight, it's sometimes better to switch to your pistol to finish a weakened opponent off.

There is no such thing as "kill stealing" in free-for-all games, despite the protestations of certain opponents – it's every man and woman for themselves. In squad-based matches (particular those that are objective-oriented), the good of the team comes first. Essentially, when you get the chance to put an opponent down, don't pause for a second.

In *MGS4*, crawling is often the safest way to go. In *MGO*, the gameplay is too fast-paced for this approach, especially as you (usually) do not have OctoCamo to mask your movements. In most situations, crouch-walking is best. As ever, running should be avoided unless you're in direct combat, storming a base as part of a team when there's no need for stealth, or when you're attempting to escape with several enemies on your tail.

Don't always hurry to charge into battle. Smart players often profit by surveying the scene and judging the correct moment to strike.

As with *MGS4*, use your eyes and ears – listen for footfalls or cries of pain. The sound system is so sensitive and realistic that you can trust your senses as much as you would in real life. If you hear steps close to you, it means that the enemy is very near and you should be on your guard. Watch for shadows moving, and be aware that your own sounds and movements can give away just as much about your position to the enemy as theirs do to you. Play with the volume too low, and you'll miss some of these critical prompts.

Wandering more or less aimlessly in free-for-all games tends to be rather ineffective. Until you familiarize yourself well with all maps and their subtleties, you can start by exploring simple routes or loops that are easy to memorize. This way, you will feel less naked and know better what to expect, and how to react accordingly. If you notice that your opponents get used to your patterns, though, be prepared to adapt them immediately, or you'll become laughably predictable.

Try to use cover as much as you can. Any time you spend in an open area exposes you to attack from multiple angles. As a general rule, staying behind an obstacle is the most efficient strategy. Survey the surrounding area by rotating the camera, and leap out to attack as an unsuspecting enemy approaches (Fig. 1).

Use the Solo Training facility to really get to grips with a map. You can develop interesting strategies to use during combat, scout for good sniping or ambush positions, and gain an instinctive "feel" for the environment. Being familiar with a map's many features will make you a much more effective player.

You can activate the Auto Aim feature in the Options menu. However, just like in *MGS4*, this is not necessarily an advantage – this function makes you direct your fire at your target's torso, which is far less effective than aiming at their head. If you do choose to use it, turn Auto Aim on ( ) only when it makes tactical sense to do so. It's great for offering suppressing fire when your team is being attacked by multiple assailants, or at very close range when standard aiming can become a little unwieldy. Don't overdo it, though: using manual aiming and/or the FPS mode is something that everyone should practice, because the ability to make lethal headshots is the mark of a true adept.

Try not to constantly creep round with [L1] held, as this slows you down significantly and restricts movement. Unless you're actively lining up a shot or sneaking up on an enemy, you should be using the free camera to look around you at regular intervals. If you don't do this, you leave yourself extremely vulnerable to attacks from behind.

Get into the habit of using explosive devices in the environment to your advantage. If your quarry is foolish enough to move next to an object with the potential to detonate, you are practically obligated to shoot it in order to start or end a fight with a bang (Fig. 2).

Memorize the positions where you respawn during your first few weeks of play, especially during free-for-all matches. Knowing where enemies are likely to appear from can help you to avoid unexpected attacks.

Firearms and CQC are not the only means of attack you have at your disposal: you can also roll into someone to make them fall down, and then follow up with a headshot. If you see someone around a corner waiting to roll into you, approach the corner in the crouching stance. Should that character go ahead and roll (and miss you), you can either shoot them with Auto Aim while they roll, shoot them in the head as they get back up, or perform a CQC move.

Similarly, when you knock an opponent to the ground, you have several options: you may finish them off either manually or with Auto Aim, or alternatively shoot them with a tranquilizer dart and then roll into them as they are getting up, which will stun them straight away.

If you attempt to hit someone with a roll and miss, hold ⊗ in order to go prone. This will confuse them if they're about to strike back, and will prevent them from hitting you with CQC or a roll. You can even try to shoot them while lying down.

If you get knocked down and you see your adversary lining up a shot, try to surprise them: instead of getting up immediately, remain prone or roll over on your back to shoot them; or, for that matter, roll to the side to dodge their shots.

To lower your chances of being shot in the head, move in an unpredictable fashion. Strafe, roll, go prone, slow down – any variation in your motion patterns can help confuse your opponents.

TEAM TIPS

Communication is absolutely essential in objective-based games, and helps in all team-oriented matches. It's important to be clear and concise, so use simple descriptive terms to identify areas and specific positions.

Camping enemy spawn points can cause confusion and irritation that will hamper their efforts to plan and execute a cohesive strategy. If you realize you are being targeted in this way, communicate the danger to your teammates and cooperate to neutralize the threat immediately. If you don't, the results can be disastrous.

In Team Death Match games, don't forget that your wellbeing is of paramount importance, and aim to have a positive kill-to-death ratio. Every single demise you suffer is a point for the opposing team, so it's extremely unwise to throw your life away in skirmishes that you have little chance of winning.

If you get the impression that you're a late addition to a well-organized group, don't just give up and go fight on your own – you'll be wasting your time. Instead, follow and observe your teammates, and try to identify the tasks that you could accomplish to make a contribution to their overall strategy.

The SOP System adds an enormous amount of tactical depth to each battle. However, there are instances where teams will benefit if players making risky solo sorties into contested territory are not actually linked into the network. This way, if a scout or sniper is captured and probed with the Scanning Plug, they won't have any sensitive location data to reveal.

METAL GEAR SOLID 4
GUNS OF THE PATRIOTS TACTICAL ESPIONAGE ACTION

HOW TO PLAY

WALKTHROUGH

INVENTORY

▶ METAL GEAR ONLINE

EXTRAS

GETTING STARTED

BASICS

▶ TIPS

GAME MODES

MAPS

03

04

05

EQUIPMENT TIPS

All equipment types that are available in multiplayer matches are functionally identical to their counterparts in *MGS4*.

You can safely crawl over deployed Claymores (Fig. 3), though this is a dangerous trick to use – you're effectively doomed if an opponent spots you while you are creeping up to or past one.

The Shield is a weapon that you will find useful mainly in team games. In itself, a Shield provides mediocre protection and only enables you to strike out at very close quarters. But if you use it to protect a teammate carrying Kerotan (Fig. 4), for example, it can make a huge difference.

You can use the Cardboard Box to protect yourself from headshots – not that it acts in any sense as armor, but because it prevents your opponents from actually *seeing* your head. Naturally the same goes for the Drum Can.

When you knock an opponent out, place a magazine at their feet: this way, they'll be trapped by it the moment they wake up.

WEAPON TIPS

Throwing grenades to soften up opponents before you launch an attack is a highly profitable tactic (Fig. 5). The damage and momentary disorientation can enable you to seize the advantage against virtually any adversary.

Grenades can also be employed to deter assailants from giving chase, especially when you run through doors.

If you are confronted by an enemy sniper, concentrate on keeping your adversary "descoped" – that is, shoot them in measured bursts to prevent them from zooming in and making a precision shot.

Feel free to practice "no-scope" kills with sniper rifles. Even a basic proficiency can be valuable as sniper weapons tend to be extremely powerful.

Place Claymores at key locations to take your enemies by surprise. Position them around a base, for example, and you can create an effective (and potentially deadly) "early warning" system. Needless to say, you should warn your teammates about such surprises when playing team-based games.

In Death Match games, your objective is to kill as many enemies as you can, so make sure you choose lethal weapons. If all you have at your disposal is equipment such as a Shield or the Mk. 2, dispatching opponents will prove problematic.

Conversely, in objective-based games, don't underestimate the potential of anesthetic weapons. You might think that killing your opponents is always more effective, but this is not necessarily the case. Rendering them unconscious works wonders as well, especially as your victims will remain asleep longer than it would take them to respawn.

Tactically, stunning or tranquilizing an opponent can be a great way to create an ambush if you suspect that the opposing team lacks coherent leadership or communication skills. When the inevitable lone hero arrives to save his or her comrade… well, you know what to do next.

If you are hit by a tranquilizer dart, or are rendered unconscious, you can wake up more quickly by rapidly pressing buttons on your controller.

Use all the information that is presented to you on the screen, especially which weapons are achieving regular kills on a map. Take note of what other players are using and emulate them if you're struggling to make an impact. It's always smart to watch and learn from others. There's no end to the useful tips you can pick up just by seeing how other people play the game. Usually this will be from bitter experience as you get sniped from a position you neglected to observe, ambushed by unseen opponents, or nonchalantly dispatched by a better-prepared adversary. Look at it this way, though: any pain and humiliation you endure in one round is knowledge that you can use to your advantage in those that follow…

GAME MODES

There are various types of game modes in *MGO*, each with particular sets of rules and objectives. There are three variations for each of these:

- **Normal:** no special conditions.

- **Drebin Points Enabled:** players can spend DP during games to use weapons that would not normally be available, or to customize certain firearms. You earn DP depending on how well you do in battle.

- **Headshots Only:** when a player is not taken down by a headshot, a penalty is handed to the shooter.

DEATH MATCH

To win, you simply need to rack up more kills than your opponents in this carnage-focused game mode (Fig. 1). Pacificists need not apply.

Tip: If you're experiencing too many deaths, pick different areas to frequent, and study the Multiplayer Maps section (page 144).

01

RESCUE MISSION

The defending team must protect a target, while the attacking team must rescue it (Fig. 2) and bring it back to its goal. You can also win by defeating all members of the opposing team.

Tip: When the target is stolen from your team, be quick to chase the thieves down and request the help of all your teammates.

02

TEAM DEATH MATCH

Killing is still the primary objective, but this time it's more organized, and you need never work alone for too long. Instead of being a solitary angel of death, you get to team up with associates and make coordinated attacks on your opponents.

Tip: Always stay with your teammates. Together, a group is stronger than the sum of its parts.

CAPTURE MISSION

Teams compete to capture Kerotan or GA-KO, and must then defend it at their goal for a set period of time (Fig. 3). If both goals have a Kerotan or GA-KO, the timer is reset.

Tip: Attack really is the best form of defense in this mode. You'll need to be aggressive both to steal your target, and to try to retrieve the other should it be grabbed by the opposing team.

03

SNEAKING MISSION

Participants are divided into two teams, red and blue as usual, with one person being designated as Snake; their name is displayed in orange on the list. Snake wins if he collects the specified number of dog tags after knocking down or killing players (Fig. 4). The teams win either by eliminating Snake a specified number of times, or by having killed the most members of the opposing team when the timer expires. When Snake is discovered, you will hear the familiar "alert" sound from the single-player game, and see a big orange exclamation mark.

When you are lucky enough to be randomly selected to be Snake for the first time, you will note that you don't have the opportunity to pick your own equipment. Don't despair, though – you are given Snake's basic sneaking gear, including the Solid Eye and Threat Ring. Your default weapon is the Mosin-Nagant. Though you can use this for sniping it's not always a good idea, as you need to be close enough to collect your victim's dog tag before they wake up. It's best to rely on sneaking and hand-to-hand combat, or to simply point the Mosin-Nagant at the enemy to hold them up and get their dog tag.

Tip: If 11 or more players join, one of them plays as Metal Gear Mk. II and can support Snake. Press ⊗ to engage the cloaking function and △ to shock an opponent.

TEAM SNEAKING

The attacking team is equipped with stealth camo and must capture an objective, while the defending team protects the target (Fig 5).

Tip: As the defending team, focus on protecting key areas, using experience and intuition to judge where your opponents will attack from.

BASE MISSION

Bases are easy to identify as they are surrounded by a frame and a small sphere floats over them. In order to achieve victory in this game mode, you will have to secure as many Bases as possible, which involves staying within the specified boundaries for a set period of time (Fig. 6). The first team to capture all Bases or with the highest total when the timer expires wins. Note that a captured Base can be won back by the enemy.

Tips:

- Capture times are reduced when two teammates occupy a Base simultaneously.

- If you leave a Base that you are in the process of capturing, the gauge will remain unchanged in your absence. This means that you can dive out to take cover for a while if required, and then resume the capturing process where you left off.

- When a round time limit is up, the team with the most Bases wins, even if someone was in the process of capturing a Base.

- It's usually far more effective to try to conquer each Base methodically – with a large group, you can overwhelm divided enemy forces.

- When a Base is being seized by the opposing team, its icon will flash on your screen as a warning.

- If an opponent contests a Base you're trying to capture by stepping inside its boundaries, the gauge will stop filling until you engineer his or her departure from either the Base, or (ideally) this mortal coil.

HOW TO PLAY
WALKTHROUGH
INVENTORY
▶ METAL GEAR ONLINE
EXTRAS

GETTING STARTED
BASICS
TIPS
▶ GAME MODES
MAPS

MULTIPLAYER MAPS: AMBUSH ALLEY

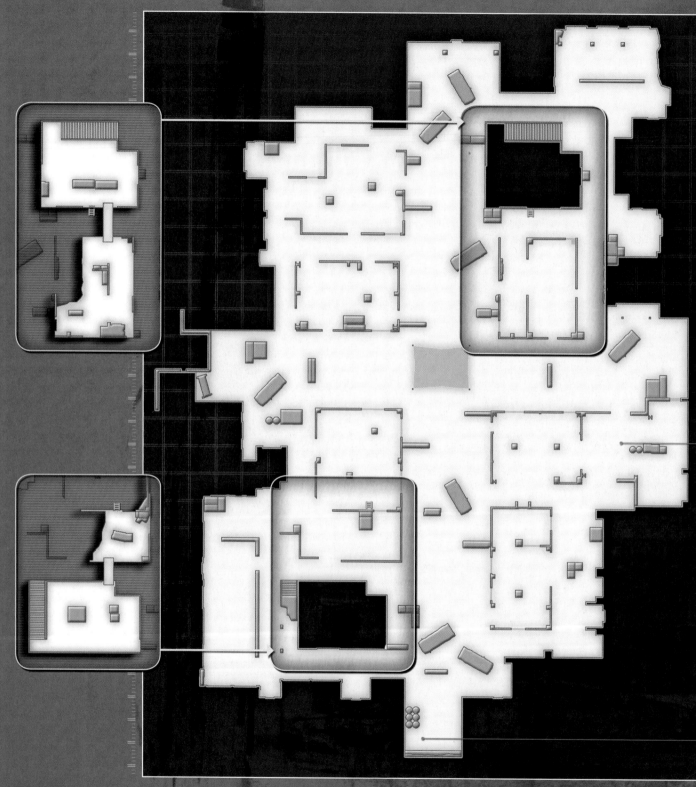

Ambush Alley definitely deserves its name: apart from the central roadway, it's a map with narrow winding paths where enemies can jump out unpredictably and stalk you. If you need to run away from a pursuer, there are countless windows and low walls that you can roll through or over. If you roll diagonally, you are usually pretty much safe during the process, and may end up behind a wall offering cover long enough for you to turn around and fight back.

There are grey barrels all over this map. Shooting them with a lethal firearm triggers a big explosion – anesthetic weapons or the Stun Knife have no effect on them. If you wield a sniper rifle, you can actually use the scope feature to zoom in from afar on those barrels and destroy them whenever a target runs by. Note that the spot where a barrel has just blown up remains on fire for a while. Should you step on those flames, you will catch fire yourself which reduces your Life gauge at an alarming rate. The easiest way to stop this is to make a few forward rolls.

This map features a dead end in the south that makes an excellent defensive position. From here you cannot be attacked from the rear, your are protected by walls on both sides, and sandbags as well as a van offer cover from the front. On top of this, if your opponents drive you to the back of the dead end or if you are attacked from the upper floor of the nearby building, you can retreat behind the pile of tires while firing back.

If you decide to opt for close-range weapons such as shotguns, you will naturally need to avoid open-air areas and rooftops. You should instead stay under cover as much as possible, and limit your stalking to the tunnel section in the north-east. In this corridor your firepower will give you an edge over everyone else; furthermore, you can use not only the explosive barrels, but also the crates and corners to jump out and crush your targets.

METAL GEAR SOLID 4
GUNS OF THE PATRIOTS TACTICAL ESPIONAGE ACTION

HOW TO PLAY
WALKTHROUGH
INVENTORY
METAL GEAR ONLINE
EXTRAS

GETTING STARTED
BASICS
TIPS
GAME MODES
MAPS

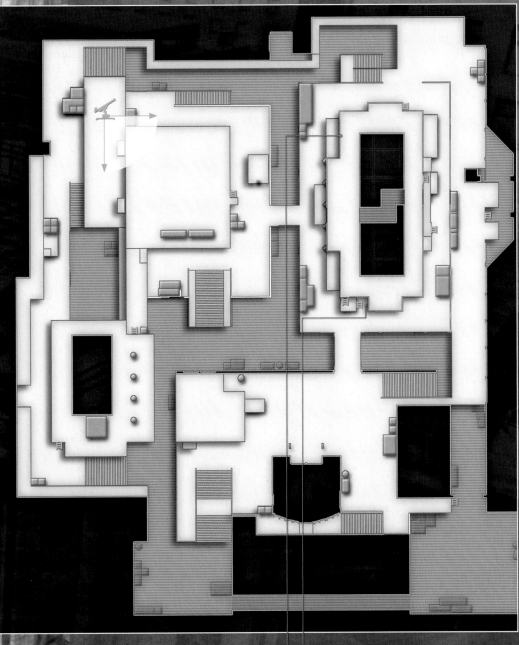

Sniping spots are abundant on the rooftops, though most of them offer very little cover. You have a good view of your enemies – but they too can easily spot you. There is one position that combines both advantages. Once on the roof of the north-east building, go to the north-west corner, hop over the railing and drop down to the small balcony below. Here you have an excellent view of the red roof and the catapult, which provides many sniping opportunities, while you can only be shot at from that roof or from the street below, which is quite manageable.

Urban Ultimatum is a sniper's dream, with tall buildings offering a great view of the scenery below. However, to access the roofs of the two highest buildings you usually need to expose yourself dangerously, either when using the catapult or when climbing up one of the long ladders. There is a way to (partly) avoid this, though. If you take the ladder on the south side of the north-east building, you are effectively protected by metal boards which make your ascent far less risky.

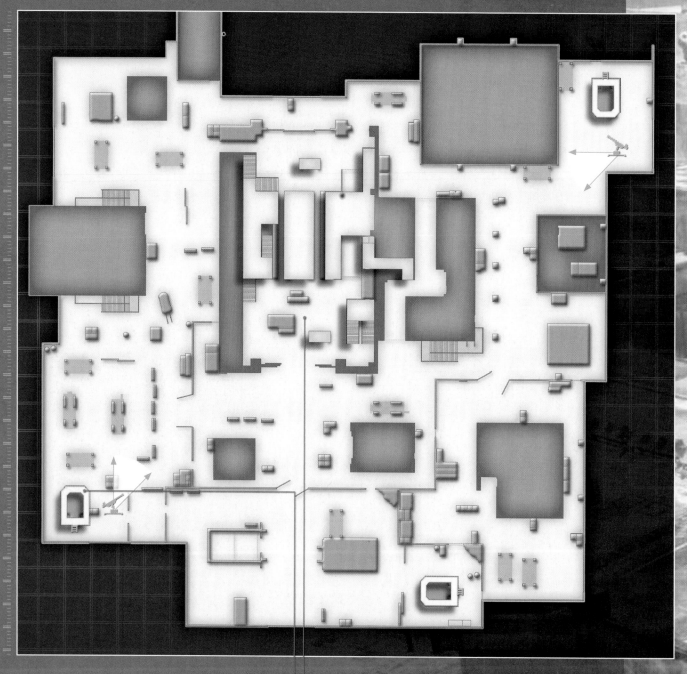

There's a tower in the south-west corner of the map that you can climb up. It's a fantastic sniping spot where you are safe from shots from the ground, but be aware that people can (and frequently will) snipe down on you from the two large buildings in the middle of the map.

You are very vulnerable in the wide open spaces (both to firearms and grenades), so you need to limit your exposure. Look out for holes in walls that you can crawl through to maintain cover. There are also lots of tanks, vehicles, large shipping containers and so on that you can crawl under or hide behind for cover. Bunkers offer good protection as well.

Being stealthy is hard inside the large central hangar, as your feet clank on the metal walkways. The best way to enter this building without making yourself an easy target for snipers on the gangways is either to catapult onto the roof, or to climb up via the building to the west. You can then make your way methodically downstairs, which is infinitely preferable to entering from the ground and working your way up. Note that there are catapults in the south-west and north-east corners of the map. Be careful, though: you will often be sniped when on a catapult, though this is marginally less likely to happen with the unit in the north-east.

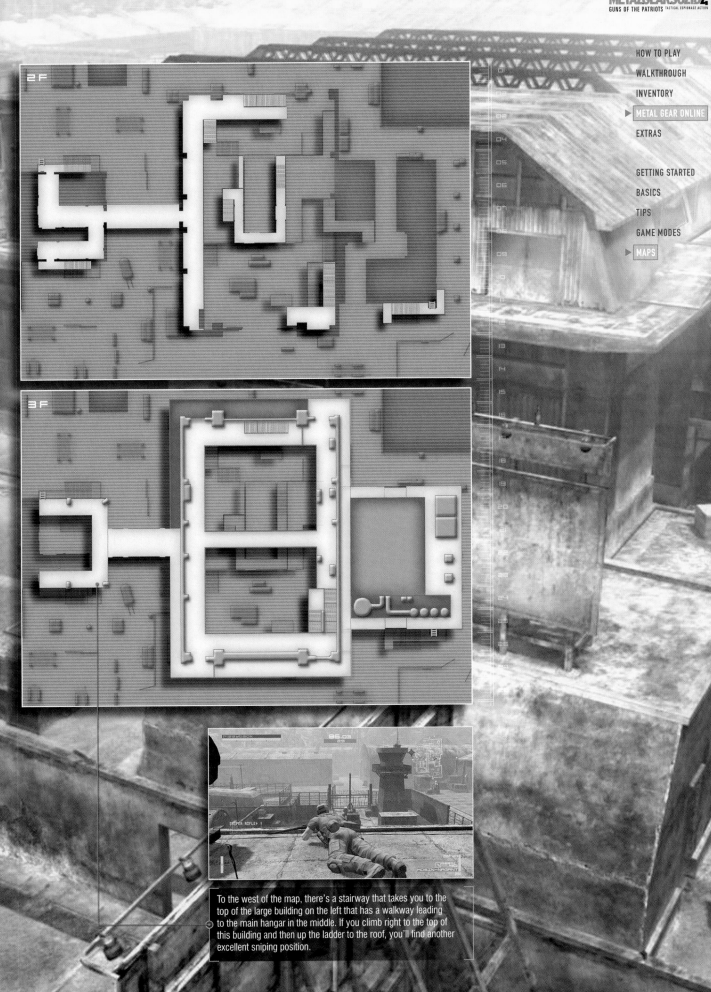

2F

3F

To the west of the map, there's a stairway that takes you to the
top of the large building on the left that has a walkway leading
to the main hangar in the middle. If you climb right to the top of
this building and then up the ladder to the roof, you'll find another
excellent sniping position.

BLOOD BATH

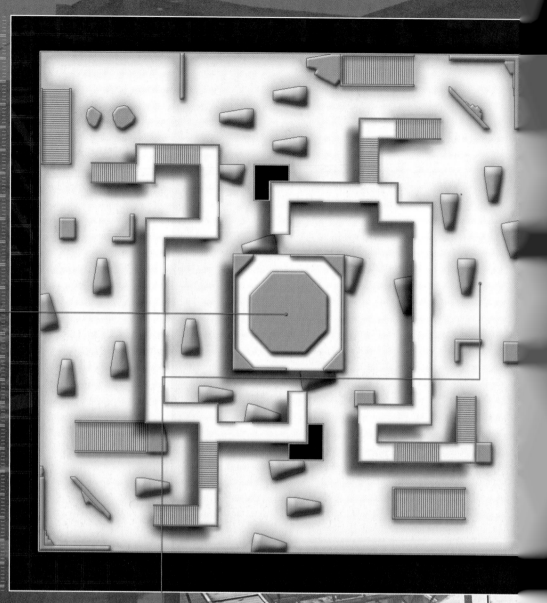

This map features a dilapidated building at its center, surrounded by walkways. You might think that the walkways are good sniping points, but they're not – you're actually a sitting duck, as they're not high enough to keep you out of harm's way.

On the ground, there are lots of large rocks and blast shields to hide behind, and you'll find moving between them and carefully stalking your prey to be one of the most satisfying experiences in *MGO*. Keeping as close to the edge of the map as possible and inching along is probably the safest way to go. Crouch down and roll to the next rock or shield to remain under cover. You should regularly pause and look around to ensure that you're not being followed, as the soft muddy ground makes it difficult to hear anyone creeping up behind you.

b1

There are steps at all four corners of the map leading down to a basement bunker level. This is a good way to get across the level without exposing yourself, but stay alert, as others will obviously have the same idea. You'll find an excellent spot in the north of the basement where you can stand with an SMG and ambush anyone coming from one of three different directions before they get a chance to see you. You could even place a magazine here to distract any approaching enemies.

MIDTOWN MAELSTROM

This map is actually taken from the single-player mode, and more precisely from the Downtown section of Act 1. As danger potentially lurks around every corner, avoid swaggering down the main boulevard which runs from the south-east to the west. Sniper rifles such as the SVD are very effective for this map, especially as they can be profitably used for both long-range shooting and close-quarters combat.

On the south side of the boulevard, just beyond the first trench, there's a very good rat run that enables you to sneak around the back to the north end. You need to climb up two small walls to reach it. Alleyways lead off it right back to the main road, and you can hide in them and wait for anyone passing down the central street.

Climb up the first ladder you come to in the alleyway on the east of the main road to reach the rooftop. This is a great sniping spot where you are well-hidden and get a good view of the whole wide thoroughfare. Alternatively, you can camp by the ladder leading up to the spot and ambush any would-be snipers. A little way further along there's also a large building that you can enter, which is a perfect spot to snipe and ambush anyone taking this route. Enter the building by jumping in through one of the ground-floor windows and go upstairs to the second floor, where you'll find more sniping vantage points to the front. You can jump out onto the rooftops from a third-floor window and hop down to another excellent sniping point behind a wall. Wait here long enough and you'll bag plenty of kills.

01
02
03
04
05
06
07
08
09
10
11
12
13
14
15
16
17
18
19
20
21
22
23
24
25

2 F

E X T R A S

S

▶ **SPOILER WARNING!** This chapter is practically bursting at the seams with secrets and spoilers. Do not, *under any circumstances*, read any further until you have completed *Metal Gear Solid 4* at least once. **YOU HAVE BEEN WARNED!**

Cutscene Interactions

Before we dive into the more momentous secrets at the heart of *MGS4*, we begin with a brief recap of the various instances where you can interact with cutscenes. These may come in useful at a later date, should you choose to revisit the entire story on a subsequent playthrough.

L1 SCENES

Bar a few "secret" interactions (particularly with Naomi in the Research Lab during Act 2), an ⓛ1 prompt appears whenever you can look through Snake's eyes during a cutscene.

ACT 1	Ground Zero	Snake looking up at a Gekko carrying a dead body above him
		Hidden Snake watching a Gekko stamping the "No Place for Hideo" box
	Downtown	Snake looking at the inside of the oil drum used by Johnny as an emergency toilet
	Advent Palace	Johnny pointing his weapon at Snake with the safety enabled
		View of photo
	Crescent Meridian	Screaming Mantis
	Millenium Park	Liquid on the balcony
ACT 2	Power Station	BB Corps
	Research Lab	Snake sneaking around the outside of the lab
		Snake thinks he saw something (it's Laughing Octopus)
		Snake picking up a cigarette and checking Naomi out (with Psyche increase)
		When Naomi sits on the bed next to Snake and attempts to pick up the cigarette (secret, no button prompt; restores Psyche)
		When Naomi kneels in front of Snake and says "I have something to tell you" (secret, no button prompt; restores Psyche)
		Naomi shocked by Snake's old body
		Snake in CT scanner
ACT 3	Church Courtyard (after Midtown N Sector)	Resistance member pointing gun at Snake
		Just after the ⓛ1 scene by the van (secret, no button prompt)
		Triumph motorcycle
	Echo's Beacon	Snake looking at Raging Beauty's bottom
	Volta River (end of Act 3)	Snake slowly walking around the corner with weapon
ACT 5	Missouri (Mission Briefing)	Snake's blurred view after using the Syringe
	Command Center	After Psycho Mantis leaves (secret; view of The Sorrow from *MGS3*)
	Missile Hangar	Snake almost losing consciousness

FLASHBACKS

You receive an increasing amount of post-Act Drebin Points bonuses in accordance with the number of Flashbacks you view. When the ⊗ prompt appears, tap the button rapidly to cycle through as many screens as you can before the interactivity ends.

ACT 1	Ground Zero	Snake saluting
		FOXDIE
		Naomi
		Liquid
	Red Zone	Metal Gear REX
	Advent Palace	Weapons pointed at Johnny in the past
		Meryl in *MGS1*
		Johnny relieving himself in oil drum
ACT 2	Nomad (Mission Briefing)	Solidus and The Patriots
		Vamp
	Power Station	Sniper Wolf, Vulcan Raven, Psycho Mantis and Decoy Octopus
		The Patriots
	Research Lab	Naomi at Shadow Moses (*MGS1*)
		ArmsTech president, Liquid
		Drebin
	Mountain Trail	Naomi
	Marketplace	Little Gray
ACT 3	Nomad (Mission Briefing)	Olga (Sunny's mother)
		Emma Emmerich
	Church Courtyard (after Midtown N Sector)	Big Mama
	Echo's Beacon	Young Snake and Liquid
		Big Boss
ACT 4	Heliport	During "secret" surveillance camera cutscene
		Otacon in *MGS1*
	Nuclear Warhead Storage Building B2	Naomi's past betrayal
		Metal Gear REX's old underground hangar
		Key cards in *MGS1*
	Snowfield & Communications Tower	Sniper Wolf
	Underground Supply Tunnel	Metal Gear REX
	Port Area	During the remembered conversation between Rose and Raiden from *MGS2* (secret, no button prompt)
ACT 5	Missouri (Mission Briefing)	Naomi
		Emma/Sunny
	Command Center	Psycho Mantis flying after the Screaming Mantis battle (secret, no button prompt)
		Memory Card/PlayStation 1
		DualShock controller/rumble feature
		MGS1 codec call
		"The Spirit of the Warrior"
	Missile Hangar	Johnny

METAL GEAR SOLID 4
GUNS OF THE PATRIOTS TACTICAL ESPIONAGE ACTION

HOW TO PLAY
WALKTHROUGH
INVENTORY
METAL GEAR ONLINE
EXTRAS

CUTSCENE INTERACTIONS
EMBLEMS
SPECIAL EQUIPMENT
SECRETS
SYNOPSIS
INTERPRETATION
BIOGRAPHIES

Emblems

At the end of each *MGS4* playthrough you will be rewarded with one or more "emblems", special accolades that acknowledge your performance in a variety of ways. The emblem with the highest "value" will always be chosen as your post-game title (Fig. 1). The higher this is on the list, the better you did.

Over the following pages, we look at all 40 emblems. Some are quirky; others monumentally difficult to obtain; a few, towards the lower reaches, might leave you feeling a little disappointed. Don't be disheartened if your initial rating is less than stellar, though – *MGS4* is a game that takes time to master, and your first playthrough is essentially a dress rehearsal for the fun that follows.

Note: the Race Gun, Suit and Command Vests are unlocked as standard after your first playthrough, so we don't mention these in the "Special Completion Bonus" sections.

Final Results		THE BOSS EXTREME
Total Play Time	88,850 DP	05:50:11
Continues	100,000 DP	0
Alert Phases	200,000 DP	0
Kills	200,000 DP	0
Recovery Items Used	100,000 DP	0
Weapon Types Procured	34,550 DP	47
Flashbacks Watched	6,810 DP	38
Special Items Used	50,000 DP	Not Used
Total Bonus		780,210 DP
Current Drebin Points		2,008,538 DP
Confer the title of...		"FOX"
Press the START button to exit		

01

EMBLEM LIST

 1.

 2.

 3.

BIG BOSS	
TYPE	Elite
DIFFICULTY	10/10
CRITERIA	
Number of Alert Phases	0
Number of kills	0
Number of continues	0
Game time	< 5:00
Rations, Regain, Noodles used	0
No use of Stealth Camouflage or the Bandana	
The Boss Extreme	

Notes: This is the ultimate accolade, and will be the sole preserve of expert players willing to hone their skills on several playthroughs. Playing a "perfect" game on the unlockable The Boss Extreme setting is ridiculously hard, but it's actually the maximum time requirement that will make it almost prohibitively difficult for most. If you're determined to beat this challenge, you can find a collection of useful tips and guidelines on page 170 of this chapter.

Special Completion Bonuses: Patriot, Big Boss FaceCamo, Big Boss iPod® song

FOX HOUND	
TYPE	Elite
DIFFICULTY	9/10
CRITERIA	
Number of Alert Phases	< 3
Number of kills	0
Number of continues	0
Game time	< 5:30
Rations, Regain, Noodles used	0
No use of Stealth Camouflage or the Bandana	
Big Boss Hard or higher	

Notes: An ambitious goal even for highly skilled players, obtaining the Fox Hound emblem is the perfect training exercise for those intending to try for the Big Boss accolade. If you can beat Fox Hound, Big Boss is within touching distance. The slightly less stringent time requirement is a real blessing, but knowing how best to beat the Beasts with a minimum of fuss is vital.

Special Completion Bonus: Thor .45-70

FOX	
TYPE	Elite
DIFFICULTY	8/10
CRITERIA	
Number of Alert Phases	< 5
Number of kills	0
Number of continues	0
Game time	< 6:00
Rations, Regain, Noodles used	0
No use of Stealth Camouflage or the Bandana	
Solid Normal or higher	

Notes: If you're determined to unlock every emblem and bonus feature, this is a good place to start on a second playthrough. Even though a few Alert Phases are allowed, it's good practice to avoid them entirely. The easier route taken through Midtown in Act 3 means that the game time requirement is still tough, but within your means once you know your way around.

Special Completion Bonus: Desert Eagle (Long Barrel)

HOUND

TYPE	Elite
DIFFICULTY	7/10
CRITERIA	
Number of Alert Phases	< 3
Number of kills	0
Number of continues	0
Game time	< 6:30
Rations, Regain, Noodles used	0
No use of Stealth Camouflage or the Bandana	
Naked Normal or higher	

Notes: There's no real point in aiming to specifically unlock the Hound emblem, as you'll obtain it automatically if you unlock Fox (or, indeed, the grades above it). The lower difficulty setting makes it a much more approachable challenge if you're not yet confident enough to go for the higher emblems, though.

Special Completion Bonus: Type 17 Pistol

MANTIS

TYPE	Elite
DIFFICULTY	7/10
CRITERIA	
Number of Alert Phases	0
Number of continues	0
Game time	< 5:00
Rations, Regain, Noodles used	0

Notes: An amazingly tricky emblem to get and not really worth the trouble, given the lack of additional rewards. If you can beat the game time requirement, you'll receive it automatically when you gain the Hound emblem or higher.

WOLF

TYPE	Elite
DIFFICULTY	5/10
CRITERIA	
Number of continues	0
Rations, Regain, Noodles used	0

Notes: This is a very approachable goal on lower difficulty levels. Once again, though, it's better to set your sights higher and gain this emblem when you obtain Hound or above. As there is no time limit, this is actually the best rating that a player could hope to win on a first playthrough – even if it's very implausible that anyone actually will.

RAVEN

TYPE	Elite
DIFFICULTY	4/10
CRITERIA	
Game time	< 5:00

Notes: This is the easiest Elite emblem to obtain. On Liquid Easy, skilled players with a good knowledge of the map layouts will be able to practically run to the exits of many zones. The Beasts and Midtown infiltration sequence will slow you down a little, but these are inconsequential hurdles if you've faced them before on higher difficulty levels.

OCTOPUS

TYPE	Elite
DIFFICULTY	6/10
CRITERIA	
Complete *MGS4* with zero Alert Phases	

Notes: The lowliest of the Elite emblems, but an admirable achievement nonetheless. This is obviously easier on the less challenging difficulty settings, but you'll still need to save regularly – even a single Alert Phase is one too many.

Special Completion Bonus: Stealth Camouflage

BEAR

TYPE	Unique
DIFFICULTY	5/10 (1/10 with Stealth Camouflage)
CRITERIA	
Defeat 100 or more enemies with CQC chokeholds	

Notes: Hard to obtain on its own (yet an absolute breeze with the luxury of Stealth Camouflage), some players might opt to try for this emblem at the same time as Assassin.

10.

EAGLE

TYPE	Unique
DIFFICULTY	3/10

CRITERIA

Perform 150 headshots or more

Notes: A good rating for those who like to shoot first, and then forgo the traditional questions at a later date in favor of yet *more* shooting.

11.

ASSASSIN

TYPE	Unique
DIFFICULTY	5/10 (1/10 with Stealth Camouflage)

CRITERIA

Enemies defeated with knife kills or knife stuns ≥ 50

Number of CQC holds ≥ 50

Number of times discovered ≤ 25

Notes: This is a rather tricky endeavor – successfully defeating 50 opponents with CQC holds and a knife kill finish, with a maximum of 25 Alert Phases during the entire playthrough, is a tough proposition. You'll need to hit the specified total before the end of the sequence where you trail the resistance member in Act 3, as there are few practical opportunities to engage in CQC after that point. The easy solution, of course, is to unlock the Stealth Camouflage gadget first…

Special Completion Bonus: Altair Disguise

12.

PIGEON

TYPE	Unique
DIFFICULTY	5/10

CRITERIA

Number of kills	0

Notes: To win this emblem, play through the entire game without killing a single soldier, and defeat each Beauty with non-lethal ammunition or Stun Grenades. Destroying Gekko (both varieties) and Sliders does not count towards your kill total. This is actually an easier goal than you might think. With a Mk. 2, Mosin-Nagant and a shotgun loaded with V-Ring ammunition, there's no challenge that you can't overcome.

Special Completion Bonus: Bandana

13.

BLUE BIRD

TYPE	Unique
DIFFICULTY	3/10

CRITERIA

Number of items given to militia/rebels ≥ 50

Notes: You can give healing items to militia and rebel soldiers in Acts 1 and 2. To do so, simply ready an appropriate restorative object in the items menu, approach a militia or rebel soldier, and then press ④ when the onscreen prompt appears. Repeat this a further 49 times, and the emblem is yours. This is much easier to achieve on lower difficulty settings, as Snake can collect and carry far more curative items. It's also a good idea to get the Hawk emblem at the same time.

14.

HAWK

TYPE	Unique
DIFFICULTY	3/10

CRITERIA

Number of times praised by militia ≥ 25

Notes: This is one of the most unusual Unique emblems. You may have already noticed that the militia and rebel forces (in Act 1 and Act 2 respectively) will praise Snake if they consider him an ally. The best way to earn their favor is to help them to win battles, annihilating PMC soldiers whenever you see them fighting the local forces. Once their name tags are colored blue, militia and rebel soldiers may celebrate Snake's achievements when they encounter him. All you then have to do is run around courting their adulation. If you successfully destroy the two Strykers and mop up the PMC infantry in Red Zone (Act 1 – see page 34), the Militia Safe House zone that follows effectively becomes the Snake Fan Club HQ.

15.

LITTLE GRAY

TYPE	Unique
DIFFICULTY	6/10 (10/10 if you don't use Extras menu passwords)

CRITERIA

Acquire 69 unique weapon types (excluding 1911), or 70 (including 1911)

Notes: Essentially, the only way to get this emblem is to acquire every last weapon in *MGS4*. This is much easier if you use Extras menu codes (see page 180) to get the weapons that can usually only be obtained after the award of the Big Boss, Fox Hound, Fox and Hound emblems.

16. ANT

TYPE	Unique
DIFFICULTY	6/10 (2/10 with Stealth Camouflage)

CRITERIA

Perform 50 or more body searches during hold-ups

Notes: This requires a lot of advance planning, as tracking down 50 lone soldiers to hold up (which can include militiamen, rebels and resistance members, if you wish) really isn't a trivial undertaking. An excellent understanding of soldier locations and patrol routes is a must. The unlockable Stealth Camouflage gadget makes this much easier to get.

17. GIBBON

TYPE	Unique
DIFFICULTY	5/10 (2/10 with Stealth Camouflage)

CRITERIA

Perform 50 or more hold-ups

Notes: You'll receive this automatically if you fulfill the criteria for the Ant emblem.

18. TORTOISE

TYPE	Unique
DIFFICULTY	3/10

CRITERIA

Spend more than 60 minutes hidden inside the Drum Can or Cardboard Box

Notes: There's no reason why an agoraphobic hero can't save the world – it just takes a little longer, and requires specialist equipment.

19. RABBIT

TYPE	Unique
DIFFICULTY	1/10

CRITERIA

Turn the pages of Playboy or the Emotion Mag 100 times or more

Notes: A reward for truly *dedicated* connoisseurs of specialist publications.

20. BEE

TYPE	Unique
DIFFICULTY	4/10

CRITERIA

Scan or inject PMC solders with the Scanning Plug or Syringe respectively on 50 occasions or more

Notes: This is an emblem that players are unlikely to get on a first playthrough, as by the time that you have the Syringe, there are relatively few opportunities to capture lone soldiers. Given the high requirements (50 injections/scans with the Scanning Plug is a fairly huge total), this is definitely an emblem that you need to intentionally play for.

21. GECKO

TYPE	Unique
DIFFICULTY	2/10

CRITERIA

Spend 1:00 hour or more clinging to a wall

Notes: As crawling is clearly the best infiltration technique, the likelihood that any player will comfortably spend over two hours pressed up against walls is extremely slim. Like so many other Unique-class emblems, though, it's easy to win once you know how.

22. SCARAB

TYPE	Unique
DIFFICULTY	1/10

CRITERIA

Perform over 100 rolls

Notes: One hundred forward rolls is a lot, but it's a simple requirement to meet once you know about it.

23. FROG

TYPE	Unique
DIFFICULTY	1/10

CRITERIA

Roll or jump to the side 200 times or more

Notes: Just find a safe spot and dodge to either side (hold L1, then press ⊗ and ⬤ left or right) until you reach the specified total. You can also get this by rolling from side to side in a prone position.

24. INCH WORM

TYPE	Unique
DIFFICULTY	2/10

CRITERIA

Crawl for 60 minutes or more

Notes: Over an hour of crawling may seem like a lot, but it's a fairly likely eventuality on the first occasion you play a "pure" stealth playthrough in order to obtain the secret Stealth Camouflage gadget.

25.

LOBSTER	
TYPE	Unique
DIFFICULTY	3/10
CRITERIA	
Crouch for 2:30 hours or more	

Notes: You're much less likely to encounter this during a general playthrough than Inch Worm, so you'll probably need to leave the game running with Snake crouched in a safe spot while you attend to other things.

26.

HYENA	
TYPE	Unique
DIFFICULTY	1/10
CRITERIA	
Pick up 400 weapons/items or more	

Notes: Not a hard emblem to obtain, even on a pure stealth walkthrough – just regularly find a decent hiding place wherever you encounter combat between PMC forces and local dissidents during the first two Acts, and then send Metal Gear Mk. II out to act as a battlefield scavenger.

27.

HOG	
TYPE	Unique
DIFFICULTY	3/10
CRITERIA	
Enter a Combat High 10 times or more	

Notes: This is a reasonably tricky accolade to get unless you're actively playing for it. You need to fire a weapon over 100 times during a full Alert Phase to experience a Combat High. The Confinement Facility zone in Act 2, with its infinitely respawning soldiers, is a good hunting ground.

28.

PIG	
TYPE	Unique
DIFFICULTY	2/10
CRITERIA	
Use 40 or more Rations, Noodles or Regains	

Notes: Gluttony: the tastiest of all sins. To unlock this accolade through "artificial" means, play on a lower difficulty level. Once you have a full collection of healing items, set one as your default item, pick a fight, and leave Snake to soak up the damage. When his stocks of one restorative object run out, switch to another. Just before you're in danger of running out of stocks, move on to the next zone and begin collecting anew.

29.

COW	
TYPE	Unique
DIFFICULTY	1/10
CRITERIA	
Number of Alert Phases	> 100

Notes: Stealth ("*stelth*"; noun): "Avoiding detection by moving carefully".

30.

CROCODILE	
TYPE	Unique
DIFFICULTY	2/10
CRITERIA	
Number of kills	≥ 400

Notes: If you have obtained this emblem, congratulations on a display of brute force "for the greater good" that would have made Machiavelli wince. You had an omelet to make (for which, read: world to save), so you weren't reluctant to crack a few eggs (for which, read: heads). We're not about to disagree with an individual who has just taken down entire battalions single-handedly, but you might – just *might* – consider moderating your use of brute force if you want to unlock any of the Elite Emblems.

31.

GIANT PANDA	
TYPE	Unique
DIFFICULTY	1/10
CRITERIA	
Game time	≥ 30:00

Notes: An accolade for either those who complete *MGS4* at an incredibly leisurely pace or, more likely, people who leave their PS3 and the game running for long periods while off doing other things.

32.

SCORPION	
TYPE	Common
DIFFICULTY	3/10
CRITERIA	
Number of Alert Phases	≤ 75
Number of kills	≤ 250
Number of continues	≤ 25

Notes: The most probable reward for those who generally favor use of non-lethal weaponry, or generally avoid potential enemies, and by far the most noteworthy of the "Common" emblems.

33.

TARANTULA	
TYPE	Common
DIFFICULTY	2/10
CRITERIA	
Number of Alert Phases	≤ 75
Number of kills	> 250
Number of continues	≤ 25

Notes: The "silent but deadly" emblem, awarded to players who generally remain out of sight but mercilessly execute all soldiers that potentially threaten them. If this was your final title, you'll probably be in good shape for a no-kill, no-alert playthrough if you can rein in your trigger-happy instincts for the next playthrough.

34.

CENTIPEDE	
TYPE	Common
DIFFICULTY	1/10
CRITERIA	
Number of Alert Phases	≤ 75
Number of kills	≤ 250
Number of continues	> 25

Notes: For players who tried to remain unseen, but were frequently trodden on when discovered.

Special Completion Bonus: Though there are no rewards specific to the rating, you'll get the Corpse Camo in the (rather unlikely) event that your total continues exceed 41.

35.

SPIDER	
TYPE	Common
DIFFICULTY	1/10
CRITERIA	
Number of Alert Phases	≤ 75
Number of kills	> 250
Number of continues	> 25

Notes: Much like Tarantula, but with one principle difference – you were much easier for your opponents to kill when discovered.

Special Completion Bonus: Though there are no rewards specific to the rating, you'll get the Corpse Camo in the unlikely event that your total continues exceeds 41.

36.

JAGUAR	
TYPE	Common
DIFFICULTY	2/10
CRITERIA	
Number of Alert Phases	> 75
Number of kills	≤ 250
Number of continues	≤ 25

Notes: An emblem for players who didn't feel obliged to blast their way out of the many Alert Phases that their frequent bouts of elephant-grade stealth led to.

37.

PANTHER	
TYPE	Common
DIFFICULTY	2/10
CRITERIA	
Number of Alert Phases	> 75
Number of kills	> 250
Number of continues	≤ 25

Notes: We don't need the powers of Psycho Mantis to discern that those who get *this* particular emblem spend a lot of time playing FPS games – and beating them.

38.

LEOPARD	
TYPE	Common
DIFFICULTY	2/10
CRITERIA	
Number of Alert Phases	> 75
Number of kills	≤ 250
Number of continues	> 25

Notes: The emblem for pacifists with subtlety issues, or for those who regularly chose to simply run for the exit when (frequently) discovered. It's by no means a terrible rating to have, as an unwillingness to engage in brute slaughter bodes well for future playthroughs.

Special Completion Bonus: Though there are no rewards specific to the rating, you'll get the Corpse Camo if your total continues exceed 41.

39.

PUMA	
TYPE	Common
DIFFICULTY	1/10
CRITERIA	
Number of Alert Phases	> 75
Number of kills	> 250
Number of continues	> 25

Notes: Despite being named after a cat that usually avoids human contact, this is a likely emblem for players who attempt to play *MGS4* as a straight shoot 'em up during their first playthrough, and don't fare too well as a consequence.

Special Completion Bonus: Though there are no rewards specific to the rating, you'll get the Corpse Camo if your total continues exceed 41.

40.

CHICKEN	
TYPE	Joke
DIFFICULTY	2/10
CRITERIA	
Number of Alert Phases	≥ 150
Number of kills	≥ 500
Number of continues	≥ 50
Game time	≥ 35:00
Number of uses of life restoring items	≥ 50

Notes: Though it's actually intended to be the worst of all emblems, Chicken actually requires quite a lot of effort to obtain. As an additional reward for your protracted (and messy) labors, you'll also receive a few Unique emblems. Though ostensibly positioned at 40, Chicken actually lies between 20 (Bee) and 21 (Gecko) in terms of prominence when it comes to determining your final "title" at the end of the game.

Special Completion Bonus: Though not directly tied to the rating, you'll definitely get the Corpse Camo with the Chicken emblem.

EMBLEM ITINERARY

There is actually a small bonus for unlocking all 40 emblems: you receive the (frankly marvelous) Snake Eater iPod® tune. As you can unlock multiple emblems on a single playthrough, we've prepared the following basic "playthrough itinerary" that you might like to follow. Naturally, this is purely a suggestion, and you're free to unlock each accolade in the order you see fit. However, the logical progression we offer here will help you to reduce the potential number of individual play sessions to a manageable number.

The "Big Boss Hard" Playthrough

Emblems Unlocked: Fox Hound, Fox, Hound, Wolf, Octopus, Pigeon, Scorpion

Requirements: Number of Alert Phases < 3; Number of kills = 0; Number of continues = 0; Game time < 5:30 ; Rations, Regain, Noodles used = 0; No use of Stealth Camouflage or the Bandana; Big Boss Hard or higher

Notes: As you'll need to both hone your skills and (ideally) acquire certain items for an attempt at the Big Boss emblem, this is excellent preparation – and an approachable second playthrough for seasoned Metal Gear Solid veterans. Though The Boss Extreme is much tougher than Big Boss Hard,

Requirements: Take a deep breath, brace yourself accordingly, and... *here we go.* Number of Alert Phases ≥ 150; Number of kills ≥ 500; Number of continues > 50; Game time > 35:00; Number of uses of life restoring items ≥ 50; Number of times in Combat High ≥ 10; Pick up 400 weapons/items or more; Spend 2:30 hours or more crouching; Spend 60 minutes or more in a prone position; Jump or roll to the side 200 times; Perform 100 or more forward rolls; spend 1:00 hour or more clinging to a wall; Scan or inject 50 soldiers or more with the Syringe or Scanning Plug; Turn the pages of a Playboy or Emotion Mag 100 times or more; Wear the Cardboard Box or Drum Can for over 60 minutes; Perform hold-ups on 50 soldiers or more; Perform body searches on 50 soldiers or more; get praised by militia or rebel soldiers on 25 occasions or more; Give 50 items or more to militia or rebel soldiers; Perform 150 headshots or more; defeat 100 enemies with CQC chokeholds

Notes: There's no reason why you can't unlock the vast majority of the Unique emblems in one playthrough, so that's precisely what we advise you to do. You'll need to spend over ten hours doing something else while working on the time-dependant accolades, and you'll really need the Stealth Camouflage to beat some

you'll have a chance to perfect many of the tricks that will enable you to beat the highest difficulty level. You will also have a chance to unlock or acquire the tools that will help you on the next step, including Emotion Bullets and the Solar Gun. See page 164 for more details.

The "Ultimate" Playthrough

Emblems Unlocked: Big Boss, Mantis, Raven, Little Gray

Requirements: Number of Alert Phases = 0; Number of kills = 0; Number of continues = 0; Game time < 5:00 ; Rations, Regain, Noodles used = 0; No use of Stealth Camouflage or the Bandana; The Boss Extreme; buy all weapons from Drebin's Shop before your playthrough ends

Notes: You can find a guide to completing The Boss Extreme on page 170; our main walkthrough also features an enormous amount of helpful tips and tricks. If you're supremely confident in your abilities, you can jump straight into your The Boss Extreme playthrough, completely skipping our suggested Big Boss Hard session. If you don't practice beforehand, though, there's a very high chance that you'll fail with the ultra harsh time requirement...

The Grand "Chicken" Playthrough

Emblems Unlocked: Chicken, Puma, Giant Panda, Crocodile, Cow, Pig, Hog, Hyena, Lobster, Inch Worm, Frog, Scarab, Gecko, Bee, Rabbit, Tortoise, Gibbon, Ant, Hawk, Blue Bird, Eagle, Bear

of the combat-oriented emblems with relative ease. As it's hard to keep track of how you are faring with certain requirements, note that you can watch the scrolling message during the Mission Briefing cutscenes to learn certain pertinent statistics. You'll need to complete most of them during Acts 1 and 2, but the Confinement Facility, obviously, is a good place to hunt PMC soldiers.

The "Assassin" Playthrough

Emblems Unlocked: Tarantula, Assassin

Requirements: Enemies defeated with knife kills or knife stuns ≥ 50; Number of CQC holds ≥ 50; Number of Alert Phases ≤ 25; Number of kills ≥ 250; Number of continues ≤ 25

Notes: Tarantula and Assassin go **reasonably** well together, so this is both a practical and enjoyable combination. Be careful not to exceed the maximum Alert Phases specified above – Tarantula allows for 75, but Assassin demands no more than 25.

The Bad News

Unfortunately, there's no way to group the remaining emblems (Centipede, Spider, Jaguar, Panther and Leopard) into a single playthrough. However, as all of these can be easily obtained on Liquid Easy, it's simply a case of having sufficient stamina for the final leg of your *MGS4* marathon. It's also a great opportunity to try out all the weapons and gadgets that you've neglected so far.

■Special Equipment

GAME COMPLETION DATA

When you save your progress for the last time after completing *MGS4*, a "Game Completion Data" file is created (Fig. 1). This is always named "Epilogue: The End". To start a new game in which you both retain all existing weapons, ammo and items, plus any rewards you unlocked in your previous playthrough, select "Load Game" and select this file. You will then be taken to a screen where you select the difficulty of your new play session.

All existing equipment and bonus items are made available for use after the meeting with Metal Gear Mk. II in Red Zone, early in Act 1.

SECRET WEAPONS

1911 CUSTOM

Unlock Conditions: Enter a special password in the Extras menu (see page 180).

- It doesn't have any special features, but the 1911 Custom is a solid, highly powerful handgun. Unlike other unlockable weapons, you can add an optional Suppressor at the Customize screen. It makes a good replacement for the Operator on higher difficulty levels, where enemies can sustain greater damage before they fall.

DESERT EAGLE
(LONG BARREL)

Unlock Conditions: Obtain the Fox emblem, or enter a password in the Extras menu (see page 180).

- The Desert Eagle (Long Barrel) (or "D.E (L.B.)" as it appears in the in-game menus) is very powerful – a single shot to the body of a PMC soldier will knock him from his feet.

- Headshots are instantly lethal against PMC soldiers, even on The Boss Extreme.

- The most noteworthy (and best) feature of the Desert Eagle (Long Barrel) is that it comes equipped with a scope. With 3x and 10x zoom modes, it's a more efficient medium-range weapon than most dedicated sniper rifles, with the added benefit that each shot knocks the target over. Even if your first squeeze of the trigger didn't have the desired result, this gives you the luxury of a few moments to make your second shot count. However, you should note that its power decreases quite dramatically with range.

EMOTION MAG

Unlock Conditions: Buy from Drebin.

- As Emotion Mags are available for purchase at Drebin's Shop during your first playthrough, you may wonder why we are mentioning them here. During a subsequent playthrough, though, the pictures of Beasts are replaced by the Beauties hidden within the suits (Fig. 2).

- Just in case you haven't experimented with them, Emotion Mags cause PMC troops (and, if you care to try, militia and rebel soldiers) to develop emotions that correspond with the Beast or Beauty displayed on the open pages. Hold **L1** and **R1**, then tap △ to enter FPS Mode, and finally press ◎ to select a page before you release all buttons to place it on the ground. Haven Troopers will instead salute the magazine. As with Playboys, Emotion Mags have no effect during Alert Phases.

HOW TO PLAY

WALKTHROUGH

INVENTORY

METAL GEAR ONLINE

▶ EXTRAS

CUTSCENE
INTERACTIONS

EMBLEMS

SPECIAL EQUIPMENT

SECRETS

SYNOPSIS

INTERPRETATION

BIOGRAPHIES

EMOTION BULLETS

Unlock Conditions: Available in Drebin's Shop from second playthrough.

- When Drebin's Shop reopens once you reach the end of the Militia Safe House zone, Emotion Bullets are offered for purchase for the first time. This unique form of ammunition is fired via the Mk. 2 pistol (.22 rounds) and Mosin-Nagant (7.62 mm rounds), and comes in four distinct varieties.

- If your chosen difficulty level is The Boss Extreme, you cannot purchase Emotion Bullets (or, indeed, any form of non-lethal ammunition) from Drebin. They don't even appear in his list of wares.

- Emotion Bullets have a profound effect on PMC troops (and, if you choose, militia, rebel and resistance soldiers encountered in the first three Acts). For an immediate effect, you'll need to make a headshot.

- Laugh bullets (yellow) cause targets to be seized by almost uncontrollable mirth. They keep hold of their weapons, and may fire intermittently (and often inaccurately) in Snake's direction if they can see him.

- Rage bullets (orange) make targets roar with anger. If they can't see Snake, they'll stand on the spot and struggle against the powerful emotion. After the initial hit, they're still highly dangerous – they can (and will) fire if Snake is in their field of view.

- Cry bullets (blue) make soldiers drop their weapons and fall to their knees instantly, where they will wail uncontrollably.

- Scream bullets (green) cause solders to drop their weapons and howl with anguish. They may even attempt to flee.

- After the initial effect period is over with all four types of Emotion Bullet, the victim will lose consciousness.

- Two headshots with this ammo type will render a target immediately unconscious.

- Emotion Bullets knock Haven Troopers out, but have no other effects. This makes them extremely useful when you play on The Boss Extreme, but you'll need to prepare (and save) a full supply in a prior playthrough to take advantage of them.

- Finally, if you hit a Beast or a Beauty with an Emotion Bullet that corresponds with her signature emotion (for example, Laugh Bullets for Laughing Octopus), it reduces her Psyche level. However, the amount depleted is lower than standard tranquilizer rounds. If you're attempting a non-lethal takedown, it's much better to stick with basic anesthetic darts.

MANTIS DOLL

Unlock Conditions: Defeat Screaming Mantis in Act 5.

- Though you obtain the Mantis Doll as standard during a playthrough, there aren't any targets (other than, naturally, the Beast herself) that you can use it on. However, this weapon is carried over to future sessions when you start a new game with your Game Completion Data.

- The Mantis Doll enables you to manipulate the bodies of the living. As Snake isn't a skilled "psychokineticist", though, his clumsy attempts to control targets shakes them to death instead. Aim at targets with **L1**, then fire with **R1**. When the slow-moving projectiles fired by the doll hit their target, an onscreen prompt will appear. Hold **L1** and tilt your controller back and forth to throw your unfortunate victim around (Fig. 3).

- Shake a soldier hard enough, and they will usually drop ammunition, grenades, or a healing item.

PATRIOT

Unlock Conditions: Obtain the Big Boss emblem, or enter a password in the Extras menu (see page 180).

- This is the most deadly submachine gun in *MGS4* – its power rating of 425 puts it just ahead of the M10, and its effective range is much higher than any other weapon in its class.

- However, the true beauty of the Patriot is that it never needs to be reloaded, and has infinite ammunition. You literally don't need to stop firing for a second.

- There is a random possibility that the opening strains of the Snake Eater song will be played when Snake fires it.

RACE GUN

Unlock Conditions: Complete *MGS4* once.

- With its poor stopping power and rather pitiful range, you might wonder how the Race Gun can be viewed as a bonus, and initially dismiss it as some form of joke. However, it is actually a truly remarkable pistol, as its bullets ricochet from any surface they hit. This enables you to shoot enemies when they are behind cover or around corners. The potential for mischief should be obvious to all…

SMOKE GRENADES
(Y, R, B & G)

Unlock Conditions: Available in Drebin's Shop from second playthrough.

- Like Emotion Bullets, these special grenades have a powerful effect on PMC soldiers who inhale their smoke (Fig. 4). If sufficiently intoxicated, targets will display unusual behavior before losing consciousness.

- For your reference, "Y" is Laugh, "R" is Rage, "B" is Cry, and "G" is Scream.

- These grenades cannot be purchased if you are playing on the unlockable The Boss Extreme difficulty level.

04

SOLAR GUN

Unlock Conditions: Collect all four Beast dolls and the Frog Soldier figurine.

- The criteria for obtaining this unusual weapon is a little more complicated than other items, so it warrants further explanation. As revealed in the main walkthrough, there are five special "figurines" that you can collect by using non-lethal weaponry in five separate battles. These are the Haven Trooper fight in Advent Palace, and all four Beast confrontations. With the exception of the Frog Soldier Doll and Crying Wolf Doll, these must be collected before the first stage of the subsequent Beauty fight ends. Collect all five, and the Solar Gun is rewarded after the final credits.

05

- If you miss one or more figurines, you need only collect those that you failed to acquire in your previous session. If you're a little sketchy on which ones you need, you can check the table opposite the kitchen area on the Nomad during the Mission Briefing cutscenes, as this is where Sunny proudly displays them. Once you complete the game again, the Solar Gun will be yours to use.

- The Solar Gun has two effects: it depletes Psyche gauges when you hit targets with single shots, and (perhaps more significantly) causes soldiers or even corpses to drop items that they would not usually possess.

- For best effect, you should hold down L1 until the Solar Gun reaches full charge (Fig. 5). Shooting an enemy with a fully charged blast will render them instantly unconscious (which can take several non-charged shots), and cause them to drop up to four items. Shooting a corpse with a fully charged shot will make them drop all potential items at once. Once a soldier or body has dropped its maximum quota of rewards, you will receive no further bonuses.

- Note that the Solar Gun's current charge level will be lost if Snake changes posture or is hit by a bullet. This makes it rather ineffective during pitched battles.

- Using charged shots is essential, because they make lower demands on the Solar Gun's limited battery life than ill-advised barrages. The Solar Gun's battery can only be replenished outdoors in direct sunlight. Move out of the shadows and into a brightly lit area, and then hold ◎ to begin the recharging process. The battery is automatically restored to full power at the start of each Act.

- Despite the noise and obvious visual disturbance, preparing to shoot the charging Solar Gun has no effect on Snake's Camo rating. However, on no-alert playthroughs you should note that the relatively slow-moving projectiles may draw attention towards him, with obvious consequences.

- The Solar Gun is extremely useful on a The Boss Extreme playthrough, especially if you're attempting a "perfect" game. Stun Grenades and Anest. (.22) ammunition are dropped fairly regularly when you hit soldiers or corpses, which makes it a great tool for obtaining vital non-lethal ammunition. It's also unbelievably effective in the fight against Vamp, and can be a real help during the motorbike sequence in Act 3. You can disable a Beauty with two charged shots, though – obviously – you'll need to fire from close range.

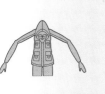

SORROW DOLL

Unlock Conditions: Collect the Sorrow Doll in addition to the Mantis Doll before you defeat Screaming Mantis in Act 5.

- Though you can obtain the Sorrow Doll during your first playthrough, there are no targets you can use it on before the final credits. However, this weapon is carried over to future sessions when you start a new game with your saved Game Completion Data.

- The Sorrow Doll enables you to manipulate the bodies of the dead in exactly the same way as the Mantis Doll enables you to take hold of the living. Shake corpses to find hidden items.

TANEGASHIMA

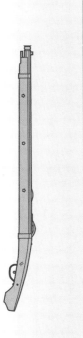

Unlock Conditions: Purchase from Drebin.

- The Tanegashima is the most expensive weapon in *MGS4*, with a basic retail price of 1,000,000 DP. This is reduced to 800,000 DP on Wednesdays and Sundays, or a (rather more manageable) 500,000 DP during Act 5. If you decide to buy it, Outer Haven is the place to make the purchase.

- So: what do you get for your significant investment? Initially, the answer seems to be:

not a great deal. To be frank, the Tanegashima is an awful weapon in general combat. As an antiquated matchlock gun it can only hold one bullet at a time; worse still, the reloading process takes several seconds, with Snake frozen on the spot for the entire time.

- The true beauty of this weapon, though, is its secret effect. Every time you fire the Tanegashima, there is a one in three chance that it will initiate a brief "kamikaze" (divine wind), which will carry any soldiers within its effect radius away (Fig. 6). You don't actually have to hit them with the weapon – it's the direction that counts. As they are buffeted by the howling gale, soldiers will drop an astonishing number of items. The variety isn't great (expect common ammo types and Rations, as a rule), but it's a remarkable way to gain new supplies if you're running low.

- The Tanegashima's special effect will only occur if Snake is outdoors, and if there is sufficient space around him. The latter is a rather broad definition, but as a general rule of thumb: a road would be fine, but an alley probably would not be.

06

THOR .45-70

Unlock Conditions: Obtain the Fox Hound emblem, or enter a password in the Extras menu (see page 180).

- This mighty "hand rifle" combines the power of the best shotguns with the portability and range of a pistol. It comes equipped with a built-in dot sight.

- The Thor .45-70 has one principle drawback: it can only hold one bullet at a time. However, as its reload rating is a perfectly respectable "A", you never need wait too long for your next shot. Headshots are always lethal, though you may need to make two body shots to make a PMC soldier stay down on The Boss Extreme.

TYPE 17 PISTOL

Unlock Conditions: Obtain the Hound emblem, or enter a password in the Extras menu (see page 180).

- This machine pistol carries 10 rounds, and can be fired in Full Auto or Semi Auto modes.

- It's a strange feature, but you cannot manually reload the Type 17 – you need to use the entire clip for Snake to replace it automatically. This means that you'll need to think tactically when you use it.

BANDANA

Unlock Conditions: Complete *MSG4* without killing a single soldier (of any type) or Beauty. Also available from Drebin's Shop for 5,000,000 DP from second playthrough onwards.

- The Bandana provides Snake with infinite ammunition for all weapons when equipped as his active item.

- It has no effect on Batteries or Suppressors.

- The Bandana counts as a "Special Item", so you cannot obtain the Big Boss, Fox Hound, Fox and Hound emblems if you use it. You'll also lose minor DP bonuses at the end of each Act, though this is a lesser consideration.

CAMERA

Unlock Conditions: Found on board the Nomad during the Mission Briefing cutscenes.

- This gadget is extremely easy to use, but it has two secret applications that you might not be aware of.

- If you point the Camera at a Beauty during the "white world" phase, she will strike poses for you (Fig. 7).

- The Camera can be used to hunt "ghosts" hidden throughout Act 4. You can find a full list of their locations on page 176.

- If you don't obtain the Camera until the Act 4 mission briefing, you'll find an exclusive picture of Naomi in the Photo Album (accessed via the Main Menu).

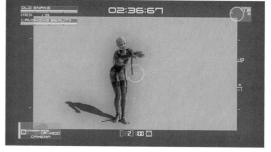

07

SCANNING PLUG

Unlock Conditions: Available for purchase in Drebin's Shop for 10,000 DP after you have played 10 hours of Metal Gear Online, or by entering a password in the Extras menu (see page 180).

- The Scanning Plug (or S-Plug, as it is referred to in the menus) can only be used when it is equipped as the current active item, and Snake has a PMC soldier held in a CQC choke-hold.

- Hold ④ to interface with the nanomachines inside a PMC soldier's body (Fig. 8). While the button is held, you will be able to see the outlines of all soldiers linked into the SOP System in the current zone.

08

STEALTH CAMOUFLAGE

Unlock Conditions: Complete *MSG4* without initiating a single Alert Phase. Also available from Drebin's Shop for 5,000,000 DP from second playthrough onwards.

- Stealth Camouflage makes Snake effectively invisible to the naked eye (Fig. 9). However, he can still be detected by the scanning beams used by Gekko and Dwarf Gekko.

- Even though enemies cannot see Snake, they can still potentially hear him.

- If Snake bumps into enemies, or is hit by stray bullets, the device is disabled immediately.

09

- During an Alert Phase the effectiveness of Stealth Camouflage is vastly reduced. A slight green tinge to Snake's body indicates that enemy soldiers can see him, and will actively fire in his direction. If you find a place to hide and elude your adversaries, the full effect will resume once the Evasion or Caution Phases begin.

- During certain battles where opponents are actively seeking Snake (such as the fracas with the Haven Troopers in Advent Palace, or boss fights), Stealth Camouflage has limited utility. At best, it merely increases Snake's Camo rating; at worst, enemies will see him clearly at all times. Again, a green tinge (and a Camo rating of less than 100%) indicates that Snake is not perfectly concealed from view.

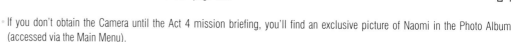

META/GEARSO/ID4
GUNS OF THE PATRIOTS TACTICAL ESPIONAGE ACTION

HOW TO PLAY

WALKTHROUGH

INVENTORY

METAL GEAR ONLINE

▶ EXTRAS

CUTSCENE INTERACTIONS

EMBLEMS

▶ SPECIAL EQUIPMENT

SECRETS

SYNOPSIS

INTERPRETATION

BIOGRAPHIES

SYRINGE

Unlock Conditions: Available after the meeting with Naomi in Act 2.

- The Syringe isn't a secret per se, but this seems as good a place as any to reveal how it works.

- For the first ten uses, its effectiveness is slightly reduced on each occasion.

- For the next ten applications (11 to 20), Snake will lose an increasing amount of Psyche once the effects wear off. He will also vomit, which can be dangerous if you're keen to avoid nearby assailants (Fig. 10).

- All further uses of the Syringe will lead to a reduction in Psyche *and* Life, with further bouts of vomiting to emphasize just how badly Snake is faring.

SECRET APPAREL

Note: the requirements/locations for optional fixed FaceCamo and Disguise types are detailed in the Inventory chapter (see page 106). In this section, we only cover rewards that are obtained by completing *MGS4*.

ALTAIR
(DISGUISE)

Unlock Conditions: Acquire the Assassin emblem, or enter a secret password in the Extras menu (see page 180).

- Those who enjoyed (or, better still, briefly fell for) Hideo Kojima's April Fools' joke can use this disguise to play their own version of Assassin's Solid, or whatever you'd like to call it (Fig. 11).

- Of all optional disguises, the Altair costume seems to have the highest average Camo rating.

BIG BOSS
(FIXED FACECAMO)

Unlock Conditions: Obtain the Big Boss emblem.

- This fixed FaceCamo looks pretty gruesome, but it has amazing properties befitting of the effort required to obtain it…

- If Snake moves close enough for any standard soldier type (PMC, militia, rebel, resistance member) to see his face clearly, they will begin screaming (Fig. 12). They won't stop until they lose consciousness.

- If you approach Haven Troopers while wearing the Big Boss FaceCamo, they will faint immediately.

SUIT (DISGUISE)

Unlock Conditions: Complete *MGS4* once.

- It's absolutely lousy if you're keen to stay out of sight, but completing *MGS4* without being detected while wearing the Suit would be an incredible feat…

- Like the Altair disguise, the Suit is available in almost all gameplay situations.

Secrets

THE BOSS EXTREME

Completing *MGS4* for the first time unlocks a new difficulty level: The Boss Extreme. In this section, we outline the key differences between it and the Big Boss Hard setting, offer a variety of tips for those looking to unlock the Big Boss emblem, and finally provide area-specific guidance for situations where our main walkthrough doesn't fully take this optional difficulty level into account.

Gameplay Differences

The Boss Extreme is preposterously hard in places, and demands nothing less than an encyclopedic knowledge of enemy behavior, numbers and locations. Here are the major challenges you will face:

• The PMC troops, Haven Troopers and anti-governmental forces you encounter have improved sight and hearing, and are more sensitive to anything that seems at all incongruous. You really can't crawl boldly past them in the same way as you might on Solid Normal or even Big Boss Hard.

• There are a greater number of potential assailants. You will encounter more patrols, and a larger number of opponents during set-piece battles (such as the fight against Haven Troopers in Advent Palace – Fig. 1 – or the Crying Wolf confrontation).

• A greater number of reinforcements may enter a zone during a Caution Phase, and an Alert Phase is little short of a disaster.

• All opponents you potentially face are stronger. On no-kill playthroughs, you'll find that tranquilizer darts will immobilize soldiers for a disturbingly short period of time. Additionally, if you opt for lethal force, headshots are a must.

• Snake's permitted allowance for restorative items, ammo and grenades is vastly reduced. The maximum resources you have to work with are detailed in the Inventory chapter, but the most important consideration is that Mk. 2 ammo is limited to a mere 50 rounds.

The most notable difference is that Snake is far less robust. His Stress level rises at an accelerated rate (and significantly so during an Alert Phase), and his Life gauge can be depleted with a brief caress of a trigger during a pitched firefight. Use of cover is an absolute requisite, and you need to employ patient, methodical tactics for all major battles.

Last, but not least, Drebin does not sell non-lethal ammunition on The Boss Extreme. This introduces an element of intelligent resource management to a no-kill playthrough (especially if you're attempting to obtain the Big Boss emblem), and means that you need to be clinically accurate with the Mk. 2 and Mosin-Nagant.

META/GEAR SO/ID 4
GUNS OF THE PATRIOTS TACTICAL ESPIONAGE ACTION

HOW TO PLAY

WALKTHROUGH

INVENTORY

METAL GEAR ONLINE

▶ EXTRAS

CUTSCENE
INTERACTIONS

EMBLEMS

SPECIAL EQUIPMENT

▶ SECRETS

SYNOPSIS

INTERPRETATION

BIOGRAPHIES

Obtaining the Big Boss Emblem

The stringent requirements for this top accolade are tough, especially when you consider the heightened difficulty of The Boss Extreme, but the two things that truly make it a nightmare are the time limit (no more than five hours), and the inability to buy non-lethal ammunition from Drebin.

As preparation, we strongly suggest that you make a practice run through Big Boss Hard beforehand. Unlock the Solar Gun if you haven't already done so (see page 166). The Middle East Militia Disguise (found in the Militia Safe House zone of Act 1) and South American Rebel Disguise (found in the secret Cove Valley Village storeroom at the start of Act 2) will also be useful. When you reach Act 5, buy 10 Stun Grenades, and 10 of each type of colored Smoke Grenade. Ensure that you have 30 V-Ring rounds, and 50 bullets for each category of Mk. 2 and Mosin-Nagant ammunition (anesthetic rounds, and the four types of Emotion Bullets). When you save your Game Completion Data at the end of your playthrough, you'll be ready for The Boss Extreme.

02

- First things first: the game clock only pauses during loading, on the results screen, and throughout the *MGS1* dream sequence. The rest of the time it never stops ticking. Skip all cutscenes, and save regularly. If you need to take a break, if only for a few minutes, wait until you reach a checkpoint, save your progress, and then reset and reload once you're ready to resume. Every second counts.

- Even if you skip all cutscenes, it takes a minimum of 17 minutes to reach the post-game ratings screen from the end of the fist fight against Liquid Ocelot. You'll need to budget for this in your time calculations.

- If you suspect that you have taken too long in a boss battle, it's probably worth the effort to replay it.

Pick your shots carefully – Mk. 2 and Mosin-Nagant ammo is (literally) priceless. Aim to collect additional supplies whenever they are available. The Emotion Bullets can be used in emergency situations.

- Use Stun Grenades against Beauties (Fig. 2). You need to judge each throw carefully to catch your opponent with the full effect, but it should take no more than six to knock her over. As Stun Grenades are relatively plentiful, this will help you to conserve vital stocks of tranquilizer darts.

- As tranquilizer darts have a very temporary effect on your opponents, consider placing a Playboy or Emotion Mag at their feet if you need them to remain distracted for a longer period of time.

- Some players find that it helps to increase the Movement Speed setting in the Options menu during the two on-rails shooting sequences in South America and Eastern Europe.

- Use the special Sailor and Rock Me Baby iPod® tunes to accelerate the healing process whenever Snake is injured.

The Boss Extreme: Walkthrough Addendum

The following table reveals all instances where differences encountered on The Boss Extreme aren't explained in our main walkthrough. We also provide additional tips, where appropriate, for players attempting to win the Big Boss title.

ACT	ZONE	PAGE	TIPS & OBSERVATIONS
MIDDLE EAST	Red Zone	34	When you crawl to the south-west corner after first arriving in the zone, there's an additional soldier in the downstairs room before you climb the stairs (Fig. 3). He'll only begin his patrol when you approach the door, so be ready to retreat and hide when he does.
			After the meeting with Otacon and Metal Gear Mk. II, you'll retrieve all items, weapons, disguises and FaceCamo (Fig. 4) collected during previous playthroughs – including all the non-lethal ammunition you (hopefully) stockpiled at an earlier date.
	Militia Safe House	36	Unless you disable at least one PMC soldier with a tranquilizer dart (or equivalent), the militia in the Safe House zone (and potentially others that follow) may attack Snake on sight.
			If you collected the Middle East Militia Disguise in a previous playthrough, you can equip it straight away. This makes the journey through this zone much quicker.
	Advent Palace	42	This can be savagely hard. There are far more Haven Troopers to deal with – you'll really need to know when to take cover and recuperate, and it's essential that you stick with (and, indeed, protect) your companions at all times. To conserve Mk. 2 ammunition, only fire when you're confident that you can land a direct hit, or you'll soon run out. A shotgun loaded with V-Ring ammo will be extremely useful for moments when you get cornered and need to escape, especially towards the end when Akiba is knocked out. A fully charged Solar Gun or strategically placed Sleep Gas Mines can also be handy, if you have either to hand. Certain Haven Troopers are equipped with the XM25 grenade launcher.
	Millennium Park	46	There's an additional soldier patrolling around the fountain after you go through the building, which makes it slightly harder to successfully sneak into the final area.
SOUTH AMERICA	Cove Valley Village	50	There are additional PMC soldiers guarding the houses and on the slope. If you have sufficient Mosin-Nagant ammunition, you'll benefit by using the alternative strategy of helping the rebel captives to escape. For the section after the checkpoint, the South American Rebel Disguise will help you to save time.
	Power Station	54	You should definitely destroy the control panel inside the substation before you go to meet Drebin. You'll need to take a little more care sneaking inside, but it's plain sailing thereafter.
	Research Lab	64	There are more Haven Troopers in the initial attack wave, but the tactic of hiding under the bed still works well. When you face Laughing Beauty, it's vital that you use Stun Grenades – don't waste your (absolutely essential) anesthetic ammunition.
	Mountain Trail	68	There are two new soldiers in slightly different positions just before and after the river crossing, so be vigilant. The Solid Eye and Threat Ring will help you to locate them, and they can be easily neutralized with tranquilizer darts.
	Stryker Escape	71	The PMC "zombies" are quicker to climb onto the Stryker, especially on the first leg of your journey. It's essential that you prevent the soldiers in powered suits from firing by deploying Chaff Grenades.
EASTERN EUROPE	Midtown S Sector	75	Use the shortcut suggested in the walkthrough. This can shave a few minutes from your time, though you'll probably need to wait until the resistance member approaches the top of the ladder before you tranquilize the PMC soldier.
	Midtown N Sector	79	The route taken by the resistance member through Midtown is identical to Big Boss Hard, but there are generally a few more soldiers dotted around – full OctoCamo is a must. However, there's one additional soldier in particular that might take the unwary by surprise. After you pass the guard on a short patrol route in an alley just before you reach the zone exit (where the resistance member changes back into his standard clothes), there's an additional PMC soldier guarding the final road to the right.
	Bike Escape	80	This is probably the hardest part of a The Boss Extreme playthrough, as reaching the end without using a single healing item is unbelievably tricky. It may take countless attempts, but trust us: it's possible. The most important thing is to have the correct tools at your disposal. You'll need a colored Smoke Grenade (we suggest either the "B" or "G" variety), the Mk. 2, the Twin Barrel loaded with V-Ring ammo, and the Solar Gun. The Smoke Grenades are indispensable for the sequences where the bike stops (just throw them relentlessly – Fig. 5), and areas where you pass large concentrations of opponents; the other weapons should help you to overcome all other challenges. As Snake's Life gauge isn't replenished between the first and second sections of the escape, you can cheat a little by saving your progress, then advancing your PLAYSTATION 3's clock by a few days to restore the bar if necessary.
	Echo's Beacon	82	Raging Raven is much more aggressive, as are the Sliders that accompany her. She'll use her dangerous barrage attack more regularly, so you'll need to rely on your observational skills and intuition to avoid this. When she flies away and returns on a diving approach vector, that's your prompt to run.
SHADOW MOSES	Canyon	88	The two Gekko are awake, alert and patrolling the moment you arrive. Finding your way past isn't hideously difficult by any means, and besides – there's actually a checkpoint moments before.
	Snowfield & Communications Tower	90	There are a few more Haven Troopers to worry about when you face Crying Wolf. They also appear to move more frequently.
	Underground Supply Tunnel	94	Vamp is ridiculously belligerent on this difficulty setting, but has a hidden weakness: he's extremely vulnerable to the Solar Gun (Fig. 6).
			The Suicide Gekko fire more regularly, so it's vital to use cover as the Rail Gun charges.
	Surface Tunnel	94	Don't hang around to harvest Gekko for Drebin Points. Note that Gekko fire more rockets than on other difficulty levels, so there's a degree of danger in this section that is pretty much unique to The Boss Extreme.
	Port Area	96	Liquid is more direct in his tactics, and Metal Gear RAY can take far greater punishment before it falls. The most important difference is that you'll really need to use the Gatling Gun to shoot down the missile barrages – they travel at a greater pace, and a mere three hits can rob you of half a Life Gauge. Under no circumstances should you let RAY get too close – the melee attack is devastating, and you're offered no quarter if knocked over.
OUTER HAVEN	Ship Bow	100	The final Gekko before the entrance door might not be destroyed, but it usually moves away long enough for you to get in. Oh, and crawl at all times – you're being watched from above.
	Command Center	102	You might think that having the Psycho Mantis doll from your previous playthrough will make this a breeze, but no – you can't successfully use it until you knock Screaming Mantis's doll from her hand and collect it. This fight is vicious on The Boss Extreme: Screaming Mantis moves her human "puppets" with greater regularity, so we can't understate how vital it is that you keep moving at all times.
	Ship Exterior	104	Liquid Ocelot uses lots of annoyingly quick and powerful single-hit attacks, and will also employ five-punch combos with an awkward delay before the final two blows. A counter-attacking strategy is a must and, as with Big Boss Hard, use of ⓐ to heal is the key to beating him.

iPod® Tunes List

The following table details the location or unlock conditions for every single iPod® song in *MGS4*. If you need a little help with finding those that are placed in fixed positions, refer to our maps in the Walkthrough chapter.

SONG	ACT	ZONE	CONDITIONS/LOCATION
Takin' On The Shagohod	1	N/A	Available from first play.
Backyard Blues	1	N/A	Available from first play.
Sea Breeze	1	N/A	Available from first play.
Calling To The Night	1	N/A	Available from first play.
Oishii Chuhan Seikatsu	1	N/A	Available from first play.
Metal Gear 20 Years History (Part 1)	1	N/A	Available from first play.
Metal Gear 20 Years History (Part 4)	1	N/A	Available from first play.
Who Am I Really?	1	N/A	Available from first play.
Test Subject Burns	1	N/A	Available from first play.
MGS4 Integral Podcast 01	1	N/A	Available from first play.
Inori no Uta	1	Nomad, Mission Briefing	Choose Mission Briefing from the Main Menu, then select your current save file. You can find the tune in the kitchen once you gain access to Metal Gear Mk. II.
Show Time	1 & 2	Red Zone onwards	Militia and rebel soldiers may give you this gift when you offer them healing items (as long as they regard you as an ally).
MGS4 Love Theme (Action Version)	1 & 2	Red Zone onwards	Militia and rebel soldiers may give you this gift when you offer them healing items (as long as they regard you as an ally).
MPO+ Theme	1 & 2	Red Zone onwards	Militia and rebel soldiers may give you this gift when you offer them healing items (as long as they regard you as an ally).
Destiny's Call – Break for the Fortress	1 & 2	Red Zone onwards	Militia and rebel soldiers may give you this gift when you offer them healing items (as long as they regard you as an ally).
Theme of Tara	1	Militia Safe House	In a small alcove after you pass through the makeshift hospital room.
Zanzibarland Breeze	1	Urban Ruins	In a "secret" area to your left just before you make the final drop down to the zone exit.
Level 3 Warning	1	Advent Palace	On the 3F level.
Theme of Solid Snake	1	Millennium Park	Inside the building, behind the crates as you enter.
Boktai 2 Theme	2	Nomad, Mission Briefing	In the kitchen area upstairs.
The Fury	2	Cove Valley Village	Inside the fire-damaged house.
Rock Me Baby	2	Confinement Facility	On the "island" at the center of the water in the south-east area.
Metal Gear 20 Years History (Part 3)	2	Confinement Facility	Inside the main building; it's on a bed in the dormitory.
Sailor	2	Vista Mansion	Between a shipping container and the east wall of the compound.
Bon Dance	2	Marketplace	This appears when one of the market stalls just in front of your starting position is destroyed.
Shin Bokura no Taiyou Theme	3	Nomad, Mission Briefing	In the kitchen area upstairs.
Test Subjects Duality	3	Midtown S Sector	On the road to the east of your starting position. Run back and collect it after the resistance member arrives.
Bio Hazard	3	Midtown	Perform a hold-up on a resistance member, then make a full body search.
One Night in Neo Kobe City	3	Midtown	Perform a hold-up on a PMC soldier, then make a full body search.
On Alert	3	Midtown N Sector	When you follow the three PMC soldiers and the resistance member, it's in the dead-end where the final soldier departs.
The Essence of Vince	3	Echo's Beacon	On the top floor, in a corner of the outer balcony.
Lunar Knights Main Theme	4	Nomad, Mission Briefing	In the kitchen area upstairs.
Warhead Storage	4	Tank Hangar/Heliport	At the end of the upper ventilation shaft just before you drop down into the Tank Hangar.
Beyond the Bounds	4	Tank Hangar	Located in a locked room accessed via the upper walkway. This is only unlocked once Metal Gear Mk. III opens the zone exit in Nuclear Warhead Storage Building 1F, so you'll need to backtrack to collect it.
Flowing Destiny	4	Canyon	In a small hole in the rock wall to your left just before you reach the zone exit.
Opening Title "Old L.A. 2040"	4	Nuclear Warhead Storage Building B2	Enter the password 78925 in Otacon's old laboratory.
"Policenauts" End Title	4	Nuclear Warhead Storage Building B2	Enter the password 13462 in Otacon's old laboratory.
Metal Gear 20 Years History (Part 2)	4	Nuclear Warhead Storage Building B2	In the laboratory you sneak through on your way back to the elevator.
The Best Is Yet To Come	4	Snowfield & Communications Tower	Just inside the building that you enter to reach the zone exit.
Yell "Dead Cell"	4	Casting Facility North	Just before you reach the zone exit after you cross the conveyor belts.
Metal Gear Solid Theme (The Document Remix)	5	Ship Bow	Use the hatch near your starting position; it's just a short crawl away.
Subsistence Action	N/A	N/A	Enter at least one game of Metal Gear Online.
Big Boss	N/A	N/A	Reward for obtaining the "Big Boss" emblem.
Snake Eater	N/A	N/A	Reward for unlocking all 40 emblems.

HOW TO PLAY

WALKTHROUGH

INVENTORY

METAL GEAR ONLINE

▶ EXTRAS

CUTSCENE
INTERACTIONS

EMBLEMS

SPECIAL EQUIPMENT

SECRETS

SYNOPSIS

INTERPRETATION

BIOGRAPHIES

Special iPod® Tunes

Certain iPod® songs have unique properties when played, as we reveal in this table. When we use the phrase "ordinary soldiers", we're referring to PMC troops and the militia and rebel forces encountered in Acts 1 and 2.

SONG	EFFECT(S)
Oishii Chuhan Seikatsu	If you play this during the "white world" phase of each Beauty battle, your opponent will start to dance (Fig. 7). They may still attack if you get too close, though. Additionally, you'll get to enjoy Sunny dancing in the video feed in the bottom left-hand corner of the pause menu.
Bon Dance, MPO+ Theme & One Night in Neo Kobe City	When you capture an ordinary soldier in a CQC hold, he may begin to laugh.
Sailor & Rock Me Baby	Snake's rate of Life recovery is increased.
Show Time & Bio Hazard	When you capture an ordinary soldier in a CQC hold, he may begin to scream.
Opening Title "Old L.A. 2040"	This song helps to steady Snake's hands.
"Policenauts" End Title	When you grab a soldier with a CQC hold, he will fall asleep instantly.
Love Theme – Action Version & Flowing Destiny	When you capture an ordinary soldier in a CQC hold, he may begin to cry.
Beyond the Bounds	This increases the amount of stun damage inflicted on ordinary soldiers when you use certain weapons (such as the Mk. 2).
The Fury & Destiny's Call – Break for the Fortress	Ordinary soldiers may be seized with uncontrollable rage when captured in a CQC hold.
Subsistence Action	Snake's hands shake less, and ordinary soldiers may be seized with uncontrollable rage when captured in a CQC hold.
Big Boss	Snake's hands shake less, stun damage against ordinary soldiers is increased, and there's a chance that PMC troops will scream when captured in a CQC hold.
Snake Eater	Increases the rate of Life recovery, reduces hand shaking, increases stun damage inflicted on ordinary soldiers, and will cause PMC soldiers to fall asleep immediately when they are captured in a CQC hold.

GHOSTS

There are 30 hidden ghosts in the Shadow Moses maps. Over the following pages, we'll reveal where you should go to find each one. Ghosts can only be seen if you are looking through the viewfinder of the Camera, and have the Sorrow Doll equipped as your current weapon (see page 102 and 167). When photos containing these mysterious apparitions are studied at the Photo Album screen, you'll find a new option: Exorcise. This removes the ghost from the current picture, with a suitably ominous (though amusing) sound effect played to mark its passing.

Just in case you're curious, some ghosts are famous faces from *MGS1*; others are members of the *MGS4* development team. You may need to wait for a moment before they become visible, especially if they are outside when the snowstorm is at its worst.

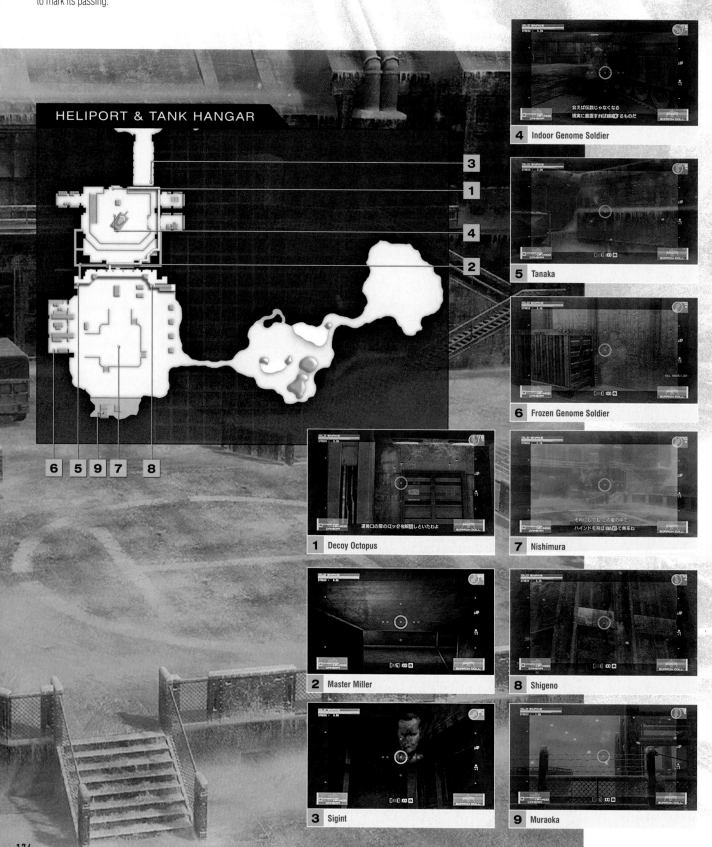

HELIPORT & TANK HANGAR

3
1
4
2

6 5 9 7 8

4 Indoor Genome Soldier

5 Tanaka

6 Frozen Genome Soldier

1 Decoy Octopus

7 Nishimura

2 Master Miller

8 Shigeno

3 Sigint

9 Muraoka

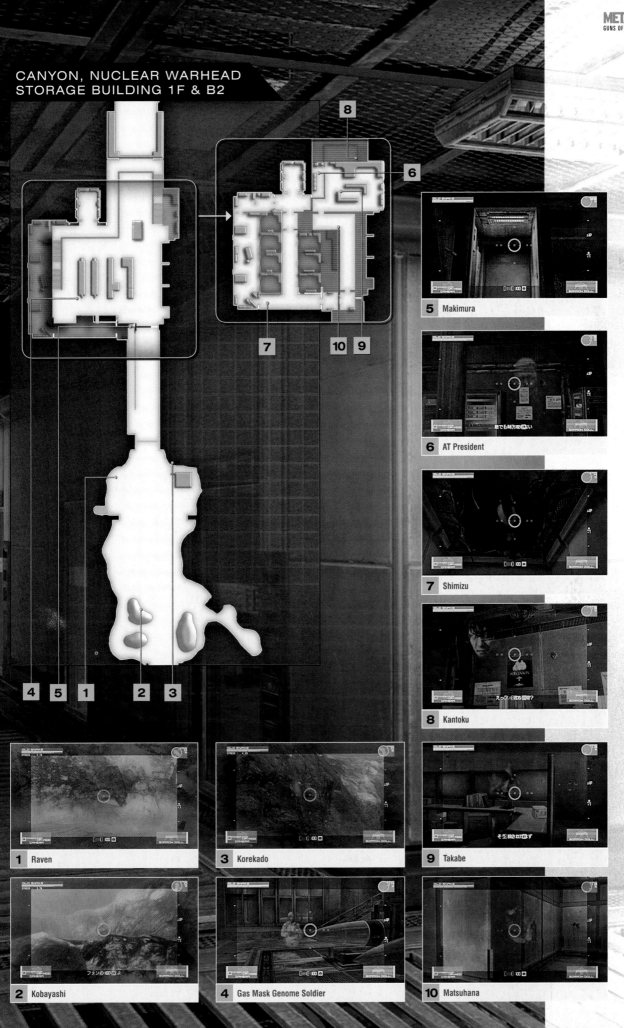

CANYON, NUCLEAR WARHEAD STORAGE BUILDING 1F & B2

METAL GEAR SOLID 4
GUNS OF THE PATRIOTS TACTICAL ESPIONAGE ACTION

HOW TO PLAY
WALKTHROUGH
INVENTORY
METAL GEAR ONLINE
EXTRAS

CUTSCENE INTERACTIONS
EMBLEMS
SPECIAL EQUIPMENT
SECRETS
SYNOPSIS
INTERPRETATION
BIOGRAPHIES

5 Makimura

6 AT President

7 Shimizu

8 Kantoku

9 Takabe

1 Raven

3 Korekado

2 Kobayashi

4 Gas Mask Genome Soldier

10 Matsuhana

SNOWFIELD & COMMUNICATIONS TOWER & CASTING FACILITY

1 Sniper Wolf

3 Shinkawa

5 Sasaki

2 Sato

4 Nakamura

6 Hirano

UNDERGROUND BASE & SUPPLY TUNNEL

5

4

3

1

2

1 Negishi

3 Liquid

2 Kaneda

4 Cyborg Ninja

5 Kimura

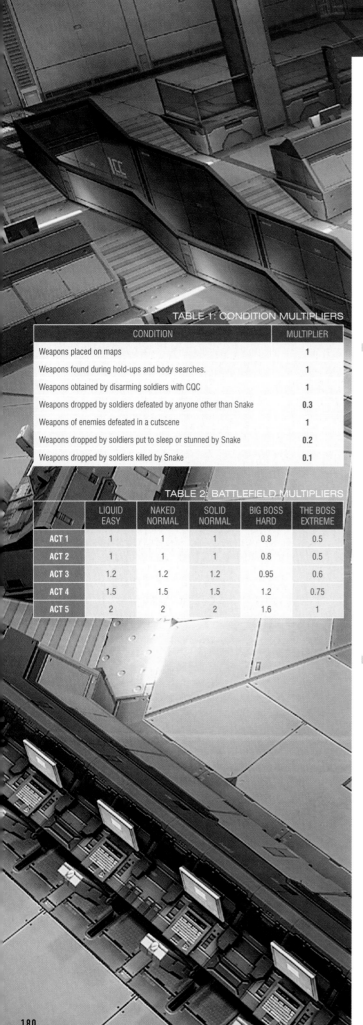

EXTRAS PASSWORDS

You can use the Extras option at the Main Menu to enter secret passwords that will unlock certain special weapons or items (Mk. 23, Type 17, Desert Eagle (Long Barrel), 1911 Custom, Thor .45-70, Patriot, Altair Disguise, Scanning Plug). These passwords will be revealed by Konami at a later date, so don't count on using them straight away.

Once you enter a password (which requires that you go online), you will receive the corresponding item. All you have to do then is load a saved game or start a new session; with the latter instance, you'll need to wait until after the meeting with Metal Gear Mk. II to try out your new weapon, disguise or gadget.

DREBIN POINTS

If you have been agonizing over how Drebin Point awards are calculated, sit up straight and pay attention – the answers you seek lie in this section.

■ Collecting Weapons: Drebin Point Calculations

Whenever you collect a weapon following the meeting with Drebin in the Urban Ruins zone, you receive a DP bonus that is adjusted in accordance with the following criteria:

1: The weapon's basic value.
2: The way the weapon was obtained (Table 1).
3: The difficulty level you are playing on (Table 2).
4: The current Act (Table 2).

The calculation, with 1 representing 100% of the basic weapon value, works in the following way:

Basic sale value **×** *condition multiplier* **×** *battlefield multiplier* = total.

For example, if you obtain a P90 by tranquilizing a Haven Trooper in Advent Palace on the Big Boss Hard difficulty level, the maths looks like this:

1,500 DP **×** 0.2 (soldier stunned) **×** 0.8 (Big Boss Hard, Act 1) = 240 DP

■ Post-Act DP Bonuses

The Drebin Point bonuses you receive at the end of each Act are calculated with a simple formula. With each of the eight categories, you have a *maximum bonus* for a "perfect" playthrough (that is, if you meet the *maximum bonus criteria*), or a general bonus for any other totals above or below that (as applicable) up until a cutoff point (in other words, if you are within the *general bonus criteria*).

Confused? Don't be. Look at the following simple examples.

- If you complete Act 1 with 0 kills, you meet the maximum bonus criteria, so you will receive the maximum bonus for that Act – 20,000 DP. Anything over 0 kills prevents you from receiving this reward.

- If you complete Act 1 with 1 kill, you will be given the full general bonus of 10,000 DP.

- If you complete Act 1 with 2 kills, you are still within the general bonus criteria, but you are further from your target, so your general bonus will fall to 9,000 DP.

- If you complete Act 1 with 10 kills, you are at the lowest degree of the general bonus criteria, so your general bonus will fall to 1,000 DP.

- If you complete Act 1 with 11 kills, your performance falls beyond the general bonus criteria, and you will receive 0 DP.

TABLE 1: CONDITION MULTIPLIERS

CONDITION	MULTIPLIER
Weapons placed on maps	1
Weapons found during hold-ups and body searches.	1
Weapons obtained by disarming soldiers with CQC	1
Weapons dropped by soldiers defeated by anyone other than Snake	0.3
Weapons of enemies defeated in a cutscene	1
Weapons dropped by soldiers put to sleep or stunned by Snake	0.2
Weapons dropped by soldiers killed by Snake	0.1

TABLE 2: BATTLEFIELD MULTIPLIERS

	LIQUID EASY	NAKED NORMAL	SOLID NORMAL	BIG BOSS HARD	THE BOSS EXTREME
ACT 1	1	1	1	0.8	0.5
ACT 2	1	1	1	0.8	0.5
ACT 3	1.2	1.2	1.2	0.95	0.6
ACT 4	1.5	1.5	1.5	1.2	0.75
ACT 5	2	2	2	1.6	1

HOW TO PLAY

WALKTHROUGH

INVENTORY

METAL GEAR ONLINE

EXTRAS

CUTSCENE
INTERACTIONS

EMBLEMS

SPECIAL EQUIPMENT

SECRETS

SYNOPSIS

INTERPRETATION

BIOGRAPHIES

ACT	CATEGORY	MAXIMUM BONUS CRITERIA	MAXIMUM BONUS	GENERAL BONUS CRITERIA	GENERAL BONUS RANGE
ACT 1	Total time	Within 50 minutes	15,000	50 to 150 Minutes	10,000 to 10
	Number of continues	0	10,000	1 to 5	5,000 to 1,000
	Number of Alert Phases	0	20,000	1 to 5	5,000 to 2,000
	Number of kills	0	20,000	1 to 10	10,000 to 1,000
	Number of healing items used	0	10,000	1 to 5	5,000 to 1,000
	Weapons owned	69+	10,000	68 to 1	5,000 to 70
	Flashbacks	40+	10,000	39 to 1	5,000 to 120
	Special items	Unused	5,000	-	-
ACT 2	Total time	Within 100 minutes	15,000	100 to 300 Minutes	10,000 to 10
	Number of continues	0	10,000	1 to 10	5,000 to 500
	Number of Alert Phases	0	20,000	1 to 10	5,000 to 1,000
	Number of kills	0	20,000	1 to 20	10,000 to 500
	Number of healing items used	0	10,000	1 to 10	5,000 to 500
	Weapons owned	69+	10,000	68 to 1	5,000 to 70
	Flashbacks	105+	10,000	104 to 1	5,000 to 40
	Special items	Unused	5,000	-	-
ACT 3	Total time	Within 160 minutes	15,000	160 to 450 Minutes	10,000 to 10
	Number of continues	0	10,000	1 to 15	5,000 to 340
	Number of Alert Phases	0	20,000	1 to 15	10,000 to 670
	Number of kills	0	20,000	1 to 30	10,000 to 340
	Number of healing items used	0	10,000	1 to 15	5,000 to 340
	Weapons owned	69+	10,000	68 to 1	5,000 to 70
	Flashbacks	143+	10,000	142 to 1	5,000 to 30
	Special items	Unused	5,000	-	-
ACT 4	Total time	Within 210 minutes	15,000	210 to 600 Minutes	10,000 to 10
	Number of continues	0	10,000	1 to 20	5,000 to 250
	Number of Alert Phases	0	20,000	1 to 20	10,000 to 500
	Number of kills	0	20,000	1 to 40	10,000 to 250
	Number of healing items used	0	10,000	1 to 20	5,000 to 250
	Weapons owned	69+	10,000	68 to 1	5,000 to 70
	Flashbacks	207+	10,000	206 to 1	5,000 to 20
	Special items	Unused	5,000	-	-
ACT 5*	Total time	Within 300 minutes	15,000 × Multiplier	300 to 750 Minutes	10,000 to 10 × Multiplier
	Number of continues	0	10,000 × Multiplier	1 to 25	5,000 to 200 × Multiplier
	Number of Alert Phases	0	20,000 × Multiplier	1 to 25	10,000 to 400 × Multiplier
	Number of kills	0	20,000 × Multiplier	1 to 50	10,000 to 200 × Multiplier
	Number of healing items used	0	10,000 × Multiplier	1 to 25	5,000 to 200 × Multiplier
	Types of weapon collected	69+	10,000 × Multiplier	68 to 1	5,000 to 70 × Multiplier
	Flashbacks	273+	10,000 × Multiplier	272 to 1	5,000 to 10 × Multiplier
	Special items	Unused	5,000 × Multiplier	-	-

Difficulty Level	Multiplier
Liquid Easy	x1
Naked & Solid Normal	x2
Big Boss Hard	x5
The Boss Extreme	x10

* The Drebin Point bonuses for the final Act are calculated in the same way as those before it, but with one key difference – a multiplier is applied to your final total in accordance with your difficulty level.

SECRETS CHECKLIST

In this section, we take a visual tour of the many optional secrets, Easter eggs and miscellaneous features that can be found in *MGS4*. The vast majority of these are mentioned in the main Walkthrough chapter, so don't feel obliged to continue reading if you'd prefer to find and see them for yourself.

■ **Mission Briefings**

There's much more to these interactive cutscenes than you might initially suspect.

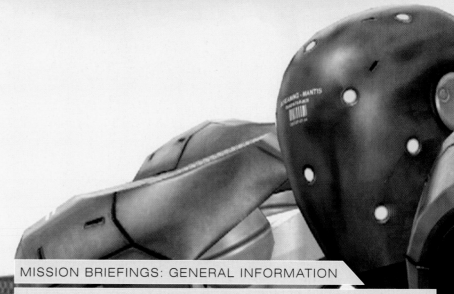

MISSION BRIEFINGS: GENERAL INFORMATION

- You can carry a maximum of six Batteries, all collected during the Mission Briefing cutscenes. They will continue to appear in each subsequent Mission Briefing until you hit this limit.

- Once the Camera or iPod® tunes have been collected, they will not appear on future playthroughs if you start a new session by using Game Completion Data.

- The Frog Soldier Doll, Laughing Octopus Doll, Raging Raven Doll, Crying Wolf Doll and Screaming Mantis Doll are all displayed on the table in front of the television in the upstairs room once collected.

- You will often find "general" supplies such as Rations, Noodles and ammunition during Mission Briefings.

- There is a remote control that changes position between each Mission Briefing. Hit it with R1, and the video screen downstairs will display a slideshow of Akina Minami.

- You can switch on the stereo in the kitchen with R1, and then cycle through the available channels by pressing the button again.

Act 1 Mission Briefing: As soon as you can save your game at Ground Zero, you can exit to view the Mission Briefing for Act 1 from the Main Menu. You'll find the Camera, a Battery, an iPod® tune, a box of ammo and a Ration. Save your game when prompted. When you resume play, you'll only have access to the Ration and iPod® tune; the ammunition becomes available once you collect a weapon, and the Battery once you acquire the Solid Eye and Metal Gear Mk. II. If you reload this Mission Briefing and use a save file after you acquire FaceCamo from Laughing Octopus in Act 2, you can bump Metal Gear Mk. II into Campbell to obtain his fixed FaceCamo type.

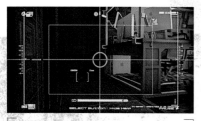

Act 2 Mission Briefing: If you didn't collect the Camera earlier, you can do so now. There's also an additional Battery and an iPod® tune.

Act 4 Mission Briefing: As usual, there's a Battery and an iPod® tune to collect. There's also a new picture on the wall upstairs next to the snapshot of Olga. This changes on every day of the week, so there are seven individual photos to see in total. If you refrain from collecting the camera until Act 4 on your first playthrough, you'll find a unique picture of Naomi in the Photo Album.

Act 3 Mission Briefing: There's another Battery and iPod® tune to collect. You can also obtain the Cyborg Raiden – Visor Closed, Cyborg Raiden – Visor Open, and Otacon fixed FaceCamo types by bumping Metal Gear Mk. II into Naomi, Sunny and Otacon respectively.

Act 5 Mission Briefing: You don't get to explore during this Mission Briefing, but you can look around the room and move the position of the projected image with the two thumbsticks.

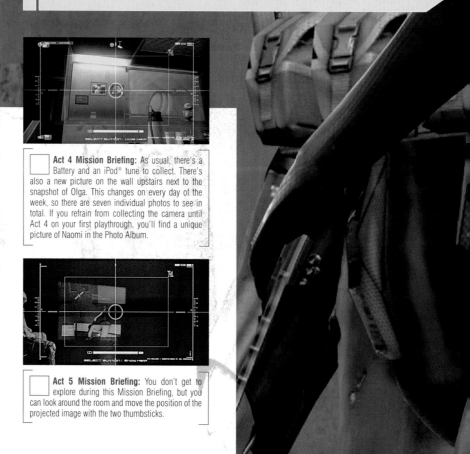

Act 1

Ground Zero: In the second short gameplay section, you can view a different cutscene depending on which end of the short street you run towards.

Militia Safe House: The Middle East Militia Disguise is hidden inside a locker in a room to the north-east of the zone. When Snake wears this, militia soldiers will ignore him completely. This can only be equipped in Act 1.

Downtown: You can blow up the helicopter that arrives when you reach the entrance to Advent Palace.

Ground Zero: If you attempt to hide on the upper floors of the broken buildings, a Gekko may climb onto the outer wall and scan the room.

Militia Safe House: This actually applies to both Acts 1 and 2. Once you endear yourself to militia or rebel soldiers, they will then (almost automatically) give you items whenever you encounter them. It's invariably a package of instant Noodles, though…

Advent Palace: You can crawl through the ventilation shaft on the roof of Advent Palace to attack the second wave of Haven Troopers from above. There are also collectible items to find.

Red Zone: You can climb onto the plinth just in front of the zone entrance; hold ▲ to make Snake imitate the missing statue.

Advent Palace: Once Johnny disables the explosive device, you can run and roll over the gap to find a hidden cache of items.

Red Zone: If you have used Game Completion Data to start a new game, all of Snake's equipment from your prior playthrough(s) is returned after you meet Metal Gear Mk. II. You also have access to FaceCamo well before the Laughing Octopus fight.

Militia Safe House: You can improve your relations with militia and rebel soldiers by giving them Rations, Regain or Noodles. Once you reach maximum allied status, they will usually reciprocate by offering ammunition, healing items and even iPod® tunes whenever you hand something over.

Advent Palace: If you reach Advent Palace Garage without killing a single Haven Trooper, you'll find the exclusive Frog Soldier Doll in plain view when you arrive.

Militia Safe House: If you backtrack to Red Zone having failed to help the militia forces out earlier, the battle outside is slightly different. A Stryker will drive along the road and stop just ahead of the sandbags where you start.

Downtown: Once you acquire the Drum Can, you can roll around inside it and even cannon into soldiers, but using this trick for more than a few seconds at a time makes Snake vomit and lose a large chunk of Psyche.

Crescent Meridian: If you safely escort the militia tank to the end of the street, it blasts the road block, which opens an alternative path to the next zone. There's no way to prevent its subsequent destruction, but you can help the local soldiers win the battle against the PMC forces.

Cove Valley Village: Look through the window of the house to the left of your starting position – you'll see a PMC soldier perusing a copy of Playboy.

Power Station: Disabling the control panel also allows access to a secret area. Climb to the top of the metal tower outside, then traverse along one of the two wires to reach the adjacent pylon.

Research Lab: If you defeat Laughing Octopus by reducing her Psyche gauge to zero, you can find the Laughing Octopus Doll on top of a bed during the Laughing Beauty fight.

Cove Valley Village: If you attack the PMC soldiers and protect the captives as they scramble to their feet, the rebels will open an otherwise locked door in the building to the right of your starting point. You can find some useful items inside, including the South American Rebel Disguise.

Confinement Facility: You can improve your relationship with the rebels by freeing the four captive soldiers. This also increases the number of rebels who will fight alongside you in the Vista Mansion area.

Research Lab: If you move onto a bed and lie down when you face Laughing Beauty, she will climb on top and embrace Snake.

Cove Valley Village: Equip the South American Rebel Disguise, and you can join the rebel soldiers as they attempt to sneak to the next zone once you pass the checkpoint. It's much too tricky without the disguise.

Vista Mansion: Once the bulldozer smashes through the gates, all PMC soldiers are removed from every map prior to Vista Mansion. This is a good opportunity to backtrack for items you might have missed earlier.

Research Lab: If you equip the Camera during the "white world" phase of every Beauty fight (not just this one), your opponent will pose for pictures. If you play the Oishii Chuhan Seikatsu iPod® tune, she will dance.

Power Station: If you destroy the control panel inside the power transmission substation, the entire zone (and Cove Valley Village) will be under rebel control after the cutscene. If you don't, and you reach Drebin before the rebels can cut the power, the zone will be under PMC control.

Vista Mansion: You can find two pictures of Akina Minami inside the mansion. The first is hidden behind a painting in the reception area (shoot to reveal it), and the second is in plain view above the bed upstairs. Viewing either in FPS Mode will cause Snake to acknowledge the model by name; if depleted, his Psyche gauge will be replenished at an accelerated rate.

Research Lab: Beat Laughing Beauty with non-lethal weapons, and you'll receive the Laughing Beauty FaceCamo.

Act 3

Mountain Trail: As you cross the bridge, look to your right to see a PMC soldier relieving himself into the river. You can also sneak up behind him to make a surprise attack.

Midtown S Sector: You can climb onto the plinth in the park area and disguise Snake as a statue, just as you did in Act 1, with obvious consequences if you do so before the resistance member relieves himself.

Midtown Central Sector: You only need to visit this area on Big Boss Hard and The Boss Extreme. The resistance member can be found admiring yet another full-color shot of Akina Minami at the start.

Midtown Central Sector: Just to the left of the poster, there's another (albeit smaller) pedestal that you can climb on top of to pose as a statue.

Mountain Trail: If you take the left-hand path to reach the river, you'll encounter a circular patch of flattened grass that resembles a crop circle. Stand at the center of it until the audio sequence ends to receive a 1,000 DP bonus. (Dedicated fans of the series will recognize the voice as being the AI-generated Campbell from *MGS2*.)

Midtown S Sector: Using the standard camera control (don't hold L1 to aim, or use FPS Mode), look around regularly as you make your way through Midtown. You should spot a shifty-looking individual in a trench coat and hat peeking out from behind cover at various points of your journey. Just in case you haven't realized the significance of this, it's actually the disguised Dwarf Gekko encountered inside the church – they track Snake from the very start of the mission (and, indeed, this is how Liquid learns the location of the resistance HQ). There's no point in attempting to shoot, as they have an uncanny knack of leaning back behind cover before you can line up a shot, and will depart long before you run over to investigate.

Echo's Beacon: If you allow Raging Raven to complete three grab attacks (with at least one of these ending in a floor slam), you can view a semi-secret attack where she carries Snake above the building and attempts to drop him to his death. If you follow our strategies in the Walkthrough chapter, you're likely to miss this event.

Mountain Trail: When you encounter a PMC soldier poised over a live Claymore, take the path to the north-east. The metal plate on the ground is covered with signatures and handprints from the *MGS4* development team. If you stand on top of it and go prone, you can acquire the unique "Hand Print" OctoCamo pattern. Go to the Camouflage menu to register it for future use.

Echo's Beacon: If you beat Raging Raven with non-lethal weapons, you can find the Raging Raven Doll on the outer balcony of the top floor during the Beauty fight.

Marketplace: When market stalls are destroyed, collectible items are left in the wreckage – including, in one instance, an iPod® tune.

Midtown S Sector: There's another poster of Akina Minami before you leave the zone – you'll usually find the resistance member gazing at it before he crosses the road.

Echo's Beacon: Defeat the Beauty by reducing her Psyche gauge to zero, and you'll be rewarded with the Raging Beauty FaceCamo.

Heliport: If you approach one of the two inactive security cameras while "The Best is Yet to Come" is still playing, you'll see a brief "secret" cutscene. This also includes an optional ⊗ Flashback interaction. There is a unique sequence for both cameras, but you can only see one per session.

Nuclear Warhead Storage Building B2: There are three secret passwords you can enter when the keypad prompt appears. 14893 leads to a 100,000 DP bonus, while 78925 and 13462 give you two iPod® tunes.

Snowfield & Communication Tower: There are four optional audio flashbacks after the Crying Beauty battle ends: just to the south of your starting point once the cutscene ends (near the corner of the north tower), by the crashed helicopter in the north-east, on the lower walkway of the south communications tower, and in the snow-covered "path" at the very south of the map.

Heliport: You can hear optional audio flashbacks at the center of the helipad, the gates to the south, and just inside the upper ventilation shaft.

Nuclear Warhead Storage Building B2: You can hear an optional audio flashback if you approach the locker in Otacon's old laboratory.

Snowfield & Communication Tower: If you annoy the four wolves, they will attack Snake. They can be knocked unconscious, but are otherwise invincible.

Tank Hangar: If you choose to enter the Tank Hangar by crawling through the upper ventilation shaft, you should notice that the rats inside have little exclamation marks that appear above their heads as Snake approaches them. This is a subtle homage to *MGS1*.

Nuclear Warhead Storage Building B2: It's possible to use Metal Gear Mk. III to electrify the floor panels in the corridor to kill the Gekko. Just press ④ when your mechanical helper approaches the flashing control panel

Blast Furnace: As long as an Alert Phase isn't in progress, you'll hear another audio flashback during the elevator ride between the Blast Furnace and Casting Facility zones.

Tank Hangar: There's an optional audio flashback trigger location on the staircase.

Snowfield & Communication Tower: If you defeat Crying Wolf with the Mosin-Nagant (or, less plausibly, other non-lethal weapons), you can find the Crying Wolf Doll just behind you once the Beauty battle begins.

Underground Supply Tunnel: Vamp is extremely vulnerable to the Solar Gun. It's laughably easy to beat him if you have it.

Tank Hangar: One of the upstairs doors is locked when you first arrive. You can backtrack here to access the room after Otacon restores power in the Nuclear Warhead Storage Building zone, after your battle against the two Gekko.

Snowfield & Communication Tower: Defeat Crying Beauty with non-lethal weapons to obtain her FaceCamo type.

Underground Supply Tunnel: Try to shoot Vamp as he fights Raiden on top of Metal Gear REX, and Snake will refuse.

METAL GEAR SOLID 4
GUNS OF THE PATRIOTS TACTICAL ESPIONAGE ACTION

HOW TO PLAY

WALKTHROUGH

INVENTORY

METAL GEAR ONLINE

▶ EXTRAS

CUTSCENE
INTERACTIONS

EMBLEMS

SPECIAL EQUIPMENT

▶ SECRETS

SYNOPSIS

INTERPRETATION

BIOGRAPHIES

Surface Tunnel: You can earn a six-figure sum of Drebin Points by hanging around to shoot Gekko when you sit at the helm of Metal Gear REX. You only need to make a break for the exit when there are approximately two minutes remaining.

Command Center: The conclusion of the Psycho Mantis cutscene is slightly different if you have a DualShock 3 controller.

Otacon always seems to have something to say to Snake when contacted via Codec – there are literally hundreds of optional conversations. His wisdom tends to run dry after a few contacts in each area, but he's full of new ideas once you reach the next zone. Assigning the Codec menu to SELECT in the Options menu is a good idea if you intend to make regular contact.

Act 5

Ship Bow: There are four hatches that you can use to gain access to objects hidden below the deck. The first, near to Snake's starting position, contains an iPod® tune.

Ship Exterior: When Liquid Ocelot makes his signature gesture, press and hold ▲ to replenish Snake's Life gauge.

There are two different cutscene conclusions to each of the four Beauty fights. The one you watch depends on whether you beat her by draining her Life bar or Psyche gauge.

Command Center: You can enjoy a number of Codec conversations that reference the Psycho Mantis battle in MGS1 if you refrain from using the Syringe straight away. There's also a secret Codec exchange between Otacon and Snake if you change your controller number.

Ship Exterior: If Liquid Ocelot catches Snake in a chokehold during the third stage of the fight, don't press anything. Eventually, Liquid will plant a kiss on Snake's cheek.

In many cutscenes, you can use ◯ to zoom by a variable amount (it's pressure sensitive), and ⊕ to move the camera slightly while the view is magnified.

Command Center: The Screaming Mantis Doll is located by the door at the north of the room during the Screaming Beauty fight.

If you press R2 when a character is introduced in a cutscene for the first time, the motion capture actor's name is displayed instead of the voice actor's.

Miscellaneous

Command Center: Beat the Beauty with non-lethal weapons, and you'll receive the Screaming Beauty FaceCamo.

If you kill over 50 soldiers during a single Act, Snake will hear an accusatory voice from the past and be overcome by nausea.

When Snake's Psyche gauge is reduced during a cinematic sequence, rapidly tap ✕ to replenish it.

■ SYNOPSIS

The story of the *Metal Gear* series spans over one hundred years, from the origins of The Philosophers to the conclusion of *Metal Gear Solid 4*. Each game in the series is, broadly, a self-contained episode, yet they are all intricately interwoven; to have missed an installment can rob certain encounters or revelations of their full impact. In this synopsis (and the following interpretation) of the entire *Metal Gear* narrative, we explore its key moments and developments to enable readers (die-hards and newcomers alike) to better enjoy this absorbing tale.

COLONEL VOLGIN

NAKED SNAKE

MAJOR ZERO

I – THE DAYS OF IDEALS

The starting point of the *Metal Gear* saga, the creation of The Philosophers, occurred during the early 1900s. This unique and deeply secretive organization was established by a select group of eminent figures from the three countries that were to dominate the century that lay ahead: the United States, Russia and China. Together, these individuals gathered a practically boundless sum of funds, known as The Philosophers' Legacy, that they believed would be sufficient to win any present or future world conflict. Those who wield the resources to wage war also possess the means to prevent it, and The Philosophers sought to achieve this noble goal by using their incredible resources and powerful influence to steer world history away from brutal, needless warfare. However, with time and the death of its founding members, the raison d'être of this clandestine committee was gradually corrupted; The Philosophers' philosophy was not passed on to posterity. In the confusion and chaos that ensued after the Second World War, the USSR – or, more precisely, an individual named Colonel Volgin – recovered and gained sole possession of The Philosophers' Legacy.

Much of the story behind *Metal Gear Solid 3* (the first episode in the chronology of the series) concerns the fight between the three countries that created The Philosophers' Legacy to claim it for themselves. During the Cold War, the growing nuclear arsenals

possessed by the US and USSR led both nations to adhere to a doctrine of *mutual assured destruction* – the fact that a strike by one nation would lead the other to retaliate with equal or greater force. With a full-scale ground war deemed impractical (and, moreover, a catalyst for the inevitably lethal escalation that would surely follow), and any potential nuclear strike certain to trigger "launch on warning" (or "fail deadly") systems, both sides instead engaged in proxy battles on both actual and ideological battlefields. The events of *Metal Gear Solid 3* take place in 1964 following the Cuban Missile Crisis, a breakdown in diplomacy that brought both nations closer to Armageddon than ever before or since.

An American agent (Naked Snake) is sent in to Soviet territory by the US secret services to facilitate the defection of a scientist (Nikolai Sokolov) who is poised to finalize the creation of a weapon so powerful that it could disrupt the delicate balance that prevents nuclear warfare between the two superpowers. To accomplish his mission, Naked Snake has the support of a remote team that includes his commander (Major Zero), a medical adviser (Para-Medic), an expert in technology and intelligence (Sigint), and his former mentor, a legendary female warrior known, with due reverence, as The Boss.

PARA-MEDIC

SIGINT

THE BOSS

A master in the arts of infiltration and survival techniques, Naked Snake succeeds in making contact with Sokolov. When attempting to escape, however, they are confronted by The Boss who, against all odds, chooses to join forces with Colonel Volgin, and provides him with two US-made portable nuclear warheads as a token of her sincerity. Volgin, in possession of The Philosophers' Legacy and aided by The Boss and Ocelot (a young prodigy of the Russian military), plans to overthrow Soviet Premier Nikita Khrushchev's government and use the Shagohod weapon created by Sokolov to enable the USSR to win the Cold War. In a distinctly one-sided fight, The Boss seriously injures Naked Snake and leaves him near death. Volgin and his allies then leave with Sokolov in order to force him to complete his invention. Gravely wounded, Naked Snake witnesses the explosion of the research center where the Shagohod was developed when Volgin activates one of the two nuclear devices.

As Naked Snake is convalescing in hospital in the week following his rescue and extraction, the President of the United States receives a call from Soviet Premier Khrushchev. Aware that the destruction of the research center was caused by an American bomb, Khrushchev demands that they make amends by eliminating Volgin who, being an ally of his political rival Leonid Brezhnev, he regards as a dangerous adversary. Major Zero and Naked Snake are given the opportunity to find redemption for their earlier failure by helping to avert a major global crisis. The objective of their mission (dubbed "Snake Eater") is to retrieve Sokolov, destroy the Shagohod, and execute Volgin and The Boss.

SOKOLOV

THE SHAGOHOD

OCELOT

E V A   G R A Y   F O X   N A O M I   H U N T E R

Naked Snake is sent back to Soviet territory, where he is told to expect the assistance of two local agents, Adam and EVA. On arrival, he finds EVA – but not a trace of Adam. A CIA mole operating within Volgin's organization, EVA reveals where Sokolov is detained. Naked Snake eventually succeeds in destroying the Shagohod and killing Volgin after a protracted and spectacular battle. One last task then awaits Naked Snake: to fulfill his mission, he must bring down his mentor, his spiritual mother, his former lover, The Boss. As they stand poised to fight she talks of her life, and relates many of the numerous sacrifices she has made as a soldier. Naked Snake battles with his emotions and wins the duel to the death, and is given the microfilm containing the access codes to The Philosophers' Legacy just before The Boss dies. Naked Snake then escapes with EVA, who steals the microfilm as he sleeps. In the message she leaves behind, it is revealed that EVA was actually an agent of the Chinese government, tasked with the responsibility of gaining control of the Legacy for her country.

The closing moments of *Metal Gear Solid 3* provide answers to many questions. It appears that the defection of The Boss was a huge deception to enable her to approach Volgin and retrieve the Philosophers' Legacy. Her final duty was to accept her role as a traitor to the last, and die at the hands of her apprentice in order to conceal her true mission. For killing The Boss, Naked Snake is promoted to the rank of living legend, Big Boss, and is entrusted with the command of the elite FOXHOUND unit. It also becomes clear that EVA (having served the United States, Volgin and, ultimately, China) was not unique in her status as a triple agent. In a startling twist, it is revealed that Ocelot was actually working for the United States government, despite his involvement with the two Soviet factions in the story. The microfilm he left for EVA to steal was a fake; the genuine article is returned to the US.

The events of *Metal Gear Solid 3*, as we learn during its denouement, are all due to a complex yet slickly executed series of maneuvers devised to retrieve The Philosophers' Legacy from the clutches of Volgin. The Boss irrevocably tarnishes her reputation by defecting in order to infiltrate Volgin's organization, her gift of two nuclear warheads an irredeemable act of treason, a point of no return; the clinically brutal (yet, as we understand with hindsight, subtly restrained) humiliation of her protégé in their first battle underlines her apparent dedication to Volgin's cause. Volgin's use of one of the two miniature nukes to destroy Sokolov's research centre leads to a rapid chain of events that enables the US Government to return Naked Snake to Soviet soil to play his unique (and unwitting) role in the Byzantine ploy. Ocelot, loyal to the Americans (and, incidentally, the biological son of The Boss), is the contact that Naked Snake is supposed to meet (under the moniker "Adam"). However, Ocelot chooses to remain deep undercover, allowing the Chinese agent EVA (ostensibly a second American spy, but in truth attempting to gain control of the Philosophers' Legacy for her country) to greet him instead.

For Volgin, the defection of The Boss was to be the final ingredient in his plan to overthrow Khrushchev and employ Sokolov's Shagohod weapons platform to gain a

decisive advantage in the Cold War. Ironically, he simply succeeded in introducing another enemy agent to his ranks, and instigated his own downfall. The Boss and Ocelot were loyal to the United States, and EVA to China; as for Sokolov, he would hate to see his weapon in the hands of the Colonel. The Boss and her son Ocelot cleverly steer events in the required direction, all the while knowing perfectly well the game each protagonist is playing. The Boss assists EVA because she knows the microfilm EVA seeks will ultimately prove to be a fake; she also "protects" her apprentice Naked Snake, as she intends for him to take over her role after her death. Ocelot, meanwhile, does his part to ensure that the Shagohod and Volgin are eliminated before he carries off the Philosophers' Legacy on behalf of the United States. In doing so, he additionally satisfies the agendas of Khrushchev (Volgin is dead), of Brezhnev (Khrushchev's position as Soviet Premier is weakened by the crisis, with Brezhnev his most likely successor) and, most pertinently, of the US (whose recovery of the Legacy is concealed in the aftermath).

The Boss was certainly the one who knew best what the whole incident had in store for her. A patriot to the very last, she chose to die for her country by assuming the mantle of traitor. Naked Snake understands her gesture and the significance of her sacrifice at the end of the adventure. His grief and disenchantment are heightened by the sheer perversity of his elevation to the rank of Big Boss by the superiors that so casually discarded her predecessor, the woman he worshipped above all others.

This was the price of The Boss's ideal, the cost of her commitment. She was ready to die for the way of life she freely chose, the expression of liberty that she lived for: love and loyalty to her country. It was this ideal that led to the birth of the infamous "Patriots".

II – THE DAYS OF CORRUPTION

Individuals may die, but their contributions, their actions and ideas, can abide long after death. Major Zero and Big Boss (Naked Snake's new name) chose to embrace the ideals that The Boss held dear. Her willingness to sacrifice all for the protection of her country left a lasting impression, and led to the creation of The Patriots in the early 1970s. This elite organization, bankrolled by The Philosophers' Legacy and dedicated to the protection of the United States, originally consisted of six founding members: Major Zero (the group's senior figure), Big Boss, Ocelot, EVA, Sigint (later known as Donald Anderson) and Para-medic (alias Dr. Clark).

In order to ensure the supremacy of the United States, The Patriots envisaged a radical solution: a process of imposing the political, economic and social model of the US on the rest of the world. By standardizing other nations through subtle manipulation, nurturing facsimiles of their own cultural and political landscape, they believed that they might prevent future opposition or outside threat. In doing so, they misinterpreted (or, perhaps, simply lost sight of) the true passion behind the principles of the woman that inspired them: her belief in individual liberty, which underpinned her desire to defend her nation at all costs, even at the expense of her own life. Where The Boss might

ROY CAMPBELL

SOLID SNAKE

have led by example, The Patriots (and particularly Zero) increasingly sought total control to achieve their ultimate goals; the ends, in their eyes, would justify the means.

With the practically inexhaustible resources that The Philosophers' Legacy put at their disposal, the influence of The Patriots grew as banks, foundations, corporations and, indeed, governments came to rely on their investments. With the iconic Big Boss promoted as a living legend, helping to guide the opinions of the masses and the rich and powerful alike, The Patriots began to shape the development of the world's political and social landscape. As the organization's power grew, so too did the disillusionment of Big Boss, who felt manipulated and exploited by Zero, and repulsed by his methods.

Realizing the growing distance between the two friends, Zero secretly launched the "Les Enfants Terribles" project. Through the expertise of Dr. Clark (alias Para-Medic), an egg donation from her Japanese assistant, and with EVA acting as a surrogate mother, three clones of Big Boss were created in utmost secrecy: Solid Snake, Liquid Snake and, later, Solidus Snake. When Big Boss learnt of this betrayal, he came to realize that his friend attached little, if any, significance to the founding principles of The Patriots, and that his thirst for power would eventually suffocate all freedom in the world.

The estrangement of the two friends was now complete. Where Major Zero dreamt solely of control over minds and information, Big Boss began to obsess over freedom; a total, anarchic, furious freedom; the drastic removal of all constraints and rules, an open and permanent battlefield where men could let their impulses and desires flow recklessly. Zero desired total order, and Big Boss the very antithesis: total chaos, extremes of individual liberty.

Big Boss left The Patriots and disappeared for several years, enabling Zero to consolidate his power and influence. The games *Metal Gear* and *Metal Gear 2: Solid Snake* tell the story of how Big Boss (assisted by Frank Jaeger, alias Gray Fox) seized control of two [fictional] nations with an army of mercenaries – first Outer Heaven, and later Zanzibarland. On both occasions, Big Boss would be foiled by Solid Snake, his son (or, to be more precise, clone – though this was not clear to Snake at the time). Despite being unaware of their existence, Solid Snake unwittingly acted as a tool of The Patriots – and, specifically, Zero. Once Snake completed his mission in Zanzibarland, The Patriots secretly retrieved the bodies of Big Boss and Gray Fox. The former was kept in a state of perpetual coma; Gray Fox was made a test subject for experimental body enhancement surgery, eventually becoming the Cyborg Ninja.

For Zero, the perceived betrayal of his friend heightened his contempt for humanity. Rather than hand control of the organization to a subsequent generation of secret governors, he instead chose to initiate the development

of a computerized system that would, ultimately, manage world affairs in accordance with his beliefs: in particular, his belief that society could only function through uniformity with restricted individual will.

The Boss's deeply human ideals of freedom and personal commitment were therefore profaned, neglected under Major Zero's command until they degenerated into a perverted and pathological obsession with control and order, a fear of unanticipated innovation or initiative, and a belief in the power of enforced conformity to engender perpetual, manageable repetition. Naturally, such an appalling betrayal of The Boss's legacy could not go unchallenged.

III – THE DAYS OF REVENGE

For Ocelot and EVA, the two founder members who still understood and appreciated the true nature of the sacrifice made by The Boss, a growing unease with the methods and corrupted ideology of The Patriots solidified into a sense of outrage. But how might they strike out at an omnipresent enemy, an organization with agents embedded within political, military and economic hierarchies throughout the world? To conceal any evidence of their involvement, they devised a sophisticated conspiracy of bewildering complexity.

The first step in their clandestine fight to destroy The Patriots from within was accomplished by Gray Fox, who (with the assistance of Naomi Hunter, recruited by EVA) escaped from the laboratory where Patriot scientists had transformed him into the Cyborg Ninja. His assassination of Dr. Clark, better known as Para-Medic, was vengeance for years of monstrously cruel medical procedures and experiments.

That said, the true beginning of their grand plan took place in 2005, with the events of *Metal Gear Solid*. The story begins as a group of terrorists seize control of an Alaskan nuclear weapons disposal facility ("Shadow Moses"), which secretly houses a radical new weapon: Metal Gear REX. In response to the crisis, the US Secretary of Defense commissions Roy Campbell (former commander of special forces group FOXHOUND) and Solid Snake to neutralize terrorist leader Liquid Snake (Solid's twin brother) and his men – with Ocelot counted among their numbers.

LIQUID

METAL GEAR REX

The Shadow Moses Incident, as it would subsequently be known, was initiated by United States President George Sears (Solidus Snake, the third Big Boss clone), who sought to obtain test data from the Metal Gear REX project as part of a plan to escape the control of his masters, The Patriots. He commissioned Ocelot to retrieve the required disc from the Shadow Moses facility, unaware that Ocelot himself was a founder member of The Patriots. Ocelot, in turn, was of course working to achieve his own ends.

To gain control of Metal Gear REX, Liquid attempts to obtain access codes held by two directors of the REX project: Donald Anderson (or Sigint, a founder member of The Patriots) and Kenneth Baker. Having taken both hostage during the takeover of the Shadow Moses facility, Liquid interrogates Anderson without success. He instructs Ocelot to torture him but, naturally, Anderson immediately recognizes his fellow Patriot; the clinical Ocelot kills him and passes it off as an unfortunate accident. Liquid then attempts to elicit the codes from Solid Snake by instructing one of his men to pose as Anderson. Snake is fooled by this subterfuge, but does not hold the information that Liquid requires, and is perplexed when Anderson suddenly dies of an apparent heart attack. Snake, it transpires, is the unwitting vector for a nanomachine-based virus called FOXDIE, created and introduced into his bloodstream prior to the mission by Naomi Hunter, a member of his support team.

Unable to gain the access codes, Liquid has only one option left available – to use special security keys to activate Metal Gear REX. Snake obtains these when he rescues rookie soldier Meryl Silverburgh from a prison cell. As he fights his way through the complex, Snake encounters individuals such as the Cyborg Ninja, (Gray Fox, the Patriot guinea pig seeking both vengeance and redemption for past crimes), Hal "Otacon" Emmerich (in the first meeting of an abiding friendship), and Ocelot. In a confrontation that would have lasting repercussions, Ocelot's right arm is severed by Gray Fox during a gunfight with Snake.

Once the keys are activated, Liquid takes control of REX. In the battle that ensues, Gray Fox sacrifices his life to enable Snake to triumph against the war machine. As Snake escapes with Meryl, a final confrontation occurs between the two brothers before the FOXDIE virus finally kills the previously relentless Liquid.

Details of the Shadow Moses Incident are leaked to the press, and the existence of Metal Gear REX is revealed on the eve of a planned nuclear disarmament agreement. President George Sears, we learn, is actually Solidus Snake – the third child of the "Les Enfants Terribles" project. Now in possession of the Metal Gear REX test data, as secured by Ocelot, Solidus abandons his presidency and disappears from public life.

In the two years between the Shadow Moses Incident and the continuation of the story in *Metal Gear Solid 2*, Solidus hides from The Patriots and prepares a plan of vengeance against them. Meanwhile, Snake and Otacon join forces to found Philanthropy, an independent non-governmental organization dedicated to preventing the proliferation of Metal Gear technology.

In 2007, Snake and Otacon learn that a disguised oil tanker transporting a new, inordinately powerful amphibious model of Metal Gear (Metal Gear RAY) is due to pass close to New York City. Snake infiltrates the vessel and obtains footage of the robot, but matters take a turn for the worst when Ocelot activates a series of explosions to scuttle the tanker and then suddenly, inexplicably, suffers a series of convulsions that seem somehow connected to his replacement right arm. It becomes apparent that he is seemingly possessed by the spirit of the deceased Liquid Snake – the original owner, in fact, of Ocelot's new limb. Under the control of Snake's brother, he escapes aboard Metal Gear RAY before apparently regaining control of his full faculties.

The story resumes two years later in a water purification complex (the "Big Shell") built on the site where the tanker sunk. Once again, the events that occur do so due to the meticulous and multifaceted designs of The Patriots, with Ocelot again serving his own separate and artfully concealed interests.

In fact, while central character Raiden initially appears to have been deployed to combat a terrorist threat, the entire setup is a bewilderingly elaborate real-life simulation, modeled on the Shadow Moses Incident and devised to push its principle protagonist (Raiden) to the very limits of his mental and physical endurance. This experiment is a part of the "Solid Snake Simulation" plan (abbreviated simply as "S3"), contrived to enable The Patriots to explore the complexities of the human psyche so that they might better control it. By studying Raiden's responses (and, indeed, those of other players in the charade) to the evolving challenges and conditions, The Patriots ultimately hope to refine an AI system created to select and filter the overabundance of information that defines the digital era.

The Big Shell purification facility was built on the pretext that the sunken tanker had leaked oil, but is actually a mobile fortress and home to Arsenal Gear, the latest development in Metal Gear technology. The Big Shell is controlled by GW, a Patriots AI system engineered by Emma Emmerich (Otacon's step-sister) to manipulate the free flow of ideas and data throughout the world. When Solidus and his followers attack the facility to take control of Arsenal Gear to aid their fight against The Patriots, the shadowy organization has – naturally – anticipated and encouraged this attack.

Indeed, almost every party involved in the Big Shell experiment has been unknowingly manipulated by The Patriots to act out the principle events of the Shadow Moses Incident. Solidus and his cohorts play the role of Liquid and the "terrorists"; Olga Gurlukovich, blindly following orders in the hope that she might see her kidnapped daughter Sunny again, dons a sophisticated body suit to become the Cyborg Ninja; Raiden, ostensibly deployed to thwart Solidus, is their principle test subject, and is therefore given the role of Snake. Even the deception of Raiden in Codec conversations with his superiors and support team broadly replicates the lies that Snake was forced to endure in his fight to stop Liquid and Metal Gear REX.

Only Ocelot and Solid Snake (and, perhaps, Otacon) appear to be outside the operational parameters of this most sophisticated simulation – Ocelot still seeking

RAIDEN

MERYL

OTACON

the downfall of the organization he helped to create, Snake searching for a meaning to his life outside the narrow confines of the values embraced by his former paymasters. As rogue variables in an intricate program, it is they that cause the simulation to "crash" – their actions and involvement lead to a situation where a computer worm created by Emma Emmerich attacks GW. Though it does not destroy the AI as planned, Emma's program seriously impairs its functionality.

By the end of the drama aboard the Big Shell, virtually all of its actors are dead bar Raiden, Ocelot, Snake and Otacon. In the final battle of *Metal Gear Solid 2*, Raiden complies with the wishes of The Patriots and eliminates Solidus, despite learning the real purpose of his "mission". Devastated by the sheer spirit-crushing import of their revelations, and his submission to their lies, he is nonetheless inspired by a speech made by Snake. Raiden, the veteran warrior explains, is free to commit to (or, indeed, fight for) any way of life or action he has faith in, and his humanity stems from the sincerity of his faith. Strangely, this is strongly reminiscent of the beliefs held so dear by The Boss; the very principle of individual liberty which has inspired the ongoing attempts of Ocelot and EVA to destroy The Patriots from within. Perhaps this is why Ocelot does not attack Snake during the story of *Metal Gear Solid 2*: that, despite their different roles and methods, both fight for the same cause.

In the aftermath, we can reflect that Ocelot has gained the most from the Shadow Moses and Big Shell Incidents. Of Solidus, only a body remains, but like that of Big Boss, it still has an important role to play. The Patriots fear the bizarre eruptions of spiritual possession that cause Ocelot to act under the control of Liquid Snake,

but do not understand that they are merely an exquisitely conceived subterfuge used to conceal Ocelot's true objectives. Ocelot and EVA have engineered the deaths of two active founders of The Patriots, and stand poised to confront the last of them: Major Zero, whose demise lies at the end of their path to redemption.

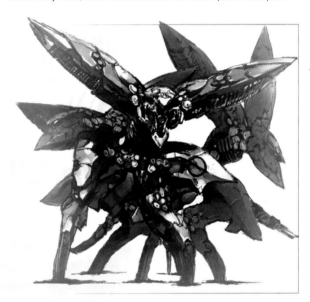

METAL GEAR RAY

EMMA EMMERICH

OLGA GURLUKOVICH

SOLIDUS

LIQUID OCELOT

IV – THE DAYS OF REDEMPTION

Almost every protagonist in the *Metal Gear* saga bears a burden, and seeks atonement for past sins, or fights to settle a score. From Naomi, who cannot forgive herself for her dire inventions (particularly the FOXDIE virus), to Ocelot and EVA, who strive to bring an end to The Patriots (the organization they helped to create), to Raiden, who is haunted by memories of life as a child soldier, it is a desire for redemption that drives the events of *Metal Gear Solid 4*.

After Arsenal Gear runs aground on Manhattan Island in 2009, the international community unites in its condemnation of the United States Government. To address the growing fear of powerful state-run armies being used to satisfy questionable political agendas, it is deemed safer to entrust Private Military Companies (PMCs) with a greater degree of control in future conflicts. Technically bereft of ideology or motive beyond a drive to increase profitability, and held to account by both shareholders and public opinion, the meteoric growth of these corporations leads to an unforeseen development: the "war economy", where all aspects of armed conflict (from weapons R&D and manufacture, to the salaries paid to individual mercenaries) becomes an integral dynamo that drives global financial markets. War, in short, becomes the key to prosperity and growth.

The mechanism that facilitates the growth of the war economy is called Sons of the Patriots (SOP): a secured system of real-time battlefield control. All soldiers and PMC mercenaries under its watchful eye are injected with nanomachines that identify each individual, monitoring and essentially controlling their behavior, interacting with a host's metabolism and manipulating body chemistry to vastly improve combat ability. Controlled by a central AI, these nanomachines are used to engender a "combat high" to suppress natural human instincts, negating potential anxiety, apprehension or remorse as soldiers engage their opponents. Other benefits include heightened awareness and improved teamwork; on a strategic level, SOP is the culmination of every military tactician's most feverish dreams.

An additional application of the System is to restrict the use of military hardware, from small arms to vehicles, to approved subjects only. Combatants can only use a weapon if their ID authorizes them to do so; the central AI ensures that a soldier's rifle is deactivated in the hands of any other individual, even his colleagues. Throughout the world, virtually all weapons – both previously existing and newly manufactured – are modified or designed for exclusive use with the SOP System.

On a micro level, SOP breeds a new generation of more compliant, peerlessly efficient soldiers; on a macro level, military officials can monitor and instantly react to developments on the battlefield. This is the realization of the "clean" conflict ideal, a perceived end to human rights violations, whereby weapons can be deactivated (or soldiers restrained on a biological level) to prevent acts of barbarity. Another attraction for governments is that conflicts fought by PMC contractors are cheaper, and remove the need for states to maintain large standing armies.

A side-effect of the "war economy", however, is that armed conflict becomes a business like any other. The PMC corporations, unfettered by nationalist sentiment or political dogma, begin to offer their services to the highest bidder: be that nation state, guerilla movement or even terrorist faction. By 2014, PMCs control more than half of the world's combined military forces.

As the story of *Metal Gear Solid 4* begins, five PMC corporations, each one a multinational with unprecedented influence in world affairs, dominate their shared marketplace. However, all five are controlled by a single parent company, Outer Heaven, whose principle director is none other than Liquid Ocelot: Ocelot possessed by Liquid.

After the story of *Metal Gear Solid 2* ended, Snake and Otacon located Olga Gurlukovich's daughter, Sunny, and rescued her from the clutches of The Patriots. This fragile prodigy now lives with them permanently aboard their aircraft, the Nomad, where she contributes her extraordinary computer skills (and, it soon becomes apparent, rather less miraculous culinary ability).

Metal Gear Solid 4 begins as Roy Campbell, now retired, contacts a prematurely ageing Snake to request that he undertake a new mission. Unusually, this will not

SUNNY

DREBIN

conclusion of events in the Middle East. Rather than manipulating the nanomachines within each soldier's body (as initially assumed), Liquid Ocelot had simply deactivated them. Freed from the influence of these microscopic yet powerful devices, the soldiers were instantly subjected to the full force of the psychological and physiological effects that the SOP System had previously repressed. It might take a war veteran a lifetime to barely come to terms with their role in a conflict. Stress, pain, remorse, fear, revulsion, anger, and more: all these extremes of feeling were unleashed *within a second* at Liquid's command, suffocating the soldiers' minds and causing them to cease to function beyond a basic animal level. The SOP System, in essence, operates as a prophylactic. Beyond this barrier, the blood, brain and flesh of each subject remembers and stores every detail. Outwardly the very epitome of calm, capable professionalism, the biological reality for each soldier was anything but sanguine – the utilitarian SOP System being designed to repress effects, not address causes.

Perplexed by Snake's vulnerability to this phenomena – as someone who should lie outside the command of the SOP System – and his premature ageing, Naomi takes a blood sample and performs a battery of tests on the veteran soldier. From this, Snake learns a dizzying barrage of revelations. Firstly, his accelerated ageing is not a side-effect of FOXDIE, but a biological inevitability. The Les Enfants Terribles project created copies of the greatest soldier in the world. What might happen if that genetic material fell into enemy hands? For that reason, Snake was designed to be sterile and fast-ageing. By Naomi's calculations, he has little more than six months to live.

Moreover, this ageing process is causing the FOXDIE virus to mutate. Naomi estimates that this previously target-specific, weapons-grade nanovirus might begin infecting ordinary humans within three months. After a life of fighting weapons of mass destruction, and those who might seek to wield them, the

be under the mandate of a specific organization or government, but merely for the greater good. It appears that Liquid Ocelot is planning to use the five PMCs under his control to launch an insurrection; Snake's mission is to eliminate him before this can happen. The manhunt begins in the Middle East, Liquid Ocelot's last known location. Arriving in a warzone where PMC forces battle against a local guerrilla faction, he meets Drebin: a dealer of "laundered" weapons with no fixed ID codes, and therefore usable by anyone. Drebin injects Snake with suppressive nanomachines to negate the effect of older models introduced into his system many years previously.

As he stealthily progresses through the conflict zone, Snake meets his designated contacts: Rat Patrol Team 01, a special forces unit commissioned to monitor and report on the battlefield activities of PMCs. The leader of this unit is none other than Meryl, daughter of Campbell, who assisted Snake during the Shadow Moses Incident. She's accompanied by three men, including Johnny (AKA Akiba), famous for his gastrointestinal adventures throughout the *Metal Gear* series. Meryl and her team are on a mission to assess the danger that a potential insurrection by Liquid Ocelot could represent.

When Snake locates Liquid Ocelot, he attempts to line up a clear shot, but is interrupted as the surrounding soldiers are suddenly subjected to enormous pain and confusion. Struggling through this sobbing, convulsing, agonized crowd, Snake also falls afoul of the mysterious effect, missing his opportunity to assassinate Liquid Ocelot, and only barely noticing the presence of Naomi Hunter at Liquid's side before losing consciousness. When he awakes aboard the Nomad, Otacon reveals that he has received an encrypted message from Naomi. In it, she reveals that she has been taken prisoner by Liquid Ocelot, and is being forced to work on the SOP System.

Snake travels to South America and infiltrates the compound where Naomi is detained. When the two meet, Snake learns the true nature of the inexplicable

JOHNNY

irony does not escape Snake. Furthermore, Naomi detects a new strain of FOXDIE, clearly a recent introduction into his system.

Snake understands that Liquid Ocelot's plan isn't to destroy the "Sons of the Patriots" system, as doing so would cause the collapse of his own army. Instead, his objective – dubbed "Guns of the Patriots" – is to gain sole control of the system, leaving him with the only valid army in the world. Liquid Ocelot performs a second SOP "experiment", causing the same effects witnessed in the Middle East. In the confusion, Snake and Naomi escape with the assistance of Raiden, now evidently a cybernetic hybrid much like Gray Fox before him. The incredible battle takes a terrible toll on the white-haired warrior. Leaking white blood from countless wounds, barely clinging to life, Raiden implores Snake to seek out Big Mama in Eastern Europe.

As the Nomad travels to its next destination, Sunny and Naomi develop a close (and, in the context of the story, rather pivotal) bond as we learn more about Liquid Ocelot's plans. In order to take control of Sons of the Patriots, he needs to obtain Big Boss's genetic code and biometric data: the keys to the virtual castle. The two disruptions of SOP in the Middle East and South America had been Liquid Ocelot's attempts to use code and data derived from Liquid (through his replacement arm), and then Solid Snake (from the tests performed by Naomi). The unsatisfactory results were the consequence of Liquid and Solid Snake's status as incomplete clones – the modifications (infertility, short life span) common to the brothers actually caused both attempts to fail, as only Solidus was an authentic clone of his "father".

To realize his goal, Liquid Ocelot needs to locate Big Boss's body, apparently maintained in an artificial coma as a "biomort", at a secret location. Big Mama currently acts as its caretaker – and, as Naomi divulges, their enemies know this, and are already en route.

In Eastern Europe, Snake trails a member of the local resistance forces and enters Big Mama's hideout. He discovers that she is in fact EVA, one of the Patriot founders who first met Big Boss (then Naked Snake) while working as a Chinese spy over half a century before. EVA explains that Liquid Ocelot is waging a war to eliminate Major Zero, and that The Patriots are attempting to exert total control via a system of AI programs: GW (believed defunct), TJ, AL and TR (the initials of the four American presidents represented on Mount Rushmore), all controlled by JD ("John Doe"), the master AI. Following the neutralization of GW on the Big Shell in 2009, these AI programs continued to monitor and filter the flow of information through world networks. From politics to finance, law to social values and, latterly, the war economy, nothing escapes the attention of these indefatigable sentinels. However, GW was merely "fragmented" by Emma Emmerich's digital attack, and is now held by Liquid Ocelot. By using GW in conjunction with the data derived from Big Boss's body, Liquid Ocelot will have everything he needs to cross otherwise impenetrable security barriers and take control of The Patriots' system.

Despite Snake and EVA's best efforts, Liquid Ocelot succeeds in obtaining Big Boss's body, which is subsequently consumed by fire. Meryl's armed intervention with a

VAMP

RAGING RAVEN

! RECONSTRUCTION

Ultimately, the story of Metal Gear Solid 4 is the conclusion of a vast conspiracy through which Ocelot and EVA (with Naomi's help) exact their revenge on Major Zero, and open the doors of redemption for themselves. We should be under no illusions as to the true role of Ocelot from the very start. As Big Boss reveals, "In order to fool the system, Ocelot used nanomachines and psychotherapy to transplant Liquid's personality into his own mind. He used hypnotic suggestion to turn himself into a mental doppelganger of Liquid." Foreseeing every step Snake would make, every likely outcome, Ocelot allows his apparent adversary to complete the most integral parts of his plot because he understands, fundamentally, that Snake is the tool of The Patriots, and therefore above suspicion in their eyes – whether he knows it or not. The evidence that underlines Snake's status as an unwitting agent of The Patriots is abundantly clear. Drebin, of course, is a Patriot employee with a clear assignment to assist Snake whenever necessary; the name "RAT PT 01" (an anagram of "PATR10T") should leave no uncertainty as to the true benefactors behind Meryl's special forces team. Snake is the weapon wielded by The Patriots in the fight against Liquid Ocelot, and the new FOXDIE virus injected by Drebin a bullet with Ocelot's name on it.

Ocelot knows that the only way to bring down The Patriots is to infect the central AI, JD, with a virus. However, there are prerequisites that must be met for this plan to work: one, that the virus code be of a sufficiently high standard, and two, that he have access to a system protected by an unprecedented degree of security.

Naomi creates a first draft of the virus, but is unable to complete it. Ocelot therefore consents to her apparent "escape" in order to deliver the code to Sunny, a child prodigy with a

preternaturally instinctive understanding of technology, to finish Naomi's work. In her dying moments, only she understands the import of Sunny's message. "I cooked them right" is not a child's touching acknowledgement of earlier culinary tips, but the confirmation that the powerful virus is complete. Her objectives satisfied, Naomi could finally allow herself to die. Like Vamp, her grip on life was dependent on the artificial assistance of nanomachines; once this was removed, she – like Vamp – exhales her last (suddenly visible) breaths in the cold Alaskan air before succumbing to the effects of the cancer within her.

As for how to deliver the virus into the heart of The Patriots' AI system, Ocelot knew that the only way to break through its security was to use a unique key: the genetic code and biometric data of Big Boss. In actual fact the body seized and then burned in Eastern Europe is not that of Big Boss, but Solidus – the only one of the three brothers to be an exact clone. (Observant viewers may have noticed that this is foreshadowed long before the actual revelation by the fact that the eye patch is on the body's left eye – Big Boss, of course, lost his right eye.)

The rest of the story is a series of deceptions designed to drive Snake ever onwards, and allay the suspicions of the Patriot AI systems. Ocelot, despite the presence of Liquid Snake within his consciousness, has no intention of using the rail gun retrieved from Metal Gear REX. Neither does he truly plan to become leader of the Patriots himself, despite his assertions to the contrary. Ocelot simply wishes for an end to The Patriots' control system, and leads Snake, their trusted yet unknowing tool, to become the agent of their ruin. For greater verisimilitude, at no point does Snake enjoy an easy ride: the sheer ferocity of the forces ranged against him (soldiers, the Gekkos, the BB Corps, Vamp) underlines the apparent

large force of soldiers is for naught; taking control of SOP, Liquid Ocelot locks the weapons of his would-be captors (and, for that matter, of all troops other than his own, worldwide). Few survive the resultant carnage as even vehicles fail to respond to the frantic interactions of their operators, and Liquid Ocelot calmly departs the scene of this grizzly, one-sided melee.

Liquid Ocelot's control of the system is still limited, though: to fulfill his objectives, he must destroy JD with a sufficiently powerful weapon. With WMDs still locked away by the master AI, he travels to Shadow Moses to retrieve the rail gun from the remains of Metal Gear REX: the one weapon outside of the System and within his grasp capable of destroying his intended target. With JD destroyed, control of The Patriot's system would revert to GW – and, therefore, Liquid Ocelot.

In hot pursuit, Snake infiltrates Shadow Moses as he did nine years before, but on finding REX – still lying as Snake had left it so many years before – he discovers that its rail gun has already been removed. Snake and his companions therefore have no choice but to infiltrate Outer Haven, an Arsenal Gear-style vessel that Liquid Ocelot had previously seized from The Patriots. Only by destroying Outer Haven's central server, home to GW, can Snake prevent his adversary from achieving his goal.

After a withering series of ordeals, an exhausted Snake escorts Metal Gear Mk. III to Outer Haven's server room and enables Otacon to upload the virus initially developed by Naomi, and later completed by Sunny. Surprisingly, though, the virus does not focus exclusively on GW, and spreads to the rest of the system, even affecting the central AI, JD. As Snake lies gravely wounded, fatigued beyond rational measure, alive through sheer brute force of will, he witnesses a recording hidden in the virus code by Naomi. In it, she reveals that she designed her virus to destroy all of the AI programs. The Patriots, she explains, were planning to extend their control network to govern not just soldiers, but all mankind.

In his final confrontation with Liquid Ocelot, Snake learns that it was this outcome that his opponent had sought from the very beginning: to release mankind from the twisted auspices of The Patriots, and the prison of their rational, micro-managed world. Liquid Ocelot dies after contracting the new FOXDIE virus carried by Snake; the AIs created by The Patriots are also disabled, but not in the way that anyone could have envisaged. In a touch of precocious genius, Sunny had altered the virus to destroy the control system, yet leave all processes that administer vital elements of society's infrastructure (energy, transportation, communications, et al) intact. With the death of Major Zero and the AI programs that were to succeed him, The Patriots – and their ideals of standardization and social control – are no more.

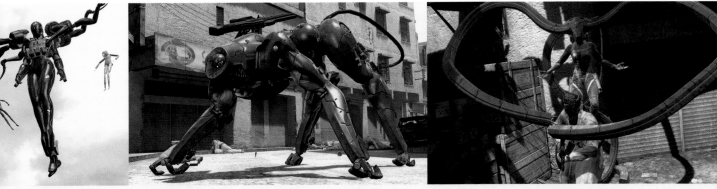

SCREAMING MANTIS   CRYING WOLF   LAUGHING OCTUPUS

sincerity of Liquid Ocelot's desire to slay the legendary soldier. And yet Ocelot, significantly, fails to dispatch Snake when given several opportunities to do so, in a manner that clearly surpasses the traditional cliché of villainous arrogance.

Ocelot, then, is not a nefarious figure, a tyrant seeking endless power, but the mastermind behind a plan to break the authoritarian web that The Patriots were weaving over the world. From this perspective, Ocelot (even in his guise as the pitiless Liquid Ocelot) is as much a hero as Snake. Even his vicious rout of the forces brought by Meryl to capture him in Eastern Europe bears further examination. At the very moment that he froze military hardware throughout the world with an apparently nonchalant wave of his hand, didn't Ocelot effectively end all ongoing conflicts at once, becoming the main architect of peace and the man to end the war economy? Despite their mutual antagonism from the first time they met, Snake and Ocelot actually worked together to stop The Patriots' rule.

Only once the virus has been deployed does Ocelot reveal hints of his true self. There is an almost cathartic quality to the brutal unarmed combat that ensues between the two before Ocelot's life is extinguished by the FOXDIE that courses through Snake's veins. Ocelot's valediction confirms that he actually played Liquid's role all along: "I am Liquid's doppelganger."

The unforeseen variable in the story of **Metal Gear Solid 4**, the protagonist that

The Patriots completely neglected to acknowledge as a threat, is Sunny. It was her precocious genius that enabled the virus to consign The Patriots to history. As an additional, inspirational touch, she engineered it to destroy the AI routines that governed the world, and yet preserve the smooth running of infrastructures essential to modern civilization. By offering society a second chance, Sunny also gains a new beginning, this time "outside".

The symbol of this renewal, Meryl and Johnny's wedding, is marked with several reconciliations: that of Meryl with her father Roy Campbell; that of Raiden with his wife and son, and ultimately with his life; that of Snake with his father, presumed long dead after Zanzibarland; and that of Big Boss with The Boss's legacy, which he finally understood.

Some, like EVA, Ocelot, Naomi and Big Boss (who deliberately breathes the FOXDIE virus exhaled by Snake), find redemption in death, both their own and in that of The Patriots' corrupted ideals. Others, such as Otacon, Meryl and Campbell, find redemption in life through their atonement for past mistakes. As for Snake, he finds himself poised between life and death, trapped between the past and the future, between Snake and David. There is, perhaps, a hint of a future, however short, for the tired soldier before the end credits roll. With the knowledge that the new FOXDIE virus has supplanted the one before it, Big Boss encourages Snake to start over, to embrace a new (albeit short) life as a fresh era dawns.

■INTERPRETATION

Big Boss and Major Zero, the catalysts for the stories of the *Metal Gear Solid* series, are polar opposites, extremes of the same scale. While the former thirsts for anarchy (as demonstrated by his actions in Outer Heaven and Zanzibarland), the latter desires total control. Both misinterpret and corrupt the teachings of The Boss, losing sight of the reason behind her final sacrifice. Big Boss believes in an ideology that promotes individual liberty at the expense of stability, security and structure, thus restricting the true freedom of citizens to speak, to grow, and even to exist. Conversely, Zero's obsession with order, and the perceived need to preserve society by means of standardization and intrusive governance, leads society to the brink of disaster. His AI successors begin to create a future where individuals would unknowingly suffer not only restrictions in their freedom to act or express themselves, but also in their freedom to *feel* beyond the confines of managed boundaries. A perverted liberty of a kind might still exist in such a civilization, but in the narrowest, least genuine sense of the word.

For Zero, freedom would be preserved by imposing a set of constraints and offering individuals liberty within this context; for Big Boss, it could be assured through the absence of constraints. The latter was, it could be argued, a delusion; even an absence of limits would prove to be a constraint in itself. Both could only define freedom in relation to boundaries, to limitations, and this was the core of their betrayal of The Boss's legacy: she saw liberty, in a far more positive light, as the result of personal and collective commitment.

From the day they founded The Patriots, the way of Zero and Big Boss was that of oblivion – by forgetting the sense The Boss had shown them, they forgot who they were. This led both to instigate a chain of events in which the same tragedy is repeated over and over, a series of questions that always seem to elicit the same replies. This explains why the *Metal Gear Solid* games follow a palpable blueprint: the same themes (death, vengeance, deception), the same actors (a hero, a designated enemy, a ninja, an elite unit), the same goals (freedom, redemption). It took the child, Sunny, perhaps the least expected agent for change, to break the endless cycle to create a spiral, where the story leads from the centre to the outside. Though each episode's narrative offers a similar scenario, it is clearly different from all others, marked by deviations in the series DNA that make it unique. This, it could be said, is a reflection of life itself, and mankind in particular: reproducing fundamentally the same things, and yet never reliving exactly the *same* thing.

After Big Boss's failure to create his warrior's utopia in Outer Heaven and, later, Zanzibarland, Zero lost both his dearest friend, and the force that kept his principles and beliefs in check. As a consequence, he ceased to believe in mankind, in the concept of open society. He refused to entrust the world's reins to a new generation, instead favoring the creation of autonomous artificial intelligence systems to govern in his stead. The Patriots became a power depersonalized and fundamentally inhuman, attempting to apply order to mankind by seeking the continual reproduction of the same, an administrable repetition without end. Its behavior can be likened to a dog chasing its own tail or, more pertinently, a

A-001

64654474 464 1684 6

S-02

METAL GEAR SOLID 4
GUNS OF THE PATRIOTS TACTICAL ESPIONAGE ACTION

HOW TO PLAY

WALKTHROUGH

INVENTORY

METAL GEAR ONLINE

▶ EXTRAS

CUTSCENE
INTERACTIONS

EMBLEMS

SPECIAL EQUIPMENT

SECRETS

SYNOPSIS

▶ INTERPRETATION

BIOGRAPHIES

computer program stuck in an infinite loop. This explains why the Patriots (or, rather, the AI that succeeded its founder members) use Snake as the primary agent of the system, and the same stratagems (for example, FOXDIE) every time.

On every occasion bar the last, the circle is refreshed, the hegemony of The Patriots challenged (though not broken) when the AI fails to take an unseen variable into account. Of greatest import is the reality that, in each episode, Ocelot's true role, his betrayal, is never anticipated or understood. However, every time the story is told, certain distinctions and innovations abide; the surviving protagonists grow, and certain things live on (for example, the influence that Snake has on those he meets). This may be what Nietzsche meant by the "Eternal Return of the Same" and especially by his famous motto, "Become what you are", so often misinterpreted. This is echoed in Big Boss's words once he finally understood what The Boss wanted: "It's not about changing the world. It's about doing our best to leave the world the way it is."

If, as Big Boss asserts just before he dies, the world is at the dawn of a new era, it remains to be seen what mankind will manage to do with this second chance, especially the most direct casualties afflicted by the machinations of The Patriots. When the soldiers are freed from the SOP system, the effects of the accumulated emotions, thoughts and memories that were repressed by their nanomachines suddenly resurface. Clearly, the consciousness, the ego, forgets, but the mind and body retain, collect, *suffer* things, whether we realize it or not. In the new age, many things will thus need to be learned afresh. This is all the more true for the victims of the Sons of the Patriots Syndrome (SOPS), but also for the others, all those that were affected by the Patriots' censorship, and whose lives were thus stolen, if only in part. The adjustment might be especially hard on Snake, and impossible within his limited lifespan, as he has been at the fulcrum of The Patriots' deceptions throughout.

So what will Snake do with his father's legacy? What will he pass on? Not his "genes", not the "memes" of his bygone epoch, not a "scene" given that the times have changed; perhaps the "sense" of his existence, then? Perhaps his perseverance, his endeavor, his fighting spirit, his unwavering will might inspire others to live by his example. With the new challenges that await mankind now that the Patriots are gone, no doubt they will need such values to avoid past mistakes. It is the significance that we attach to our deeds that enables us to achieve the best results: this is what Meryl and Johnny prove by being perfectly synchronized on Outer Haven without SOP; Snake by getting back to his feet a thousand times out of sheer willpower; Raiden by finding the strength to accomplish miracles even though his artificial body is cracked and broken.

Nevertheless, the few months that remain for Snake (or, rather, David) to live will barely allow him to catch a glimpse of the horizons of this new beginning. He is a clone built for conflict, a "blue rose", an aberration: a thing that does not occur naturally, an orphan of a dying epoch. In the post-credits dialogue, however, we hear Otacon dissuade his closest friend from spending his final days alone; an encouraging first step for a new world order.

The following biographies should explain everything you need to know to better understand all major (and many minor) plot developments that occur during *Metal Gear Solid 4*. These central protagonists, organizations and concepts are all relevant to its compelling narrative, though we have abbreviated or omitted entries for individuals who play no significant role in shaping the events of this conclusion to the long-running Metal Gear storyline.

THE BOSS

A legendary American secret agent, the foremost soldier of her generation, The Boss was regarded as an exemplary patriot until her shocking defection to the USSR during the Virtuous Mission in 1964. In actual fact, her apparent betrayal was made at her government's behest, a subterfuge designed to enable her to infiltrate Colonel Volgin's organization. Her objective was to retrieve The Philosophers' Legacy, and to secretly support her designated successor, Naked Snake, in his mission to assassinate Volgin and destroy the Shagohod weapon. Having achieved both goals, The Boss made a final sacrifice for her country: to die at the hands of her protégé, accepting death and disgrace in order to conceal the true nature of her involvement (specifically, the transfer of the coveted Philosophers' Legacy to United States control). The teachings of The Boss, and her final expression of devotion and commitment, inspired a small cabal of those who knew the truth to found The Patriots to perpetuate her legacy.

BIG BOSS alias Naked Snake

Originally known as Naked Snake, he was forced during Operation Snake Eater to assassinate his spiritual mother, The Boss, thus becoming even greater than The Boss and earning the title Big Boss. After he prevented a nuclear strike on the US in the 1970 San Hieronymo Incident, Big Boss joined Major Zero and Ocelot (the conspirators behind the aforementioned episode) to found The Patriots. However, though a firm friend of the organization's leader, Major Zero, Big Boss's gradual estrangement from Zero and dissatisfaction with his methods – seen as a betrayal of the message of liberty bequeathed to them by The Boss – caused him to leave the group.

After secretly (and illegally) re-forming the elite FOXHOUND special forces unit (formerly under his command), Big Boss aspired to create a "warrior's utopia" by overthrowing the governments of Outer Heaven and, later, Zanzibarland. His goal was to free himself from the rapidly encroaching influence of The Patriots, and to create a nation defined by a charter of total liberty for all citizens. In both instances The Patriots sent his cloned "son", Solid Snake, to foil his plans. Gravely wounded after their second clash in Zanzibarland, Big Boss's body was retrieved by The Patriots and maintained in a perpetual artificial coma. His unique genetic code and biometric data would later be used as the sole key to a sophisticated AI system conceived by Major Zero. Though initially designed to filter the digital era's free flow of information, this system would later develop and manage the Sons of the Patriots program. ▶▶

▶▶ EVA, with Raiden's assistance, was eventually able to reclaim Big Boss's body. Reconstructed with organs and limbs harvested from the corpses of Liquid and Solidus, Big Boss was restored to life in 2014. Finally comprehending the true sense of his former mentor's legacy, he took the opportunity to pass this message on to his son, intentionally contracting the lethal FOXDIE virus during their brief, yet significant reunion, before dying on the grave of the woman he had worshipped.

MAJOR ZERO

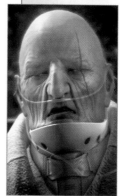

Commander of Naked Snake (the future Big Boss) during Operation Snake Eater, Major Zero was deeply moved by The Boss's sacrifice and inspired by her final act of selfless patriotism. After orchestrating the San Hieronymo uprising – whereby he obtained more information about the Philosophers and their Legacy – he created The Patriots (with Big Boss and other key figures in the events of 1964) to protect and advance the interests of the United States in world affairs. However, variations in personal doctrine drove a wedge between Major Zero and Big Boss; where the former sought to achieve the group's perceived aims through overt manipulation and, ultimately, control, Big Boss instead developed an obsession with a dream of absolute freedom for all.

Big Boss's departure from The Patriots initiated a cycle of violence where these two ideologies would clash over several decades. This began with the events in Outer Heaven and Zanzibarland; later, Liquid and Solidus would firmly grasp the torch lit by their father in the subsequent Shadow Moses and Big Shell Incidents. In each instance, Major Zero triumphed through the intervention of Solid Snake, his (albeit unwitting) agent; every success reinforced his hegemony, with his increasingly malign and dictatorial influence a product of a growing contempt for the human race.

Unwilling to foster a new generation of Patriots to steer the course of world history, Zero instead created an autonomous AI system capable of interpreting and filtering the free flow of information in the digital age. Initially a subtle means of shaping human behavior (from governments to individual citizens), the AI system became a tool for the direct control of bodies and minds with the advent of the Sons of the Patriots (SOP) program. Though soldiers would be its primary focus at first, The Patriots stood poised to extend its reach to encompass all mankind, creating a future where internal nanomachines and centralized management would deny mankind the natural, unfettered emotional responses that constitute the very essence of humanity – and, indeed, of individual liberty.

The irony, as was later revealed when Big Boss met with Solid Snake, was that the decrepit Major Zero had long existed in a vegetative state. By 2014 and the events of *MGS4*, The Patriots existed purely as the authoritarian, autonomous and rapidly evolving AI system that Zero created.

Bankrolled by the practically inexhaustible funds of The Philosophers' Legacy (retrieved by Ocelot at the conclusion of the Snake Eater mission), The Patriots increased their influence in world affairs through measured investments and subtle lobbying. In time, entire governments and corporations would effectively (and often unwittingly) fulfill their every bidding. The role of Big Boss, elevated to the status of a global hero through media manipulation, a figurehead celebrated by all, was to help shape the opinions of the social elite and common citizens alike. Noting Big Boss's growing disenchantment with The Patriots as a concept, however, Zero initiated the Les Enfants Terribles project to create clones of his valuable but volatile ally as an insurance policy. This led to the birth of Solid Snake, Liquid and Solidus, with Para-Medic the principle engineer behind this feat of advanced science, and EVA acting as surrogate mother. His discovery of this betrayal led Big Boss to finally leave The Patriots in pursuit of very different ideals. This marked the beginning of a conflict that would last for decades.

Big Boss was not alone in despising what The Patriots (and, specifically, Zero) had become. Unbeknownst to Zero, Ocelot and EVA covertly conspired to bring the organization down from within. Through their direct intervention, Para-Medic was killed by Gray Fox; during the events at Shadow Moses, Sigint was murdered by Ocelot himself.

Though The Patriots already had pawns within all major institutions in the world, Zero sought to increase his domination with the advent of the digital age. By creating a software system to filter and control information travelling through global networks, he ultimately aspired to directly manage society as a whole through selective censorship. But the role of this network of autonomous AIs (GW, TJ, AL, TR and JD, the master AI) evolved beyond its original parameters, eventually creating the Sons of the Patriots System, and the "war economy" that accompanied it.

With Zero's descent into physical fragility and senility, eventually alive only in the purely physical sense of the word, sole control of The Patriots reverted to these unfeeling computer programs. Perhaps lacking any true comprehension or appreciation of society or its constituent members beyond a superficial mathematical level, perceiving human culture as an equation to be solved, the AIs began to implement a new world order. Conflict was encouraged as the principle mechanism for economic prosperity simply because it worked – a practical yet unflinchingly callous conclusion. The planned extension of the SOP System to the general population would have been made to improve the efficiency of society, not as an expression of cruelty or dominance. The Patriots, in its post-Zero incarnation, was not inherently evil; merely inhuman. It was not motivated by nationalist sentiment, religious ideology, or a thirst for profit or revenge, but by a basic digital desire for practical functionality, for variables operating within simple, predictable, malleable routines.

Ultimately, though, this AI system was prone to colossal errors of judgment, with a tendency to repeat the same routines or mistakes (and a curious affinity for cyborg ninjas). It was this fallibility that Ocelot ultimately exploited. Focusing their attention on him, JD and its associated AIs failed to notice that their weapon of choice (Snake), the sharp blade wielded so successfully against previous challenges to the supremacy of The Patriots, had been slowly, imperceptibly rotated to face the organization's beating heart.

THE PHILOSOPHERS

The Philosophers was a committee created in the early years of the 1900s by preeminent figures from the three nations that would dominate the century ahead: the United States, Russia and China. This secret organization amassed a colossal sum of funds, the Philosophers' Legacy, which was originally dedicated to a broad ideal of ensuring world peace. With the death of its founders, however, this noble aim was forgotten as their successors fought to gain sole control of the Legacy in the aftermath of the Second World War.

THE PATRIOTS

A clandestine organization founded by Major Zero in the early 1970s, joined by Big Boss, EVA, Ocelot, Sigint and Para-Medic, The Patriots could be regarded as the direct successors of The Philosophers. The six committee members (led by Zero) originally intended to act on the teachings of The Boss, who had given her life to serve her country's interests. However, an initial desire to protect the United States soon became a concerted attempt to impose its social, political and economic mores on other nations; a belief that standardization, a global uniformity of culture emulating the American model, was the means by which they might achieve their desired ends.

OCELOT
alias Adam, General Ivan, Shalashaska, et al (also see Liquid Ocelot, page 204)

The son of The Boss and The Sorrow, Ocelot was an integral part of the conspiracy that returned The Philosophers' Legacy to the United States in the aftermath of Operation Snake Eater. He cemented his relationship with Major Zero by acting as co-conspirator during the San Hieronymo Incident. A founder member of The Patriots, he eventually became disillusioned with the organization's gradual drift away from its original ideals, particularly after the departure of Big Boss. Though still ostensibly acting as a Patriot agent, he secretly plotted and labored to destroy the group from within.

During the Shadow Moses Incident, Ocelot used Liquid to retrieve test data from Metal Gear REX in order to deliver it to Solidus (the third Big Boss clone, and then US President) while still technically serving the interests of The Patriots, but in fact manipulating all parties involved. However, Gray Fox (the Cyborg Ninja) unexpectedly severed Ocelot's right arm during a confrontation with Snake; this was later replaced with the equivalent limb from the corpse of the late Liquid.

During the Big Shell Incident in 2009 (and, for that matter, the theft of Metal Gear RAY two years previously), Ocelot again concealed his true intentions from his enemies, allies and Patriot masters alike through a series of audacious deceptions. His principle innovation was to periodically assume the identity of Liquid, as if somehow possessed by the dead clone. The Patriots, though alarmed by such behavior, at no point doubted his integrity – as he had planned.

Eventually adopting the full-time persona of "Liquid Ocelot", thus severing his ties with The Patriots, Ocelot feigned a desire to create a world of lawless freedom (much like Big Boss before him) as a foil to hide his true objective: the end of The Patriots' tyranny. As he knew that the systems established by The Patriots were unassailable by means of a direct assault, he endeavored to destroy them with the one person they would least suspect: Solid Snake, their own agent. His behavior in *Metal Gear Solid 4*, then, was a devious, elaborate ploy to drive Snake towards an eventual goal of disabling the Patriots' AI network with a computer virus. Having achieved his aims, he engaged Snake in hand-to-hand combat, perhaps relishing one last opportunity to test his prowess against the progeny of his great friend and idol, Big Boss. By doing so, he voluntarily contracted the FOXDIE virus, choosing death (and, you sense, peace) as his reward for ushering in a new era.

EVA alias Big Mama, Tatyana

As an agent serving the United States, Russia and, ultimately, China, EVA assisted Big Boss (then Naked Snake) during Operation Snake Eater, yet secretly planned to snatch The Philosophers' Legacy for her masters in Beijing. Later reconciled with (and, indeed, rescued by) Big Boss, she was invited to become a member of The Patriots. She volunteered to be the surrogate mother for the Les Enfants Terribles project, but – with Ocelot – felt an overpowering fury towards the organization following the departure of Big Boss, and Major Zero's drift towards absolutism. Retreating to the shadows, she became Ocelot's co-conspirator, and took control of the resistance group Paradise Lost, recruiting former members of PMCs. She eventually succeeded in recovering Big Boss's body with the assistance of Raiden, and led the efforts to reconstruct and revive the legendary warrior by using body parts from Liquid and Solidus.

EVA died believing that Liquid Ocelot truly existed, as convinced as any other that her friend had become merely a vessel for Liquid's malign spirit. This was the true extent of the price that Ocelot had to pay in order to succeed: not even EVA could know the true scope of his plan.

SIGINT alias Donald Anderson

A member of Big Boss's support team during Operation Snake Eater, Sigint specialized in technology and intelligence acquisition. Among the many technological developments he created or managed, one of the most important was ARPANET: the predecessor to the Internet that enabled The Patriots to plan their control over the future digital society. As one of Zero's closest and most dedicated allies within the organization, he became head of DARPA – the Pentagon research agency responsible for developing Metal Gear REX. More commonly known as Donald Anderson, he died at the hands of Ocelot during the Shadow Moses Incident; his death was passed off as an unfortunate accident during interrogation.

The Donald Anderson who later died before Snake's eyes when infected by the FOXDIE virus was, in fact, Decoy Octopus: one of Liquid's men disguised as Anderson in an attempt to glean information from Snake.

PARA-MEDIC alias Dr. Clark

The final founding member of The Patriots, Para-Medic also played an important role in Operation Snake Eater. Later, known as Dr. Clark, she led the Les Enfants Terribles project and ran The Patriots' gene research program, among other scientific endeavors. After Snake's victory in Zanzibarland, she used her expertise to place Big Boss in a permanent coma, and used advanced cybernetic surgery to transform Gray Fox into the Cyborg Ninja. Freed by Naomi Hunter, Gray Fox murdered the morally bankrupt scientist as revenge for the pain and suffering she had subjected him to.

SOLID SNAKE alias David

Of the three products of the Les Enfants Terribles project, Snake was deemed to be the inferior specimen when compared to his more robust twin, Liquid, and the "pure" clone Solidus. An adulterated copy of his "father", Big Boss, he was designed to be sterile, with a limited life expectancy.

Snake served as an agent of The Patriots throughout his life (up until the conclusion of *MGS4*) without realizing it; only aboard the Big Shell was he perhaps a variable that existed outside their calculations. After defeating Big Boss in Outer Heaven and Zanzibarland, Snake aspired to take an early retirement. Instead, he was called into service once again to eliminate his twin, Liquid, during the Shadow Moses Incident. Liquid erroneously (and jealously) believed his brother to be his genetic superior and, but for the timely intervention of the FOXDIE virus introduced into Snake's body by Naomi Hunter, might have succeeded in killing him. One beneficial result of the events at Shadow Moses, however, was that it introduced Snake to Otacon and Meryl Silverburgh.

After choosing not to work for his government (yet never moving far beyond the indefatigable gaze of The Patriots), Snake co-founded "Philanthropy" with Otacon: an independent organization dedicated to preventing the proliferation of Metal Gear technology. This led to his presence on the Discovery tanker where Ocelot – and, in his first performance, Liquid Ocelot – stole Metal Gear RAY. Two years later, he assisted Raiden in his successful attempt to thwart Solidus aboard the Big Shell.

Afflicted by the ravages of premature decrepitude programmed into his genes, Snake was called back into action by Roy Campbell, his former commander, for the events of *MGS4*. As in all prior instances, Snake was again unknowingly acting as a Patriot tool – though, with Ocelot's oblique assistance, he this time became the weapon responsible for the organization's absolute destruction.

OTACON alias Hal Emmerich

A scientific genius, Otacon was manipulated by The Patriots to create Metal Gear REX, a weapon of mass destruction. Snake's intervention at Shadow Moses helped Otacon to learn that he had been exploited; he then dedicated his life to the admirable goal of securing world peace. After co-founding Philanthropy, he assisted Snake in his subsequent missions – first at the Big Shell, then again in the fight against Liquid Ocelot in 2014. Regularly a victim of fate, Otacon appears condemned to always lose the women he loves most dearly: Sniper Wolf at Shadow Moses, his step-sister Emma on the Big Shell, and – finally it must be hoped – Naomi Hunter.

EMMA EMMERICH alias E.E.

Otacon's step-sister, Emma held a grudge against her brother for his inability to prevent the accidental drowning of their common father, but was oblivious to the fact that Otacon was conducting an illicit affair with her mother at the time – and that her father's death was actually suicide. Emma developed GW, the AI at the heart of Arsenal Gear, but later developed the "worm" program that disabled it. She did not live long enough to witness its effects: stabbed by Vamp, she died in her brother's arms. Her life extinguished, her genius nonetheless lived on: the worm code she devised became the basis of the virus Naomi Hunter and Sunny created to destroy The Patriots' central AI.

LIQUID

On discovering the partial truth of his heritage, and the Les Enfants Terribles project, Liquid developed a pathological obsession with realizing his father's dream, and an irrational hatred of Snake.

Manipulated by other parties (particularly Solidus and Ocelot) throughout the Shadow Moses Incident, Liquid was killed at its conclusion by Naomi Hunter's FOXDIE virus. In the broader scheme of the series narrative, the transplant of Liquid's arm to Ocelot is arguably of greater significance than its original host. It was this limb that facilitated the Liquid Ocelot subterfuge, a fiction that enabled Ocelot to steer Snake towards his destiny as the man to end the rule of The Patriots.

LIQUID OCELOT

To all intents and purposes, Liquid Ocelot and Ocelot were the very same person. In a performance of superlative quality, augmented by advanced psychotherapy techniques, hypnotherapy and nanomachines, Ocelot used his fake Liquid Ocelot persona to disguise his true intentions from The Patriots. By 2014, he had gained control of the world's five largest Private Military Companies, all owned by a holding corporation named Outer Heaven. Liquid Ocelot used Solidus's body to snatch control of The Patriots' SOP System, and subsequently lock all weapons of troops not under his direct command. He then conspired to destroy the central AI program satellite (JD) with Metal Gear REX's rail gun, but was stopped by Snake. However, this was yet another deception through which Ocelot fooled The Patriots and led Snake, their own agent, to eliminate them on his behalf.

SOLIDUS alias Geoge Sears

Third product of the Les Enfants Terribles project, Solidus was the only identical clone of Big Boss. President of the United States under the name George Sears, he took advantage of his position to obtain the test data of Metal Gear REX in the Shadow Moses Incident. Having seemingly aroused the ire of his masters, The Patriots, he escaped and organized the attack on the Big Shell. As with Big Boss and Liquid before him, he wished to create a free state beyond the influence of the organization that created him but, like his forebears, he failed. In actual fact, The Patriots had orchestrated his rebellion from the very beginning, using it as an integral part of their S3 research plan. The whole Big Shell crisis, it transpired, was nothing more than a live-action recreation of key moments from the Shadow Moses Incident designed to improve the Patriots' technology, with Raiden the Patriot guinea-pig scripted to slay Solidus. Solidus's body would later be used by Liquid Ocelot to take control of the SOP System.

VAMP

Right-hand man to Solidus in the attack on the Big Shell, Vamp apparently died from a gunshot wound to the head. However, this fearsome (and gleefully perverse) warrior was rendered effectively invincible by nanomachines invented by Naomi Hunter. These microscopic devices accelerated his natural cellular processes to successfully (and, often, near-instantaneously) heal even the gravest injuries. This prodigious advantage was removed when Snake, on his return to Shadow Moses, injected Vamp with nanomachines that suppressed his unique ability, allowing Raiden to kill him once and for all.

ROY CAMPBELL

Though a key protagonist in the San Hieronymo Incident, where he helped Big Boss to resolve the crisis, Campbell acted as Snake's commander during his two assignments to stop Big Boss; he later reprised this role during the Shadow Moses mission. However, the Colonel Campbell who assisted Raiden on the Big Shell was actually a virtual impostor created by a Patriots AI program.

In 2014, made aware of Liquid Ocelot's schemes through his work for the United Nations, Campbell implored Snake (in a purely private capacity, though doubtlessly manipulated in secret by The Patriots) to assassinate Liquid. Campbell's relationship with Rose, Raiden's former girlfriend, led others to question his character and view him in a far less sympathetic light, and caused his complete estrangement from Meryl. This partnership was later revealed to be a deceit of Campbell's design; a generous and fiercely guarded secret that protected Rose and Raiden's son from The Patriots.

MERYL SILVERBURGH

Daughter of Roy Campbell, Meryl long pretended to be his niece due to a family quarrel. Taken hostage during the Shadow Moses crisis, the young soldier escaped and assisted Snake in his struggle against the terrorists led by Liquid. Later in her career she was assigned as the lead operative in Rat Patrol Team 01, a special unit charged with the responsibility of observing Private Military Companies during their battlefield operations. In 2014 she would again play an important role by assisting Snake in his fight against Liquid Ocelot.

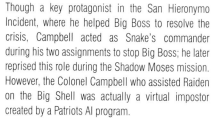

JOHNNY alias Akiba

Infamous within the *Metal Gear Solid* saga for his innate clumsiness and abdominal eccentricities, *MGS4* reveals that Johnny was so afflicted due to the absence of nanomachines in his body. Unlike other SOP-augmented soldiers, he did not enjoy the benefits of a regulated metabolism, nor the advantage of artificially enhanced reactions. However, this weakness became his strength when Liquid Ocelot disrupted the SOP System. Enjoying a natural, human degree of control as an individual free from SOP influence, he was able to save Meryl's life at a pivotal moment. As he and Meryl held out against colossal odds to defend Snake at the end of *MGS4*, Johnny won the love of the woman he had adored since their first encounter at Shadow Moses.

GRAY FOX
alias Frank Hunter, Frank Jaeger, Null

A soldier from an early age, Frank Hunter was responsible for countless deaths. Seized by a powerful sense of guilt after killing a young child's parents, he adopted the little girl and named her Naomi. The subject of experimental enhancement surgery, he was used as a combat weapon in the San Hieronymo Incident. Later enlisted to FOXHOUND, he first fought against, and then for, Big Boss, but was defeated on both occasions by Snake. Restored to life as the Cyborg Ninja but again subjected to hideous experiments in the process, he escaped from the laboratory of Dr. Clark, alias Para-Medic, killing her as retribution for the indignities he had suffered. Having developed an obsession with Snake that comprised extremes of outright fascination and utter hatred, he intervened in the Shadow Moses Incident to both aid and confront him. After severing Ocelot's arm in one such moment, he eventually sacrificed himself to enable Snake to defeat Liquid.

NAOMI HUNTER

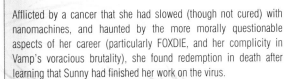

As an orphan, Naomi Hunter was adopted by Frank Hunter/Jaeger, alias Gray Fox – the man who, unbeknownst to Naomi, had killed her parents. After he was defeated by Snake and reconstructed as the Cyborg Ninja by The Patriots, Naomi craved revenge. Recruited by EVA, she helped instigate his escape. Naomi later injected Snake with the FOXDIE virus at the beginning of his Shadow Moses mission, hoping to cause his death, but instead making him a simple vector for the disease. Her anger was tempered when she realized that Snake was merely an instrument used by The Patriots; she later joined forces with Ocelot, contributing her incredible technical acumen to his secret cause. She created the first draft of the virus that would eventually disable the Patriot AI network, which she later gave to the child prodigy Sunny to complete.

Afflicted by a cancer that she had slowed (though not cured) with nanomachines, and haunted by the more morally questionable aspects of her career (particularly FOXDIE, and her complicity in Vamp's voracious brutality), she found redemption in death after learning that Sunny had finished her work on the virus.

OLGA GURLUKOVICH

A Russian soldier who assisted her father in the sinking of the Discovery tanker in 2007 while heavily pregnant, Olga later became an unwilling but compliant Patriots operative when the organization kidnapped her daughter. Compelled to obey The Patriots to protect her new-born baby, she played the role of the "cyborg ninja" substitute as part of the S3 simulation on the Big Shell. In a cruel twist, she was obliged to die at the hands of Solidus in order to save Raiden – a precondition for the survival of her daughter, Sunny.

SUNNY

Daughter of Olga Gurlukovich, Sunny was abducted at birth by the Patriots. Set free by Raiden, she then joined Snake and Otacon aboard their airship, the Nomad. Blessed with an instinctive understanding of technology, and possessing a genius that might be considered precocious for an individual ten times her age, she changed the course of world history by completing the virus developed by Naomi Hunter. Her most incredible contribution, perhaps, was to modify its code structure to ensure that it destroyed the virtual "minds" of the Patriots' AI programs, but preserved systems essential for the operation of society's infrastructure – a development that not even Ocelot appeared to have presumed possible.

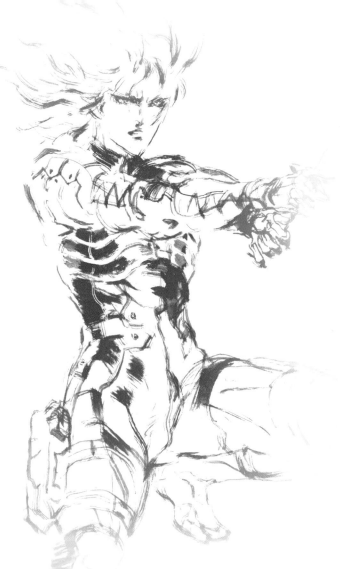

ROSE alias Rosemary

Raiden's girlfriend, Rose hid the birth of their son by claiming to have had a miscarriage. By conducting a sham marriage with Roy Campbell, she succeeded in escaping the notice of The Patriots, who might otherwise have used her and her son as leverage against Raiden. Convinced that her love would return to her once his mission was complete, she waited until The Patriots had been eliminated before revealing the truth.

The Rose that spoke to Raiden via Codec during the Big Shell Incident was an AI-generated impostor designed by The Patriots to mislead him.

MEI LING

A member of Snake's support staff throughout the Shadow Moses crisis, Mei Ling remained loyal to him once the mission ended. She worked closely with Philanthropy in the lead up to, and during, the Big Shell crisis, supplying Snake with equipment stolen from her then-employers.

She once again came to Snake's aid in 2014 while serving aboard an old war vessel, the Missouri. As the ship was not under the control of the SOP System, Mei Ling used it to convey Snake and his allies in their pursuit of Liquid Ocelot's mighty ocean-bound fortress, the Outer Haven. With her help, they were able to board the colossal vessel and release the AI-killing virus created by Naomi and Sunny.

RAIDEN
alias Jack, White Devil, Jack the Ripper, et al

A former child soldier during the Liberian Civil War under the command of Solidus, Raiden grew up repressing abhorrent memories. He believed he was a FOXHOUND secret agent, but was in fact a guinea-pig used by The Patriots for their S3 research program.

Though he ultimately survived the Big Shell crisis, Raiden could not escape the ghosts of his tragic past. Troubled and increasingly irrational, he left his partner, Rose, convinced that she had suffered a miscarriage; later, he believed the (sadly necessary) fiction that she and Roy Campbell had married. Raiden first went in search of Sunny, freeing her from the clutches of The Patriots, and then retrieved Big Boss's body on behalf of EVA. In a desperate attempt to cleanse himself of past sins, he submitted himself to cybernetic enhancements in a process that made him more machine than man. Only in his fight alongside Snake to defeat The Patriots did he rediscover his humanity. His mission complete, his reward was to be reunited with Rose and his young son.

METAL GEAR

A bipedal tank first conceived by a Russian scientist named Granin, it was overshadowed by Sokolov's "Shagohod", encountered during Operation Snake Eater. Several decades later, Otacon created an advanced iteration of the original concept, Metal Gear REX, armed with the capacity to fire nuclear warheads. This design was later upgraded to create an amphibious model, Metal Gear RAY. The Metal Gear technology reached its zenith with the advent of Arsenal Gear, a vastly expanded interpretation of the design brief that was, in essence, a mobile fortress. Liquid Ocelot's Outer Haven vessel was a modified version of an Arsenal Gear stolen from The Patriots.

FOXDIE

The product of a research project conducted at the behest of The Patriots, FOXDIE was a "nanovirus" transmissible by air and physical contact. Unlike other biological weapons, its effects were limited to targets specified by a genetic identification process designed by Naomi Hunter. When she injected Snake with the virus in her quest for revenge, she unknowingly did the bidding of The Patriots – the FOXDIE coursing through Snake's veins caused the death of many principle protagonists in the Shadow Moses Incident, including Liquid. The virus spared Snake due to the simple fact that he lacked the same genetic markers as his brother.

In 2014, Naomi revealed to Snake during his rescue attempt in South America that biological processes within his body were causing FOXDIE to mutate. The virus had the potential to begin infecting victims indiscriminately within a period of a few months, she estimated, transforming Snake into the harbinger of a global apocalypse. However, a new variety of FOXDIE injected into Snake by Drebin had the side effect of supplanting the original virus strain, thus ending – or perhaps merely postponing – the threat he posed.

PSYCHO MANTIS

A warrior with tremendous telekinetic abilities, Psycho Mantis fought alongside Liquid in the Shadow Moses Incident. Defeated by Snake – with whom he felt a curious kinship, a sense that both shared a similar emptiness at the very core of their being – his spirit nonetheless survived the passing of his corporeal form. His unique talents were employed to condition the fragile minds of the BB Corps members, and his spirit found refuge within Screaming Mantis, their commander.

Psycho Mantis made a noteworthy return after Snake defeated Screaming Mantis on the Outer Haven, and once again attempted a vibrant demonstration of his powers...

COBRA UNIT

An elite unit under the command of The Boss during Operation Snake Eater, it included notable figures such as The Pain, The Fear, The Fury, The End and The Sorrow (Ocelot's father). Naked Snake eliminated each one in turn, including their leader, acquiring both the title of Big Boss and a sense of guilt that would consume him until his dying day.

FOXHOUND

An elite unit commanded by Big Boss in the 1970s before its disbandment, it was reformed first by Big Boss, then later Liquid before the events at Shadow Moses. In the latter two incarnations, FOXHOUND was identified by the international community as a terrorist group. It included members as famous as they were unhinged, such as Vulcan Raven, Sniper Wolf, Psycho Mantis and Decoy Octopus – the last being the first known victim of the FOXDIE virus.

DREBIN

One of The Patriots' innumerable agents, but fairly unusual in that he was fully aware of his role, Drebin was given the task of selling "laundered" weaponry free of SOP restrictions. One of hundreds of designated Drebins worldwide, his job was to ensure that those who sought to fight would always have the means to do so – thus perpetuating the war economy. After injecting Snake with a new FOXDIE strain designed to kill EVA, Ocelot and Big Boss, Drebin was ordered by his Patriot masters to support him in his mission to eliminate Liquid Ocelot – proof positive, were it needed, that Snake remained the preferred instrument of the organization. It was only through Drebin's assistance that the forces that attacked Outer Haven to support Snake's infiltration had weapons at their disposal.

DEAD CELL

An anti-terrorist unit created by George Sears (Solidus) during his presidency, it was devised to launch surprise training assaults on allied bases to better enable them to protect themselves in the event of a real attack. Dissolved after the imprisonment of its leader, Dead Cell secretly reformed with Fortune, Fatman and Vamp as its principle members, and attacked the Big Shell under Solidus's orders.

SNAKEHOUND alias BB Corps

Founded by Liquid Ocelot, and based on the model of the FOXHOUND unit, this group of highly conditioned shock troops included Laughing Octopus, Raging Raven, Crying Wolf and Screaming Mantis. All four were victims of war, having suffered immensely at a tender age. The training they received left them with a slender grip on reality, but made them furiously relentless warriors.

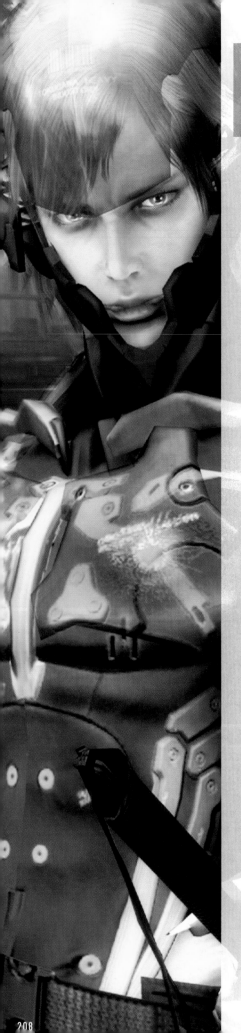

∎ INDEX

If you are looking for specific information, this alphabetical listing is just what you need. Simply search for the keyword you're wondering about, and turn to the relevant page number, which refers directly to the corresponding explanation in the guide.

Depending on how far you have already progressed in the game, be aware that the index may lead you to potential spoilers. To avoid any such premature revelations, all index entries that link to the Extras chapter are written in red. You should avoid opening this chapter at all costs until you have played through the entire game at least once.

CREDITS

Very Special Thanks to Kojima Productions

The Complete Official Guide to *Metal Gear Solid® 4: Guns of the Patriots* is a Piggyback Interactive Limited production.

KONAMI DIGITAL ENTERTAINMENT CO., LTD.

Producer:	Kenichiro Imaizumi
Assistant Producer & Guide Contributor:	Ryan Payton
General Manager, Europe Business Development:	Aki Saito
International Product Manager:	Ayako Tateyama

KONAMI DIGITAL ENTERTAINMENT, INC.

CEO:	Kazumi Kitaue
Director of Marketing:	Rozita Tolouey
Senior Product Manager:	Patrick Dillon

PIGGYBACK INTERACTIVE LIMITED

Managing Directors:	Louie Beatty, Vincent Pargney
Editorial Director:	Mathieu Daujam
Editors:	Matthias Loges, Carsten Ostermann
Lead Author:	James Price
Co-author:	Maura Sutton
Q.A. Team & Editorial Support:	Eric Ling
Art Director:	Martin C. Schneider (Glorienschein)
Designers:	Jeanette Killmann, Cathrin Queins, Jonas Radtke
Sub-Editing:	Maura Sutton
Preprint:	AlsterWerk MedienService GmbH

The Complete Official Guide to *Metal Gear Solid® 4: Guns of the Patriots* is co-published in North America by Piggyback Interactive Limited and Prima Games, a division of Random House, Inc.

PRIMA GAMES

President:	Debra Kempker
Publishing Director:	Julie Asbury
Sales Director:	Mark Hughes

Very Special Thanks to:

Hans-Joachim Amann, Wolfgang Ebert, Christopher Heck, Hideo Kojima, Yoshi Matsuhana, Tim Vogt, Careen Yapp

Special Thanks to:

Frank Adler, Thomas Altemeier, Carlos Astorqui, Manuel Auletta, Antoine Bailly, Markus Bösebeck, Giusy Drammis, Nicolas Dyan, Wolfgang Ebert, Jürgen Endres, Nadine Fieze, Carlo Fracchioni, Roberto Ganskopf, Tobias Giesener, Stéphanie Hattenberger, Ilse Hüttner, Jamie Ingram, Sépa Jolijoli, Rishi Kartaram, Anskje Kirschner, Hans-Jürgen Kohrs, Angela Kosik, Samantha Leigh, Svetlana Lührig, Lars Marquardt, Jon Murphy, Kristin Rüther, Géraldine Saint-Louis, Sebastian Schedlbauer, Klaus Schendler, Uwe Setzer, Ella Siebert, Jean-Marcel Sommer, Franco Sportaiuolo, Pete Stone, Sandra Urban, Henriëtte van Herk, Andreas Voigt, Torsten Wedemeier.